The Common Good

The Common Good

Its Politics, Policies and Philosophy

Marcus G. Raskin

Routledge & Kegan Paul

NEW YORK AND LONDON

First published in the USA in 1986 by
Routledge & Kegan Paul Inc.
in association with Methuen Inc.
29 West 35th Street, New York, NY 10001

Published in Great Britain by
Routledge & Kegan Paul plc
11 New Fetter Lane, London EC4P 4EE

Set in Garamond, 10 on 12pt.
by Columns of Reading
and printed in Great Britain
by Richard Clay plc
Bungay, Suffolk

Library of Congress Cataloging in Publication Data

Raskin, Marcus, G.
The common good.
Bibliography: p.
Includes index.
1. United States – Politics and government – 1981-
2. Political participation – United States.
3. Public interest – United States.   4. United States –
Economic policy – 1981-   .   5. United States –
Social policy – 1980-   . I. Title.
JK271.R26 1986   361.6'.'0973   86-3229

British Library CIP Data also available

ISBN 0-7102-0690-9

For Emily, Zachary and Maggie;
and to Erika, Keith, Jamin, Noah, and Eden
in hopes for their future and
that of their contemporaries.

Contents

Acknowledgments   xi

Introduction   1

Forming an alliance   8
Social reconstruction   11
A new politics   19

1 The common good   23

Freedom and the common good   29
The common good and timeless universality   30
The common good and trusteeship   33
Common sense and common good   34
The common good and private interests   37
The common good and pragmatism   39
Can trust help us find the common good?   42

2 Becoming leaders and organizers   47

Political organizers   52
Paths of organizing   62
   A guide for organizers   62
   Some strategic tasks of organizing   69
Myths and the common good   79
Bonding and linking principles   83

3 Social caring   88

Social caring   88
   Social security   94
Health and social reconstruction   102
   Organization of the health system   107

Contents

Education 115
   Vouchers, credits and choice 118
   Higher education and the knowledge problem 123
Reconstructive knowledge 125
Shelter and community as part of the person's
   guarantee to be human 131

4 Economy for the common good 142

Reorganizing the public sector for a productive
   economy: some models and problems 149
Zone One – The oligopoly and public interest sector 155
Zone Two – The public service sector 158
Zone Three – Competitive and small business 160
Zone Four – Non-profit, small-scale, worker
   control activities 161
An economic distribution in a modern democracy 164
Economic proposals for the transition to democracy 167
Inflation and full employment 168
The full employment economy 169
Free goods 172
Free goods and need 174
Social security investment trusts 175
Money and banking 178
Shaky capitalism 180
   Budgeting and taxation 181
Reconstruction economic reforms 182
   The question of tax cuts 182
   Voting by taxes 182
   The question of regulation 183
   Transportation system 184
   Design of towns and cities/ an ecological economics 184
   Protective tariffs 186
   Agriculture and rural life 187
Workers and the common good 189

**5 Securing the nation: an alternative foreign and
defense policy** 193

Overview 193
US national security and world arms limitation 207
A proposal and a policy 211
General principles for security 219
World economy and arms race 224

The question of arms control   226
Program treaty for security and general disarmament   230
The international economy and social reconstruction   255
International money market   255
International development   258

6   The next stage of democracy   269

Attributes of a modern democracy   275
Dignity of person in the nation-state   286
Democracy and personal recognition   288
Democracy and constitution   290
Reorganizing the government for the common good   294
Citizenship   296
Civil disobedience   298
Internal security   300
Crime in a modern democracy   302
A criminal code for the national security state   305
Democratic law revision and punishment for crime   307
Re-bonding   308
Ersatz social bonding   311
Police obligations   312

7   Progress and the common good   317

Notes   337

Index   364

Acknowledgments

A book does not spring from the head of one person as Minerva did from Zeus. While authors may think of themselves as lonely individualists working in solitude, there are many people whose hands are on our shoulders. In my case this is especially true.

I want to thank my colleagues at the Institute for Policy Studies and its Board of Trustees. The Institute stands as a beacon in a dark and chaotic period. Its members address themselves to social inquiry, invention and reconstruction so the last ding dong for civilization does not have to toll in our time or the foreseeable future. Indeed, we work for this period of history to be one of flowering creativity and liberation.

In my lifetime several of my friends knew and understood, indeed even contributed to, a shift in our fundamental understanding of things and ourselves. They were Leo Szilard, Paul Goodman, Hannah Arendt and Hans Morgenthau, all of whom left us too soon, as did a political ally, Martin King Jr. The reader will see their hands on my shoulders.

Over the course of several years I have had extraordinarily competent research and secretarial assistants. I want to acknowledge their help and their devotion. Ann Wilcox, Trin Yarborough and Holly Hope all worked on earlier versions of *The Common Good*. I want to thank especially Rachel Fershko and Jill Lawrenz whose assistance on this project was absolutely crucial. Susan Hart worked on an earlier draft of the book offering important editorial suggestions. My special thanks to Leif Haase, and to David Steele for note checking. I acknowledge with gratitude Michael Ferber, Douglas Ireland, Herbert Bernstein, Leonard Rapping, Jan Downey, Martin Carnoy, and Robin Hahnel for reading various sections of *The Common Good*.

I owe special thanks to Richard Barnet, Bob Borosage, Saul Landau, Isabel Letelier and Roger Wilkins, Peter Weiss, Michael Goldhaber, Bill Kaplan, Phil Brenner, Chester Hartman, Nancy Lewis, Peter Kornbluh, Barbara Ehrenreich, Noam Chomsky, Bill Arkin, John Cavanagh, Michael Klare, Barbara Raskin, and Doris Porter. My editors Stratford Caldecott and Michael Apple helped enormously in bringing *The Common Good* to completion. Professor Apple asked the right questions with sound suggestions when I needed them most.

Finally, Lynn Randels, my wife, never stopped caring and loving even as she presented skeptical arguments that would have made her Scottish ancestors very proud indeed.

Introduction

What are you doing to feed the nation, without plundering or killing another nation? What do you, as a physician, do against the chronic diseases, or as an educator for the happiness of the children, or as an economist for the elimination of poverty, or as a builder for more hygienic living conditions? Give us a concrete, practical answer or shut up.[1]

Since the Second World War most Americans assumed that the economics of growth would sustain them, that there was no end to credit, or the cheap raw materials from abroad, or the successes which the children of the white working class could have if they did what they were told in the schools, at work or by television morality plays. They could escape the factories of Gary or Birmingham, leaving the most unpleasant jobs to blacks, machines and immigrants. Not very many people guessed that the jobs and plants would run away to seek cheap labor, leaving the American working class to fall backward rather than grasp upward. The economic decline has been quick and frightening as people have learned that their prosperity has few structural roots to protect them. Most people have come to the terrifying realization that they are one paycheck away from disaster. They believe that the social security system is near collapse and that their pensions, if they have them, are by no means automatic.

As Professor Daphne Greenwood has pointed out the top 1 per cent of families in the wealth distribution in the United States held an estimated 32.6 per cent of net wealth and received 8.7 per cent of income in 1973, while the top 1 per cent of families in the income distribution held 24.3 per cent of income. The highest wealth percentile held 60.3 per cent of corporate stock, 29.4 per cent of debt instruments, and 8.4 per cent of real estate, while the highest income percentile held 47.2 per cent of corporate stock, 20 per cent of debt instruments, and 8.1 per cent of real estate. The upper 10 per cent of wealthholders held almost 70 per cent of net wealth and 93 per cent of corporate stock. The upper 10 per cent of the family income distribution held over 50 per cent of net wealth and 70 per cent of corporate stock. Only 1 per cent of net wealth rests with the lower half of the wealth distribution.[2]

This pyramid of wealth inequity will look much worse by the end of the Reagan administration. And it is so intended. One should not conclude, however, that it is only under the Republicans that the base of this pyramid is reinforced. In 1978 the richest 20 per cent took home 5.2 per cent of total family income. In 1980 there was a 5.5 per cent decline in real median income. This was the largest decline since the end of the Second World War. This meant that there was an increase of 3.2 million people below the poverty line over the previous year. Needless to say, black people have suffered the most from this decline. In 1970 the median income of black families was 61 per cent of that of white families whereas nine years later it fell to 57 per cent of the median income of white families. By 1983 the wealthiest fifth received 42.7 per cent of the total national income whereas the poorest 20 per cent dropped to 4.7 per cent of national income.[3] Nearly half of all black families found themselves in the bottom 20 per cent of the US population in terms of income.[4]

With the United States and in other nations, American corporations seek to protect this pyramidal wealth distribution by devising programs to rid the corporations and civil service of "dead wood." These are people who are not profitable to other people and who are deemed irrelevant to the productive system as defined by the more powerful group. The society as a whole supinely accepts the dominant group's definition of "profitable," "efficient" and "productive" with the most peculiar and dangerous results for the society.

We are part of an ideological system in which capitalist accounting and its valuation method assumes the importance of Tiffany Jewelers and the unimportance of sanitation systems because the former is private and the latter is public. Government officials now internalize the principle of this mode of accounting by accepting the decay of cities because they are "too expensive to maintain." As a result, sanitation engineers predict that unless major refurbishing occurs, sewage systems in the major cities will break down.[5] Is it too far-fetched to believe that the result of our inattention and skewed values will be cholera epidemics and similar diseases caused by unsanitary conditions? Air pollution within the factories is so serious that some unionists have called for applying the international rules of war prohibiting the use of chemical weapons to the situation within the stench-filled factories. They argue (correctly) that corporate managers find it more profitable in terms of their balance sheets to pollute the workers rather than provide environmental protection.[6] The attack on occupational health and safety by business is related to profit margins and management's "prerogative" to favor profits over consumer/worker health. One can only wonder whether the tragedy in Bhopal, India with the deaths of several thousand workers and the injury of tens of thousands of other people as a result of the Union Carbide "accident" prefigures other such ghastly accidents in the United States and other nations where "safety" is understood as a primarily financial problem.

As workers seek to hang on to the jobs they had hoped to escape, many of the tasks they perform add to our common misery, and theirs. How else should we think about the food additive business – or even the automobile industry?[7] How much of such activities do positive harm to the general welfare? And do we not have a positive responsibility to stand against proposals for restoring activities and industries which cause social and environmental decay?

The trade union movement declines in strength.[8] Its leaders look to a badly demoralized government to balance the capitalistic economic system from its excesses. But its only real hope has been to get government to protect the gains they have already made, or as in the case of occupation health and safety, to enable the workers to act as health inspectors in the plants.

The paradox of American attitudes toward government is that people expect – and it is – more than just another instrument to obtain fairness and competition in the economy. The state is the economic heart of the society and yet our individualist ideology refuses to recognize this social fact.

> In addition to the 11 million workers employed directly by the state, there are countless wage and salary earners – perhaps as many as 25 to 30 million – who are employed by private capital dependent in whole or in part on state contracts and facilities. Workers in such industries as military and space, branches of capital goods, construction, transportation, and others, are *indirectly* employed by state capital. Further tens of thousands of doctors, welfare workers, and other self-employed and privately employed professionals and technicians who use facilities provided by the state are also dependent in whole or in part on the state budget. Finally, tens of millions of men and women are dependent on the budget as clients and recipients of state services; these include nearly all students at all levels of education, welfare recipients, and other facilities.[9]

Under the "rules" of Democratic party liberalism, the so-called private sector of American life gives the government the task of balancing contrary tendencies among the powerful, encouraging some of them and finding means of defusing those ideas which, if taken seriously, would result in profound disruption. While it is to play the social control function, the bureaucracy is not to reject any idea from the ruling elites on moral grounds. Realpolitik clothed in calculation is its chosen language and therefore the people and their needs are judged in terms of cost balance sheets. This appearance of reality belies the fact that the public

3

consciousness is governed by the wildest and most contrary notions, certainly not very different from those ideas, fears, and fantasies which are said to occupy the bins of our unconscious. It should be no wonder that conducting our public business in this way is a failure, for it brings neither security, well-being or "order." This is not new. It is just becoming a bit more perverse.

Lewis Mumford once described the products of capitalism as law, order and uniformity.

> But the law exists to confirm the status quo and secure the position of the privileged classes; the order is a mechanical order, based not upon blood or neighborhood or kindred purpose and affections but upon subjection to the ruling Prince; and as for the uniformity . . . it is the uniformity of the bureaucrat, with his pigeonholes, his dossiers, his red tape, his numerous devices for regulating and systematizing the collection of taxes. The external means for capitalist policy; and its most typical institutions are the standing army, the bourse, the bureaucracy and the court.[10]

Yet these institutions which are so often felt by the mass of humanity to be institutions of repression are unable to interrupt the inertial plunge towards disintegration, disorder and anomie which holds sway over them. The "standing army, the bourse, the bureaucracy and the court," so often mistaken for orderly rationality require the most profound change. The center, as Yeats put it on the eve of the Second World War, is not holding. And what was true during the 1930s is again true. The breaking apart of society is not an esoteric concern. The sense of *throwness* is the concern and the plight of modern man. It is not limited to a few intellectuals on the margins of society.

Neither state socialism nor capitalism is able to secure the social affinity among people which will assure that they keep before them their common attributes and links rather than their differences. Unfortunately, people do not carry around similar social realities in their heads unless they are imposed or manipulated ones presented through image systems such as television and film. These image systems are the modern mode of developing common beliefs and bonds. But they are as fleeting and one-dimensional as the images on a screen.[11] They cannot hide or supply common purpose and common belief – profoundly existential feelings.

When a society loses its common purpose and aspirations, where the society is in danger of breaking apart into conflicting interests, classes and races and sexes without transcendent and rooted beliefs that are legitimated through agreement or verified through scientific knowledge, or where a society finds itself without its common direction, and when its defense system is predicated on the society's total destruction, we have moved into a period of appearance without substance wherein the politically necessary becomes superfluous and the imagistic takes the place of people's felt needs. Enter Ronald Reagan, image maker and actor, who is meant to restore to our heads the images and beliefs that supposedly held the society together during the depression. But harsh reality obtrudes.

Reagan and his coterie stand for the very attitudes and policies which, over the last generation, brought the American people the Indo-China war, high unemployment rates and meaningless work, militarism, a madcap arms race, the return of the fig leaf of national security to justify foreign intervention, the intensification of big business's search for markets and stable high profits (at the expense of the public and workers) and an increase in xenophobia. Reagan builds on past defense policies adding an ever more bizarre character to them. The government has embraced the power to plan protracted nuclear war by calculation and intention, in other words calculated world destruction. National security planners are to prepare for nuclear war, except by miscalculation or accident as if the victims and historians will really care or know whether civilization ended by accident or design. Under the guise of a strategic defense initiative the arms race will now reach towards the heavens.[12]

Geopoliticians concerned with Western standards of living encourage the life boat strategy, that is, the death of millions by organizing the principle of "rational starvation." According to them, if the world is "running out" of resources, it is only the aggressive and the rich that should and can survive.[13] Of course such thoughts fit well with an international economic system in which economists and bankers insist on "austerity" for poor nations, a code word for greater demands that are to be placed on the wretched of these nations.[14] These nations, from India to Jamaica, are increasingly integrated into an international economic system that entices the poor nation's richer classes into the accoutrement of expensive foreign goods, education and health at high prices in exchange for cheap raw materials. This type of development causes greater underdevelopment. The international project takes on an ever more grotesque character as the modern malthusians shed crocodile tears for the starving of Africa as Western and state socialist nations, namely the Soviet Union and the United States, privately conspire with governments that build up their military and bureaucratic apparatus at the expense of their agricultural and village sectors. (In a less horrifying guise this social project is now being run by the Reagan administration on "inefficient" American farmers and on those poor people who are the modern castoffs. Thus, we have our own pathological development.)

In the face of economic and unemployment insecurity, perhaps it is not strange that many Americans have embraced a reactionary stance on issues of human dignity hoping in this way to restore themselves to a more financially secure position. It should not be surprising that parts of the

5

middle, working and poor classes, encouraged by such leaders of the New Right as Senator Jesse Helms, Phyllis Schlafly and Reverend Falwell, have interpreted their own economic decline as caused by women's rights, or environmentalists, or the victories of the civil rights movement in the last generation.

After all, they have not heard anything comprehensive or coherent from either political party, or from the candidates in political campaigns which do much more than punctuate frustration. For there is no leadership, program or articulated ideological alternative which gives people a way out of their psychological panic and economic insecurity.[15] Nor is there one which looks directly at the puerile arms race and its foolish, wasteful technologies and states that it is now time to stop it.

That a political leadership does not exist which has sufficient political strength to lead the society to the common good does not mean that we are incapable of forging a programmatic and organizational alternative to this end. And we had better do so for prudence dictates that without using our passion and intelligence to pursue a politics of social reconstruction we will find ourselves with problems of the magnitude which caused a civil war in the United States.

There is ample reason to compare this time to the pre-Civil War period. Before the Civil War it was slavery which could not be dealt with through "normal" politics. Then there were conservative thinkers who pointed to the relative calm of the South as examples of emulation when compared to the insecurity and restlessness of the worker in the North. Now it is the profound and interlinked issues of human dignity, national security and economic justice which do not yield to the politics of interest and gimmickry, even as conservative thinkers trumpet the calm of the past that never existed. In 1860 the inability of the political system to deal with slavery and new forms of industrial capitalism led to a systemic break in the political structure.[16] In the latter part of the twentieth century it is the economic and imperial defense system which is leading to a colossal, internal crisis as it collides with the ideals and practices of human dignity and equity.

A program to arrest this slide to disaster must apply to the electoral and non-electoral aspects of public life. It must as well affect our behaviors and social relationships. The common goal of social reconstruction is not based on a utopian or abstract vision of hope. It is based on a program which people can talk about and implement in their own situations, organize with others in their work places, develop research and curriculum studies around in the unversities, schools, and argue for in electoral politics and social organizations. It is spatial and "quantifiable" in the sense that people will find their own means of measuring what they are doing according to standards that may vary from geographic place. It is both existential and objective in that it requires actions and events that others can see and judge.

It is even musical in that proper concern is given to those themes which fit together.

Those who share such a program should be aware of accidentality which in life leads to necessary but new harmonies. The program, its strategy, tactics and values, is governed by non-antagonistic principles in profoundly different areas of social existence. We have learned through political experience and psychological insights how each particular phase of life repeats certain characteristics and formulae of other areas, and how the same habits of mind are present throughout the society. Because this is so, rational politics must be practical enough to show how seemingly unrelated matters and actions can fit together either in affirmative or negative ways. It must concern itself with the relatively short-term. I believe that many of the aspects of social reconstruction can be accomplished and implemented by the beginning of the twenty-first century.

A political program, and the attempt to implement it, will not take the place, nor should it, of a Beethoven sonata, a country western dance, or questions around the mystery of God or the universe. No politics which seeks the common good would interrupt the artistic and the religious, the person's quest for seeing deeply and beyond the ordinary dimensions and explanations. Such a politics has no catechisms or little red books. It does seek to help people clear a path to ease the way of themselves and others.

A modern and humane political program will seek ways of dealing positively with the terrifying social fact that to survive in the modern world we must share in the making of each other's history because we share each other's moral responsibility. With such a program, political action need never contradict the permanent striving of people to transcend their present as they seek to retain the most noble aspects of human nature and of their past.

In historical terms the ideas, project, and patterns of development which I discuss follow a survival trend in world history. I take this trend to be the struggle to include all people as subjects and active participants with each other in making history. To this end the American covenant should be modified and redrafted.[17] To many of us this task is an uncomfortable one for it means opening the institutions of our society to participate with the incarcerated, the unseen, in forging a definition of the common good. It means changing our slightly suspect and self-serving standards of "excellence" and constipated notions of merit to include with us the not so strong, the lame, the troubled and even the more deserving than ourselves. It demands that women's social capacity to care for and weave a network of relationships to sustain others, and self with others, should become a central concern of our political life. Such a covenant requires us to surrender those aspects of one-dimensional elitism which flatten out the variation of human creativity. It counsels us to reaffirm pluralism and reject the pernicious and regressive political bureaucratic tendency to consign whole classes, races, the lame and the inexplicable to the ashheap of history. Finally, it counsels us to see property and production as economic problems which are the joint concern of the worker and the public who have the power and legitimacy to resolve them.

There are those who think that the social crafting of such a covenant can come through some sort of magic, the day after which social classes cease to exist, new knives and forks automatically appear as the old ones are thrown away and the question of man's fate in the universe is no longer one of importance. But this is and should be false.

Those pursuing political action must find means to assure themselves that the course which they follow, inquire into, analyze and seek limits to will dignify human life, recognize the playful and creative aspects of people while they embrace the objectives that the dominant spirit of politics enobles and enhances the quality of human life. When such notions are made the basis of political action, the objective of liberation and reconstruction will not be either abstract, graceless, or sentimental.

In other words a program for the common good can best begin by understanding its limits. No political program will replace anger or love. It will not replace intriguers and intrigues, although it does not have to surrender center stage to them. Social reconstruction will not make the perfect world, nor is it intended to construct a "new man." What its proponents can encourage and create is a level of equity and cooperation, activities and relationships, so that human emotions and mistakes will flow easily with minimum damage or destruction. It can show how structured greed, tunnel vision, fear and reason in the service of madness can be contained and therefore will not yield to world disaster or misery.

This program asserts the political principle that no inhuman act should be used as a short cut to a better day, and that each step of the way the program will be judged against the likelihood that it will result in linking equity, sharing, personal dignity, security, freedom and caring. In other words, it breaks with an older formulation of liberalism which asserted individualism and opportunity as the highest goods. And it shuns those terroristic or revolutionary acts which degrade or destroy others. The politics of the common good has no place for the violence of the deed whomever employs it and for whatever "noble" objective. To achieve the common good, one must reach across class, gender and function seeing the other as part of them but with the capacity to transcend and shape them into "co-responsibles" for rather than against humanity.

Forming an alliance

There are those who automatically reject a politics of reconstruction which reaches to any part of the capitalist and governing class and the officer class of the armed services. There are others who say that the splits and antagonisms, between teachers and students, small business and workers, Chicanos and Indians, public and private sector workers are irreconcilable, and that each of these groups is concerned only with itself against all others. Can diverse and disparate interests be united and then transformed?

Unless such objections by a movement are proved wrong in practice, we will see terrible tensions between groups that should in fact be allies to each other. We have already seen evidence of such tension in which white women have brought law suits alleging discrimination against them by institutions who defended themselves by saying that they gave priority of admission, whether for jobs or schools, to black men.[18]

In response to those who see irreconcilable conflicts, an alliance of reconstruction can cite the experience of civil rights and anti-war causes which showed that there are those in the business class, including the children of the business class, who reject greed, embrace democracy as an open process of persuasion and inclusion even as they enjoy their class privileges. It is not likely that many people will, like St Francis, know how or be strong enough to escape those privileges. One should remember that some people in a privileged situation are prepared to act *against* their class interests because of their conscious awareness of their inelasticity of needs and the psychological security which often comes from privilege. They have, as I suggested in *Being and Doing* (1971), a surplus of consciousness which is really their awakened, empathic sense. In the period of the Indo-China war and civil rights struggles the privileged used their own systematically conferred legitimacy to bring about a confrontation with imperialism and racism – just as young American officers and soldiers joined together and rejected the Indo-China war. This telling social event has occurred in other nations recently, notably among Portuguese officers who fought in Angola and who then were radicalized.[19]

We should not forget that the middle class spawned the anti-war generation. Being of draft age, its activists were unduly maligned about the honesty of their commitments to the anti-imperialist stance. The fact is that its actions, both out of personal interest and the despicable nature of that war, motivated this generation. While the nation's media has lurched rightward, the members of the "anti" generation are still ready to participate in actions which are meant to move beyond personal selfishness.

Is there an economic base to this strategy in the middle class? When analyzed in traditional, political terms the middle class is an organizable group for reconstruction because it does not have movable capital that defines the investment direction of the society, large enough amounts of disposable sums or property to sustain children in the middle class. We can discern an interesting social phenomenon which affects the shaky ground upon which the middle class stands. To retain their position within the middle class, its younger members postpone or give up having either children or families. At first blush this may appear to be a relatively benign result of a tightening economic situation or the embrace of zero population ideology, or a renewed dedication to the work ethic required by an art or skill, the cause of inquiry or revolution. Instead, the reason may be quite different. The middle class is in perilous danger of trading human relationships and the insecurity of having offspring for fulfilling consumer needs. Without political concern, their life actions are regressive. In a consumer society governed by market economies younger workers of the middle class are turned into somewhat selfish people who have little choice but to calculate for themselves *against* others. Nevertheless, their potential energy is present for community work once their caring attributes are linked to specific tasks and a program is generated for them to center themselves psychologically and politically.

Class antagonisms between the skilled and the unskilled, the middle class and the poor, can be mediated through political programs worked through in the problematic of political struggle and championed by political and educational leaders. As I have said, there are those who believe that the conflicts which emerged in the 1960s between the educated college student, the poor and unemployed, or the industrial worker, are irresolvable. But the differences that do exist can be resolved and transcended through a common program. We will find that intra and inter-class conflicts which do exist will tend to be mediated, even resolved each step of the way through common projects, ideas of participation, role respect and role sharing and an acceptance of one's own empathic sense.

For example, the antagonisms between organized and unorganized workers, between workers for the state and those who work for large non-competitive corporations, and those that are competitive are not irreparable. They are intertwined with ways we formulate social questions rather than fundamentally antagonistic interests between these sectors. Consequently, we are compelled to change our description of work tasks to clarify the obvious; that, for example, the work of people who outfit toilets in the "private sector" and those who repair sewer pipes in the "public sector" do not have antagonistic interests. It is absurd to believe that work at home, "housework," is not work even though those women who are working at home without pay are subsidizing their spouses' jobs and employer.

It is time that we transcend attempts at creating false categories between what is public and private, what is state and what is community-sanctioned. These ideological categories have destroyed communities and groups, alienating people from each other in profound ways for they have created an ideology that the productive process is not social. They have created a peculiar individualism, one less predicated on individual ability and productive activity than on the ideology of greed and "making it." Most important, false distinctions between, for example, the private and public sector, have resulted in work not getting done, needs going unmet and decay deepening.

In the issue of race and education few adjustments have been made among liberals to speak to peoples' fears. At present working-class white parents see no reason why their children should be bussed for reasons of integration since public education is seen by them as one of the few pieces of "property" which they can pass on to their children. Foolishly, no efforts were made to foster full employment, skills training or special scholarship programs for children who are part of the bussing system. Yet it is taken for granted, both by Democrats and Republicans, that the rich are to be bribed with tax incentives so they will "invest" or perform other publicly conditioned activities.[20] The social policy of the society made so clear by President Reagan is to use carrots on the rich and sticks on the poor. Even under Democratic administrations no attempts were made to devise programs for mortgage-free home ownership or rental subsidies for those groups who participate in integration programs.

Assuredly, generations of racism cannot be overcome with gimmicks. But it is also true that certain specific social inventions and regulations, the way we mold our cities architecturally, financially and physically, the types of knowledges which are generated and funded in the universities will move the society either more quickly or not at all from racism, sexism, economic injustice and war. These issues will take a great deal of rethinking. For while traditional liberalism may not mean fundamental rethinking, reconstruction does.

Social reconstruction

Social reconstruction is the means to find the basis of agreement and consent for a new societal covenant. It is more than pragmatic problem solving. Social reconstruction takes its cue from the human attributes of imagination and ordinariness. By imagination I mean the recognition of the playful, the serial nature of ideas which shade and then double back on each other.[21] We are required to recognize that cause and effect, and descriptions of events and processes such as profound changes, revolutions or systemic breaks, are not necessarily felt descriptions of what is happening or what is preferred by those existentially involved with the changes. We should not mistake the laws which we construct in our mind from data and intuition and assume that these are the laws of the universe independent of ourselves. Through imagination we recognize the unformed and the creative, to be formed, life itself, the possible and impossible which remind us always of our limits and incompleteness; attributes we almost always have but fail to grasp, even in our fantasy and imagination. Even so we think also of our needs, our ordinariness and applaud those political activists who as they celebrate imagination know the importance of organization and skill. The Italian Marxist, Antonio Gramsci, talked of societies' needs in time of great turbulence and what those committed to profound change should be like:

> What is needed for the revolution are men of sober mind, men who don't cause an absence of bread in the bakeries, who make trains run, who provide the factories with raw materials and know how to turn the produce of the country into industrial products, who ensure the safety and freedom of the people against the attacks of criminals, who enable the network of collective services to function and who do not reduce the people to despair and to make horrible carnage. Verbal enthusiasm and reckless phraseology make one laugh (or cry) when a single one of these problems has to be resolved even in a village of one hundred inhabitants.[22]

Beyond reflecting these purposes in our daily work, the political program is meant to establish a standard which will allow Americans to live on the planet as fellow human beings with others and with themselves in a human (ordinary plus imaginative) manner. It asserts that organizations and structures of existence such as schools or factories, hospitals or old age homes are social institutions which by their nature are public, and which besides being places of skill or production, had also better begin from the assumption of caring, a fundamental value in the feminine view of the world. According to Carol Gilligan's study, *In a Different Voice*,[23] neither radicalism or liberalism has a vested interest in decaying institutions. Where social or "productive" institutions cease to operate on the basis of caring they have failed and should be dismantled. They are no longer a benefit to the whole or to those who we are to help directly. They have become abandoned and expensive property symbolic of the problem rather than reflective of a cure.

Obviously, political programs cannot avoid the question of property, who should own it, how it should be maintained and in the modern context, what is it? The restated covenant upon which the common good is perceived encourages two propositions about property. On one level property is to be socially controlled through the political process. But the second level is to assure that each person has a measure of private ownership which allows individuals and families to be secure *against* the state, as well as the community, public associations and guilds or great aggregations of wealth. In other words, the person should not have to be dependent on associations or the state for minimums. All political actions should be of such a nature as to protect and encourage economic security and independence. Economic guarantees are critical to a modern democracy because comprehensive changes which are made in the political and economic sphere and in the sphere of foreign and national security should be made on the basis of reason and dialogue rather than the fear of loss of property, jobs, or economic retribution. A major problem of the arms race is the bureaucratic and industrial vested interest for defense contracts supported by workers who fear loss of income and jobs without the Pentagon's largesse. Economic fears and insecurities strip us of disinterested judgment. It is to be hoped that the question of "how much" property is needed for individuals and family to act beyond interest and without fear can be answered through rational dialogue rather than class war.

The rest of the twentieth century and the early period of the twenty-first century could be an era of great and peaceful experimentation in our political and economic life. If properly conceived, politically, such experimentation can create a balance between different types of social ownership and individual, economic security. Experimentation on this question should go forward through the political process and with the recognition of certain inchoate arrangements and propositions. Political leaders need not shirk these questions for they are the ones that are on the minds of the citizens. They are the basis of a new American convenant. These propositions are:

— that we require a new meaning to citizenship, one that makes sense for a society split by many conflicts, economic, social and geographic interests. In the process we need to identify the United States as a democracy, not a republic or oligarchy, and then define the meaning of that elusive term.
— that monopoly and oligopoly capital is not in the interests of the citizenry when it is held privately and that when the bulk of investment power is retained in private hands no common good can be sustained.
— that the public sector does not only include the government; it includes independent and non-profit associations such as labor unions, coops, schools and cultural institutions; that they should operate public programs with substantial funds.
— that militarism is destructive of our people and the world and that disarmament is a key to our common security.
— that ecological disasters can be avoided if we change the scientific and political ideology and the social structures which foster the institution-alized (and therefore unconscious) will to plunder nature; rather than find means of serving in harmony with nature.
— that skills must be encouraged; each of us should see ourselves as teachers and students, therefore barriers created by "expertise," secrets and specialized knowledges are to be transcended and decoded.
— that the process of political and economic equality between people should be interpreted as egalitarian interdependence in which we play out our needs and wants through joint actions, projects and jointly defined tasks.

The assumption and the goal of our covenant is that people have a practical and inherent *need* to cooperate just as they have a practical and inherent *capacity* to help others live healthily, happily, and justly. To the extent possible each person should recognize the economic value that he or she performs, has or will perform, and ask whether that activity is in fact a productive and humane one. When this recognition is made by the society, the society will assess more properly the limits of the market system, for the market system cannot fulfill the multivarious needs and wants or the actual kinds of production which occur in modern society. And this recognition will show the difference between market or monetary values and humane values. Humane values are not congruent to a market system, for the latter is a system of interest that must finally disdain the unproductive, the current misfit or the long term.

No wonder the misfits, older people, and the maimed are easily denied their humanity and possibility. The "professionals" who internalize the values of the market system, the economists, government officials, business people, see such people as only marginal in the economic and productive sphere.[24] If nothing else the totalitarian experiences of the twentieth century, the Auschwitzes and Gulags, and our own barrios and ghettos tell us that the worth of a political system should be valued only to the extent that it protects and esteems those who do not appear to have productive or economic value to those with power. For it is this sentiment which – given the present deformed definitions of productivity and production – has the greatest utility and is critical to the maintenance of civilization.

The market system becomes patently absurd when we think that it should dominate social relationships.[25] Suppose a mother charged her child or husband for her milk and the time she nursed her child. Suppose the father charged the mother a fee for service in relation to the number of times she achieved orgasm. The question of what we mean by humane utility will become ever more pressing as pathological emphasis is placed on market values. (One hopes that this pathology does not have to overtake us before we embrace vastly different definitions of production and economics which can sustain a humane civilization.)

There will be those from the left who will object to a program which espouses socialist and voluntary cooperative forms next to capitalist ones. Their view is incorrect for two reasons. First, the United States is still in the process of becoming a democracy. As I suggest at greater length, its political voting system has to be enriched so that fundamental issues are reached in the electoral process through public deliberation rather than mass manipulation. Politicians, businessmen and women, managers and entre-preneurs have not tried or worked through different economic forms to their ultimate conclusion. Different types of capitalism can now be tried within a genuinely democratic system.

The American productive enterprise would also benefit greatly from

14

experimentation and democratic participation of worker-controlled enterprises.[26] Such enterprises would be radically expanded. It would transform the class separation of owner, manager and worker. Democratic experimentation and participation reflect our commitment to dignity and equality, knowing that this commitment is best maintained by ending organizational tendencies to mystification and selfishness. Some would call this a form of socialism. Perhaps. But it is a very different type of "socialism" than one sees around us. No socialism can be worthy of the common good unless it is of the kind which is compatible with individual initiative, liberty, democratic participation, protection of the private space and even anarchism. It must be a socialism derived from the application of humane reason, natural association and affinity of people for each other. It must build on what is already there, within us, as Americans and inviolate human beings. It must even build on capitalism, not only its accomplishments but certain of its sensibilities.

We should not forget that small-scale capitalism is rooted in American experience. It spawned a large and skilled small business and working class.[27] Most members of the small business class are less interested in exploitation than they are in ensuring personal dignity and material security through their work. Their commitment to individualism or individualistic behaviors in the right circumstances is nothing more than a laudable human desire to have their "strokes" recognized in the world. Obviously, where their activities of small-scale capitalism are related to direct modes of exploitation, public discussions should be encouraged to show why and how this exploitative side can be changed. Historically, voluntary cooperation has been used as the way to pick up the pieces on the local and neighborhood level of the capitalist system. Having learned the habit of voluntarism as de Tocqueville pointed out, Americans fostered a new type of responsibility which is a powerful, political tool for securing creativity and competence among the people.

The second reason that justifies plural political and economic forums merits a great deal of attention. As any citizen of an East European country knows, socialism as mediated through state power is seriously flawed, indeed deformed.[28] It has caused a narrowing of the space of freedom, in the sense of being left to be free from groups, voluntary or state organized.

State socialism has not found how to separate social service from control and compulsion. Its compulsion extends to the assembly line as well. It is not accidental that the largest corporations in the world, groups such as Fiat, have set up automobile plants in the Soviet Union for cars called the "Togliatti"; Fiat believes, with good reason, that it will have a more pliant work force, guaranteed as such by the Soviet government. The corporate leadership knows that if Brezhnev's forces invaded Czechoslovakia to put down democratic socialism there, or sought to "modernize" Afghanistan through invasion, it is not likely that the Politburo will tolerate organized, unsanctioned work stoppages of Soviet workers. And does socialism, Chinese style, offer Americans anything? Socialism in the twentieth century has been nothing more than the national state's ideological mode to accomplish capital accumulation.

The Chinese continue in their praise of Joseph Stalin, Henry Kissinger and Josef Strauss. They are seen by national liberation movements (such as those in Angola and Zimbabwe) as favoring the colonial power. Chinese communists have dutifully recognized and supported the Chilean junta. The Chinese tell the world in terms similar to the language of the American national security managers in the Pentagon Papers that they are going to "punish" and "teach the Vietnamese" a lesson for their invasion of Pol Pot's Cambodia. And Pot's "socialism" operated according to modern Draconian principles that soaked Cambodia in blood after the land of Cambodia had been virtually salted away to prove the principles of *realpolitik*, according to Henry Kissinger. Nevertheless, certain socialist practices in Western Europe have more than a passing interest where they attempt to bring together socialism (the economy of the society in a participative way) and democracy (the political system in a participative and collective way). These are not alien to cooperative aspects of American life or our present needs. But more to the point, the diversity, deformation, conflict and anarchic methodologies of socialism across the world liberates Americans to reach into our own experience and history to follow our own brand of reconstruction according to our needs and culture.

Like many sound ideas, socialism has been a victim of twentieth-century murderers. It was used by the Nazis to justify their bestial political formations, while the Stalinists used "socialist legality" to devour their own revolutionaries. But beyond such perversions certain basic questions arise in those nations that could honestly be called socialist. They have to do with the fact that socialism, a concept which referred to the potential for everyone's liberation, has not taken into account the person or unofficial group's freedom to say *no* without the fear of terrible retribution. The result of not having this right, or of having it in an atrophied or truncated form, is to decrease the possibility of vital debate and differences, mixing fear, truthful statements, power and cowardice together in a stew which ultimately pushed the common good further into the sunset. This failure of socialism, therefore, requires a clearly defined and recognized corrective. A movement for the common good and one which seeks correctives to the way state socialism has evolved in the twentieth century is a problem for workers' groups and intellectuals in socialist nations as well.

In the United States our task is easier. We can easily protect the whiggish right to say no through a constitutional right of civil disobedience which protects the person and group as the society goes through changes either favored or fought by the dominant group or spirit.[29] It is in that "no" that those committed to the common good can find the possible, the power to say "yes" to the changes we need. The individual's power to say *no* through civil disobedience is his or her power to see beyond the faceless role that others have chosen for him or her, just as acting as a citizen is a way to be seen, heard and felt in changing the nature and operations of power. Both functions, citizenship and civil disobedience, serve as the way for the modern political system to *humanize* itself, to see that it must change its assumptions, namely that people are expendable as unemployment rates or body counts.

Being free of the ideologies of state socialism as they are practiced, except to study them, we are able to promulgate specific ideas and a coherent program which grows out of our own experience, often a local experience which is unreplicable. The relevant political path will vary at each political stage. And emphasis on different projects will vary from place to place for reasons of climate, and local culture. This fact is often submerged by another social fact. Cultural homogeneity in the United States is preempting sectoral differences. Through technological communication and the will of Alexander Hamilton to organize national markets, transportation, telephone, the requirements of technology and the national consumer market system have created national complaints and, possibly, solutions which can be generalized. As important as these factors have been to the national consciousness, the rise of the military since the Second World War has assured the power of the national state and the national solution. Thus, the consumer culture, both the criticism of it and its own trajectory, has become national, even international in character, as has the American military system. Consequently, the program must be comprehensive in scope. The new left of the 1960s was accused of not having its ideological house in order, for it railed against national power with no progressive alternatives especially around the issue of production. Some referred to the period of the 1960s as the politics of the unpolitical, arguing that it generated changes in consciousness but not in practice. Its adherents were accused of being characters out of an existential novel who had given up their trust in the mangled reasons and knowledges so assiduously prepared by old state Marxists, bourgeois political thinkers and pragmatists. During the height of the student movement no less a figure of the American ruling elite than George Kennan accused the New Left of not having a program and coherent ideology as if he were about to join up if it had one.[30]

This attack continues against the left side of the political spectrum. In recent years it has been said that progressives no longer had "ideas," that they had lost their way. To the extent this is true the left has lost its moral authority in society. This "loss of face" occurred because established liberalism has accepted the big business and military system as a given and assumed that politics had to be played between the big business and military goalposts. It is the task of those committed to the common good to change

17

the playing field. They – we – must offer alternatives and strategies that do more than present cold war liberalism in the guise of neo-conservatism or neo-liberalism.[31] The crisis we face requires us to rethink our fundamental purposes and values, indeed our very definition of politics.

In *The Common Good* I have formulated a program that takes account of the gains of the past, protects them and moves forward from them. Plans and programs are important aspects of profound social change. The evidence for this point of view is too great to cite. Charles Beard reminds us of what James Madison said in *The Federalist*:

> It is impossible for the people spontaneously and universally to move in concert toward their object; and so in times of stress changes and plans for them must be instituted by some informal group and unacceptable propositions made acceptable by some patriotic and respective citizens or number of citizens.[32]

Of course I am aware that we are at a stage of history where people need to present themselves rather than be represented or explained by others. Nevertheless, I have taken the liberty of describing the contours of a social and political movement for the common good which by its nature and practice could bring about profound, sustained and positive social reconstruction. The ground for it already exists and it is being worked by separate groups: environmental, civil rights, anti-war, labor, artists, and media workers. The movements of social progress of the last twenty years, their purpose, and most important the people in them, can and must be linked and connected through ideas, action and program to ongoing institutions, churches, labor unions and universities.[33]

I do not want to fool the reader into thinking that once certain universally accepted principles of social reconstruction are acknowledged and affirmed, such as anti-racist, anti-imperial, and anti-sexist principles, there is a "correct" political line to follow. Rather, social reconstruction is an open inquiry which must be constantly pursued through the sharing of talk, analysis, empirical facts from "out there," not to mention the play which one has between half-formed and understood fantasies or recollections of experiences and purposes as well as those of others on the operation of these principles in practice. Social reconstruction can take advantage of the middle-class concern with self and psychology stimulating a new process of psychological inquiry in structured reality and its contradictions as well as within ourselves and our own contradictions. Such notions require a new meaning to politics.

A new politics

By politics we usually mean the distribution of power, the means of wielding it, whether for good, bad or an indifferent end. I do not believe that politics is synonymous with power. Those who do are creating a poisonous stew in practice and theory. The concoction, once imbibed, destroys the person or group's ability to sustain a liberating change. The result of the conventional equation of politics as power has been a series of imperfect and failed revolutions. At this point I am sure that some readers will say that I am hopelessly naive, although I would urge them to ponder different examples from history. Identifying power is not quite as simple as the arms manufacturers or military strategists claim. There are very few outside of the military world who would argue that the $2 trillion spent on "defense" by the American taxpayer in recent years, or the $2 trillion we intend to spend between 1982/7 will make us more secure, more "happy" or "powerful." Yet this arms spending is the primary means states use to extend power and control over others. Martin Luther King, Jr had no power on his side except that of mobilizing the feelings and needs of people. The People's War of the Vietnamese had powerlessness as its source of power, just as the second-century Christians had enormous power due to their willingness to die. (When a Christian martyr met a Roman soldier on the street, he would challenge the soldier to kill him or convert. Otherwise, the Christian would kill himself before the soldier's eyes.) The women's movement and its projects of networking and consciousness raising introduced a new dimension to politics which transcended traditional conceptions of power causing men to have to invite women into the corridors of power, if not their rightful seats.

Power is the mobilization of resources to obtain a specific end. Its means may include manipulation, persuasion, coercion, verification (scientific inquiry) and magic. Economic resources, both the object and means of power, is often the "means of the means" to accomplish any specific objective. When politics is reduced to a synonym for power, other necessary ingredients for political practice – love, hope, and justice – are lost. Once relieved of these attributes, politics is reduced to a brutal series of actions (transactions) in which force, fraud, and fear dominate the lives of society and its people. Whatever our definition, politics *is* the means by which people create relationships to live with others.

In practical terms, politics for the common good can mean organizing a person's feelings and passions for purposes which are decided upon with others. These feelings and passions venture beyond the mere assertion of power because they include other characteristics, sometimes viewed as irrational, "inexplicable," like love, generosity or empathy.[34] Democratic politics, the most likely form to obtain the common good, should be recognized as bonding of such feelings to other people and a yoking of them with the mobilization of material and work resources for a particular series of ends. Obviously, this point of view does not envision a smaller role for politics.

Technology and scientific discovery *force* a different meaning to politics from the one that comes to us through present Marxist or bourgeois social science. Marxists believed that politics reduced itself to never-ending struggles between classes which would be swept away once revolution against the exploiting class was successful. No recrimination, just scientific administration would result. And American social scientists of bourgeois persuasion adopted a version of this point of view. The eminent political scientist, Harold Lasswell, believed that politics was useless and dirty; that it was better to forge policy practices which were measurable, technocratic, "precise" and apolitical. Interests would then be mediated through the bureaucratic mind in a kind of Hegelian transcendance.[35]

Social reconstruction rejects social engineering by encouraging everyone to be "political," to organize public and private activity and formulate the line between them, develop institutions, make mistakes, choose projects, while constructing a program and a path which helps the person locate himself or herself. In social reconstruction, power remains only one aspect of politics, not its total meaning. Nevertheless, power is recognized as the problematic of history, of organized existence. One cannot escape from it through a utopian door or by saying it does not exist.

Some will object that this changed definition of politics is too comprehensive and therefore puts too heavy a load on it. Others might say that such a definition of politics has fallen out of favor at least since Machiavelli. I am conscious of the charge that politics in my meaning of it is virtually "metaphysical" because it encompasses an almost ontological meaning, giving politics religious functions. There is truth to the criticism. As consciousness and political revolution increase (perhaps reflecting Hegel's belief that history progresses toward freedom and therefore all people seek to change their status and become free-liberated), and as organized science increases its hold on people's minds by creating alternate explanations and operations about the way nature works and could be conquered, the power of organized religion recedes. Unfortunately as the objective problems that humankind is left with continue to expand exponentially, a void is left in the lives of people. (And yet there is the mocking and inescapable humanistic piece of folk wisdom: "Pray to God, but keep rowing to shore." Why is that, why should we believe in ourselves, especially now? "Eli, Eli lama sabach-tani." If God forsook His son surely he will not remember me, or us.) The person's needs have not been met either through scientific explanation or organized religion. From the eighteenth century forward, happiness, usually defined as progress (an increased amount of material goods, choices, and leisure), has been a prime purpose or pursuit of politics without inquiry into the meaning of either happiness or progress. While the goal of progressives in politics was happiness, few took seriously the inner feelings of people, the need to comprehend them, fashioning them into cooperative activity, a *sine qua non* for happiness. While the Greek citizens of Plato and Aristotle's time assumed the importance of property they rejected any idea of "inner feelings" or conscience which was not acted out. What they did was what they felt. What they felt was who they were.[36]

Modern societies can develop institutional forms and spaces which allow and encourage people to integrate feeling, action and being in the world. It is in this way that the "pursuit of happiness" and the common good can be more than a rhetorical flourish of the American covenant. This attempt at social and personal transformation is now the central but unstated concern of politics. It is late enough in the twentieth century to acknowledge that politics is not merely the distribution of power, nor is it merely action unchained from conscience. It is the statement of inward and outward relationships, including the person's activities and fears, of people to themselves and to others. When politics is presented in this way there is a tendency to think about it holistically since it is assumed that each activity reflects this inward and outward relationship, including the person's fears about him or herself in relation to others.

In practical terms people mediate their relationships through work and love.[37] It is their way of expressing and allowing for the expression of these fundamental needs. Thus, politics must now be an attempt to recapture and express this fundamental yearning of people, and to transform or initiate new institutions so they reflect this type of politics. Before Zimbabwean independence, a black minister of justice left his post because he knew that there was no way for black people to exercise their conscience through white-controlled police and courts. He understood that the politics of liberation cannot be grafted on to institutions whose assumptions and practices are meant to reproduce the old meaning of repression and domination.

But just because the politics of liberation and participation is more than the struggle between classes for distribution of power and wealth, there should be no illusion. If economic relationships are not transformed and we do not show how economic redistribution can be accomplished through action, if we do not find a way of taming power through law and justice, the broader and primary meaning of politics is lost and democracy either as an end to itself or as an instrument to obtain the common good is reduced to a cruel joke. On the other hand, if we adopt a politics of the common good which struggles against class oppression and authoritarianism, we can reach to the sacred reality of human dignity and solidarity; which may seem invisible but is immediately and continuously present when we try to deny its existence. If we continue war preparation and such perverse habits as

Introduction

cataloging nuclear strategy under political science rather than criminal law in our libraries and universities, the sophisticated renditions of thinkers will mean nothing. If we seek to act only in response to events which are not understood, yet caused by the madness of a dying class or the hubris of an emerging one, we will have again lost the battle of politics which is related to reason and grounded in empathy and dignity. If we do not understand, and neglect to organize, the events which are likely to occur will inspire horror, war and for our time the hangman's tolling of the fascist bell. Without jobs but craving excitement people will eagerly queue up for employment on firing squads. I believe that the questions and program which I have raised here are part of the dialogues that are inescapable for this generation. Intellectual handymen and political leaders bring these questions together. It is the people who will answer them.

1
The common good

It is a curious irony that the phrase "common good" which should find itself in all spheres of human existence is more likely than not restricted or banished from the harsh world of politics and everyday life. We come to believe that such ideas cannot apply to the actions of states, and that conscious efforts at projecting the common good in the marketplace are held to be disastrous. Some offer the silent judgment that the common good is best served when there is none. Others take the view that a common good with government as the engine leads to authoritarianism or even totalitarianism. But this flimsy catechism is not helpful when we consider the activities of modern day life. The purpose of this inquiry is to resurrect the common good and present the contours of a public philosophy to this end. Such a philosophy requires us to escape false or irrelevant dichotomies and categories which obscure the policies and paths of social reconstruction.

We are prone to believe that actions of people are centered in two different realms each with its own code. In one realm it is taken for granted that men dominate; namely in the realm of the state. In the other realm, that of society, women are expected to have a central role, albeit a support and maintenance one. They are to care for the family, religious institutions, schools and provide the non-remunerative subsidy to the economic corporation while they act as the caretakers of the young. In capitalist society they are to act as the organizers of consumption.

In society relationships sometimes can be associative and unburdened by hierarchic or administrative control with natural affection and cooperation enhancing the quality of individual life. Thus, in society there are spaces for action where the actors seek their own social, political and economic combination. The actors can even recognize the intimate, unmediated through extrinsic state demands – often but not always.

Such societies are permissive, and usually they are democratic. Yet, even democratic societies do not escape coercion. Coercion is often clothed in traditional social roles and rituals that are suffocating and tend toward the relationship of dominator and dominated.

The carrier of these roles is often the family although it can be passed on through religion and the law as it is used to protect property. In the past racism which is laced through the society was supported by the state's administrative and legislative regulations. Sexism is also passed through the way institutions are structured and the values they propound. Most states are never far from their central roots, namely the control and use of violence and coercion. The state uses its organization of power, its "monopoly" of violence to coerce or mandate outcomes, although other modes of suasion are used as well. Depending on the character of the society or the nature of the constitution the state will either be limited or seek to be coextensive with all aspects of society. Wielders of state power may strike a separate peace with churches, or there may be a pious, hands-off attitude towards family. However, the state is thought of as the instrument to command, when it wants to, the resources of the society for its purposes and it may insist on all manner of invasive activity into all institutions.

According to the anarchists, whether Simone Weil or Paul Goodman, the state is so suffused with violence and war preparation and war making that it cannot escape its origins and the purposes that those with power, invariably men, place on the process of governing.[1] The state leaves virtually no room for an internal, self-corrective mechanism to operate. Once a government begins arming it loses proportion and the society, including its various institutions, legitimates the state through passive or active support. The institutions of society find it difficult to correct the state and its activities. This is why some anarchists dislike global concepts such as Society for they play into the hands of the "statesmen." Such concepts miss the diverse and irremediable differences of groups. According to Goodman, for example, people live in societies and groups of associations not in a Society. Others have argued that it is a mistake to think that freedom can be authorized or mandated through the state. Freedom is bonded through direct relations which, as Martin Buber would have it, are optimally face to face and precede modes of governance.[2]

Such ideas are sprinkled around in modern thought and practice. The Marxists talked about the withering away of the state: the anarchists insisted on it, the conservatives demanded it. Political pragmatists argue that governments should have limited powers. The Founding Fathers describe spheres of power which different levels of governments should have, believing that the federal system is the one most likely to protect individual liberties.[3] The purpose of the delineation of power both within the government and between the government and society, it is said, will limit the possibility of total power of the state. In its extreme view this belief holds that governments should get out of the way of the natural industry of the people, and in its modern form, governments should get out of the way of the corporations so that well-being may be attained.

While some of these ideas have an attraction and a certain charm to them and some may be more right than wrong they are not very useful once we look at the developments of society and governments and once we introduce the notion that human beings have needs and rights which precede their relationship to the Other or to a group irrespective of political category. There is now recognition that needs can only be fulfilled through relationship with the group. Self-independence, if it ever existed, is certainly not a condition of modern industrial societies where dependence, interaction, and trust are integral to the group or another for virtually everything.

When there is a recognition of personal need of the other and the realization that we are born into relationships, institutions, problems and potentialities we either seek our own personal interest at the expense of others or we seek the common good, realizing that the common good itself begins from an ensemble of prior rights which human beings can concretize in their relationship to each other and through each other as well as through and against social and state institutions. Once people say that there should be a common good and when we say that everyone is endowed, as American thinkers and statesmen have said, with certain inalienable rights, namely life, liberty and the pursuit of happiness, we have curious but altogether felicitous results. Each institution is constantly challenged to line up in that pursuit, whether public or private, and the power of government is to be used for that purpose. It becomes an actor and is acted upon. According to this view the institutions of the society and the state fall under intense scrutiny from each other, from other groups and institutions for they too are to have the common good in mind as they fulfill the revolutionary charge of pursuit of happiness. In this framework power is shared and free-floating within a force field of the government, institutions and peoples. Government is challenged to secure the common good as institutions become aware of their shortcomings, as individuals and other groups press claims against each other and the government for new rights or old ones reinterpreted and applied more broadly.

When the consciousness of submerged humanity awakens, the motive force is present for profound change which then reshapes the purposes of government and other controlling or central institutions of society. Boundaries, protocols and customs shift in the struggle of power, authority and autonomy between private institutions and the government.[4]

Throughout the struggle between the society and the state runs the issue of the economic underpinnings for all citizens. The common good begins from the principle of a common social product to be equitably shared. How this is to be accomplished reflects a continuous, sometimes dialectical relationship between the institutions of society and the state as they come together in new shapes and forms with each element of society challenging the other to make good, to find a common good for everyone to pursue happiness. This includes the challenge of direct action and the constitutional response of protecting that direct action. The modern world has chosen, for the most part, democracy and democracy is a system knowing no bounds and encouraging those who had no apparent voice to find their voice. It seeks the common good throughout the society enabling people to find themselves. Of course such concepts as democracy and the common good are not set in concrete. They too change and they do so through inquiry and struggle.

In Chapter 6 I discuss the character of the modern democracy with specific emphasis on what could happen in the United States. But I will begin with the common good and its meaning for when we think about the common good we know that it should be throughout the society and in the government, not separated by boundaries or false dichotomies. We intuitively recognize that common good encompasses all humanity in its entirety and recognizes the 'morality of liberation' to attain a measure of happiness for all. The common good calls us to escape categories which have worked as instances and institutions of oppression. Actors for the common good seek means (that of social reconstruction) to find a path and networks that defeat those dichotomies and institutions which keep people from themselves and each other and which do not recognize the inherent dignity of all. The task of social reconstruction is a continuous affirmation of potentiality and practical hope. This optimism is not easy to maintain.

In a time when so many of us feel thrown, or alone and sinking, and in a time when our institutions and knowledge seem to reflect our problems rather than offer any cure or amelioration to them, is there any sense at all in talking about the common good for and among us? In an age of narcissism, selfishness and inattention, is there any value to proclaiming the need for a common good beyond class, or family or self – and trying to show how it just might be achieved?

In an age of deformed institutions and economic turbulence, is there any sense to reinvigorating our social and economic institutions, transforming them so that they will serve the economic, social and psychological dignity of all people? In an age of mass manipulation where politicians package themselves like commodities and where politics is synonymous with power, is there any value to concerning ourselves with a different, humane conception of politics and leadership?

In a system which is both complex and vulnerable where the expert and specialist give the false appearance of knowing and governing wisely but where the citizenry may be aware of even less, is it responsible to argue for a principle of inclusion which allows all to participate in decision making beyond their social role, class and function? In an age where reason is detached from feeling and ethical consequences where we allow ourselves to become slaves of an almost autonomous drive to civilization's extinction, is there any value in relying on our collective reason and common sense as the primary way of saving ourselves and the future of mankind?

And in a time where people are told to hug old social structures, assert fundamentalist dogmas, and seek the repeal of social gains made by women, poor people, workers, since the French and American revolution, should not people argue for more rather than less democracy, for more participation rather than trusteeship and oligarchy to protect and extend the gains of the past?

And finally, should the thrust for social reconstruction be made at all during a time of conservative orthodoxy?

The answer to each of these questions is "yes" if we want civilization to last beyond the twenty-first century. Every activity of politicians, artists, scientists, workers, religious people, farmers, business entrepreneurs, even those whose vocations are not obvious, like intellectuals, must incorporate the way these questions can be affirmatively answered. This inquiry is meant as one key to answering these questions. They are meant to show that the common good as a path can be found.

The common good is not static; it shifts with our understanding and our discoveries of what is possible, of what humankind can positively create. In the day to day search for the common good those concerned with political action and those having to make conscious choices soon become aware that the common good is made up of contradictory and antagonistic elements. Often these antagonisms are between the new and the old. But no one should assume that the "new" or the "old" is *a priori* preferable over the other. In the age of modern science there is always a tendency to dismiss the old for the new. Indeed, the market system stimulates this tendency and there is enough that is rotten in tradition, or decaying in the old which justifies revolutionaries and capitalists alike in wanting to begin from scratch to erase history and its artifacts. But the reality is that the path of the common good encompasses the culture of the past, not in the sense that people should be controlled by another time, but in the sense that the accomplishments and struggles of the past, of other generations, are not to be treated lightly. The accomplishments of others reflect the cumulative power and wisdom of civilization.

The terror of nuclear armaments and the seemingly autonomous direction that institutions involved in the arms race are taking is that they are placing the accomplishments of the past on the butcher block. They oblige those committed to social reconstruction to stay the hand of those who would be our butchers. There is no other choice but to defend what has been built and struggled for over the generations, namely, our cities, technological, religious and artistic treasures.

It is more important than ever for people to understand that with thermo-nuclear weapons as the vanguard of instruments to destroy civilization, a radical position must be that it is not only the destruction of the future that we oppose, but the destruction of the cultures of the past that we live within which we cannot countenance. In any case, it is hard to know what is past and what is future. (J.D. Bernal has correctly pointed out that the basic engineering of the twentieth century is the work of nineteenth-century scientists. They made it possible for us to hear both rock and Palestrina at home conflating the centuries.)[5] If people do not remember their yesterday, or that of others, they become alienated from themselves and their work. Indeed, they have lost consciousness of themselves and of others. They are rootless, given over to anything and anybody. And those who act irresponsibly with power, taking on the ways of cultural vandals, thrive on the destruction of any consciousness of the past.

This is not to say that "talked about" history is the full history. Our understanding of events of the past is invariably incomplete and flawed. Often the descriptions are mythical, screened through the dominant fashions of one's own time. This obvious observation should help to free us from assuming that reported history is the only history. And that what others say happened in the past should dominate our future actions. Thus while on the one hand we must guard humankind against the destroyers of civilization for the sake of the common good, another element in seeking the common good contradicts those reactionaries and conservatives who dote on tradition, turning formerly functional forms into fetishes. Once we recognize and realize what others have accomplished we do not have to be governed by their successes or failures. By comprehending and protecting the past, finding and protecting traditions and styles of art, music, law, politics, science and literature we learn that it is not necessary to build our shelters of thought and practice in completed traditions. We can transcend them because we will know what we do not want, what shelters we cannot fit into.[6] With this recognition we do well to pay close attention to the cyclical aspects of natural history, namely the seasons and their repetitive character, the menstrual cycles of women, the seasons of plantings, the invariability of the individual's death and the personal need that people have to socially belong throughout their lives.[7]

As I will suggest in the last chapter of this book, where we seek wrenching political actions we must never forget the cyclical nature of day to day life.[8] Otherwise we will not comprehend the vulnerability, limits and perpetual needs of humankind. Our political actions will not be successful for we will demand too much or too little of ourselves and others.

There are five important questions which comprise the common good and which should be kept in mind as political change is accepted. The first is how should freedom be integrated into the common good? The second is whether there is a universal definition of the common good which all people would readily recognize? The third is does responsibility for the common good rest with everyone or with trustees? The fourth is how does the common sense lead to the common good? The fifth is if it rests with everyone, does that mean the common good is derived from adding people's private interests with pragmatism being the way to find the additive common good?

Freedom and the common good

The cyclical nature of life does not contradict the need and impulse for freedom. It means, however, that in the generation of the common good a variability to the meaning of freedom will be championed by different people and groups who have differing needs and appetites.[9] While there are variations in the meaning of freedom,[10] the common good should begin with the concept of freedom as the power of the person to do and act according to his or her own purposes, with or without others. This definition assumes that the person is social *and* autonomous. It allows for self- and group-generated activity of which the initiators and participants are the "objects." Thus, for example, in the productive sphere the common good is premised on recognizing a variety of activity and means of organizing work. It encourages worker-controlled activities as well as small and micro-business and self-employment enterprises. It even celebrates the skills of the individual entrepreneurs but within socially and legally defined limits. Analogous to this type of freedom is the modern democracy's guarantee of artistic freedom.[11]

Freedom includes the person's right to choose between different courses of action which might lead to mistakes. Obviously, there is danger involved in this view. While we must cherish the right of error and the right to make mistakes, it is also obvious that such a definition of freedom incurs substantial risks. For example, the development of modern technology and science is predicated on virtually no concern for consequences, or knowledge of how the public might be affected by a particular invention or idea. Part of the reason for this point of view is that it is believed that technological advance does yield human progress and any interference with the right of inventors – except for the patent right – is thought of as undercutting productivity and the advancement of human kind.

In the twentieth century socialist, and even capitalist, states define freedom in relation to the productive process and growth.[12] It is usually thought that nations which have a high and sustained productive economy will either automatically grant more freedom to their people in the sense of more choice or they will be forced to do so by an "itchy" populace that has an economic surplus or social product that should be shared. But it is not clear that high productivity necessarily results in more political freedom. Indeed, in some places high productivity is seen as a contradiction to freedom as, for example, in South Korea, Brazil, and South Africa. Rather than the productive process serving to ennoble freedom the process is reversed. Freedom becomes a prisoner of the productive process and the consumption practices which the productive process engenders. The worker becomes an instrument of those who interpret the productive process to the rest of society.

In state socialism, where emphasis rests on production rather than the human process of it, freedom also becomes a victim. Ironically, so does productivity. Freedom is not found in the wrong answer it is said, nor even in the right to have a wrong answer since each answer is supposed to count toward greater productivity. Thus, in Poland the struggle of the Solidarity group revolved around the participatory right to organize production as a dependent system to freedom whereas the communist party concerned itself with production. In state socialism where so much emphasis is placed on the productive process individual rights and self-definition are victims of supposedly common needs: really needs and wants established by "trustees," i.e. the Party. Because this is so, individuality breaks out in highly eccentric and egoistic ways as, for example, the case of Solzhenitsyn. One cannot blame the victim of a system where people cannot reason *against* and apply their criticial faculties. Because everything is public, the victims become silent, sullen, and privatized. And too often what is not permitted or authorized is illegal. There is little spontaneous social energy which is not channeled, sanctioned or repressed. This is the central problem of socialism, Soviet style. If the institutions of the state or the caring institutions are totally relied upon for one's social existence, both one's feelings and daily actions become deadened – hierarchically managed processes. Often people are repelled by this situation but they have no way of channeling their anger except through selfish acts. Nevertheless, to talk of freedom as separate from people's work is absurd and a carry-over from the type of philosophic idealism which controlled class-oriented societies.

The platonic vision in which work had nothing to do with freedom as an absolute, unsullied ideal because only the slaves did work (indeed this is how slavery came to be identified) is the most pernicious characteristic of ancient thought which controlled Western ideas until the French revolution. Because work and production are essential to our freedom and dignity it is obvious that the common good must relate to the transformation of the situation at the work place including the productive process. The common good can only be acted upon by the person in terms of a particular time or place, as felt experiences which the person helps to bring about through the exercise of rational choices.

The common good and timeless universality

Social reconstruction assumes that people have a natural propensity for the common good which precedes their identification with any particular institution. The common good precedes the class appetite of the individual, group or the appetite of any particular institution. Nevertheless, because classes, families and institutions exist, the person mediates the common good through these institutions. The individual instinct for the common good – caring for the Other – is manifested by the dialectic which a person develops through his or her social and natural environment. It is this dialectic which determines the direction and pace of the common good.

It remains a question, however, whether, as Teilhard or Marx and Hegel might have believed, entering into history means that there is one common good irrespective of place. Political philosophies are contingent on place. That is, they are most applicable to particular historical times and geographies. For example, Hume sought to depend on one's sense and concluded that moral and political questions stemmed from the particular case and from non-rational feelings and unexamined habits. For Plato or Kant, as examples, character and virtue remain unchanged throughout history. But for Hegel, freedom and the common good mean the unfolding of consciousness (the necessary but free choice), as humankind walks through history. It is a changing conception.

I conclude that the practice of the common good is not the same everywhere for all time. Nevertheless, there is a common good everywhere and the present test of international practice is to assert the existence of that common good everywhere. In other words there is not a separate common good for the person, the family, the neighborhood, the city, the nation and the world.

It is to say, however, that the way humankind has fragmented one person from the other in their history and social relationships, creating socially imposed categories, power-dominated knowledge systems and systems to protect property for some over others, the struggle for the common good cannot be contained for very long. When we speak of ending domination and subservience, colonizer-colonized relationships whether between individuals and individual or between group and group, we are seeking new paths of complementarity, and networks of relationships that bind us to each other and which are based on political and social principles of egalitarian interdependence. When we seek basic minimums for social and personal existence with the means of sharing the social product of the society or civilization; when we assert the protection, development and regeneration of culture and the humane defense of it we reflect our emotional and felt need to find a practical meaning to the common good for humankind. To attain personhood and to align institutions and relations with this objective is the purpose of politics.

Personhood is not a concept outside of history which holds true for all time; it is a developing one which knows no final end and which can only be guessed about at any particular time. In other words, personhood is part of a historical process through the generations and is effected by how the earth and nature have been transformed by humankind. The historical

31

process is made up of billions of incompletions, of unfinished hopes and interrupted lives that are propelled forward by an interaction of themselves with others. And so when we think of the common good it can only be seen as a developing and incomplete process. When Aristotle said that man was a political animal, needing others and expressing himself through his relations with others, he should have added that good ends towards which political action attempts to propel us are never fully achieved; they are only sketched, too often erased, and yet there is a cumulative sense of world accomplishment. As the great mathematician Norbert Wiener pointed out, it is a world of malleability and structure:

> The world is an organism, neither so tightly joined that it cannot be changed in some aspects without losing all of its identity in all aspects nor so loosely jointed that any one thing can happen as readily as any other thing. It is a world which lacks both the rigidity of the Newtonian model of physics and the detail-less flexibility of a state of maximum entropy or heat death, in which nothing really new can ever happen. It is a world of Process, not one of a final dead equilibrium to which Process leads nor one determined in advance of all happenings, by a pre-established harmony such as that of Leibnitz.[13]

The common good is a victim and beneficiary of process. We bring to it our constantly unfolding understanding of what the good is, for society is a system of relationships that produces a common and changing understanding. When humankind allows it, society produces a memory of interactions that ground us in a process of seeking, knowing and creating. Process is the end itself. It means that there can be no one left out of any part of the society's process as subject actor or as cared for. It means, as Pope John Paul II said, "that the first principle of the whole ethical and social order" is the common use of goods and the "socializing of the productive process in the way that that process can best serve humankind."[14] This cannot be achieved through the wisdom or power of a communist party, the Trilateral Commission or a hierarchic church. It comes only through energy and sharing each other's knowledge, common sense, and continually reshaping our institutions, whether the state or society (societies).

Politics, then, is seeking the common good which emerges from the consciousness of the person as a person and not as a commodity. The politics of the kind I am describing is a bit like a feedback loop. The conscious person sustains the common good just as the common good organizes social life to encourage people to attain consciousness and the common good. The knowledge and inquiries pursued must therefore be aimed at seeing the person in all of his or her aspects as person, not through one-dimensional roles or institutions. Unrestrained market or oligopoly capitalism, bureaucratic or theological orthodoxy enchain people into single dimensionality thereby distorting our gaze and diminishing our personhood. In their present form each of these processes serves as an impediment to humankind making a humane history. Understanding that this is so merely defines the political problem. We do not wave our wands, beat drums and watch the disappearance of institutions and ideologies which people commit themselves to or roles which define who they are. People need roles and protection because nakedness is a frightening thing for people. There can be very little direct economic activity if people do not have social roles. And while we now talk against "cover ups" and "covers" giving the appearance that we wish for nakedness and total honesty once it is there as the fundamental element of governing, we become frightened. We mediate ourselves through masks and roles. And we are encouraged to do so by law, our economic system and our other social institutions.

We can reject nakedness and instead embrace the truth of looking at the Other which rends for both the unspoken truth. We must learn to feel our commonness with others in their vulnerability and humanity; and our own. This quality of openness will cause the other *not* to avert our gaze. It is this kind of tracking which should be present in the undertaking of social reconstruction. It is this point of view which should help in "humanizing" our institutions. This then is a process for all people capable of participating in it. But who are the ones deemed capable?

The common good and trusteeship

When we examine the political structure of nations we see that nations are run by trustees who supposedly define the common good for their respective nation. What they really do is no more than broker between contending interests among powerful elites. In the political realm trustees are either elected, selected, or are chosen through war, revolution, coup, family connections or "heredity right." Through history, often knocking at the back door or presenting itself in spasms, is the populace which seeks direct participatory inclusion. The assumption of the participatory mode is that, to the extent possible, each person wants to participate in a process which affects him or her, and thus is more likely to accept the consequences of choices in which they participated.

Even in the best of circumstances where planners may believe they speak for the whole and where they believe they are in fact performing for others, the likelihood of failure is very great. The most dangerous case is where the one or the few decide for the many about whether life on the planet should continue, or where hundreds of millions should perish in war, all justified by a misplaced notion of trusteeship. The other is the more obvious and correctable situation. In 1972 a public housing project in St Louis, Missouri was destroyed by the US army because it was too hard to maintain – the people who lived in the project hated it and vandalized the project because they could not control it. Yet twenty years before this project had won an architectural award for its design. The same is true of other such projects where they were torn down forty years after they were built because the people did not feel that the projects were theirs either in terms of ownership, architectural design or participatory control.[15] Trustees of activities are bound to fail where the priniciple of inclusion is not accepted and where the notion of sovereignty and ownership is not shared by those who in fact live their lives in the particular institution. In modern democracies the nature of what is known and the possibility of new forms of communication make the formerly impenetrable distinctions between government and citizen, teacher and student, worker and consumer no more permanent than a mark drawn with one's hand in the sea.

The assumption that trustees know or knew more than others, a principle held strongly in state socialist nations where the communist party is thought to operate as the embodiment of the historical process and the truth giver, much in the manner of Plato's guardians, cannot be taken seriously any more.[16] The same is true of the trustee system in Western nations. Too many bad decisions have been made by the few for the many which the many have to live out in their lives.

There are those who criticize the trustee system because it distributes power and legitimacy to too many trustees. For example, Hitler believed that he was the embodiment of the people: they would have to do his will.[17] Those who believed in him did so on the principle that they were extensions of him, just as he was the instrument of their desires.

In modern democracy, however, there is a strong predisposition to believe in the people, both as they act for themselves and as they act with others. The reason for this is a belief in people's judgment and common sense.

Common sense and common good

Our common sense allows us to live in the world by teaching us that we are utterly dependent on each other from the moment of birth. Our perceptions, how we interpret those perceptions and certainly our preferences are learned through and with others. They may either be shared understandings in which each person in her or his fullness contributes to seeing and understanding others, or the person may in fact be living solely the life of someone else's understandings and perceptions. As we grow older, if the social structure and the political situation allow it, we become interdependent in the sense of giving and taking love, exercising productive capability with and for others, helping others to perceive particular situations as potentially mad or dangerous or life affirming. We do so automatically and uncritically, operating only on common sense. A relatively benign social and political structure helps us lay up a personal and collective bank of experiences and perceptions which may be the ground for the common good. Our individual senses are not enough to seed the ground for the common good. Aquinas was right when he referred to the individual senses as needing a sixth sense, "sensus communis," the common sense which holds sway over all others. Before she died, Hannah Arendt said that

> This same sense, which is a mysterious sixth sense because it cannot be localized as a bodily organ, enables the sensations of my strictly private five senses – so private that sensations in their merely sensational quality and intensity are incommunicable – to fit into a common world shared with others, though its mode of appearance may be different.[18]

But the common sense, which the other senses report to in the individual, cannot exist in a vacuum. The common sense of the person needs other people in their fullness, not as images on television screens or as isolated, inert individuals. Our common sense reaches out to others in fulfilling desires and in perceiving that the world is "an intersubjective space" which remains unrecognized or is dessicated unless it seeks with others the common good. The common sense cannot operate fully unless there is a collective willingness within a society and government to cherish this capacity and not abuse it by institutions and knowledge which operate purposely to frame the unsuspecting. How treacherous it is that so many activities – and technologies – of modern life are meant to betray or befuddle us.

Bernard Lonergan correctly said that "Common sense knows, but it does not know what it knows nor how it knows nor how to correct and complement its own inadequacies. In other words, it can never know enough to help the world out of its present crisis."[19] We should not think that holding on to the experiences of the people, already warped and emptied by television and every conceivable manipulation, we will be able to rely on people's common sense to reach the common good. This fact puts us at a fork in the road. It is either platonism, where only the trustee can know, or towards reconstruction, where each person with others can debate what is to be known and what is to be done. Lonergan hopes for the platonic solution to the civilization:

> What is both unnecessary and disastrous is the exaltation of the practical, the supremacy of the state, the cult of the class. What is necessary is neither class nor state, that stands above all claims, that cuts them down to size, that is founded on the native detachment and disinterestedness of every intelligence, that commands first allegiance, that implements

35

itself primarily through that allegiance that is too universal to be bribed, too impalpable to be forced, too effective to be ignored.[20]

But no such people exist. Surely they are not the neo-conservatives around *Commentary* magazine or the triumphalists in the Moral Majority or even the mock gothic world of the Committee on Social Thought at the University of Chicago. Lonergan's notion is not the politics of a democracy. It is the esthetics of Herman Hesse's bead player who dares to think that his game played by the elite of the elite keeps the world from spinning off its axis. No elite can speak successfully for the whole. Nevertheless, from Plato's reactionary and elitist views there is something that can be taken.[21] It is the dialogic method. We can champion the Socratic dialogue and conversation form which will stimulate all people into entering the public space, sharing and generating a social common sense. Such dialogues will help us know and inquire into what we do not know and help us talk through programs of intention with those who are the objects of such intentions. This is what mass communications should help to generate. Unfortunately, the purpose of the communications and propaganda industry around the world fits more with the trustee view in which a few ostensibly know the truth or the "facts" while the rest are framed into them. They use a distancing language which masks and mystifies – a condition that must be remedied if we are to attain the common good. Knowledge and opinions are filtered through the prism of the dominant class and one's own senses are thought to be less trustworthy than the received information which is presented by the dominant class. As a result of the Reagan counter-revolution the underclass is not expected to be heard in the public space let alone take part in reshaping social institutions. People are not to be noticed except through the categories created by the dominant class. Is it by intention or accident that the two interlinked estates of the modern large corporation and government have the capacity to transform people into passive facts, objects to be categorized, pieces of human beings which are dealt with upon demand? In the films of the 1930s there was a routine which the comedian Jack Benny had with his black sidekick "Rochester," played by Eddie Anderson. The screen would go dark and Benny would ask, "Are you there, Rochester?" He would respond and say, "Ah's here, boss" and one would see only the whites of Anderson's eyes. Blacks were not present unless asked to be noticed. Blacks were not to be seen or heard.

In the elitist trustee view, people do not exist for those in the dominant class (whether they are liberal or conservative) except when they are called upon to exist. (Labelling and categorizing of course have become a big business.) They then are wanted and used as an armed force or a pool of workers. It is taken for granted that people in these categories have no shared common sense. Nevertheless underclasses can frame the conditions of the master and in the end change the nature of who gets to decide basic questions of everyday life. In his autobiography Booker T. Washington tells how, as a freed slave, he did everything and therefore learned everything while his former master did less and knew how to do less.[22]

By definition, modern democracy is committed to all people being active subjects of their own history. Democratic adherents accept the potentiality and the common sense of all people. The result is that a common good may be forged. In the process class and social roles will be transformed. The wretched, those not heard from, can define their world and ours – with us. This is what I have attempted to suggest in my comments on law and justice. It means job and task sharing. It means continuous learning. It means no artificial barriers. When we transcend class we can begin to see that we have a capacity for shared understanding which can build through experiences in which we manifest loving, caring and compassion. Strengthening, through use, of this capacity finally determines the long-run success of human beings. We have not stimulated the face to face relationship or those relationships which command caring. Instead scientists and technologists have invented systems of categorizations through pigeonholing, believing that this is progress. This dangerous tendency contradicts our common sense and instead fits with the authoritarian/totalitarian mode which has been central to social organization. As William Hocking has said,

> Organization is in its nature impersonal: it can deal only in the common denominators of personality, the abstract elements of will. If it touches men powerfully, it invites them to accept its generalized human being in place of their concrete selfhood, and thus dehumanizes those with whom it converses.[23]

But modern democratic organization does not have to be authoritarian in its form. It can look to augment and generate those attributes of civilization which allow us to see things in new ways, somewhat more gently and more empathetically. Democracy then *changes* government into a participatory function which encourages all of us to see things and events in new ways.[24] Through the participatory function our definition of private or personal interest necessarily changes.

The common good and private interests

British philosophic thinking held that private interests could be added together to make the common good. But this insight only seems to apply when the people are members of the same social and economic class, one that is a bourgeois class. At their most incisive, utilitarians like Bentham sought to find a rhetoric, an agreed upon method of compromise, to resolve conflicts that emerge from members of the same class. Utilitarian ideas have not successfully solved problems across class lines. They do not tell us how the private interests of the capitalist owner and the worker, or the broken tenant farmer can be added together to make the common good. Utilitarian theory worked only to the extent Great Britain's political leadership submerged its class conflicts at home by encouraging technological and geographic expansion, exodus and colonization.

The reader should not think that it was only the Marxists who saw the contradictions between capitalism and the common good. A half-millennium before, Thomas Aquinas saw it when capitalism was a mere gleam in the eye of traders. According to him there was no way to be involved in profit enterprises in a moral manner because they result in wealth leaving the society and ending either in the hands of the individual or the corporate organization *against* the society itself. No wonder R.H. Tawney called Marx the last of the *Schoolmen*.[25] He was in his time rejecting the learning of his predecessor Ricardo to favor that of Aquinas who values the group over the individual. Taking their own cue from Socrates in *The Republic*, Marxists argue that the common good for all cannot be found in a capitalist society since what is thought to be "good" or "just" is dictated by the private interests of the dominant class. As a result, the capacities *there* in people for goodness and creativity cannot be exercised because the collectivity is not nurtured. The collectivity exists only as strangers who happen to do particular things together like wait for a bus or buy things from one another in unrelated transactions.

Modern utilitarians, namely John Rawls, have sought to curb the rough edges of capitalism by laying down a standard to which it must repair. For Rawls the common good is that set of activities which maintains conditions and achieves objectives that are similarly to everyone's advantage.[26] But this definition begs the question. What do we mean by advantage? Since not everyone starts in the world equally, whether for reasons of personal endowment, class advantage or good luck, what can it mean that everyone's advantage should be served? The only way that the definition can have ethical meaning is if we begin from a reconstructive position. For example, a just economic policy must assume that there should be no social arrangement which causes inequality because that arrangement adds to the unequal condition which exists or is caused by nature.[27] To make such a policy work in practice it is necessary that the educational and social system emphasize the importance and centrality of service by those who have great gifts. They are to be encouraged and socialized to use those gifts not only for themselves but primarily for others. It would then not matter that some have greater judgment or leadership capability or scientific agility than others, or that they live longer than others for they are socially educated to serve others with their endowments and abilities. In American society this sentiment is lost even among knowledge workers who are taught to be in service of themselves or a particular vested interest. They are expected to surrender their critical capacity. Knowledge workers become deputies and hired guns without consciousness beyond their most particular need and comfort.[28] They are hired to justify or operate a certain type of school, or build a cruise missile or make and manage nuclear weapons or devise inequitable (or equitable) taxing schemes. They are expected to seek advantage for themselves using their knowledge as pieces of private property and personal capital. And the advantages they seek are for those who already have advantage. One has only to note the nexus between leading law schools, bright law students and Wall Street law firms to understand how advantage and sacrifice work together to increase the wealth and power of the propertied. In a capitalist society it is taken for granted that professionals are to be rewarded with property and a certain amount of wealth. As I suggest in Chapter 2, before we can expect any particular group in the society to accept less for the advantage of others, a different attitude towards property is required to seep into our conscious-ness. I do not believe that a pragmatic or utilitarian attitude will change the consciousness of people so that a common good will be sought, let alone achieved.

The common good and pragmatism

Pragmatists and utilitarians see particular goals to be achieved. They operate incrementally. They are not interested in the interrelationship between the particular problem they have carved out as "the problem" to the force field in which the problem exists. This is thought to be unnecessary because the principles of the pragmatists are given and accepted. In a time of crisis this is politically unwise for there are no guideposts (sturdy principles). Although John Dewey might have hoped otherwise the pragmatic experiment requires us to believe that there are ends to be achieved from a related set of means in which everything else around the particular "experiment" is to be held constant. Pragmatists are like surgeons who set themselves an order of priorities when performing an operation. The surgeon's concern is to hold everything constant in the patient and the situation in such a way as to avoid any dramatic change. Curiously, John Dewey started from the assumption that everything is in flux. Other pragmatists gave the appearance that they were prepared to change everything because their belief was that change is the law of life. This remains the ideological point of view of American scientists and technologists in their approach to their experiments. Yet in political matters pragmatists' views of change and of purposes such as equity are very narrow. They are bounded by a willingness to accept the distribution of power as a given and to operate in a brokering way between the powerful and the powerless. The charges that Dewey levelled at the utilitarians *in practice* could be laid at the doorsteps of the pragmatists: concern with the product rather than the productive process, fostering the class interest of the capitalist to the virtual exclusion of everyone else, protection of the business activity so long as it followed legal rules, rules which business owners were central in devising. Dewey's critique that utilitarianism narrowed the definition of the good to a bottom line mentality was true. But the pragmatists also lost any moral compass so that they had no means to judge either capitalism or nuclear war. The defects of pragmatism were finally played out in the thoughts of Sidney Hook who made false dichotomies between "red" or "dead" as if both were logical and biological opposites of each other. The pragmatists, who were for a time the essence of liberalism, have become the neo-conservatives whose role justified power as it was used and executed by the corporate and military powerful. Changes gave way to stability and experimental diversity gave way to order.

Max Horkheimer understood the limits of pragmatism at a time when it was hard for others to see the direction it would finally take when its humane masters had died.[29] This refugee from Nazism who came to the United States with a critical philosophic vision proceeded to question the liberal pragmatic dogmas of Robert Lynd and Dewey. He saw that as much as it might want to, pragmatism was not dealing with the cultural contradictions that had arisen as a result of capitalism. And he saw that utility and pragmatism had become a cover story for the domination of the status quo.

> Paradoxically, a society that, in the face of starvation in great areas of the world allows a large part of its machinery to stand idle, that shelves many important inventions, and that devotes innumerable working hours to moronic advertising and to the production of instruments of destruction – a society in which these luxuries are inherent has made usefulness its gospel.[30]

Horkheimer was anything but an idealist and yet he understood clearly the fatal flaw in the utilitarian-pragmatist method which failed to show how to get out of the contradictions that the self-justifiying ideas of capitalism had put Western societies. The glorifiers of the incremental approach did not see that pragmatism can easily degenerate into a method of convenience and expediency for the powerful because there are no fixed principles or purposes which themselves can be directly judged. Such expediency, degenerative pragmatism, is the practice of any working hierarchy which takes for granted its own assumptions and structures and those of other organizations with which it must deal. Needless to say, incremental pragmatism does define the crisis of the modern American politician on the liberal side of the spectrum. It is also the crisis of others as well.

Whatever the social system, pragmatists who wield power in the name of different ideologies often see social stability as a good unto itself, believing that too much change or moral turbulence is dangerous. As a political method pragmatism is serviceable so long as a system's first principles hold (whatever they may be). But when there is a turning, that is, when the social system is under serious attack, when it does not perform *according to its purposes*, as vague or contradictory as they might be, when it does not deliver materially, then the first principles of the system do not hold. In a social upheaval where principles are under serious and sustained attack from all sides, it is then that pragmatism fails because there is no framework for it to operate within. While pragmatists may pride themselves on their openness and disdain for fixed principles, their fixed principles are derived from the "reality" of the distribution of power. Where power is in flux their actions descend to principles of convenience. I do not want to imply that pragmatism does not have its place. Indeed, people drawn to politics invariably have a strong pragmatic streak. Politicians invariably adopt a pragmatic view of human nature. It may be important, as William James has said, to know the beliefs of another person with whom one deals for good material reasons, but political people constantly shift their beliefs where power is the sole object.

Each period of history, each ideology emphasizes different aspects of people's nature exploiting or strengthening one attribute over another. The purpose of those committed to the common good must be to emphasize those aspects which result in the common good. But such emphasis may in fact contradict the pragmatic mode of politics for it assumes that the common good is both a process and fairly clearly defined both in quantitative and qualitative terms. It is prepared to fix such goals and not surrender them. If those of us concerned with reconstruction find pragmatism as often contradicting equity, sharing and dignity when faced with the realities of political power, what philosophic method should be thought about as compatible with our purposes?

Some would say that the method to be used should be a dialectical one. But the problem with the dialectical method is that it is evanescent like a film of a series of appearances which keep changing before one's eyes. The content of the film is often lost because what appears to be is not. And vice versa. The dialectical method fashions a truth until it is stated, then is found wanting. It becomes a lie after it is uttered or revealed. Because pragmatism is insufficient, leading to ad hoc convenience, and because it tails off into a utilitarianism whose advantage is given to those who already have, and because dialectical thought leads to lies or splitting the difference between "opposites," calling the difference the synthesis although there may be thousands of other choices and shades between the thesis and antithesis, we are still left needing a method which is beyond that of muddling through on a case by case basis.

The common good

Because of the continuing, profound changes in modern life, political philosophy must be *projective* to the extent that it helps us know what we don't want as well as what we need and want. A projective method should tell us something about how to get to common, ethical purposes. It would seek to end the gulf between objective and subjective knowledge. In this way we can reduce the number of tragic errors that this gulf has produced. A projective mode will include the need to comprehend the nature of trust as a fundamental human and social attribute. It will also include our rethinking the role of scientific inquiry and its character. Finally, a projective mode will require concern with a new type of leadership and bureaucracy which is institutionally arranged to invite more freedom, creativity and participation. These matters I concern myself with in later chapters of this book.

Can trust help us find the common good?

We should be aware that people are able to live and survive with that which is less than good or not in their interest. Unless a system is hopelessly pathological the oppressed will not think to overthrow it or change it. Contrary to Sartre it is not because people are part of the practico-inert that they do not act, it is because they are acting on their innate sense of trust and confidence. Indeed, the most outrageous practices will continue and will be acceptable to people with exploiters building on people's innate sense of trust and confidence. Such practices and pathological social systems continue *only* through the goodness of people who operate according to natural systems of trust which are independent of the social system and inhere in each individual. To the extent that a social system destroys trust, insisting on distrust, competition and meanness (thereby damaging people's innate decency) the people as a people will be destroyed. Thus, political and social systems serve at the pleasure of the people. They trade on their good sense, until the people's humanity is so deformed that they have become as beasts, or until people cannot recognize what is happening to them. Their pain, circumstance, technology and social organization overwhelm them. It is then that they become broken-spirited or totally other worldly and the social system in which they live takes on utterly pathological characteristics. The political irony is that the people who perform slavish work are often the ones who must be trusted as, for example, the miners of South Africa.

When the dominant organized social system becomes intolerable, the ties of trust and affection are broken. There is a physiological – almost instinctual – belief either in the Eschaton, the group's end or in a new possibility. Our "sixth sense" does not choose for us. Our bodies choose for us. This is why so many women stopped menstruating in the concentration camps of the Nazis, for inmates knew that human relationships were broken.[31] The Nazis enforced a policy that was meant to destroy trust and affection among people and their collective future as well. Scientists pursued the course of breaking social bonds with much alacrity since the nineteenth century.

It is painful but true that the practice of the Nazis is presaged in the social thought of the nineteenth century with its social darwinist ethics, its eugenics, and its fashionable belief that those who were lazy, stupid or incompetent had no place in society and should be "let go."[32] This anti-communal feeling which often hid behind the rhetoric of community social welfare and progress persists in some modern states. Similarly, scientists have jumped at the chance of enhancing their power through the state giving the state weapons which destroy the common world heritage of knowledge and material resources in exchange for an alliance with state power. Unwittingly, they encouraged people to trust in their creation, weapons, rather than in humankind.

Modern states, encased in bureaucratic and technological paraphernalia and rhetoric, often with the support of police, corporations and political parties, undermine the impulse of people's trust and affection. Therefore, they destroy the caring attribute which sees beyond the Other's flaws or personal handicaps to the core of human existence. Destroying these sentiments and the means for expressing these sentiments has the gravest consequences for world civilization. For it means that there can be no rules or laws that interrupt or control conflict. This situation also has profound implications among those who fall out with one another in politics irrespective of their political purposes.

My emphasis on "trust" may remind some reader of free market capitalists who insist that depressions occur because trust and confidence are undermined by the state. There is truth to this "charge." It is not inaccurate to say that capitalism has learned to package the qualities of trust and caring in human nature as money, price and commodities. We know that the world's banking credit system trades on people's sense of responsibility and trust of each other. The banking system exists because there is a human impulse to trust and that most businesses are conducted on the basis of a handshake, hand signals at an auction, or agreements over a telephone.

There is no way to comprehend the relationship between parents and infants except as systems of trust and affection. When a person drives a car he or she is involved in a thousand different decisions which can harm the driver and others moment by moment. The driver is involved in continuous trust of others. We are all prepared to embrace stringent if not repressive controls over ourselves so that we will not hurt others, and so that others can trust our driving. We also know that institutions which start from the assumption that others cannot be trusted exist on the basis of trust and affection among their members. Armed forces must trust their soldiers not to kill each other or their officers rather than the enemy. And when the reverse begins to happen, it is clear that the nature of the war has changed to one of rebellion or revolution. A hospital, to the extent that it operates as a hospital today, must start from an operative assumption of trust and affection between the medical workers, and then with the patients. Where technical knowledge is "cold" and unattached and deviates from commonly accepted meanings of trust and affection, there will be a failure of the knowledge itself. It will not be an elixir but a poison.

We may recall that Marx and Engels had a good way of describing how the social system frittered away the very core of people's humanity. Engels pointed out that "there was a time, as in the Middle Ages, when only the superfluous, excess of production over consumption was exchanged." But this was only the half of it. It was a natural right that a person expected to eat. On the other hand, "There was again a time, when not only the superfluous but all products, all industrial existence, had passed into commerce, when the whole or production depended on exchange."[33] And then there came a time when everything was for sale:

> Finally there came a time when everything man considered inalienable became an object of exchange, of traffic and could be alienated. This is the time when the very things which till then had been communicated, but never exchanged, given but never sold, acquired but never bought – virtue, love, conviction, knowledge, conscience, etc.[34]

When everything is for sale, including aspects of a person's being, the person is both selling or renting part of himself. This is the modern political meaning of alienation. But to make the commodity system work, trust and affection must be part of each commodity. Modern economic systems trade on the very aspects of people's nature which *cannot* be alienated. Suppose a martian looked at the way capitalism or state socialist bureaucracy affected a person. He would see that people who produce and use products internalize in their products and relationships love, conscience, trust and responsibility. The money-price system and the legal system, he would note, trade on these qualities. *However rotten the particular system is, it must be grounded in the essence of human goodness*. It is true that human love and responsibility may end up being misplaced and misused. But surely no one will deny that the qualities Engels talked about are present.

When I buy food in a store I am trusting the persons who grew the food that I am not going to be poisoned. Even where laws exist which supposedly punish people who grow poisonous food, I buy the food on the basis of my trust of those who handle it before me. The intervention of the state's laws is merely a deterrent which does not affect my trust or the conscience of the food producer. Furthermore, I am forced to trust the laws, lawyers, the men of state and their intentions, that they are acting on my behalf. Any exchange relationship is preceded by need and trust. Before people can engage in exchange they must first have a need or a desire for something and also trust each other that the goods are what they seem to be. People are tricked just because their natural tendency is one of trust. It is in our nature. But what is in us individually as an empathic sense must be brought out as a political sentiment where all share in it and build on it. ·

I am not so naive as to believe that people will not seek economic advantage or political advantage at the cost of others where there is no program or ethic to do otherwise. Surely people will adopt principles of convenience where they have not generated principles which govern beyond any particular situation with which they might be faced. In his essay on the Pan-African revolt, C.L.R. James points out how even race prejudice is surely a principle of convenience.

> Before the revolution Negroes were so despised that white women undressed before them as one undresses today before a dog or a cat. Ten years after, when former slaves were now ruling the country, most of the whites accepted the new regime, fraternized with the ex-slave generals and dined at their tables; while the white women, members of some of the proudest families of the French aristocracy, threw themselves recklessly at the black dictator, sent him locks of hair, keepsakes, passionate letters, etc. To the laboring Negroes, however, they showed as much of their old hostility as they dared. When the Le Clerc expedition came, the whites rushed to join it, and took a leading part in the gladiatorial shows where dogs ate living Negroes, etc. But when they saw that Le Clerc's expedition was doomed to defeat, they disentangled themselves from it and turned again to the blacks. Dessalines, the new dictator, declared the island independent, but promised them their properties. This was enough for them.[35]

This terrifying quote shows that we must be agnostic about how human nature interacts in situations where social structures are crumbling. All we can say is that people have certain capacities which social systems attempt to use and which people hope to find to their advantage. If we hold to the principles of the common good as unfolding through history we begin with the political choice that there is a natural capacity within people for trust and empathy. By choosing as an assumption paths for human happiness we are able to judge goals, consequences, and purposes in our political actions and the actions of others.

The legitimacy of social reconstruction stems from the power of dialogic reason and empathic sensibility to project into the future what is commonly desirable now, what we feel to be desirable and what so many others have struggled for and what can be talked out. We find out these desires through the democratic process of participating and deliberating in the public space in society and then we find ways of implementing our choices through the government – or against it. The dialogue which must be continuously held is the one which generates new political, social and economic instrumentalities that call upon our natural sensibilities and which tell us, through our reason and passion, what is inhuman and out of bounds. Of course, man's attraction to violence and revenge is great, often greater in any particular case than his interest in justice. In Homer's *Iliad* we learn of the brutality and ugliness of war, also that it excites us and that we are attracted to violence and violent action. We are excited by the technology of destruction whether with nuclear weapons or the sight of cleats digging into the flesh of football players. But given the nature of modern organized violence is it not obvious that the fascination for it must be put to an end? And to the extent we act must we not choose for empathy and trust, risking our own alienation and failure in the bargain? This is the only tolerable way of confronting our personal and social bondage which surely will come with the destruction of civilization. I doubt that we need more than common sense to see this, although to recognize our plight does not effectuate the insight into changing reality. There are, however, examples where common sense insight may change reality. The work of people in the disarmament movement, whether physicians who use their social or technical power or the religious who call on faith and trust as the correct way of averting ruin, are now appealing to our common sense. And in so doing common survival if not the common good may result – through changing what physicians and theologians are ordinarily expected to think and talk about. Then they become citizens and catalytic leaders in all spheres of the body politic.

2
Becoming leaders and organizers

In the 1960s the movements in motion had a positive aversion to leadership. Those who worked in the barrios and slums, or turned out people for street demonstrations believed that leadership was merely a form of ego tripping. While celebrities were expected to attend meetings and demonstrations it was taken for granted by all concerned that they would not be part of the planning or organizing strategy whether it was for a demonstration or to obtain a street light. There was a shared belief that leaders would seek to "run things" and they would confirm the iron rule of oligarchy taking on to themselves the status and power to decide and channel the more localized and spontaneous directions at the local or grassroots level.

There was also an unstated fear that any national organization which generated leaders would result in leaders who would become like trustees, that is, worthies who would perpetuate people as an inert mass representing, sanitizing, and reinterpreting people's needs and views to their own ends. Organizers were favored (especially by organizers!) over leaders for it was often said that they were more responsible to the political base.

The organizer's task was one of "revolutionary patience," often to wait or sit in silence as the local group groped to a decision. Unfortunately, there was little interest in national politics except in a whiggish way so characteristic of Americans. Demands were usually negative, for example get the government to stop doing wrong, in this case the wrong was the Vietnam war. No national program emerged from the 1960s and early 1970s and national leaders, those who did come to the fore, invariably did so around a particular issue. The movements themselves failed at generating a national program sinking leaders whose task should have been that of catalyzing people into action. To have denied the need for leadership even as enablers was to deny a requirement for national political action and social reconstruction.

Leadership is an undeniable aspect of social existence. And it comes in a variety of forms. Some people are natural leaders as a result of their authority and mastery over a particular field. Thus, Albert Einstein was a towering leader in scientific thought. He was able to lead on the basis of his proofs, reasoning, openness to empirical verification and sweetness of disposition. Others lead by acting as spiritual catalysts in organizing social groups. They see the possibility of making connections, of taking imaginings and putting them into practice with people who quickly recognize the central truth of what is being attempted. Martin King was such a leader. Such persons are to be distinguished from trustees; those who "govern" on the basis of inheritance, wealth, or social status. It does not matter whether they are entitled to that position. It is because they are *in* that position, self-appointed, elected and chosen by others, or as a result of wealth that they are looked to by others. For example, many of the members of the US Senate who are multimillionaires are mistaken for "leaders" although they are really trustees for wealth. Often as not they have little capacity and when they lose their position they have nothing but their wealth or their former position as the basis for their "leadership".[1]

The process of political leading on more than one issue or in more than one situation is the process of seeing far, of seeing the wholeness and interrelation of things, of seeing seemingly unrelated things and processes which come together in a future, of advantages which can be taken, of limits which must be set, and purposes to be achieved. Above all, leadership seeks to get others to act and to lead, to become part of a chain of moral creativity. The United States in its inception was blessed with a number of men who were such leaders.

The question about leadership is whether it can now be yoked with moral purpose or whether leadership is related to power alone which only accidentally might have a moral purpose. The success of the American revolution was that a moral purpose was clearly defined by its leaders through a palpable situation generally felt. It was yoked to deist or religious purposes which went beyond the particular special capacity of the particular economic interest the leader might have had. Leaders were meant to define a new order of justice.[2] In the end of an epoch and the beginning of another where do leaders find moral purpose? It is found in taking responsibility for the problems of others. These problems may not have been those of the leaders but as a result of a surplus of consciousness they are understood existentially and taken up as his or her own, just as Freud's Moses took on the Jews' struggle for freedom. Leaders learn that the problems of the Other are theirs as well. The Bible depicts Joseph as a born leader because he was able to reach to the hearts of others. He had a gentle disposition, had suffered much himself and was willing to fail rather than commit a dishonorable act. In this way his supporters trusted him for they knew that he would not betray them or change course for expediential reasons.[3] He seemed to be free of personal anxiety and therefore he had a calming effect on others. (The reader might want to stop and ponder a comparision between Joseph and Henry Kissinger on these points.) The leader gets people to see themselves in new ways and then to act to fulfill themselves. Imaginative leaders know that vision needs practical steps which ennoble and embolden others. Without such steps the alienation that people feel between their lived experience and what people hoped or thought will create immobilization. The born leaders act as catalysts. Through their imagination of a possible future they create enthusiasm, articulating the felt needs of others. But leaders must also have practical wisdom so that others will know that their vision can be fulfilled without superhuman effort, or suffering.[4]

Leaders who seek the common good in a democracy do so through the dialogic method and the clear understanding that there are limits which they cannot cross and human social purposes that must be analyzed and publicly deliberated. They bring questions forward which otherwise would not be considered. And they lead in the moral search for the good of the whole. On the other hand, the citizen's task is never to be overwhelmed by leadership and to understand that it is a quality which is of value only where there is a strong attachment to achieving the common good on the part of the leader and the group that he or she may represent.

The role of leaders is critical, however, especially so during a period where society seeks to reorder its priorities and values.

Clever political leaders study the weaknesses and strengths of their friends and adversaries. Activists and politicians alike spend a great deal of time analyzing the character of people, what to ask for, how to ask it and how to get people to do certain things which will serve the petitioner's purpose. If they are skillful at their work and they live in a time where there is not a common feeling of great expectancy or urgency, they will never ask someone to perform a task which is out of character, that is, what a person's behavior would be under normal circumstances. Political brokers and leaders are concerned that their requests are not refused since such refusals set up tensions that are likely to breach normal and relatively successful patterns of relationship which are "skin deep." Even worse, the person may grant the favor or do the task, but he or she may exact a price which the politician will not be able to pay at another time.

It may be possible to cajole a rich man into confronting his class on a particular set of issues, but he cannot be cajoled against his own character.

American leaders (when they operate domestically) start from the principle that people are not infinitely malleable. This is an important and altogether tolerable trait of American politics. The disaster of revolutionary leaders is that they often give up the notion of human limits of endurance and purpose, in part out of the difficult situation which revolutionary leaders are faced with after a revolution, but also because revolutionaries often believe that man's nature is a bare slate upon which one can write anything.[5] As revolutionaries have learned in this century, the political consequences of righting wrongs or promulgating comprehensive purposes can be disastrous. The rhetorically skilled are often able to conceptualize problems and transform the difficulty of lived experiences into ideas and images that appear easier or less tormenting than they really are. Thus, Mao's cultural revolution may have been a way to keep the flames of revolution burning and was intended to interrupt the bureaucratization of the revolution by the Chinese mandarins with little pain, but the costs on the people were overwhelming. Similarly, the mistaken willingness to favor the workers over the peasants in the Russian revolution may have been seen as an easy task but it turned into terrifying bloodshed because the peasants would not go along.

Of course, revolutionary leaders have many problems to sort out. They attempt to see beyond immediate problems and the institutional oppression which they inherit from the old regime. In the Third World they may think about distributive justice first and then political freedom.[6] Their task becomes the establishment of practical methods that production can increase, that culture can be liberated for production, and that a new surplus, socially shared, can be created. This surplus is meant to include material goods and spirit, the latter being generated through exemplary action, creative energy and good will. Hence, revolutionary leaders define their purpose as the encouragement of shared actions which can obtain a measure of equity between the various classes which continue in existence long after a radical revolution. To this end the revolutionary leader does not distinguish between the public and private space.[7]

Once a revolutionary fervor is released everyone believes that time has stopped for a moment. It is then that leaders must act quickly, know what they are doing. Otherwise, they and others tend to fall back on old ways, or they mistake the reforms toward centralization of the last regime as the revolutionary process. If a revolutionary leadership is lucky enough to avert a civil war or the hostile alliance of other nations, the leadership, no matter how decent and righteous, no matter what they might have planned for, are in danger of being entrapped in the vise of the past, be confronted by previously repressed and bottled up passions which are often quite mad, and which they did not imagine existed. This madness scares the new leaders just as their old assumptions about human behavior do not appear to fit the new realities. Yet the revolutionaries are stuck with a bureaucratic apparatus which is lost, insecure and not quite sure how it can do the bidding of the new masters. The Tsarist state, for example, was the "front" for authoritarian forms such as the Orthodox Church and the army, the great landed gentry, a police bureaucracy, a nascent market system which protected the rich and powerful but punished the rural classes. Yet Lenin depended on this apparatus for his changes just because revolution is chaotic by its nature.[8] Revolutionary leaders concerned with governing follow one of two courses: (a) they depend on past ideas which might not have any relevance to current conditions or (b) they pursue a dogmatic view of the world. Yet their official dogma requires that they *not* believe in power except as a transitory thing. Their inability to deal with how to limit and legalize their own power once they seek a "new man" and "new society" is why revolutions usually fail in achieving the common good. Finally, their interest is in melding violence and power. The result is the victory of violence over reason. Activists and people's movements such as the Maghdevites were swallowed up by the wave of revolutionary turbulence and ideological insecurity. The party could not see farmers and shopkeepers as groups which could be brought into the process of social transformation. They were considered enemies not because they agreed with any part of the old regime, but because they did not agree with the anti-democratic, hierarchic nature of the new regime. Revolutions in our time are social constructs. They make little sense to the processes of radical change which are now necessary. It is mistaken to believe that a particular end, justice, can be accomplished by doing its dialectical opposite, violence. It may be that omelettes can be made with broken eggs; chickens cannot be made that way. It is life that revolution should seek to protect, not omelettes. Thus, it is hardly possible to believe that the decimation of a class of peasants, or putting one's faith in an expanded police system or elite will result in greater democratization and liberation. It is also true that Third World nations need to be liberated from the bureaucratic weight of Western institutions and consumer goods as the indicia of success. As Ivan Illich has put it,

> we have embodied our world view in our institutions and are now their prisoners. Factories, news media, hospitals, governments, and schools produce goods and services packages to contain our view of the world. We – the rich – conceive of progress as the expansion of these establishments.[9]

Both communist and capitalist roaders continue to use essentially the same measuring rods for success although changes can be detected in capitalist and state socialist ideas.

The leadership of the Spanish and Italian communist parties argue that the people must act and engage themselves, develop their own institutions and protect them from any state apparatus by nurturing and protecting voluntary institutions.[10] This would necessarily mean choice of what institutions to have. This view is one shared generally among non-Marxist radicals. It assumes a devolution of leadership to the grassroots and removes from it any mysterious qualities. It further grounds itself in the anarchist belief that since government derived its influence from force, it is an overrated mechanism for bringing about human happiness. It is through voluntary arrangements and institutions which are autonomous, but themselves democratic that human happiness can find its way.

One reason that left parties failed in the United States was that they were unable to understand the depth of voluntarism in America and its profound importance. When, for example, American communists thought about how to organize American society in the 1920s and 1930s, they favored a very powerful, centralized government which was to be modelled after the "efficiency" of the giant monopoly oriented American corporation.[11] There was no sense of liberation in such ideas. They stopped people from believing that politics could be anything more than a grab for power. Where profound change does occur which promises personal and group liberation the leaders of such change must know how to live by such thoughts and be prepared to implement them in practice. Otherwise, such ideas will be as meaningless as the Soviet Constitution of 1936 which promised freedom and delivered Gulags. In very little time the liberation (whether as a reform, revolution or reconstruction) which so many hoped for is experienced as wooden and inauthentic. People mouth slogans and go through the motions of solidarity and obeisance. They give up. This happens in modern life where relatively spontaneous and voluntary forms which people initiate are crushed or negated by political leaders. For example, the worker councils which emerged after the Russian revolution were undercut and then destroyed by communist party leadership just as the flowering of art in a dynamic relationship to culture was also decimated.[12] When conflicts and antagonisms are replaced by a unitary-dogmatic view of the world, the result will most likely end up reactionary in practice, buttressed by institutionally sanctioned violence. Political organizers of social reconstruction are committed to avoiding dogmatism. Their task is the generation of creativity and freedom with responsibility for others.

Political organizers

Political organizers know that to move people "beyond themselves" it is necessary to organize small groups and sustain them through practical discussion, action and hope measured by cumulative success. This is true of whatever social strata are being organized and whatever the purpose. To organize for the common good we need political techniques. But they are not the kind which John Dewey spoke of and which led to polling and surveying; nor do we need the system of focus groups from which the ambitious and the marketeer learn how to package themselves more successfully. Our need is for experiential guides from which political meaning can be usefully extracted. They are meant to conduct reconstruction in the context of moral limits.[13]

Political organizers of social reconstruction act as entrepreneurs and catalysts, magicians, social scientists and maintenance persons to assure that non-material conditions, hope and spirit in fact shape and change material reality. They know that people are painfully aware that modern institutions have failed them. Schools do not necessarily give education or guarantee jobs to the degree holders. They may not even give the correct ideological line which would allow students to live in peace with the social system. They know that hospitals only marginally improve the health of people and that neither diagnosis nor medical technical equipment will substantially improve their health condition. Political organizers know that the military has purposes other than defense of the nation, and that it is an instrument of the status quo. They also know that people feel helpless in the face of nuclear war, war preparations and ecological destruction. As the philosopher Rudolf Bahro has put it,

> Our collective practices break up and destroy natural conditions, degrade energy potentials, suffocate the earth's surface and isolate human beings from spontaneous energy cycles. The result is inevitably a distortion of both body and mind, whose consequences range from cancer to crime.[14]

The political organizer who seeks the common good must establish a catalytic and dialogic mode of communication which stimulates other people's thought and their creative, empathic sense through the terrible problematic in which we find ourselves. The organizer's creative sensibility is meant to encourage actions that will change institutions and behaviors. In other words political organizing with a reconstructive purpose is meant to change facts into values and values into facts so that a new consciousness will emerge which will make change easier to attain and moral change an obvious necessity. To this end no project for social reconstruction can be very successful unless its participants evidence qualities of *will*, *judgment*, *caring* and *rationality* which they integrate within themselves emotionally and politically.

By *will* I mean the ability of people to transcend their "objective situation." In other words it is utterly linked to subjective notions of purpose and action. It is through willing that people set purposes for themselves which transcend their daily lives or give meaning to them in ways which otherwise are not present. Willing changes the social context and its own self-definition. In the process it causes others to see the "objective situation" differently.

> Our will is the originator of actions that are not explicable by preceding causes. Such actions spring from the incalculable power of willing and are as spontaneous and unpredictable as life itself, which the will closely resembles.[15]

Becoming leaders and organizers

The will manifests itself in all aspects of life. We see it every fall Sunday on our television sets where battered and injured men play football at great physical cost to themselves. It can be noticed among scientists when they work day and night in their laboratories on experiments. It can be admired in men such as Martin King Jr in their search for justice and in their ability to revise the definition of freedom in the social situation that they live within. Will by itself is blind and dumb. We may see will at its dumbest in war. It is used for destructive purposes often by leaders who mask their psycho-neurosis as political or military necessity. Soldiers are expected to act without critical thought, suspend their own will and act on the basis of what they are told to do by their leaders. It is the will of their leaders which they follow and therefore they do damage to their own will and their own capacity for independent thought. In war it is taken for granted that the will is to be divorced from judgment for the individual is expected to act automatically according to the views of leadership. Wars, since they are made from the "top down" do not require or expect critical thought from the troop combatants.

For example, imagine the unhappy lieutenant who is directed to shoot off a nuclear-tipped missile. He is expected to obliterate politics and reality itself with no questions asked. He is expected to see all of humanity as his potential victims and perpetual hostages. On the other hand, those committed to reconstruction and liberation dare reality to change and seek to will into existence a social reality which will transform people from their will-less victim status. In its early stages, reconstruction and revolution may seem similar because both build on the consciousness of change. Both build on an undeformed will to bring about change. But revolution does not seem to sustain a continuous critical aspect, an openness. This narrows and ultimately diminishes its initial purpose.

The will to start and to continue is not often encumbered with critical reason and ethics. It is more in the nature of a heroic act which we think of as flying in the face of history, denying its own obvious roots in the situation and the past from which it springs. But heroism (will aligned with reason) is short-lived and individualistic. It is quickly deformed unless it is harnessed to a covenantual purpose which aims toward a common good. When heroism is found in the group as a whole, or in the community and not only in a particular individual, it is tempered with judgment and an ethical purpose which governs social relations.

American colonists began with the principles of a heroic convenant between themselves and with God. Heroism and personal need were to be subsumed under the common moral purpose of the community. Without this common bond for good all individuals would be destroyed. John Winthrop's sermon, *A Modell of Christian Charity* tells us as much.

But if our heartes shall turn away soe that wee will not obey but shall be reduced and worship . . . other Gods, our pleasures, and profitts, and serve them it is propounded unto us this day, wee shall surely perishe out of the good Land whither wee passe over this vast Sea to posses it: Therefore lett us choose life, that wee and our Seeds may livve, by obeying his voyce, and cleving to him, for hee is our life and our prosperity.[16]

The early American theologian-politican, William Ellery Channing, believed that political will could be best controlled through the community, but the community would have to find a way of being constantly and deeply critical and self-reflective.[17] The democratic system allows for such a critical model for its community is constantly in motion and constantly changing. It must arrange itself so that each person participates in the dialogue of right and wrong. Needless to say, in our time this method is not found among the Right where people are urged to accept order without dialogue. In right-wing fundamentalism with its roots in fear, greed and authoritarianism people are to admire heroism but are to see it as highly individualistic and in service of the reactionary order. Unfortunately, the spiritual need of individuals and communities is not often recognized by modern left thinkers and activists. It is as if they are ashamed of this emotional attribute of humankind. An important exception was Martin Buber who understood that will could be transmitted into a positive spirit for the community.

He argued that unless this yearning was dealt with directly by those who wanted to change the material basis of existence, then man's spiritual needs of the community would have to find a way of being fulfilled. Those like Paul Tillich who knew pre-First World War and Weimar Germany and were not blinded by the success of the Russian revolution realized that the spiritual impulse, especially in Germany, would have to be met. Otherwise, people's need to transcend would be used for violent and fascist ends. The violent never underestimate the need for man to die for a cause beyond himself, even if that cause is an atrocious one.[18] It is only through calling on God in a covenantual way and emphasizing the attributes of judgment and caring that men and women teach will its humane purpose.

The quality that political organizers committed to the common good are to call upon to harness the will is that of *judgment*. They must stimulate judgment in everyone. Judgment is the most difficult learned attribute to recognize and transmit for it requires those who act towards freedom to do so spontaneously *and* yet assess the consequences of their actions. Judgment involves relating seemingly unrelated events in the future and gauging their effects. When this attribute is not present among political activists and leaders incalculable damage is done to others. One aspect of the Vietnam war was that the American leadership followed those who operated from calculative reason and will without judgment, and devoid of caring.

The managerial elite symbol of the Vietnam war, Robert McNamara, reflected this technocratic deformation to the chagrin and pain of the rest of us. Those with limited judgment tend to know the likely effects of particular means used and the likely immediate results. They believe that any judgment is time and space specific, relating only to the situation at hand. They follow the rules but they see no way to go beyond the situation, and they invariably accept the constraints, whether good or bad, that are handed to them by authority. This is what Kant refers to as determinative judgment. The person with good judgment knows that the possibilities of success and failure in any situation are not only dependent on himself or herself, or their respective analyses, but on the judgments and plans of many others who operate out of their own purpose, perceptions and separate motivations. Those who act and act out of good judgment must be prepared for either good or bad fortune beyond the given frame of reference. And those with good judgment teach others how to live *through* bad fortune. Even more important, those with good judgment must act where there are no rules or where the rules which the society or the state concocted may themselves be criminal or crazy as, for example, in totalitarian nations. Arendt understood that Eichmann could follow rules but he could not determine right from wrong beyond rules that themselves were quite mad and odious to humanity. Modern states which are warlike need the mentality of the order taker.[19]

Like the morally blinded bureaucrat or military man the unreflective citizen follows the rules and orders of the powerful. The result is disastrous for civilization and nature.

Elitists argue that the mass of humanity has poor judgment. And what is adduced to prove this point is that they have had no experience in judging; that democracy itself suggests the limits of their capacity to judge. But the time and place that people have to exercise judgment is neither often or many.

Judgment is exercised for humanity by the few either through laws, regulations or custom, thus framing people into situations and questions which by the nature of how they are posed deny people individual judgment. No referendum is taken about the use of nuclear weapons and no one is given the chance to exercise judgment or any othr human value beyond dumb revenge in the present system of defense which states have devised.

When we examine relations outside of those having to do with struggle for power, and we seek the most important element to sustain humanity, we come upon the human relationship of *caring*. This too must be taught and engrained in political organizers who dare to set social reconstruction and the common good as their objectives. As I look out of my window I see a man hurrying in the cold. He sees a broken but large branch in the alley. He stops, picks it up and puts it on the side of the alley. Why? Probably because

56

he cares about the unseen Other, namely the person driving a car who would ruin his or her tires and chassis if they did not see the branch. There is an identity between that person and the unseen Other upon whom humanity predicates its future existence.

Those who emphasize caring as part of their calculus of politics seek activities that relate the person's individual sensibilities to that which is needed by another. This sensibility goes deeper than any particular social role and is there in all of us. "Caring is the antithesis of simply using the other person to satisfy one's own needs."[20]

Because this is so, caring is essential to social reconstruction. The good citizen who picked up the branch did not expect anything in return. He did not start from the market principle of "I use you, you use me." Instead, he exercised affirmative interdependence. Traditionally, the feminine sense of morality is predicated on "the ability to care for and protect others." According to Carol Gilligan it includes the notion of resolving conflicts without anyone getting hurt, a system of relationship and recognition of interdependence which is outside the masculine framework of hierarchy and authority too quick to assign praise and blame. The caring attribute, which is more likely to be found in women than men is absolutely essential in bringing about social reconstruction. To the extent possible a political organizer should emphasize the non-market feminist image of interdependence. When such interdependence exists people are stimulated to create, to recognize worth in themselves – beyond social function, and to grow in a direction they define with others. People who are so motivated call upon their own caring sensibility.

In his *Politics* Aristotle says that which is common has the least care bestowed on it. He says that it is better to have parents who feel that they are truly responsible for their children than to have 10,000 parents who in some abstract way are "responsible" for the caring of childen.[21] There is much in this argument.

Usually the walls of an apartment building are bleak with nothing on them. They exude a desolate quality with no murals, or paintings or "humanizing" objects. Whenever I ask apartment dwellers why they don't pay more attention to their hallways I am told that they don't "own" the building. They are saying that because they have no property rights there is no need to "improve" the worth of their daily existence because it might improve the economic worth of the owner. Even where the building is cooperatively owned, the building will often remain emptied of care in the common spaces. Part of this reason must surely be that in a capitalist society a person's social instinct is subservient to his or her selfish property instinct. Yet, in children of my friends I notice that they are prepared to do more things for a greater whole than for themselves and without necessarily receiving property benefits from their actions. They would rather clean up an alley than their own yard when they are asked to do one or the other.

And as second best they are prepared to clean up the yard of a friend than where they reside. Political organizers may build on the caring sensibility.

Before we embrace taking care of things we must first know why *taking care* is a central value for the common good. After all, the assumption of the nineteenth century and most of the twentieth is that there is little if any value to taking care of things and people. In America we have made a fetish of *using up* things, and sometimes people as well, and then throwing them away. Consequently, we should first explore why we should take care and how people should discover that process within themselves. It will help us to understand the relationship between personal responsibility and property.

Taking care is a simple conception. Really, it means no more than being conscious of, and in the first instance, paying attention. Without consciousness of the web of interdependence and relationships there can be no caring for caring must be an utterly conscious activity of the actor who seeks to correlate the requirements of the situation, or of another with one's understanding of what is required. And, of course, taking care is also an exemplary activity, creating in others this humane sense. It is a process of touching and critically trusting which should be learned from childbirth.

When we seek to translate this conception into matters concerning production and property we should not feel stymied. Should it not be the case that a person or entity can retain property, machinery, etc. only to the extent that they are used and cared for? Our present meaning of property, whether socially or individually, seems to be that property rights include the right of destruction and abuse. Let us say that a person who cannot care for a thing, whether land, house or whatever is in mortal danger of losing that thing, for that person has already constructively abandoned it.[22] On the other hand, to the extent that a person joins with others in caring and making a thing, he or she acquires it as, for example, where a family might improve on their shelter in a public housing project thereby getting joint title for what they have produced. It seems obvious that where governments, and certainly corporations, have abandoned facilities and property their use falls to those prepared to operate them thereby achieving title to what they work and transform.

Surely groups of people can reassert rather traditional Lockean conceptions of land and production in our cities; that legal rights follow use and that rights in property are determined through the relatively objective standard of use and taking care. By this reasoning, squatter-workers in the South Bronx have all sorts of rights which attach to them.

It should be obvious to anyone who cares to see that capitalist enterprise depends on subsidies from the public sector such as training of workers, roads, police, etc., which always make the government, acting as the society's agent, a joint owner in the enterprise. Once this is understood, the only question becomes the relative weighting between the partners. These are matters that a political organizer can point out to groups. Obviously, one's capacity to care must be integrated with rationality just because the common good requires the reattachment of "head to heart" in our public activities.

In social reconstruction *rationality* plays a central role. Rationality usually means that which is measurable and that which can be described empirically by logical, linear formulations.[23] This definition has been described by a number of feminist scholars as a masculine view of rationality. They are correct when they see this notion of rationality as a highly restrictive one which rejects factors that must be taken into account whenever a "problem" or experiment is analyzed.

Modern rational thought begins with the distinction between that which is "hard," measurable as against secondary characteristics which are thought to be soft and subjective. The works of Bacon and Descartes lead us to this bifurcation. But now the very nature of the problems caused by the bifurcation of the subjective and the objective which eliminates any moral or ethical sensibility, any relational sense between the person and the object made, measured or used demands a very different definition of rationality. Because we downplay the subjective aspect to logic and rationality we miss the obvious point that logic, like science and rationality, is in history. Since the person or the group does the describing of reality through science, history, logic or novels, it is not possible nor should we want to escape the subjective or qualitative sensibility.

Political organizers in their own work know that rationality includes the subjective qualitative attribute. Perhaps this element could be taught to scientists. Once science accepts the subjective we are then able to reattach reason to ethical concerns. Rationality does not remain the neutral twin to will, one having to do with the head, the other with the body, both being devoid of critical ethical purpose. Instead, reason learns its own limits through *including* what science once rejected as unimportant or off point.

Political organizers either lead directly or act as catalysts. They do so with an alternative political program. But the question is whose alternatives, whose objectives. Some will say that it is better that alternatives come from the people themselves, their experiences, without guidance or mediation through political parties, movements or the prodding of organizers. Is it not better that things just happen as spontaneously and naturally as possible? Is it not preferable that such ideas be implemented after debate by the people themselves, without "guidance"? Perhaps. Such were the ideas of movement activists in the 1960s. But history is not overly solicitous of spontaneity as a means by which political structures endure. An anarchic form needs its own boundaries which will allow people to organize their raw experience into a net of interconnected paths for their cumulative benefit. The raw experiences of people are data which often are varied and contradictory, divided by socially constructed categories of gender, race and class not always reflecting the potentiality toward equity and caring which is within us beyond these categories. Thus, a skilled political organizer opens up the possibility of "moving" people to struggle for new social definition by their own efforts. In this sense, skilled political organizers learn to reflect what others think and feel privately. As political people committed to liberation, they are the ones who get the news of caring early. Like the abolitionists on the slavery issue, they then set the moral and political ground which over time cannot be denied by others.

Organizing does not have to be the person's first or primary occupation, although often this task overtakes the person and other work becomes secondary. In all cases, if one is to be a successful political organizer the person must engender trust and then action from others. He or she helps persons "come to themselves" in the public space. This objective may be accomplished in three ways. One is that organizers should listen to others with respect and talk little. This does not mean that they have to agree with those with whom they speak. It means that organizers should not dismiss what is said to them, grimace foolishly or burlesque the culture of people who operate on sometimes paranoid schizophrenic assumptions and vastly different conceptions of time and space: assumptions that the oppressed and wretched – even if they are "middle class" – need in their daily struggle to explain to themselves what is happening to them. One should remember that neurotic formations are also instruments to maintain humanness in the face of extra-ordinarily difficult circumstances.

The political organizer must be able to teach practical skills. These skills should be taught with clearly defined political purposes as a way of helping people command their life situations. In other words, there must always be a "political" component to the skill taught. Otherwise, the skill will not be of ready use in helping the person understand much beyond a particular skill.

Organizers, therefore, are required to have practical skills which they can pass on to others in the immediate circumstances in which they and others find themselves, but they should be taught in the context of exploring a more fundamental transformation.

The political organizer's task is to recognize the time use of the person or group noting those "times" which can be transformed that are controlled times even though they are not readily perceived as either important or oppressive. Organizers with a middle-class education are invariably amazed at how the poor can wait and be silent. They wait in hospitals and at bus stops, to be processed in courts, welfare and unemployment lines and prisons. Such waiting is time used by institutions to make persons dumb and immobile, turning each of them into a part of a mass, an unthinking, unaware and undifferentiated group, unconscious of what is happening.

By defeating the hidden ways time is used in institutions, political organizers can transform "waiting" institutions in favor of forms of self and group controlled time. If the nature of how time is used is changed, the possibilities of people spending time in affective functions will increase. I mean by affective activity creating autonomy and caring among people through a mutual educational function.

The third concern of the good political organizer is how to handle intersecting space by which I mean that ideas have social weight and can change material conditions once people are alert to making intellectual and practical connections that otherwise would not be made. On the whole, skilled political organizers show how to make things happen out of "abstract" connections. Thus, they show how credit unions can leverage loans to set up community land trusts or how an empty building can be occupied and fixed up – guaranteed by the common law of squatters' rights – or they show how to set up a midwife clinic. The political organizer's competence is also judged on whether he or she can help confront those who attempt to occupy all the spaces emotionally and intellectually, or materially own the ground upon which everyone has to stand. It is often the case – and understandable – that the control of rational, emotional and material space by either institutions or dominant groups will cause the political organizer to restrict his or her interests to specific, narrow issues which are immediate and which are thought to have immediate payoff or relief.

The political organizer for the common good must find ways of developing those cultural instruments which will enable people to make alternative ideological connections freed from dependence on any single institution or group, but yet in contact with a vision of what the entire society should be like. Where can such creativity and talent be found? Clues may be taken from the most independent, autonomous and hard working group in the society, namely, the artists. As a group artists are politically the most unappreciated and underutilized. They have profound political skills just because they make surprising and useful emotional and ideological connections. They often have a vision of the whole, unexpressed, sometimes inarticulate. Nevertheless they hold a vision of how the particular and the general, the direct and indirect, relate to each other.[24]

Like artists, the political organizer for reconstruction must have "revolutionary patience" not fearing to be castigated as "soft" or fear that other term of contempt, "do gooders" or "bleeding hearts." The rage and mean-spiritedness we see all around us, the renewed interest in war, even nuclear war as a noble exercise, should give us pause to ponder the Christian message – "Love your enemies, do good to them that hate you, bless them that curse you. Greater love hath no man than this, that a man lay down his life for his friends." Those who organize in the framework of reconstruction must be more willing to suffer injustice than practice it. Such a politics is known by its means and what its adherents will not do under any circumstance for it would violate the core of their existence. Yet they are to recognize full well that their patience should never be an excuse for inaction or the recognition of moral limits an excuse for injustice.

If a political organizer wants to reduce reconstruction principles to a short-hand statement, I would say that a movement for the common good believes in practical hope, "which can be learned from each event and analyzed experience," shared reason, "If I cannot understand the problem alone, maybe there is a way we can work together which will help us see the inside as well as the outside of the problem," and material well-being. "Sharing and work make for the provision of necessaries." This formula of material well-being, hope and shared reason can be applied to political action. And because this is so, political action can help us reorganize social structures which are more in line with natural impulses and capacities. Since the Birmingham boycotts in 1955-6, ongoing American social struggle has been an exercise in how to forge social relations that are non-oppressive. In the future political organizing for social reconstruction will change the nature of public space and allow natural actions that authoritarians think of as crude, dangerous, or expansive. Thus, we might expect the following: women nursing babies wherever women and children require it, encouraging hitchhiking, parents bringing their children to day care centers at work, initiating and sustaining public places such as community houses for people to find love, and music centers to hear and make music so that music may be appreciated as something other than a commodity, finding means of learning as through neighborhood science libraries and experimental centers, computer terminals in neighborhoods which would keep information in both a random and sequential way about all subjects that people wanted to learn. Other proposals such as publicly-owned businesses and schemes to keep taxes in neighborhoods are now the political property of the left and the wretched in the Third World. Such ideas are the cultural ground within the United States for the common good.

The following points are guides to a political "technology" of value which are the attitudes and style of organizing that can best fit modern democracy which seeks the common good. They are attitudes and methods of organizing which can set the terms for such a political transformation.

Paths of organizing[25]

A guide for organizers

(1) The transformation of society towards the common good is accomplished by people who do not think of themselves as political. Political transformation occurs in "everyday" transient incidents and events. It occurs where people begin to feel that the contradictions and antagonisms of their lives are too great and that to continue living out such contradictions is not "worth it." Organizers can take this feeling and turn it toward positive external ends by showing through discussion and example, how the "waste"

of society and one's life is in fact a resource. The task of organizing is to show how from our waste and contradictions it is possible to develop "energy centers of reconstruction." In the first instance, these are exemplary models, then alternatives and finally the obvious next change of fundamental transformation. Whether in the grocery store, the clinic, the bedroom, the office, with children or old people, new energy and new ways can be derived which change people's relationships to one another. Finding such energies is the beginning of liberation.

(2) Whatever project or development is undertaken or discussed, political activists and community groups must analyze whether their projects or activities will lead to democratic reconstruction or reaction and immobilism. Thus, the people involved in the development of projects or social invention must ask of their own activities whether they are meant to bring about (a) greater participation among the people; (b) an end to militarism and the war culture; (c) an end to economic exploitation in the foreseeable future; and (d) a transformation of that social focus which causes racism, sexism, and uncaring.

(3) Accordingly, it is necessary to ask how a political action will affect different groups and strata within the society. In a mass society there are two ways that this effect manifests itself. One is the images which people internalize after watching television or reading the newspaper headlines. The other is through direct participation with people in projects. In the latter case an understanding of what is happening is not molded by the media. Instead, it is shaped through existential experience and catalyzed by the organizer who knows what can be done in the short term in specific situations.

(4) A good political organizer knows that most situations have contradictory and antagonistic elements. Being aware of these elements and then knowing how to act can only come through continuous and open discussion which makes clear the practical steps that need to be taken to obtain minimum goals. There can be no social planning that makes any sense without public and open discussion.

Planning is, by its nature, a public activity. Organizers should not predict the future. It is only in understanding the lived present that people who disagree with you will listen to what you have to say and take seriously your answer to the inevitable question, "What shall I do?"

(5) The social process contains progressive and regressive aspects. Thus, for example, in the "right to life" anti-abortion movement there is fierce unwillingness to allow women the control of their own bodies (regressive) coupled with a stated reverence for children who are then to be protected and nurtured (reconstructive). The populist sounding movement of Governor Wallace was both anti-authoritarian and anti-bureaucratic (reconstructive). Its members carried on wildcat strikes in the factories, but primarily racist actions in the neighborhood. Police were

willing to volunteer their services to the community without pay as in New York to forestall layoffs. This impulse is regressive, but often police identify their human existence with their revolver, which is regressive. Open dialogue and political organizing can give impetus to the reconstructive side because this process will expose the reasons for regressive political behavior and the possibility for changing it.

(6) Political organizers committed to the common good know that human beings do not exist for abstract entities. In this regard economic systems called "socialism" or "capitalism" are judged by people on the basis of their performance in meeting their fundamental needs.

(7) In a modern democracy all authority must be stripped of its epaulets, badges and nightsticks. When there are real tasks to be performed, ways should be found to share authority so that tasks and authority are related.

No work is menial. It should never be performed or thought of as without dignity where such work serves the common good of society. To the extent possible, unpleasant work should be shared and done in small groups.

(8) Discussions of political action should be used to bring forth needs of people who live in the immediate geographic vicinity. They are to encourage discussion and action groups that have skills (doctors, lawyers, journalists, plumbers) with the understanding that such groups do not have to be members of any single political group. It is not the task of such a movement to mesmerize or hoodwink people to forget their own reason or good sense. Hence, leadership and catalytic leadership must play an anti-authoritarian role.

(9) Negotiations between community groups, activist organizations, unions and established power should be open. It is only where negotiations are open that "audiences," the public, can play to each other and see themselves as active. In such cases new relationships and understandings automatically develop. Thus, unless the membership thinks otherwise, union negotiations with managements should be open, congressional bodies should be open, deliberations should be open.

(10) Organizers should guard against interpreting their subjective needs, or well worked out political conclusions as the last word on what the entire society needs or wants. Ideas and understandings are tested through reasoned action which makes action open to criticism, correction and revision. In other words, there is a "scientific" spirit about organizing, once it is understood that science includes the empathic understanding of all those involved and that no experience or phenomenon is deemed unworthy of analysis and ethical judgment.

(11) Organizers should not assume that people believe their economic well-being is more important than their faith in "non-tangibles", such as God, justice, or the future. People's beliefs in intangibles are both the bane

and hope of reconstruction. It is crucial, however, to analyze for people what goes on in areas where they do not have direct experience. Once such analysis comes within their grasp, they will come to see that they can change social reality. People who can be bought off with privilege will be unable, most likely, to share their material well-being with others. They will take repressive and regressive actions rather than forfeit their privilege.

(12) People have a need to feel legitimate. Politically, legitimacy helps people not feel guilty about taking free or liberated actions. Organizers should show that there is ample support for their actions in the common and state laws of the United States, the laws and practices of other nations, and UN resolutions. In other words, a movement of the common good should use and contribute to the legitimacy of law and non-repressive religion. Organizers should encourage members of the professional class to become part of the movement for a common good. For example, lawyers and ministers would deepen the public's understanding of the relationship between guilt, conscience and responsibility so that liberating actions can be sought and taken without consequent guilt or repression. Obviously this quality of involvement requires "the professionals" to reconsider the fundamental principles of their craft and discipline.

(13) Organizers should never drive wedges between the working class, the poor and the middle class, the young and the old. They are to understand and explain the shaky condition of those who think they are "well off" but in fact can be wiped out by any sort of perturbation in the economy, or through imperial arrogance and wars. In other words, political organizers must formulate specific demands and proposals which will bring together groups that appear to be in conflict – like consumers and farmers, medical workers and patients, soldiers and service employees, even turnkeys and prisoners. They should show how participatory power can be shared on a daily basis. There will be attempts on the part of "vanguard" groups to split from each other. They do the political work of the rulers who try to divide groups from one another, thus giving rise to factionalism, arrogant or paranoid behavior among those who need to be allied.

(14) Cultural work is crucial to the development of a new conscious-ness. Such work includes the discovery and projection of folk and "formal" music, the artistic renovation of buildings, the repair of houses and the fostering of public crafts to fill spaces such as little vegetable parks and gardens in the city. Cultural work must also include group cooking, experimentation with waste materials, the development of technology skill centers and the sponsorship of neighborhood and community festivals which bring together the various social elements of the community. Competence should be praised and artisans should be encouraged to teach young people.

(15) No activity by political organizers should be undertaken unthink-ingly or by impulse. And when activities are undertaken, they should be

65

done with skill and craftsmanship. Artwork, leaflets and printing should be made in such a way that they will be kept (hung on walls) but not made fetishes of by the recipients.

(16) Listen to the talk and silence of people so their needs can be met and their dignity respected and preserved.

(17) It is important to think transnationally, to understand the effect of American action on other nations, even the most benign and well-intentioned actions. But it is crucial to recognize the possibility of building a regenerated American civilization in accord with a plural world civilization that lives in many different ways. As the fulcrum of world interest shifts to the Third World, the American movement of social reconstruction should set up such contacts which can strengthen an empathic understanding and relationship between Americans and people from other nations.

(18) People will be approaching the common good when they will be able to bring five elements together: (a) life situations which generate a redistribution of wealth and political power; (b) a program which speaks to immediate daily concerns and long-term transformations; (c) a leadership which changes and is open to change because it encourages heavily decentralized activity (a resurgence of cultural differences) with continuous public participation; (d) technical advice which will help people in their immediate situation to establish alternatives in the present which people can use without changing every part of their existence at once; and (e) concrete steps to avoid the unparalleled tragedy of nuclear war.

(19) The special skills and talents of people should be discovered and encouraged. They in turn are expected to teach their skills to others notwithstanding standards of accreditation. Knowledge is part of the *commons* of people.[26]

(20) Organizers are to begin dialogues in each city and state among all groups and classes to determine what is to be held in common and how that which is to be held in common is to be administered. Universities, schools and media should be called upon to begin debate on what might be commonly held. Rock and alternative media groups should be encouraged to distribute pamphlets on the common good to listeners and concert-goers. Community groups at the city and state level should encourage the development of ideas for the control of resources to remain with the people of each political subdivision. Political discussion groups should be held around public activities of others that could result in community control of resources and how this is to be done.

(21) The political credibility of any movement is not its willingness to take risks, its program or the will of its leaders. It is the willingness of its members to act differently in the roles they choose or are assigned to in society. Thus, a worker who insists that a plant should operate in a different way or sits down when laid off, or a farmer who develops his own marketing system outside of the present one with consumers or a teacher

who is prepared to write "fuck" on the blackboard to teach children how to read. It is neighborhood consumers changing as a group their consumption patterns. Altogether the strength of a movement is one which relates people in their roles to a common consciousness that transforms their roles.

(22) Organizers in a movement for reconstruction should think carefully about their lives, what parts are exploitative, how those aspects can be changed. He or she should not be afraid to ask for help, provided they are prepared to offer aid to others.

(23) Since social reconstruction seeks the common good, it starts from its own legitimacy. The legitimacy of a social system or political organization is its openness and non-secrecy. A citizens' movement for the common good must discuss its mistakes openly and be prepared to make changes openly. In this sense, decisions are a constant daily process that all members can share in so long as they live with the consequences of what they propose.

(24) Those committed to the common good should be constantly critical of leadership. However, leaders are useful, even important, when they combine certain qualities of political acumen: (a) the ability to analyze parts of a political situation and crisis putting the elements of them together: (b) a willingness to raise the contrary direction and show why it is the correct one to follow (advance when others would retreat and vice versa); (c) a willingness to do the hardest and most unpleasant work alongside of exercising leadership direction; (d) a willingness and ability to explain to others either through exemplary action or dialogue what a particular series of events means and what the next direction could be; and (e) the ability to laugh and not be overwhelmed either by reversals or betrayals.

(25) A political movement should not fear police spies or psychotics. They should be helped and exposed where there is incontrovertible proof. But no series of actions, or discussions, should be interrupted for fear of police spies. Security should not precede political necessity or openness.

(26) To the extent possible, administrative work is to be shared by group members. Work should not be made overbearing through crushing time schedules. Meetings should be informal and take up specific points which are task-oriented. Such discussions are not meant to take the place of longer discussions or interpret causes and consequences. Gossip can be destructive and should be discouraged. Although discussion of problems which people have should be open and without shame, yet a person should not be dissected like a patient etherized on a table.

(27) Organizers should see to what extent personal problems have political roots, or problems between men and women are also problems of class and privilege which neither wants to recognize nor is conscious of.

(28) A political movement which retains humane ends will set realizable goals. Its members should not be overwhelmed if they go achieved or unachieved. But we must always discuss ways of testing whether the political

goals achieved are failures, or whether the unachieved goals are successes.

(29) No movement is a substitute for love, humor, children or art. A political organization which seeks the common good recognizes the critical importance of binding ceremonies. Special ceremonies should be encouraged around burial, birth as well as occasions which are accomplishments of and for the community.

(30) Intellectuals should be prepared to "teach in the streets." They are to understand that it is more important that ideas be understood than set apart and encased. Also, their special skill should be to show the context of daily struggles, how the past has led to the present state of affairs. They should be able to analyze failed solutions and comprehend different perceptions of reality which people have at different stages of their lives.

(31) There are now many people with progressive ideas in all classes. Often they have a position of radical reconstruction as it relates to one problem such as ecology, workers' rights and consumer problems. The task of an organizer is to show how one problem is related to others.

(32) The movement of the 1960s showed the courage of many people. But there is no longer a great need for heroism in the usual meaning of that term. Heroism is ahistorical, without roots in a past or a future. The objectives of previous movements committed to liberation at the very least have entered the consciousness of society although they are under severe attack from the right. The question is whether through its discussions and practices a movement for the common good can engender ideas, programs, and new categories of understanding which will be so practical that people will see them as the obvious and necessary answer to right-wing reaction.

(33) It is important to remember that each person lives in a "contradictory" situation because the material base of the society, how most people earn their livelihood, is separate from their inner feelings and hopes. This very contradiction is the basis of profound and creative energy, if it is rooted in clear understandings of how the society is to change.

These organizing "instructions" are meant to decrease the level of political fear most people have in approaching and working with others. They are meant to allow for personal judgment, an attitude of quiet seriousness, and a feeling that reconstruction is a cumulative social process rather than a particular event which people learn about in the *New York Times* or on the television news. They assume organizing, not mass mailing.

Political activists of reconstruction should guard against a millennial streak. Organizers know that amelioration, not perfection, is a necessary condition for retaining people's loyalties, that people are more complicated than the class roles they play and that corrective measures can be invented and then used to protect the loser and the challenger from the arrogance of the powerful who soon enough assert that they are the dominant spirit of history.

Because my view of a political movement brings theory and practice together in politics through program, some people on the left and liberals committed to organizing coalitions around "specific issues" have accused me of being a "program and idea junkie." I reject spontaneity or "decisionism" in politics, a form of action made famous by the Nazis in the early 1930s, who thought it unnecessary to act from any coherent set of principles which could be judged in the light of history and shared human purpose.[27] Our task is to discuss, analyze and act, never forgetting that politics is part vision, imagination, analysis and discussion.

Some strategic tasks of organizing

When we use the word strategy in everyday conversation, we usually have in mind a set of goals, purposes and means to achieve them. While there is a surface value to this view – as, for example, businessmen or women who talk about profit-loss statements and the bottom line – a political strategy must seek to be as rich as life itself. A political strategy is a function of timing, when to act or wait. The timing process is many layered, reflecting what each of us agrees to or lives by with others in our personal lives. It intersects with our own individual biological clocks which we hardly understand or only marginally control. In 1968, a number of people who supported Eugene McCarthy's presidency wanted to begin a new political party after the Democratic party leaders caused a shambles on the streets of Chicago. But the victims and the losers were physically and emotionally exhausted. They could not move to an act of challenge and regeneration so the opportune political moment for a powerful political thrust disappeared without much of a ripple.

Even in the best of circumstances, it is hard to know when a political strategy is successful for in part it depends on who is supposed to enjoy the fruits of the strategy and for how long. Thus, short-term success may lead to long-term failure and vice versa. In the short term, Japan lost the Second World War. But forty years later the purpose for which its leaders went to war, the Asian co-prosperity sphere, was attained because it lost the war.[28] Professional football players have a lifespan which is substantially less than the average lifespan in America. Should coaches and football players concern themselves with this harsh statistic when they choose a game strategy? Because of such questions, no strategy should be hidden in the politics of a democracy for it is only in public discussion that one can tease out the likely public interest. Public discussion will add to the continuous dialogue of the society between those who agree and those who disagree. Finally, it will help people find correct *strategies* or paths which can be changed in accordance with the conditions of particular geographic regions and industrial sectors. This does not mean that fundamental purposes of a program should change. Thus, just as the abolitionists and most Republicans before the civil war understood that slavery was an evil which could not fit with either the needs or the ideals of American society or industrialism so it is that we comprehend that the arms race and imperial capitalism can only disrupt modern democracy, namely, the collective participation of all people in the decision process over their economy and government. The political task for us is to forge a persuasive and humane political strategy which peacefully moves the United States from imperial capitalism and the arms race to modern participatory democracy – the common good.

What is the specific strategy that we can organize to this end? The first political judgment which we must make is that a program grows out of real needs of a constituency which are articulated through continuous dialogue and public involvement. While the dominant powers use manipulations to obtain consent, organizing the middle class – the constituency I am addressing – requires participation. Several generations ago the Marxists appealed to the working class, but fewer Americans than ever are in the working class. They may be pensioned, unemployed, or irrelevant to the modern productive system. Furthermore, whatever their income most Americans think of themselves as middle class, especially during the false prosperity under Reagan. For purposes of organizing it is not important whether there is a subjective or objective reality to this belief since the belief is the basis upon which people act.

On the most primary level they need to be convinced of the moral importance of what is being proposed for those with political power in the society – often out of inertia – stand in direct conflict with the common good. The method of persuasion to interrupt this inertia is dialogue where the humane qualities of one's adversaries are recognized. If knowledge workers (writers, academics, engineers and ministers as well as bureaucrats) are convinced intellectually and morally, the balance of forces in power terms can be changed, with a reconstruction strategy by which I mean transcending particular interests, obtaining agreements between groups on a common program that is there and recognized as a necessity to avoid common ruin.

There are some who criticize progressives, often correctly, for their lack of timing, being militant when it is time to be conciliatory. Others think progressives shock people by asking for too much of a change, thus scaring away potential adherents. And there are those who believe that progressives are cursed by a certain rigidity and a fear of power, i.e., the willingness to take the responsibility for grappling with evil, knowing that it exacts a price when it is engaged.

The result is that people who would ordinarily turn to progressives in a time of felt powerlessness and obvious crisis cannot count on them because of their reluctance to struggle for that which it fears – state power. On the national level, movement activists reduce themselves to spectators whose

70

purposes are inordinately limited; who whine and bring havoc to others because they do not recognize the potentiality in the uses of power when there are agreed upon purposes which undeniably have positive value for the common good. I have wondered about the problem of stunted self-confidence especially given the resurgence of the right and the left's quiescence. Perhaps it is because there is a puritan streak in many who graduated from the movements of the 1960s that caused them to fear their own passions and ambitions which at all times were to be kept under tight reign, lest they lose sight of who they thought they should be. Such people disdained politics because they had a powerful but unacknowledged interest in saving their own souls, leaving themselves untouched by deal making; like the puritans who feared being wrong or tempted because of their own moralistic and pinched sense of right and wrong. This fear of risking failure and humiliation hides a certain inflexibility which could guarantee marginal relevance to future progressive politics. No perfect arrangement can be found in politics – only in fiction.

Yet one should not be unduly critical of those who might have a tendency to political immobilism because of their strong sense of moral responsibility in doubting the utility of state power. One cannot be sure that the state, with its warring groups, agencies, and contradictory government administrations serving a medley of clients, ruling class and bureaucratic interests as well as professional ideals can ever be put to positive use. Can it ever be in the service of a continuous and open process that changes social relations toward egalitarian interdependence, respect, caring and security? Since the answer can only be a tentative and hesitant yes, we should not despair about the anxiety that the most sensitive members of the left have about the exercise of power. It is an altogether healthy sign that a political movement pays homage to those who fear those who command others to do things, and suspects those who think and act about power as if it is an end in itself, neutral to be used for "good" or "bad."

The way people act when they do not contest for power, in their modes of sharing and commitment to one another and to nature itself is the measure of how to act ethically when we contest the present balance of power in the society. Nevertheless, a programmatic alternative should not represent the lowest common denominator in which each group may attempt to scuttle any particular part.

The common good can be initiated, debated and promulgated in one of four ways: (a) through the two major parties where the machinery and program of the various parties in the states, locally and statewide, would be challenged to adopt the program; (b) through union, church· and community groups that hammer out joint programs of mutual aid in a national framework; (c) through a national group of locally elected and selected officials who act with social and political movements in the daily exercise of making practical the alternative agenda; and (d) by individuals insisting that institutions in which they work set out these goals and develop the process which will make such goals realizable. In the latter case, groups already formed, or in the process of formation, should concentrate on institutions which have a self-defined moral purpose to them. Thus, institutions such as unions, hospitals, schools, government service bureaucracies committed to a high level of moral purpose and people skilled in crafts and specialized knowledge should organize to assure that their work is reflected in the program. This reflection, however, must be very carefully analyzed and debated so that those who earn their livelihood, status or obtain pleasure by ascertaining the needs of others will not descend into being a party of bureaucrats and technocrats that define others. This was the experience of the various socialist parties in Europe. They became "service" parties who often, under that guise, kept political participation from the people.

As part of a program for the common good, a twenty-year goal should be set, perhaps the year 2005, as the time in which people involved in the program can look back and see the conscious changes which they wrought as participants in history. One question remains. How are these changes going to be discussed and prepared for – in the present? Each group and community will decide its own speed so long as there is agreement that a shared framework is to be adopted.

Guides can be given or questions asked which would provide clues as to what activities should be undertaken first. In this regard methodological clues may be found in such fields of study as law and medicine which operate on the basis of example, cases and symptomatic signs. Each series of actions contains certain fundamental rules of social transformation. Consequently, the specific action to begin with is relatively unimportant. While this point of view is abstractly true, political process demands the support of certain groups over other groups at particular times even though the particular means used to obtain an end may be mistaken as, for example, in the case of bussing. Obviously, the results will be somewhat different if one method of initiation is used to the exclusion of others.

In practical terms, this means that candidates for public office should be judged in terms of their commitment to empowering the people to act in the public space as well as their presentation of a coherent program. The movement should encourage candidacies at all levels of government, with the understanding that they be committed to the program. It should be understood that candidates have a purpose beyond manipulating elections. Their task is to change the frame of reference of debate, the nature of questions considered in politics. And one way of doing so is standing for office *with* a program and building a political organization which can operate inside and outside political parties and other institutions of American life.

Groups within the largest 1,000 corporations should organize discussions of alternate modes of operation in production, administration, marketing and quality of the work place. Labor unions should take the lead in this effort. *They* should *organize* managers into seminars and discussions that are framed according to the principles laid out by workers and public interest groups. While the top 100 corporations may call themselves part of the private sector, they are not entitled to rights of privacy granted to individuals just as fourteenth amendment protections, protecting the corporation as a natural person, should be removed. Whether in the United States, Great Britain or Europe a direct legal onslaught needs to be made on the privileged status granted to corporations through the metaphysics of constitutional law.[29] Where a particular industry can affect the direction of the society economically and politically, different ways should be found to open the management and assumptions of that organization to workers and the community at large through the political process. Thus, as one example, we may think of ways to apply first amendment rights to the work place. This right should become an almost automatic one as the productive and technical process changes so that workers can relate their needs and that of the community to the production line. Another is through the process of religious organizing where clergy emphasize, as Pope John Paul II did in his Encyclical, that labor takes precedence over capital, and that both must serve the common good and the person.[30]

There is a serious question as to the nineteenth and early twentieth-century applicability of what production means in relation to our modern methods and needs. Modern technology changes the definition of worker and production. The phrase "dictatorship of the proletariat" does not adequately describe the productive process in the United States, does not comprehend the American commitment to citizenship within the nation or to the importance of celebrating humanism over production and control by the category known as "worker." This recognition requires, therefore, a new emphasis on participation which avoids any suggestion of "dictatorship." Furthermore, the question of dictatorship over whom needs to be answered. In the early stages of the Russian revolution, actually through the 1930s, proletarian dictatorship meant dictatorship over the peasantry. A working-class dictatorship within the United States would be no better, for it would be aimed at the poor and the helpless. The participatory system contradicts the dictatorship system for it extends to deliberation for all at all levels of production as well as experiment, inquiry and human relations. In practical terms, dictatorship is changed into cooperation and discipline arises out of self and group willingness to act or perform rather than prepare or hope for domination from outsiders.

Among various members of Congress there is a residual belief in transcending either class or interest group politics. As the American corporation grew alongside the state in the twentieth century, members of Congress attempted to form themselves either as interest group representatives or as groups whose interests or purposes were so broad as to escape the charge of being narrow or vested. On the other hand, some caucuses in Congress learned that to obtain their objectives it was necessary to join with other groups because their purposes could not obtain without such relationships.

Thus, Fiorello LaGuardia's group in Congress in the late 1920s was the first to focus on the importance of the cities and their needs in the United States, seeking to establish a federal responsibility for the American city. Robert Kastenmeier and his group served as the basis for new ideas in the late 1950s and early 1960s which matured into a powerful anti-Vietnam war group in Congress. A number of the members of this group were the ones responsible for the "heat" which led to Nixon's resignation.

However, as a general rule, parliamentary bodies in the twentieth century are folded into the bureaucratic and governing processes of the central state. They find it easier, safer, to "go along" with the central or bureaucratic direction of the state. Thus, there is a danger that the representative system will disappear because it does not seem to be "relevant" to the bureaucratic state, or to those who seek major transformations socially. This means that the progressive member of Congress must assume a teacher/organizer role. Because of increased staffing of Congress and the ways in which problems are defined for congressional members by the executive and staffs, the individual members' roles have been further circumscribed. Too often they are caught up in packaging themselves as commodities. The result is that staffs and bureaucracies set the terms of reference for substantive consideration of policy and legislation as members spend their time in ceremonial and vote-getting activities. This has made legislative activity a largely unaccountable affair as the party system itself has no internal program or discipline. Yet legislative bodies are by nature obstreperous, requiring special handling. President Reagan was somewhat stymied by a House of Representatives which did not find itself as a dependent body.

There is an important political point to be made. Within the nation itself, even where political organizers believe in the local process and radical "decentering" people at the grassroots level seek recognition and legitimation for their work by national leaders and specifically by Congressional members through what we might term the "echoing effect." Accordingly, one of the important national tasks which political activists for social reconstruction must relate to is a Congressional study and action group that presses a joint program of legislative and cultural action.

It has been said with some justification that the progressives in Congress have not used or been prepared to use Congressional rules to focus attention on their legislation; nor have they been prepared to use the rules of Congress to frustrate programs and policies that were contradictory to their own objectives. The Reagan victory and the victory of conservatives and the right in the Senate should have increased progressive interest in working the rules of the House and Senate to slow down the Reagan program. However, the weakness of the progressive alternative, without any long-term vision behind it, and the isolation of members of Congress as a group from a national programmatic constituency has limited Congressional effectiveness, even though liberals in the House controlled most of the subcommittees.

In the last few years I have attempted to bring together a caucus of subcommittee chairs in relation to a budgetary program of social reconstruction. This program is put into the language of the budgetary process which means that it includes analysis of conservative assumptions. Alternatives and analysis are not enough. Congressional members must also be related to significant numbers of people at the grassroots who will give these members political and social support.

A number of such people were active in the movements of the 1960s and early 1970s. They find themselves in positions to influence the direction of events from their jobs in legislatures, bureaucracies, and even corporate industry. Many professionals participated in consumer movements as lawyers, short-term organizers or public interest advocates. They carry with them the hopes of the immediate past and the willingness to address themselves to the obvious needs of the present. But without program and a moral alternative it is not likely that they will be prepared to challenge orthodoxies and immobilism in their own situation. This is especially true of the government employee who is under direct attack as "useless" by conservative ideologists and corporate interests that fear the power and ideological inclinations of the bureaucracy.

Several means of "organizing" the government worker can be found. The first and most important intellectually is through the seminar form where dialogue on theoretical issues is held. In this case institutes and universities are the natural base for discussion. The second is through open organization of the government employee into movement discussion groups which will take on discussions of practical alternatives in their area of responsibility. The third is through encouraging associations for government workers which are meant to include dealing with the specific work problems of the government employee. One such project is the whistle blowers project organized at the Institute for Policy Studies which could develop into a national association to protect the civil rights and liberties of government workers who declare their allegiance to the public at large rather than their immediate boss and will point out wrong doing and the violation of the public trust. Such activities will encourage government workers to redefine their methods and goals in relation to program. Organizing along these lines is a means to consider ethical flashpoints with which government officials may be faced, for if they are compromised, the very nature of what we are will have changed. Thus, for

75

example, the use of nuclear weapons by the United States would be such a flashpoint.

Throughout American history religious movements and individuals have sought to find an alternative path. Political organizers who do not take the religious impulse into account cannot be successful in any long-term sense – especially in the United States. These impulses are not limited to a particular class or section of the nation.

Of course, it is no news that churches and the religious profession play a powerful role in American political life. Politicians use the get-out-the-vote power of ministers. Often this power is the difference between success and failure at the polls. Churches set the framework for social action and are the major group responsible for taking care of those damaged by the economic or political system.

The style of American religious concern has changed in the past fifty years. The first style which emerged from the 1920s and 1930s was rebellion against the narrowness of theological concerns. Such advocates as Reinhold Niebuhr and A.J. Muste believed that the social gospel required action, not talk of God.[31] In other words, "Render to God what is known and to man what must be done." They and their followers believed that excessive talk about religious matters would detract from political work. Celebratory events, liturgies, and sermons took people away from purpose and struggle because there was no way to move such events from church vestries into the daily productive life of people or into direct confrontation with the state's activities. Thus, it was believed that the less time given to discussions about God, which are inevitably divisive, or working through ceremonies and communal lives around religion, the more time there would be to confront directly the ills of the secular society, and therefore to manifest the true will of God.

But there is another view which has a growing number of adherents. It is that God reflects the various aspects of our understanding and therefore any understanding of humankind and what he and she are to become has to include direct discussion of God and ways to bring together the life of religious belief and the everyday life of government, the production line and the secular culture itself. This is what is meant by religious belief suffusing a culture, and it was best spelled out by Martin Buber who believed that there are three aspects of God which affect and define people.[32] There is the spirit which "blows" all over humankind in and around all of us. This spirit moves us to act and feel. There is the physical world, nature itself, which is there and which we seek to know and discover, often conquer or put to our use. And there is God as personal being. God is within us as a force who creates a direct relation which allows us the people to have "creative, revealing and redeeming acts, and thus makes it possible for us to enter into a direct relation with him." I would add a fourth attribute which is present and of which those in politics are aware.

The attribute of "relationship" is one in which God exists between people through the caring and bonding function. It is not there in any of us except as a capacity, but it is there in all of us. It is what each of us sees in the other. Empirical studies make clear that women especially comprehend the caring and bonding function of communities and groups. From John Winthrop forward Americans have sought to find a way through secular or theocratic religion to handle humankind's solitariness with loyalty to reason, progress and the natural universe. This sensibility is forever present in politics. It is even noticeable in Third World struggles and it is addressed by Marxists and liberation theologians alike. In Latin America their complementary work makes it easy to understand the direct and vibrant connection which people feel and expect to have beyond religion and class, but for liberation.

Most political organizers see interest in God as a datum in a complex political puzzle which can only be solved if the religious sensibility is duly recognized and fitted into people's strivings. The political organizer and leader's view of people's character is calculated to exclude any element of personal shock at what people might do. Consequently, they tend to be stoical about people. This attribute is a useful one in political action for it means that organizers cannot be overwhelmed or dispirited by the bravery, cowardice or irrationality of people. They are aware that people, whether religious or not, are capable in various situations of contradictory feelings and actions which flow from them. They know that those who take part in political action are, within limits, quite malleable. The reason is that most people are quite lonely and, if they are given a task to perform or, better, are able to relate their skill to a general need, they will commit themselves to political action on matters to which they would not otherwise necessarily agree.

As a practical matter, humane political organizers do not believe that humankind should aspire to be gods or beasts. For to treat them in either way is to destroy one's own humanity. Thus, for members of a movement of reconstruction, the purpose of political action is to seek the humane which is both achievable and knowable. Their optimism should not only stem from a historic reading of events for historical examples often make people into pessimists about the possibilities of human action and good actions. More than historical example, activists for the common good should believe in the idea that shared human sensibilities do exist, that even logic can only be understood in the contextual framework of human feeling although it takes the power of mind to discover and explicate the relationship between logic, feeling and political action. What conclusions may be drawn from these disparate points? Reconstruction for the common good is possible through a "porous strategy" in which members of all social strata participate to refashion the dominant direction of the society. The porous strategy assumes that change is inherently uncontrollable, should *not* be directed and that leadership can only be accomplished through particular actions which then either fade or are picked up by others. It also assumes that most of politics is not action. It is talk and attitude.

It is worth noting that the establishment's alternative to the porous strategy of change is in consciously engineering consent. The task of the engineers of consent is to mute class consciousness and class antagonisms within the "public space."

The practitioners of public relations and advertising have been influential in pointing out how ideas could be packaged, mass distributed and moved by the same techniques which disseminated the mass production of goods. With the expansion of the communications industry, the distinction between "ideas" and "goods" as things to be distributed was erased. (The information industry is, of course, predicated on the premise that ideas are commodities.) But with this erasure came certain very interesting effects. If a ruling class intended to control the material conditions – the consumer goods made, the structure of work of the city, etc. – it would also have to control consciousness as well. Without such control of consciousness, the chance for the formation of an antagonistic consciousness was too great. Sociologists, psychologists and other social researchers found markets for their work among the great and small corporations which sought to manipulate opinion to buy certain products, have certain attitudes about oil, utilities, defense, etc. It was no accident that the great behavioralist, J.B. Watson, left Johns Hopkins to work for the Walter Thompson advertising agency. His work prepared the way for astounding changes. One professor from the University of Illinois who studied public opinion research from 1936 to 1956 concluded that in that period there was more special pleading and propaganda than in all previous cultural history. Social scientists were brought up with Harold Lasswell's idea that "Propaganda is a mere tool . . . no more moral or immoral than a pump handle."[33] Lasswell's view is mistaken.

Propaganda and advertising are the modern means for spinning out myths and morality plays. Historic struggles in politics are about which myths to accept and which social facts to embrace as true. They describe turning points in the society, moments of striving, of leaving one reality in favor of another. Obviously, such ruling ideas and myths are not limited to the political system, but they include the way we think about scientific questions and the way we organize our "specialized" disciplines. While it is more hidden today because there are so many specializations of knowledge, the fundamental ways of describing life, power and relationships are similar in all disciplines and they are set by unexamined phrases and ultimately irrational fears, half understandings and scapegoating.[34]

Myths and the common good

Organizers know the importance of visions and myths for humankind uses such devices to center itself. In reconstruction, a vision or myth is a means to present a coherent alternative "to the existing order, and represent a permanent drive to it."[35] A social myth is meant to teach people social limits. It sets reason and the passions as complementary rather than antagonistic to each other. A political program and political organizers are only as good as the myth that they reflect, the type of society which they champion and the means which are used for doing so. A myth of reconstruction presents us with a yearning, a potentiality and a taboo or warning. Consequently its generation and then the practice of it is a central political and moral enterprise which organizers, everyone, must consider deeply.

The major unstated issue for people in a period of profound instability is the search for wholeness. This pattern can be seen in unstable periods as far away from each other in time as Plato's world of the fourth century and Germany after the First World War. Throughout history this question has been addressed by radicals, conservatives, and liberals alike. In Plato's *Symposium* we learn that, in the beginning, man and nature, sensation and thought, subject and object were all united as one until a great catastrophe occurred that caused a wrenching dualism. In Platonic and Marxist terms the dialectic in thought and "material reality" is the relationship between these constituent parts. Marx and Engels believed that "integration" and "wholeness" between man and society, between work and family or personal life was the way to end dualism and individual alienation. The Marxist hope is the political analogue of certain male and female myths which are meant to show that completion occurs in the "two becoming one." There is the yin-yang story; there is the story of the androgyne and in modern biology there is the story of the helix and the double helix. Each of these interpretations of reality suggests that social existence demands complementary "male" and "female" principles and, without linking these complementary principles together, life is either incomplete or unbearable. Those concerned with reconstruction will find such myths most favorable.

It is not easy to know the specifications of myths which fall into the modern definition of the common good. In *The Republic*, Plato's operating myth dealt with the problem of the good and bad by constructing a static society. He asserted that an aristocracy of the wise was the best of all possible worlds and that society had to be ordered in such a manner as to bring forward the wise to leadership positions. Society was to be ordered from "chaos" to secure the emergence of the wise who knew justice. The actions of the wise would reproduce "justice" for each social class.

In modern liberal nationalist thought, those who followed Max Weber believed that the bureaucracy would produce community "justice" for each social class. Each class is then measured according to its respective capabilities for the good of society. There is much sentiment from the right and left which holds that the establishment of this kind of state trades the capitalist exploiter for the bureaucratic exploiter. The laws are changed, but only to the degree that they promote and protect the exploitation rendered by new groups that use force and stealth to achieve legitimacy. I am inclined to believe that bureaucracies are taking the bum rap without adequately answering such criticism.

There is little to suggest that bureaucratic exploitation is the only alternative to a capitalism which itself has become highly bureaucratized. However, to avoid the "inevitability" of state or capital exploitation we must embrace the fundamental spirit of the age. Humankind is trying desperately to shed myths of dominance: of one over another, white over non-white, man over woman, rich over poor. The myths of reactionary order and stability myths cannot be used as a basis either for a scientific understanding of the world, or of operating for the common good. In other words, a myth should reflect liberation and complementarity and, where it does not, it is a myth which should be transcended and politically rejected because it is regressive.

Myths for a modern democracy are required to *fit* the sensibilities and yearnings of our time. They can never be too far from the concreteness of science, yet they cannot rely too heavily on science and its methods. Our best scientists know that an empirical science is an

> elaborate structure built on piles that are anchored, not on bedrock, as is commonly supposed, but on the shifting sand of fallible human judgment, conjecture and intuition. It is not even true, again contrary to common belief, that a single purported counter-instance [that] if accepted as genuine would certainly falsify a specific scientific theory, or would lead to abandonment of that theory.[36]

Science is sustained by its own myths and errors. Myths are the "coordinating link": between ideas and social and physical reality. In the 1960s, as the philosopher, Rudolph Sibert, has pointed out, "New-Left groups did not sufficiently appreciate the difference which occurs if one jumps from ideality dialectic over to reality dialectic."[37] There is a vast difference between a dialectic of ideas and the "dialectic of real social conditions." Had the New Left defined a program or vision, the linkage between idealistic hope and practice could have been stronger with a more acute understanding of how to proceed politically.

The twentieth century is full of movements that have attempted to escape from duality, from alienated labor and alienated lives. The need for wholeness, while laudable, becomes another dream which in practice can be terribly devastating as those who have lived through totalitarian experiences can testify. When contradictions and antagonisms are put to rest through the truncheon and violence, the dialectic has failed. The reality of modern life is that there is no way to have either certitude or social wholeness. In the world of modern communications, ideas and information move faster than what can be accomplished in reality. Therefore, contradictions and antagonisms are a basic fact of existence. Nevertheless, this duality is an opportunity and a need. It is an opportunity to choose a basic direction with accompanying myths to sustain that direction. The myths that we must seek as socially beneficial are those that emphasize complementarity. Is it not obvious that without a vision of complementarity and one which addresses itself to limits, civilization will be destroyed?

Modern social myths of complementarity postulate that a person's biography and his or her life is a critical part of the world's history. Once we postulate that all of us are part of history as subject-actors, then it is obvious that there is a linked and complementary relationship between the person and rest of the world. Myths of complementarity in our time are those that substantiate in practice egalitarian interdependence. They recognize that each person shapes civilization and its character. In part, therefore, such myths are ethical norms or preachments meant to reshape social reality. They call for fundamental changes, for example, in oppressive or inequitable relationships that are structured into people's daily life. This situation is especially true of women and blacks. For example, in the work situation in industry, agriculture, and services throughout the world.

Women are clustered in unskilled, dead-end jobs with low pay and little potential for training or advancement. In agriculture, if cash crops are grown, women tend to do the back-breaking planting, weeding and harvesting; men to operate whatever mechanical equipment is available. In the services, women are largely in menial jobs, primarily as domestics, or in the informal sector, selling food and home grown crops. In industry, they provide cheap assembly-line labor for the rapidly growing multinational operations in textiles, apparel, and electronic products.

Women's occupational concentration is associated with unfavorable work patterns: lower wages, lower status, longer hours, fewer or no fringe benefits, and less security. A hierarchy in pay reflects gender ratios in occupations: fields in which women predominate are generally lowest, fields employing both men and women somewhat higher, and fields predominately or exclusively occupied by men at the top of the pay scale. Work done at home, and part-time, seasonal, and temporary jobs, in which women are the large majority, not only are low in pay but generally have few job benefits and inadequate social protection, such as health insurance or vacation rights, and are less likely to provide training or career development.[38]

Becoming leaders and organizers

Myths of the common good in a democracy assert that people have capacities which are invariant and which are reflected in their observed and unconscious behavior. These capacities can set the terms of the common good. Such myths must state that people are linked/bonded together as cells to each other and each recognizes the other has dignity and importance to one's self. And yet there is recognition of each person's uniqueness which is undefinable because it can only be explained in terms of another. The attraction toward each other is one which constantly develops and changes. But each changes in relation to the other, in balance. This is what I mean by egalitarian interdependence. The face of one is the face of all. The task of a movement is to urge institutions to establish practical ways in which uniqueness and sameness, as well as egalitarian interdependence, can be carried out.

This "formula" means that we should replace the two social myths which now govern American life. One is the myth of individualism which most liberals and "new liberals, neo-conservatives" accept.[39] The other is the social myth of good breeding; the language of conservatives and reactionaries. In practice the differences may be slight.

The liberal myth starts from the premise that people are an undifferentiated mass who, through personal merit, and drive, can distinguish themselves from the undifferentiated and interchangeable mass if the social system is geared to reward the winners with "opportunities" to escape their class position and supply a cushion for the losers. Americans view this as an improvement over social arrangements which consign a person to a particular status without a chance to "better one's self." But we should ask ourselves when are "opportunities" most important to the person? Opportunities are most critical for people where necessities are not given or where the social system deprives the person or group, where there is an emphasis on envy and competition, where there is little friendship or chance for it, where shared distinction is not possible, and where the social, political and economic system is separate from most people, controlled in some way by governments or groups who make "opportunities possible." The liberal position of individual opportunity does not adequately reflect the shared and linked nature of what we do and what we know. It does not take adequate account of the shared nature of resources or knowledge, either in their production, use, or their discovery.

With the election of Reagan, other, more damaging social myths are beginning to dominate American life. Reactionaries believe that it is absurd to offer educational and economic opportunities, for good breeding, as in horses and dogs, comes from the genetics of intermarriages with the right classes.[40] Thus, opportunity merely turns people's heads. Furthermore, those who do not have such education or family connections will botch things that require a sense of purpose, forbearance and surplus. Except for the unique individual who "makes it," people are replaceable cogs who should be protected only to the extent they have class importance. Social protection for everyone in the society is unwise and unnecessary because there is no inherent need to protect everyone. As a group, ordinary people should be given no control over the affairs of the society. They can and should be manipulated through the mass mails or the media. But decisions and issues which require judgment and deliberation should be limited to a very small group. Indeed, the presence in activities of large numbers of people clutters and obfuscates necessary directions that "have to be taken." Reactionaries and conservatives have no belief in democracy. They see little value in voting and seek to control or intimidate the poorer, "less educated," from voting – as events in the 1981 elections of New Jersey showed when toughs were hired by the Republican party to keep blacks from voting at the polls. One of their intellectual mentors, Paul Weyrich, makes this point to mass audiences.[41] In practice the rightist myth is the nationalization of racism and sexism.

The right's purpose is the severe limitation of the rights of citizenship by eliminating access to the public space and to information. What manner of myths do progressives have to confront the right and give people hope?

Bonding and linking principles

The democratic project to attain the common good is the political process of including everyone in egalitarian interdependence. This interdependence is fashioned through linking principles which show themselves in various events and in various institutions, whether in the day-to-day life of economic relationships, or institutional life in schools and hospitals, or on questions of foreign policy and statecraft. When prudent people talk about principles being linked they often recite principles that are opposites. Thus, some people say that there should be a balance between responsibility and liberty or that there can be no justice without authority.

I do not mean the balance of apparent opposites as the way to find the common good. Instead, what I mean is the linked relationship between certain conceptions which, if they stand alone, will invariably fail, but if they are linked together, as it were, the chances for a decent society are rather good, and the chance that any particular act will not turn out to be its dialectical opposite is fairly good. I see these linked principles as critical to attaining the common good, with the democracy as the process and an end state which tells us whether in practice we are stating the "correct" relationships and attributes. I hope that a set of linked principles is reflected adequately in the program I have outlined. In debating this program the linked nature of the principles used should be made explicit. Otherwise, people will applaud the program, but not see that to bring the program about requires a massive transformation which, paradoxically, sets limits to behavior. Without acknowledging and accepting limits in practice there will be those who think that because their task is a noble one there should be no limits to their action. Thus, the conceptions which are linked are critical in setting limits to violent action or oppressive action against others.

So what must be linked? It is loving and reasoning, just as empathy and liberty should be linked. Hope and skill also go hand in hand. Cooperation and individual dignity are also part of the links in the chain of the common good.

In reality linked principles are based on what it takes to sustain a decent society. They are meant to change society gracefully, and to let certain institutions and ways fill out their time without catastrophe, while excising others. But one should not be carried away with such ideas. Organizers and leaders must always keep in mind the differences between metaphor and reality. We must always keep before us, as a general rule, that metaphor is never reality and language hardly ever describes it.

There is a way to defend and justify the linking principle on scientific grounds. When we describe biological and chemical or atomic matter we know that atoms are bonded together and that the scientific task is to find the way they are bound together, which we then conclude is the fundamental reality. And we are also aware that the nature of the universe, so far as we can tell, is broken apart and held together by chemical and physical links. When they are split, they bring into existence new relationships and new things, sometimes horrible ones as in the case of nuclear weapons.

When we describe ourselves – our "conditions" in medical terms, our doctors look for syndromes of disease and pathology in the belief that one symptom or malfunction relates to another, and is linked to it in some way. Of course in this case we are aware of a "negative" linking which required either intervention or the encouragement of natural process that breaks down the negative linking system.

It does not seem to be too far-fetched to say that there are linked principles of political action and values which define the common good. Yet I am aware of the dangers. The meaning of the words has to be very precise and they have to stand up against an unseemly past in social science. Nineteenth-century socialists, humanists, social democrats and scientists were very eager to find those characteristics among people which determined that they were "criminal." They looked everywhere to prove their own point except to their own prejudices. Lombroso sought to show how the structure of people's heads and bodies, as well as their color, defined their criminal tendencies. This was the type of "knowledge" that the believers in progress intended to apply in institutions and law. The Comteans and Lombrosites wrote nineteenth-century laws so that those who met the negative characteristics as defined by Lombroso could be put away for long prison terms, having been scientifically defined as natural

84

criminals.[42] In our time penologists, psychologists, and administrators continue this tradition through the development of indices that entrap people who are then categorized, watched and incarcerated for their own good. This habit of mind has found its way into genetic research where some scientists talk about the "criminal" chromosome.

Once we set up a standard of "good" linked principles, by definition we exclude other ways of being and behaving. We must remember that there is no way that a political theory can encompass the uniqueness of life. And when a theory sets up any sort of standard which is not a consciously agreed upon meaning or standard, its adherents are setting up a system of repression and even racism. What does social linking mean in practice? It means that a politics of the common good has to encompass antagonism, common experience, personal ambition and felt injustice. But the problem in American society is whose injustice? The Indians, the Third World people in America? Once we say it is for their common good some would say that we have to Balkanize the United States, give back Indian lands while the chicanos would be given the Southwest and a new confederation would be drafted to supplant the present constitution.

But a redrafting of the Constitution such as the right demanded before it took power does not yield very pleasant results. It is the right which has played on secessionist tendencies just as those in the New Right seek a caesarist central government.[43] A program of social reconstruction is to achieve the common good without a breakup of the United States. We live with many grievances and injustices of history and it is all right that we do so for we must be careful to know which wrongs are the most egregious and which unravel others.

Attempts to avenge the past do not necessarily correct the present or the future. As Ivan Illich has pointed out when doctors try to correct difficult ailments of people with wonder drugs they often make more trouble for the patient.[44] So, too, in politics there is the problem of trying to correct admittedly flagrant errors or injustices through massive political surgery which is then worse for all concerned. No independent or abstract statement such as "Justice" or "Equality" has very much meaning without placing it in a context and linking it to other active principles. And redrawing the geographic map will not be salutory because it will lead to civil war, even though embracing cultural and ethnic pride in the context of American citizenship is a positive objective.

In politics there is a "grandfather clause." This is not to say that injustice need be carried into the future. It is to say that that which is settled should not be unsettled in order that politics live up to a literary standard of verisimilitude or scientific elegance. It must live up to an evolving standard of the common good. In other words, Puerto Rico, not yet a state, should be independent. But it hardly seems valid to think that New Mexico should be returned to Mexico out of a sense of compensatory justice. Yet it is obvious that "illegal" migrant labor in New Mexico or California could easily come to accept the idea that *they* are not violating any law, except that of power, since those areas were once Mexican. When such beliefs are acted on the results are painful. Tijerina, in 1967, sought self-determination as a separate entity for part of New Mexico which was brutally put down by the United States. The problem of Chicano rights will not go away but secession cannot end up in anything but civil war. The question of Puerto Rico, or the Indian claims, or the black claims are real and just, although it does not follow that cutting up the United States is the way to make good these claims. Balkanization into separate entities, the likely result had the South won the Civil War, will not solve anyone's problems or the needs of Third World people in the United States.

But one should not be too optimistic in thinking that American citizenship can overwhelm the interests of either ethnic or geographic groups who start from principles of secessionism. Once the imperialist cast of mind is broken, avoiding the breakup of the United States will require the most subtle politics and overt compensatory action. We should be clear on our own purposes in this regard. The movement to fulfill the terms of a modern democracy is not a secessionist one. Indeed, one of its major purposes is to assure that secessionism does not have to occur. But just because this is so we must be sure to take into account cultural differences and the heightened political awareness people have of their original or future identities outside the current definitions of American citizenship. To avoid such an organizational breakup our map needs to be drawn in new ways. Plato noted that in the ideal state unity is the most important concern and that to maintain unity, the state must not grow too large. And for this reason we should forswear annexationist tendencies which will surely appear if Canada splits or Mexico does not solve its economic difficulties; and imperial visions of the "free world" which supposedly the United States can control. As President Reagan has shown so well, Americans do not bind themselves by the precept of limits but pride themselves on chasing the "impossible dream", the unity which we have had among each other is belief in the impossible, the fantastic and the unlimited. As a result, our unity may be a very shaky matter for it is predicated on individual dreams of a better individual future, or at best a family future. It is not based on either a collective or cooperative future, or fundamental agreement around principles. Given the closing of the frontier and the discovery that outer and inner space will not bring either personal or collective happiness, the question is whether we can reach for community and the common good through a process democratic in ends and means which helps people recognize what is truly humane as against what is exploitive and a Faustian bargain. Political organizers, those who give catalytic leadership to the generation of a modern democracy, will play an important role in generating the principle of social complementarity and aiding the American nation to become one which recognizes a new moral and political purpose. Leaders, organizers and a movement of social reconstruction will reflect in their program and projects collective and individual responsibility for social caring.

3
Social caring

Social caring

At the beginning of the twentieth century it was taken for granted in Western Europe and among progressive groups in the United States that social welfare was a necessary activity to be undertaken by government. Indeed, socialist parties organized themselves around this principle on both continents. Leaders and organizers of social movements, both inside and outside of the established parties held to the idea that the social product should be shared in a more equitable way. It was taken for granted that increased technology, positivistic or dialectical rationality, would lead to new concepts that would better the lot of people.[1] Concern developed around everyday life and certain concepts were introduced such as standard of living and economic growth as instruments of explanation and measurement to better people's lot.

Both capitalist and state socialist thinking continue to maintain the importance of more consumer goods, schooling, housing and medical care as evidence of the success of their respective ideologies. In recent years with the idea that "more is less" and that schools or hospitals are limited in what they can do for people given their deformed institutional character, a critical re-evaluation of the utility of much of the social welfare and social democratic program has emerged.[2] Nevertheless, even with this re-evaluation there is little doubt that concern with social security, health, education, nutrition and shelter continues to be fundamental to the operations of the modern nation, and relations which groups and individuals have with one another. Public concern as manifested in social programs is an important element in attaining a decent society.

The social caring task of leaders and organizers for reconstruction is a complex one in relation to this objective. They are required to take account of the critique of social democracy, socialism and democracy which puts mistaken emphasis on measurements without coming to grips with the way social services are experienced, for too often they are experienced as social control mechanisms rather than liberating activities which would allow the person to feel dignity. The result is that the fundamental philosophic and spiritual underpinning to the human project, namely caring and taking care, is lost thus allowing conservatives and reactionaries to mobilize among those very groups that have the most to gain from social reconstruction. Political leaders and organizers of reconstruction are called upon to transcend mechanistic views about caring and dominating rationality which grew out of nineteenth-century views of progress, whether of the capitalist or socialist variety. Reconstruction necessitates new, richer forms of rationality and deeper cultural understandings if the common good is to be achieved.

The common good is utterly intertwined with the question of care and taking care. It is the obligation that human beings owe each other, owe nature and owe that which they produce that can be used positively for each other (in a life-affirming way).[3] This chapter will take up the context of the common good in a society which seeks social reconstruction and which starts from the principle that governmental organization with democratic participation is the means to assure a system of taking care between people. The two other areas of concern for humanity, namely taking care of nature, that is, acting as the trustee of it, and acting as the conservator for that which is created and produced is considered only as derivative of our political capacity to care for each other.

As we shall see the caring instinct necessitates concern with the nature of the economy, and means for assuring and allocating the protection of security, the means to assure a healthy, functioning life and the educational tools to enable the person to take part in guiding the destiny of society namely producing, creating, and enjoying the society that is jointly nurtured by its members. This chapter begins, therefore, from the assumption that humankind (adam) and nature (adama) have a mutual and interactive relationship with one another. The human relationship to protect nature and the earth is mediated politically through the way humankind in particular social and political interactors care for one another. Once this principle is taken seriously in an operational sense it means certain profound changes will have to be enacted. A caring humanity accepts the rights of animals, and controls its own predatory ways toward the environment, land, and animals. Its activities are related to living with, that is, understanding nature, rather than conquering or dominating it. A caring humanity realizes that human beings are themselves part of nature. In the chapters on foreign policy and economics I will take up the problem of maldistribution. For example, about 30 per cent of the earth's population uses 83 per cent of the earth's fossil fuel resources, leaving 17 per cent for two-thirds of the rest of the world, where basic needs are greatest. This is an important consideration for it makes clear that one aspect of the common good is the obligation owed to unseen others not part of one's own family, tribe or nation. (See Chapter 5.)

There is both a productive application to caring as well as one which reflects the sentiment of welfare and conservation. In practice these aspects cannot be separated from each other. For the fact is that caring for land and resources, animals, tools, workers, children, buildings, sewage systems, highways and maintenance is of great importance to the productive process and to the sense of well-being in the society. To lose this aspect of the common good, or not to recognize its fundamental necessity is to court social disaster. Take one case in the area of infrastructure for society. The data provided by one 1984 study prepared for Congress point out that our national needs in roads, bridges, mass transit, water and sewer systems is 1.2 trillion dollars with a financing gap of 450 billion dollars.[4]

Pat Choate, the author of *America in Ruins*,[5] stated before a Congressional committee that since 1965 the United States experienced a 27 per cent drop in public works investment on a per capita basis. This occurred *before* the Reagan administration's slashing of the non-defense aspects of the federal budget. The result of this situation is that "one of every five bridges requires major rehabilitation or total reconstruction. The nation's Interstate Highway System has deteriorated to the point that almost one of every four miles requires replacement. Conrail faces the prospect of abandoning half of its lines." He went on to point out that "half the nation's cities" could not allow substantial industrial expansion because of the inadequate water and sewage systems. Another quarter of the nation's communities, he said, "could not improve their economies because their roads, streets, and certain other public facilities were worn out, obsolete or already operating at full capacity."[6]

That a nation refuses to repair itself in a collective way is symbolic of a deformation of the caring sentiment. It is not different from parents who stop caring for their children or vice versa. Through public investment and maintenance the society states that it cares for itself as a whole. In the chapter on economic policies I have outlined how a society might begin repairing itself, reflecting its caring instinct and in the process generate necessary and productive enterprises.

Beyond the productive side of caring there remains the human welfare aspect to caring, which we find in our attitudes and policies toward health, housing and education. On the most primary level, taking care means being conscious of and paying attention. In *Death of a Salesman* Willie Loman's wife says to her sons "Attention must be paid."

And so it must be for everyone in the society. Caring is not a casual activity which is habitual or unconscious. It must be built into direct relationships, into relationships fostered through institutions, and among people who are not directly involved with one another. Is this not the definition of humanity? In *Being and Time*, Heidegger, for all his egregious political errors, stated this point well in mythical terms:

Once when "Care" was crossing a river, she saw some clay; she thoughtfully took up a piece and began to shape it. While she was meditating on what she had made, Jupiter came by. "Care" asked him to give it spirit, and this he gladly granted. But when she wanted her name to be bestowed upon it, he forbade this, and demanded that it be given his name instead. While "Care" and Jupiter were disputing, Earth arose and desired that her name be conferred on the creature, since she had furnished it with part of her body. They asked Saturn to be their arbiter, and he made the following decision, which seemed a just one: "Since you, Jupiter, have given its spirit, you shall receive that spirit at its death; and since you, Earth, have given its body, you shall receive its body. But since 'Care' first shaped this creature, she shall possess it as long as it lives. And because there is now a dispute among you as to its name, let it be called '*homo*' for it is made out of humus (earth).[7]

The human being's fundamental purpose in the world according to this myth is that of caring, for it is in caring that the body and the spirit are brought together. It is this sensibility which is to inform the making of public policy on questions concerned with social caring. In its political aspects caring must also include *equity*, namely, the distribution of goods and services to people so that individual dignity can be assured within the body politic as a whole.[8] One such distribution system is social welfare.

The system of social welfare which Americans accept does not flow from any distinct or coherent set of ideas around caring and equity. The American system grew from individual and group interest demands which then gave rise to contradictory legislation, regulation and bureaucratic entanglement. Claimants and beneficiaries found themselves to be pawns of the day-to-day practice of struggle between social welfare government officials who seek to work out complex and contradictory formulae between the various levels of government as a means of determining "citizen wages." These formulae determine the benefits that any particular individual is to get. Conservatives attempt to apply market criteria to the principle of social welfare and social security and in the process limit financial responsibility of the government, that is, of the society as a whole, for benefits to individuals while liberals moved toward guarantees to people outside of market criteria. As John Myles pointed out in "The Trillion Dollar Misunderstanding":

> Social Security is socialized consumption which provides a "citizen's wage" as opposed to a "market wage." It has been used to redistribute income within generations; it has paid out benefits on the basis of need and not just past contribution levels; it has attached income claims to persons and not just to their capital.[9]

This liberal welfare notion became more pronounced as an operating assumption of public policy in the 1960s. Indeed, except for the first participants in social security, welfare programs were usually understood as a system of benefits that were paid in exchange for services rendered. Individual claimants did not think of their benefits as gifts but rather as payment for previous service. Thus, for example, veterans believed that they were owed debts for services. They did not think of themselves, either subjectively or objectively, as in the same category as those who are the unemployed poor and who have no rights of entitlement.

In Reagan's America, whether one is on the left or right, each person carries an image in the back of his or her mind (and these are quite separate images according to gender) of what is meant by social welfare and who is entitled. There are delineated classes and hierarchies among those on welfare (the highest being people on social security and veterans' benefits to the lowest, those in AFDC (Aid to Families with Dependent Children) and food stamps). That we have pitted one category of welfare recipients against another, that they are divided against each other (those on veterans' benefits and education grants from those on welfare or social security) has meant the perpetuation of an unwieldly and irrational welfare system which in practice is expensive, inefficient and quite uncaring. A self-conscious, progressive, public philosophy of social welfare is needed for reasons of guaranteeing decency and dignity to everyone in the society irrespective of the market system, and coincidentally, for reasons of cost and efficiency.

The reader should take note that the US lags far behind other nations in its commitment to social welfare and security. Our social benefits and pensions programs are more primitive and mean-spirited than that of other Western nations, as shown below.[10]

	Prices 1970-81		Pensions 1970-81		1981 Ratio of Pension to Prices
United States	100	234	100	239	1.02
France	100	285	100	385	1.35
Germany	100	174	100	221	1.27
Netherlands	100	217	100	339	1.56
Sweden	100	271	100	392	1.44
Switzerland	100	173	100	275	1.59
United Kingdom	100	404	100	543	1.35

For pragmatic reasons American liberals have been reluctant to argue that the society as a whole should so arrange its social welfare system as to provide a decent standard of living for all members of society.[11] The official social security phrase which is used instead is "minimally *adequate* income to long-term wage workers." The fact that the commitment to a decent standard does not exist means that conservative sermonettes on "individualism," opportunity to "make it on one's own," claims that "nobody owes you a living," the denial that there are "decent living standards" and even preachments on "liberty" grow in rhetorical importance to the point that these paternosters replace sentiments which bind people to one another. But a society of individualist selfishness cannot long endure and that is one important reason why American society should dedicate itself to a common good which asserts equity, caring and a decent standard of living for all.

Consequently, we begin from a non-market principle of the common good. In a democracy all members sue to retain humanity and citizen obligation. This means that producers and non-producers are required to help the "Other."[2] This objective is to be partly accomplished through the governmental process. Government is the enabling instrument to bring out the caring tendency of people who do *not* know each other. To attain minimum standards of decency it organizes material goods, sentiment and money as a *right* for people rather than as a voluntary gift to them. What is required therefore is minimum income, free goods and an active political and economic life in which the beneficiaries participate in and democratically control the public investment trusts whose policy mission is social caring. (I have taken up the investment of social security funds in the section on economic policies.) Suffice to say that social security should not be a passive fund and should be an active investment instrument to strengthen the public sector and the free goods created in the society.

In an economy which is primarily market-oriented, such as the American system of capitalism, minimum income is the primary concern of the beneficiary for it is that amount of money which can be spent at the discretion of the person or social unit. It is to be obtained as a matter of right from the society and is to be determined by the level of production of the society as a whole and through a taxing policy that sets limits to wealth and income. In other words, the government serves as a redistributive mechanism that stops the society from flying apart for economic reasons. The political principle here is obvious.

Deep disparities of income and wealth increase envy and class conflict within a society thus cheapening the value of citizenship. People have less in common with the society as a whole as against their own class. This increases the chance of economic civil war.

There are three methods of assuring minimum income. One such method is through the negative income tax in which everyone beneath a politically determined level receives a subsidy to attain that level. Another is through the social security system which would increase payments as a matter of vested rights to each person. A third method is through the growth of special programs which are meant to cater to organized interest groups in the society such as blacklung victims.

Since much of public policy builds on institutions already in place, and since it is the case that the social security system itself is recognized by the society as the single most important anti-poverty program for most people, it is obvious that the social security program is the system upon which to build minimum incomes.

The astounding number of categorical programs, special programs and special interest groups should suggest that there is a need to establish basic guarantees and where possible to convert categorical grants into basic grants for everyone. I do not make this suggestion as a way to destroy the paltry benefits of categorical programs, or to disturb the minimum adequacy standards that people are able to paste together when they match state and federal funding for themselves, or even to interrupt the relationship of the claimant to his or her interest group, which does battle for them at various levels of the government. I put this notion as part of a general program of democratic commitment.

A society's commitment to guaranteed incomes at decent levels is meant to give flexibility to individuals to make it possible for them to choose and not feel socially or economically forced to undertake particular actions or jobs because of the whip of necessity. Economically guaranteed incomes (citizen wages) are meant to revalue unpleasant work. Politically, they empower people with the right to exercise citizenship beyond mere economic self-interest. And in this process they are able to meet standards of equity, fairness and caring toward each other because they are not personally financially burdened. In the context of guaranteed income, public social welfare must be based on the person's needs and aspirations throughout his or her life.

Some elementary points need to be made about social security since it is the social welfare program that should be expanded and activated as the primary means of abolishing poverty while financially protecting all of our citizens.

Social security

The cornerstone of the present social welfare program is the Social Security Act of 1935. Like so many political programs that grow incrementally in the context of a turbulent situation it began narrowly and was meant to counteract more far reaching proposals of the time which had a populist base to them. Thus, as Gilbert Steiner has pointed out, the Townsend Plan which called for 150 dollars a month for the elderly, financed by a national sales tax, and Huey Long's Share the Wealth campaign, the New Deal, enacted "a national program to forestall indigency and to provide support for the indigent. . .".[13] It was also used as a means of getting older people out of the work force, thus reducing unemployment, and getting the public to pick up pension costs. In its inception social security was to be applicable only to "retired workers in commerce and industry," although soon thereafter coverage was extended to:

aged wives and to children of retired workers and to the widows and young children of deceased workers. In 1950 social security coverage was extended to many farm workers and domestics, the nonfarm self-employed (except professionals), and to many employees of state and local governments and nonprofit organizations (on an elective basis).

During the 1950s and 1960s additional changes were made. Benefits were extended to self-employed farmers, professionals, and others, so that now more than 90 per cent of the employed labor force is covered by social security. Congress reduced the age at which women, and later men, could retire (although they receive actuarially reduced benefits if they claim benefits before age 65). In 1956 benefits were established for disabled workers; subsequently this program also was broadened. In 1965 Congress enacted medicare, under which first the aged and then disabled workers were made eligible for hospital insurance, and provided the option (of which almost all retirees have availed themselves) of purchasing subsidized insurance for physicians' expenses.

Under the schedule adopted in 1939, the social security benefit payable to a worker retiring in 1979 after always earning the average taxable wage would have – in the absence of changes in wage and price levels – replaced 41 per cent of that worker's preretirement gross earnings. If married, the couple's replacement rate would have been 62 per cent. Replacement rates – benefits as a fraction of previous earnings – are higher for workers with above average earnings.

In subsequent years, Congress repeatedly adjusted the benefit schedule on an ad hoc basis in order to offset the effect of inflation on the purchasing power of benefits and the effect of increases in average wage levels on replacement rates. In 1972, such adjustments were made automatic. The mechanism adopted then to adjust automatically the initial benefits of newly retiring workers as similar to the way such adjustments had been made previously. In an inflationary period, however, it proved faulty. This was corrected in 1977.

Under the 1977 law, the replacement rate at retirement for a worker who has spent a full career at the average wage will be virtually identical to the level established in 1939 for such a worker retiring in the early 1980s. In the absence of a legislated change, it will remain at that level for future retirees. After retirement, each worker's benefit is adjusted automatically to preserve its purchasing power.[14]

However, criticism from all sides is levelled at social security. Conservatives refer to federal social security as a forced savings program because there are no interest payments to the contributor. The fund has never been used as a system for capital accumulation for the type of investment that would benefit either the contributor or communities. It has been a pay-as-you-go system. As Professor Myles has put it, "Pay-as-you-go" had the further effect of preventing the buildup of huge capital funds in the program, which would have amounted to a significant transfer of economic power from the private sector to the state. Liberals accepted the conservative framework of funding but in exchange they sought substantial incremental improvements in the program. However, important regressive taxing elements remain: For example, the

> increase in the payroll tax over the years has reduced the progressivity
> of the overall tax system enormously and shifted the financing of
> government from the fair income tax to the unfair payroll tax. Thus,
> since 1960 to 1978 employment taxes (mostly social security) have
> doubled, from 12 per cent to 24 per cent of the federal total intake,
> whereas the corporate and individual income tax declined from 73 per
> cent to 70 per cent with corporate taxes in the mix declining from 24
> per cent to 16 per cent. At the individual level, a four person family with
> a single earner, in 1978, with $5000 annual earnings paid all their federal
> taxes in regressive folly at $10,000 earnings, paid out $3 in regressive tax
> for every $1 of income tax; and at $15,000 still paid more than $1 for
> $1.[15]

Even if one were to add benefits such as medicare and medicaid to lower wage earners, important major inequities continue which reflect a class and anti-family bias. Lower income workers obtain less of their previous earnings than those who earned higher incomes. Married couples get half as much as single persons with the same earnings. Young workers, "women and especially married women who work, single persons without dependents, working persons 65-72 years" all seem to be penalized for their natural condition or status. There is animosity between government and non-government workers and social security. Non-government workers are resentful that government employees do not pay into the social security system, and have a far better security system through their federal plans, which are paid by taxation. Most importantly, conservatives and reactionaries have fanned the flames of intergenerational conflict by claiming that free riders are destroying the integrity of the social security system.

It is argued that the social security system operates on a redistribution income arrangement from various segments of the middle class to the poor. But the truth is that transfer payments for social welfare are meant to foster a benevolent attitude of the body politic between its members by stimulating a benign complaisance of the poorer sectors of the society to the more affluent even though transfer payments are described as "payments to maintain the income of families whose livelihood has been cut off because of unemployment, disability, retirement, or death of the breadwinner."

Such changes do represent a shift in income from higher to lower income groups, from the younger worker to the older worker, from those who produce in acceptable ways to those who produce in any way they decide. Greater transfers *are* going to those who define their work, or are defined by the economic system as outside of the productive system.

A strong argument can be made that if this is happening (and it is more than a perception of reality) those in favor of reconstruction should applaud. Unfortunately, this perception is accompanied by increased resentment against those who receive the transfer payments. It should not be surprising that this resentment is focussed on the victim beneficiary rather than the victimizer. While there is anger on the part of the middle and working classes because they bear the brunt of transfer payments and because taxes are regressive, especially payroll taxes, the reason that they are required to pay so much emerges from the fact that in the American brand of capitalist industrial civilization there is *no room* for the victim or marginal person in the work place as presently defined and there is no room for that person in the context of social arrangements except as a ward; nor is there room for the old, sick, orphaned in extended families because these are only partly sanctioned or subsidized by the state or community. More directly, selfishness and societal dissolution is hailed as a public policy to foster capitalism. The actual taxes paid by large corporations and the very rich continue to decline while present tax redistribution schemes increase the income of the rich, their spending habits and their methods of income production.

On the other hand, the real income of the middle class has dropped in relation to the cost of basic services. Those in the middle class on fixed incomes – even where social security is a second income – are especially vulnerable. They experience a continuous and sharp increase in the cost of "basic" expenses, such as energy, clothing, food, education and health care. Middle-class people are caught in the double bind of fearing their old age and therefore wanting social security while seeking large immediate cash payments to pay current indebtedness on consumer goods. Such instabilities and paradoxes among the working and middle class engendered by unsettled economic conditions show up in doubts about the social security fund. According to a Peter Hart poll most workers doubt that the social security fund will be present for them to aid them in their retirement. And given the conservative unwillingness to raise payroll taxes or to have costs paid from the federal budget there is some justifiable basis to this fear.

When there is substantial unemployment and inflation the fund is not adequately replenished because its solvency is predicated on payroll taxes from workers. A pay-as-you-go program is dependent on a stable and relatively full employment, non-inflationary economy. If the economic history of the last twenty years is any guide, the "short-term" economic crisis of the system is in fact a structurally chronic one for the social security system. Given its present level of benefits the social security system cannot afford more than a 5.5 per cent unemployment rate. There is nothing to suggest that the American economy will operate at such a low level of unemployment without direct government intervention to transform the economy. (It is true that a conventional war could have as one of its effects increasing employment. Substantial increases in the defense budget, if reallocated and directed to labor-intensive manufacturing, would reduce the unemployment rate.) Since these conditions are not present, we may expect serious problems for social security unless there are basic structural reforms. According to the report of the trustees of the social security system, retirement benefits are virtually exhausted, by which the government means that there is less willingness on the part of Congress to raise taxes for the purpose of supplying enough funds to keep the system a pay-as-you-go system. The Carter administration attempted to save the situation by calling for multiple cuts in the program and in the categories of people covered by social security. For example, elimination of survivors benefits, parents benefits when the youngest child reaches 16, lump-sum death benefits, post-secondary student benefits and special minimum benefits. In 1981-2 the Reagan administration sought further cuts in social security ostensibly for the purpose of encouraging people to "save" and invest in pension funds which would then be available for private enterprise investment.

An argument is often made by conservatives that as the population of the United States grows older there will be a greater financial drain on the "employed" classes that pay for the system. Unless there is a change in retirement laws there will be a 50 per cent increase in the ratio of retired persons to workers by the year 2000. Thus, if the 1980 benefit structure is kept, there will be a huge increase in the social security tax to maintain the ratio of benefits to wages. For example, in 1976 32 million people received social security benefits and 100 million paid social security taxes. By 2000 with only 50 million paying benefits, some 72 million people will be receiving benefits. This is why various liberal groups have urged politicians to coopt the social security financing side into the federal budget. This reform would allow current taxes, loans and general revenues to be used to pay for the social security system.

For the last forty years various advisory councils to the social security system have recommended that general revenues be used for financing at least part of social security. Each time this request is made it has been turned aside or turned down by Congress. It is as if conservatives in Congress sought to penalize workers by insisting that the social security tax remain outside of the general revenue taxing stream and be a regressive tax to boot. Perhaps, as William Cannon, the leading social policy analyst, has pointed out the payroll tax system was the price liberals had to pay for having *any* kind of national pension program.

Under present rules of financing the employer and employee share equally in the costs of the system. (In Sweden, employers are the major source of funding for the social security system. The employer contributes about 14.5 per cent of payroll to old age, invalidity, and survivor insurance. They also contribute "about 8 per cent toward health, work injury, and unemployment insurance combined." Employees are limited to small amounts in union-related unemployment programs.) The "contribution" of the employers is illusory for in most firms the employer calculates this contribution by paying lower wages to the worker. In reality the worker contributes the entire amount. In other words, the worker is penalized with a regressive tax by the government and the corporation. In intensively organized industrial sectors employers are unable to lay off their share of social security taxes on to the workers. In such cases large corporate employers pass the cost on to consumers rather than deduct from corporate profits. An argument of sorts could be made to tax employees equally if the employer in fact used the funds for capital formation, lending to reinvestment and rebuilding the society. But this treasured goal of free enterprise is not happening.

Once social security is extended and is recognized as part of the yearly federal budget, it will be possible to revamp the entire social welfare budget so that it is folded into a comprehensive social security system. Categorical programs would be subsumed under social security and monetary allowances for each family and individual in the society would be debated on the basis of a yearly national budget which would show allocations of expenditures. With a strong security program which included allowances and free social and health services for the entire society, disposable income for social security commitments could continue at a relatively low level. The monetary aspects of the social security fund would become a "life" fund in which people would use cash payments as disposable income for study, travel, sabbatical at particular times in their work lives and some consumer luxuries. *Of course this is a far cry from our present situation where two-thirds of our retirees live only on their social security and where one-third of the retirees fall below the "poverty line."*

Once having concluded that the social security system is to be extended and consciously devised as a "citizen wage" program, we are relieved of the obligation of applying needs tests and cumbersome bureaucratic procedures which are costly and demeaning. Social security would become the gift and obligation of one American to another. It would be available for activities of the person at the end of his or her work time, or for other designated purposes such as travel, education, building, etc., at specific life times. The funds could be placed in commercial and savings banks in the name of individuals. But the funds would not be able to be withdrawn except for purposes outlined in new comprehensive social security legislation. With the changed focus of the social security fund, a contributor would have the right to withdraw and reinvest in other *designated pension funds* that would be coordinated for investment purposes through the federal government. The contributor would be required to demonstrate to social security investment trustees that particular private investment funds yielded higher rates of return than the social security investment trust. Designated pension funds would be those that invested in primarily public and community enterprise.[16]

In the short term the system can be transformed to enhance the dignity of the people, their innate fairness and responsibility for each other. This is accomplished by increasing the social wages to all those on social security. Special attention must be given to those who have no supplementary income from pensions. Thus, the millions of people who do not have any other income, or who have worked throughout their lives at low-paying, unprotected jobs are entitled to be cared for by the society as a whole at a higher rate than those with second incomes. The costs of maintaining a market system must not be paid by those who are victims of it, namely those who are unorganized and who attempt to live in an "individualistic" way within the context of the market system. There is no way to set percentage increases in dollar amounts for this group of people because the amount would have to be indexed to inflation levels.

What is the conception of the common good, therefore, as it applies to social security? We have already shown that it involves the profoundly important human activity of caring. But it also involves the evolution of an ensemble of economic, social and work rights which are protections of the individual and which additively define a decent society. To the extent possible it starts from the notion that people must be considered as ends, not means, and therefore not controlled by the accident of class, race or gender. Obviously, the concept of the "decent" which would embrace economic and social rights can and should be argued about since it involves different points of view that emanate from one's own experience or class. Nevertheless, the agreement for the policy of a decent standard should not be subject to casuistry or mystification. When tenant farmers live in hovels on the edge of starvation we are aware that they are in need, just as when older people find that they live longer but are reduced to hollow shells whose lives are taken up with medical care, fearful that they have no way to pay for such care and caught in the situation of being "patientized." Their situation leaves no doubt about their need.

Because the social security system is so central to the personal plans of individuals, and because social security should be understood as the fundamental instrument for assuring well-being within the society, changes should be undertaken as part of a continuing dialogue on the nature of obligation and rights we owe and expect of each other. In public policy terms there are two stages to reconstruction of the social security system. The first is the realization that it is the primary instrument to assure a decent standard of living for everyone in American life. (This consideration, as I explain elsewhere, necessitates the consideration of social security trust funds as investment rather than passive funds.) The first stage of reconstruction is to assure the maintenance of benefits and their extension for all members of society beyond either the safety net or adequacy formulation. Once the understanding is present in the society that caring can and should be reflected in public policy, without the interruption of benefits we can begin the second stage which is that of switching over to a new framework for social security. This framework would be predicated on the principle that a combination of services should not be dependent on the vagaries of income. For the foreseeable future priority consideration in the social sphere should be given to health, shelter and education because they define the character of modern society and the level of decency which should exist for everyone. These three needs, socially defined but personally necessary, are critical in defining the character of modern society and the level of decency which will exist for everyone in it. Because they are socially constructed and personally internalized as a need, it is likely that once the common good is sought people will recognize the special responsibilities which each member of the society owes to the other. Consequently, it should not be a surprise to see that the fulfilment of these needs can be accomplished best outside of a money-price market system.

A public policy aimed at social reconstruction does not mean that a person is unable to go to the "market" to purchase services or special goods. It is to say, however, that the primary emphasis of the society should be on recognizing that the "free goods" of health, education and shelter are guaranteed to the people. The conception of public responsibility and "free goods" does not mean that experimentation, innovation and variety are sacrificed to some dead or inert ideas of standards. Instead once there is recognition that such services are to be considered as goods collectively paid for, variety, difference and personal choice could flourish. No doubt it is difficult to present innovative ideas in a framework which eschews them. This is why it is of such importance that ideas of reconstruction be studied in depth and projects undertaken and defended in the culture that have the seeds of alternatives within them. Conceptual rethinking is also critical. Hayek makes the point that free health service, by alleviating human suffering or prolonging life, "cannot be justified on economic, but only on humanitarian grounds."[17] If one takes a restrictive, mechanistic view of health which is understood totally in individualistic terms, Hayek's terms are harsh but well taken. But being healthy is a personal and social construct resulting from dozens of decisions taken daily by the society as a whole which impinge on the individual.

As I will suggest, the problem of how the individual assures himself or herself of a healthy life relates directly to the type of medicine practiced, the personal regimen that a person follows, and most important the social and work situation in which the person operates.

Health and social reconstruction

I have stated that the social health of a nation is dependent on the shared belief that the common good is a necessary part of everyone's life. But there is another aspect to health which is usually considered to be an individual matter. Here I refer to the physical and mental well-being of each person. Obviously, the improved health of the American people will not be possible without concentrating on the society's productive, environmental and food system. This should not be thought of as surprising since these interrelated systems frame the personal life experience of the individual. In other words, an individual's health may be best understood by locating the person in a social situation and comprehending the various social causes which define the relative condition of the person. Our problem is that the American health system continues to follow a mechanistic line of thought and inquiry rather than a situational one.

The single causal agent approach to disease and discomfort, represented by the discovery of micro-organisms, a series of discoveries which have had profound explanatory power and some curative results, is now stimulating a degenerating research program which yields diminishing returns in understanding and in contributing to a more healthy population. The major causes of sickness in the United States are related to poor nutrition, economic insecurity, stress from social disintegration, air and water pollution and poisonous substances made or stimulated through the industrial and agricultural process.

Poor working or living conditions feed into a hereditary "bias" for certain infirmities which are latent in people. For example, it is not surprising that working conditions in an asbestos factory are likely to cause chronic lung conditions in workers, or tobacco subsidization by the state to farmers is likely to increase the incidence of cancer to society as a whole. Such activities would tend to explain why more than 75 per cent of cancer is environmentally caused either through foul food or air or smoking. Rather than directly confront this condition, which would mean investment reallocation, hard political decisions, such as a system of free, nutritious food, and medical care programs away from hospital-based facilities, the medical system has left unchallenged the entire productive and nutritional process. The medical profession has tended to enslave itself to the powerful drug and food business by seeking drugs as an elixir, while avoiding to an alarming extent nutritional, environmental and productive process questions in medical training and the treatment of patients. Medical reliance on drugs is relatively recent. As late as 1935 the doctor had only "six specific medicines in his 'armory'; that is, medicines capable of attacking causes."[18]

While the most popular types of research among health researchers are those which revolve around viruses and bacteria as the cause of cellular breakdown in the person, such research has its limits in terms of caring for an entire population. Bacteria and viruses are always present so the question is to what extent certain formations in the productive and environmental process increase the incidence of virus and bacteria thus generating sickness and degeneration in individuals. While it is indisputable that researches on bacteria and viruses have resulted in improvement in people's lives, this improvement can only be highly circumscribed unless accompanied by a direct improvement in working conditions in factories, stress situations, economic and social conditions. It was not until the counter-cultural movement of the 1960s that any serious public attention was given to the diets of Americans who were supposedly eating well. And it was not until the work of Ivan Illich and his interest in iatrogenesis that the public at large understood that the medical system's emphasis on certain types of cures caused debilities and disease often more harmful than the original malady.

Questions such as nutrition, full employment and security go far beyond those doctors take to be their arena of technical concern. This narrowness does not have to be the dominant spirit of the medical profession. The great nineteenth-century pathologist Rudolph Virchow said that "medicine is a social science and politics nothing but medicine on a grand scale." If we were to apply Virchow's challenge to our present situation it would mean that health workers and doctors are central to the transformation of the industrial process. For example, if they knew, they could teach workers about the medical effects of various processes and chemicals, design with workers new detection equipment and with chemists possible alternatives to substances presently used which cause deleterious effects in workers and consumers. This could be part of medical school programs, especially at medical schools located in industrial areas. Workers could begin the difficult but rewarding activity of policing their own work places – once they are given guidelines, training and instruction from health workers, OSHA (Occupational Safety and Health Administration) and their unions. In other words, medical schools with OSHA would sponsor national teaching laboratories for workers and consumers who would learn how to self-police and transform the work place.

Some experience of this type has been gained in public laboratories where materials are tested and skilled workers are encouraged to analyze the work process at factories and offices for the protection and health maintenance of employees. The work of public laboratories and medical schools could be strengthened greatly by doctors who operate in factories as "company doctors." With the aid of the National Institutes of Health (NIH) and OSHA, local medical societies, and plant workers could devise rules for the industrial process which emphasize health and security for the worker as well as the consumer.

The acolytes of Milton Friedman argues that these are questions which would best be left to the marketplace or individual judgment so that the worker has the right to risk his or her life as he or she sees fit. But this point of view neither takes account of the social and linked basis of individual existence nor does it credit the limited choices that people have in their occupation alternatives. Except for adventurers, people work at medically dangerous jobs not because they are masochists, but because they have few other economic or social choices. Consequently, the task of society is to provide full employment and lessen the burden of dangerous jobs either through redesigning them, when possible eliminating the activity itself, or offering benefits that make clear that the society has a social responsibility to those who work in medically hazardous positions. (In this sense a coalminer's work is more important to the society than that of the advertising executive, although some would see both as polluters.)

Where the dual ethos of the common good and democracy emerged as the society's dominant spirit the present narrowness to medical research and care would give way to a far more open attitude about the role of the medical worker. The medical worker would be transformed into a health worker who could move beyond narrow parameters and speak about social "vectors" as the likely ground for individual difficulty. If we state that the professional purpose of the health worker is to help create the conditions of a healthy population we then may conclude that the diagnostic signs which he or she looks for in the patient should include social stress and ways to overcome that stress by changing social institutions.

The types of concerns and knowledges which should be taught in medical schools and organized in the health system generally require a broader base of understanding between disease and social systems. While this information is often known it is not put to use as a means of rectifying poor conditions. The obvious next step in the knowledge-practice process is to encourage medical schools and public health institutions to initiate and participate in the redesign of the assembly, production, machine and office process. When medical scientists do not formulate a critical analysis of other institutions or elements of the society such as the productive process they fail in their central purpose, helping the development of healthy people. They continue the belief that people's health, in the way they feel and function, is utterly dependent on internal processes which do not have either an external relationship or cause.

Part of the reason for the increase in unresolved sickness is the Procrustean development of medical science which places great emphasis on drugs, medical technology and little emphasis on the daily life of the person. Ironically, for example, psychotherapists who should interest themselves in the work lives of their patients and the general structure of work are more fascinated with dream states or childhood memories than experiences which are presently lived – or lived through.[19] While there may be some explanation for this attitude, that people at work live lived lives, and therefore they are not "free agents" at work, the therapeutic way this can be broken is through attention being paid directly to conditions of work rather than evading the problem through prescription drugs. The American commitment to the high use of drugs helps in evading the possibility of full consciousness for the person.

American doctors use twice the number of drugs for the same illnesses than their counterparts in the second leading "drug oriented" nation. This reliance on drugs in the United States can be understood in terms of individualist psychology and diagnosis. Because events which are external to the body are not thought to be of crucial importance, patients are unable to relate their illnesses in direct terms to the social and productive situation which in fact influences, even guides, the person's relationship to his or her body. There is a history to this situation which bears mention. Prior to the Flexner Report of 1910, (a foundation study sponsored to develop a credidation system for doctors which recommended more vigorous scientific training for them) medicine and its practice in the United States was less structured and those who sought medical training came from a broad cross-section of the society. They practiced according to their own scientific and social biases. After 1910, the situation radically changed in the United States:

> The scientific mode became the sole form of training and practice;
> medicine became increasingly technological and the hospital the
> principal locus for its execution; and, because training for scientific
> medicine took place exclusively in the universities, it quickly became
> limited to sons of the upper middle and upper classes.[20]

The state was used to repress other healers, namely the homeopathic and eclectic schools, calling them quacks, closing them off from public acceptance. In the process any description of human behavior or of the human body which was not essentially mechanistic was rejected. Nevertheless, the adoption of this mechanistic analysis has neither improved the average American's health or the actual health care given.

We have become painfully aware that the theory of knowledge as it relates to disease, and is mastered in medical schools, is limited. Modern technology has absorbed modern medicine and in the process the doctors have little familiarity with the very equipment they must use (invariably not knowing how to build it, how it works, or the nature of its side-effects). Doctors are often in the same situation as car buyers who are basically ignorant of the mechanical aspects of their own cars unless they happen to be mechanics. The actual care of patients in terms of hours spent with the hospitalized patient, literally understanding and working out the basis of care is left to other health workers whose income wage is far less than that of the average doctor.

Social caring

When we are unfortunate enough to have to enter a hospital we learn to our surprise that the people who care for us are the nurses, attendants and hidden laboratory technicians. Doctors are not seen very often by the patient. In most institutions (and hospitals are no exception), administrators are prone to turn people into problems. This has the advantage of making the life of the institution easier because the person is then objectified and routinized. It is questionable whether this institutional habit of mind and the methods which flow from it are of any particular aid to the patient.

It is time to change the medical pyramid by recognizing that the doctor's role is not as central to good health or health care as we have come to believe. By de-emphasizing the role of the doctor in medical care, the medical school's role will change. Then other teachers and teaching institutions will be recognized. Part of these changes are caused by new modes of therapy and medical technology. Changes generated by technology require much more openness to the "non-certified" doctor. Once these changes are understood it is possible to see medical school as but one method of both learning medicine and being allowed to practice medicine. The de-professionalization system has begun informally. But it has taken crude forms. In a New York hospital a hospital equipment salesman was called into the operating room to help operate and fit a prosthetic appliance to the patient. The patient then sued the doctors for incompetence. The patient said that without the salesman doing the major work in the operating room he would have died.

A medical educational system built on practical knowledge and fueled by master-apprentice relations could produce a renaissance in medical learning moving from specialization to a more holistic approach. Once the curriculum and accrediting constraint is lifted by reducing the power of the medical schools and the professional associations, the new practitioners would be more open to learning other modes of medicine and inventing cures not now thought to be legitimate by the medical establishment.

Contrary to what the reader might think, standards for the practice of medicine would become progressively higher once anyone could practice medicine under the general terms set forth. In the present situation criminal laws are hard to apply against incompetent doctors precisely because the individual doctor is protected by guild licensing and the legitimated status of other doctors. While it is true that malpractice cases have increased in recent years, these cases do not reach the question of licensing and certification. An alternative system of accountability should be formulated. For example, doctors should be expected to take national examinations every ten years on their acquired medical arts. Such exams would include a review of one's work, written tests and interviews with patients. The results of these periodic reviews would be made public. They could hang in the doctor's waiting room thereby demystifying the practitioner's competence.

106

Organization of the health system

I proceed from the premise that the more people can know about their bodies and mental disposition as they relate to social, political and economic conditions the more likely it is that the person will approach a measure of happiness. The proposed national health program starts, therefore, from the assumption that health workers are critical to the operations of a society undertaking social reconstruction. Their training and education should vary, and those who are health workers should be free to organize their own curriculum with medical and non-medical faculties of universities. This liberalization of "standards" in medicine is now possible if the social milieu around health is changed. The general level of knowledge about health could be increased greatly through the high schools in preventive health programs. Special computer corners in towns and cities would be programmed with information about disease, causes and cures. We should be mature enough as a society not to have to deny psychological, religious and vitalistic components of human existence. And to the extent that a particular belief in cures and ways of healing are accepted by groups of people they need not be denied, merely understood and incorporated.

Perhaps an argument can be made against a comprehensive health system on the grounds that we are patientizing people and giving too much power to a new class of know-it-alls. But this does not have to be the result of medical care. We are challenged to remember our task. How are we to take care of each other, realizing that each of us is less than the reasonable, prudent person, the individual who is neither young nor old, never sick, never crazy, never in need, who suffers stoically in silence, believing that it is better to calculate than to hope. We can best surrender the patient in us by generating a community of relationships, by remaining silent about labels and categories which insist on divisions and by recognizing the importance of return to the community, the association and congregation of friends. This can be stimulated through the way a health system is organized.

During their education and training period health workers and the medical schools in which they are in attendance would be paid directly by the federal government. Part of the pay would be made available by communities, neighborhoods, as well as the federal and state governments. In the case of communities and neighborhoods such groups would choose people from among themselves to study medicine. They would be expected to return to their own communities for service. Communities would be given the funds from a national health trust for the education of medical students. This would assure return of the student to the particular geographic area which awarded the scholarship.

A *separate* health tax trust fund would be established as a subcategory of the proposed national social insurance fund. It would administer programs of research in sickness prevention, nutrition, social organization of the productive system and other forms of social activity which cause stress and disintegration. It would be paid through yearly tax revenues in which people voluntarily allocated part of their tax for health ecology. The trust fund would encourage studies, practices, projects and social inventions which transcended the present germ and virus theory of disease by showing how a process of attaining better nutrition and sanitation, wage raises, intellectual freedom, self-government, cooperative work conditions, and escape from the arms race would result in a healthier population. In this regard the new interest around the effects of nuclear war by doctors is a positive development.

Medical schools would be absorbed or transformed into schools of health, ecology and social organization. Their members would pursue studies of the body/mind and disease in relation to social organization. They would seek to fashion theories of health which embraced the common-sense/common good impulse of people to end their own objectification. In this process the medical profession would seek ways to escape its own assumptions by reaching for causal understanding beyond germ and virus theory.

To undertake such studies medical schools would become part of human ecology centers. They would receive endowment grants from the health tax trust fund so that independence could be exercised by them and they would be able to exercise their own judgment about matters of cause, health and medicine. We should be aware that such freedom allows the researcher to look more deeply with a "free gaze" once he or she is free of biases which may come from funding. Often these biases are not readily recognized. But they are present for they help to form the "legitimacy framework" of questions and ways to consider questions. Given the present interest of the captains of industry and education in cutting deals around profit making research arrangements the direction of knowledge in science and medicine could be skewed for another fifty years. The economic independence of health institutions, however, is meant as a way for its participants and researchers to be free of state and corporate assumptions and the type of restricted learning which is presently generated by them. Such endowments are also meant to free them from their fear of competing with those who present and develop "unauthorized" popular cures.

Health workers are concerned primarily with the question of how to retain and encourage health in the sick, and prevent sickness among the healthy. They are not charged with the responsibility of helping people live forever.[21] On the other hand, their responsibility is greatly increased by helping to formulate a healthy and creative community. This objective changes the function of the health workers somewhat for it includes a far more holistic approach to medicine, health care and definitions of health. There is a wrong way to achieve this end, and unfortunately, it is the present direction that we have taken as a society and that health workers have taken. It is by encouraging an unlimited growth market in terms of specialization, equipment, drugs, therapies, etc. The medical health industry continues to expand, but without the fundamental purposes of creating a healthy, non-patientized society. Admittedly, this objective is an increasingly complicated one for it means confronting the health bureaucratic enterprise itself which can always be justified in terms of patient difficulty and suffering, loneliness, and specific complaints. As an example, in the case of specific complaints subspecialties are initiated with attendant drugs and machinery. Such equipment, medical technology and even architecture is meant to relate to one aspect of the person. Health institutions find that their interest in disease or cell structure becomes the basis upon which institutions and technologies are established, often to the detriment of the society as a whole or to the whole body. But the quandary for health workers is that so long as they are not part of a more general movement with a program, they are stuck with a limited consciousness of their task. The result is that they have the most limited definition of crisis intervention and problem solving and they postpone the treatment of fundamental causes.

Where health workers, from doctors to orderlies, see their work in political terms, it becomes possible for them to formulate goals and purposes which transform the role of the health worker as social control repressor or "pill pusher." We may begin to see an organizationally and humanely reasonable structure for the American health system. When considering the common good it is important to be aware of those relationships and activities which are endemic to the health profession. They have grown up over the centuries and they reflect considerable wisdom behind them. At the same time, it is important to be aware of structural and organizational flaws which are relatively recent and which stem from the way in which organized medical care, the hospital and insurance system developed over the last two generations. Faulty bureaucratic arrangements and choices made between, for example, Blue Cross and Blue Shield (a national, private insurer system operating with private and government funds) with the Department of Health and Human Services; or definitions of phrases such as "reasonable charges," or the unexamined emphasis on hospitals which increases the power and authority of the hospital over the health system, and the disdain that medicaid patients are held in all qualify as relationships which can and should be corrected. If they are not corrected, we will witness a society committed to great health expenditures yet swamped by illness, disease and health delivery inequity.

The first step in reorganizing the health system of the US is to make clear the values which we intend to promote through the health system. One such value is self-independence and ability to know one's own body and relationship to surrounding circumstances. Thus, part of the program of good health is education about the body and surrounding environment which affects the person. These studies are meant to educate and transform the social and political system so people are not denied healthy lives by virtue of class, race or gender. The second is to use the National Health Planning and Resources Act of 1974 to increase greatly the number of people in the National Health Service Corps, and to specifically operate training and education programs at medical and nursing schools as well as hospitals. Members of the National Health Service Corps would then become the most important group in bringing quality medicine to Americans.[22] For these changes to occur an understanding and resistance to the entrenched interests are necessary. The politics of medicine will have to become part of the public deliberative process transcending the vested interest players. Presently, there are four "players" in the national health scene, each holding very different power cards. The first player is the hospitals. The second is the insurance companies, the third is the federal bureaucracy with a more minimal role exercised by Congress, and the fourth are the doctors. From time to time minor players are heard. They tend to be involved in preventive health, basic research or nursing, technical assistant work.

To obtain the minimum health system which was initiated in the 1960s in the United States the federal government agreed to turn over the basic charge scale and handling of payments to the hospitals, doctors and insurance companies. Congressional anxiety over the cost of the program was aimed at the patient rather than the "provider" of health care. The financing and administration of the program was given to the "professionals" whose interest has been in increasing "professionalism" and professional markets, protecting their own hold on the health system and stabilizing their own class position. Congress, on the other hand, concerned itself with costs, but it was open to institutional pressures from the professionals who gladly accepted *further* charges of patients beyond that which is subsidized. It is surprising, but true, that the poor presently pay more for medical services than they did prior to medicaid.

The political task is to change the nature of the dynamics between the health institutions and organizations. This is accomplished by undercutting the present assumptions of the institutional players. There is reason to suggest that this possibility does exist. Given the sour mood of taxpayers to high governmental expenditures there is a possibility that programs beyond those of the old Kennedy-Griffiths bill may be fashioned. It may be remembered that the Kennedy-Griffiths bill, as in other programs, began from legitimation of the players, namely, that they should be sitting at the table deciding the fate of medical care. While the Kennedy program was the one which opened up the issue most clearly to new voices, even to the extent of changing the role of the insurance companies such as Blue Cross-

Blue Shield, absorbing them into the public sector, the fact remains that this program, like other Republican and Democratic party health bills,

> repeat(s) the scenario of funnelling generous amounts of public funds through private agencies to private providers of health care, without upsetting the mode of operations of either. All of them (the proposals) also extract the greatest financial burdens from the lower middle class, both directly, through financing the program and sharing in its costs, and indirectly, through the future effects of the inflationary imperative inherent in national health insurance, as it was inherent in medicare and medicaid. All of them, in short, are essentially more of the same – the same manipulation of the political process by powerful private interests.[23]

Conservatives are reaching for a new way to continue this manipulation by following market principles. I reject the notion of the Reagan administration that good health for people can be achieved through the market system and that access to good health care is not a basic human right. The Reagan administration's plan is to give people a health allowance up to a particular dollar amount which it can redeem at different provider "stores." This program does not deal with the power of the present players in medicine. Nor does it concern itself with the character or quality of medical care. If there is competition, which is possible but not likely, there will be a marginal effect on medical costs. What is profoundly mistaken about the Reagan-Stockman proposal is that it tells the patient that he or she should be careful in going to doctors because they have a limited number of health stamps to cover their health costs. It seeks no health prevention system, and it certainly keeps in place the social causes of disease and physical distress. Thus, this proposal is another step away from promoting a healthy functioning people.

We should not escape the responsibility of understanding good health as a right which requires increased care and *medical* understanding of the implications of our social organization. This means that programs in health should be offered through the legislative and referendum process to the citizenry. They must participate in their formulation. The participation of the people can be obtained where there are clear lines which suggest a reconstructive model that has the support of members of Congress and which can then be organized among local legislators and members of the lower bureaucracy.[24]

(1) Each congressional district is to be drawn into segments of 50,000 people. On a precinct by precinct basis, a health and preventive health plan is to be devised which includes clear integrating relationships to an analysis of local conditions in agriculture, nutrition, the productive

111

process, environmental hazards, nursing care, physical fitness and education.

(2) Each congressional subdivision is to submit a health plan for approximately 50,000 people. Such plans optimally are to include one-third for preventive medicine, analysis of productive processes, and environmental problems including conditions of social stress, and two-thirds for health education, nursing and general medical care. They would provide for public clinics, public health hospitals, and wellness centers that would offer a range of services. All health programs would be free (publicly paid for) at the point of their distribution.

(3) Congress would establish a national health trust fund which would be paid from segregated tax funds and general revenue. The taxpayer would have the choice of setting aside his or her tax funds for health and preventive care. Where either necessary or useful, the drug companies would be absorbed into public laboratories which would manufacture drugs thus competing with existing drug firms. These public laboratories would have the added responsibility of studying new food processing systems which eliminate harmful additives. A further activity of public laboratories would be the testing and aiding of local programs by schools, workers, students who seek to devise new standards and techniques for better health across the productive and psychological and nutritional lines. The national health board would also aid the expansion of the National Health Service. All doctors who received medical school aid would be members of the National Health Service for a fifteen-year period. Their incomes would be limited accordingly. As Victor and Ruth Sidel have pointed out in *A Healthy State*,

It is widely believed that doctors are free to practice wherever they wish, yet the increasingly large numbers of doctors whose education is paid for by government agencies such as the armed forces or the National Health Service Corps give up a considerable degree of autonomy on where and how they will practice at least part of their careers.

It is widely believed that doctors pay for their own medical education and should therefore be free to earn as much as the traffic will bear, yet over half of the costs of medical education are already borne by government at one level or another or indirectly by payments for patient care, and for some students almost all expenses are already covered by one government agency or another.[25]

The Health Service would be expanded to include other health workers as well.

(4) A national health board would be established by Congress. Its board would be nationally elected for staggered terms. The board of nine

members would be automatically appointed by the Congress and the President upon election of the electorate. The members would oversee the insurance, financial, research and education system. It would operate and establish a national hearing and inspector system in each congressional district to ascertain how the plan on the local level was in fact being implemented. Its results would be deemed advisory to the Congress. It would work with the congressional jury system holding hearings and recommending corrective procedures locally.

(5) The health education system would establish programs for all medical workers to continuously study, learn, and be judged within the medical profession and community. Career lines would change so that medical workers who are not MDs could in fact become doctors through study and practice. There is no reason, for example, why nurses, laboratory technicians, etc., should not be given the opportunity of becoming Doctors of Medicine. In other words, the testing aptitude method which is used for students who want to enter medical school would be replaced by the "willingness" test. This would be reflected in the willingness of young people to perform different types of health work under tutorial and practitioners' supervision as well as that of a medical school.

In this way we can more easily recognize that the study of medicine is an historic and comparative cultural science as well as a "technical art." Just because of this fact there should be greater plurality of method and the definition of health worker would be far broader than it presently is, but without the status constraints internally which grind its workers into separate classes.

With an expanded public medical service and the direct intervention of health workers in helping to define and shape the productive and consumer process (changing the power balance between social costs and private profit), with medical care guaranteed to all as a free good the possibilities of building community and formulating a practical system of equity which would include the goal of healthy lives in a healthy society would no longer be the visionaries' dream but a realizable good available to all of us.

A primary way to bring down the costs of medical care is to reduce the causes for specific disease and to concentrate on those social and industrial repairs which will change the "illness base" of the population. However, even if a new consciousness were to exist which was then translated into a public policy that shifted changed emphasis from medical care to a program of social and preventive health, the costs of individual medical care would remain very high. Two methods have been proposed to bring the costs down. The Reagan administration has promoted the Prospective Payment System for medicare. The system attempts to set a flat rate for different categories of patients. The flat rate is determined by a formula which relates

113

to national average costs, whether the hospital is urban or rural and the history of past costs for similar services in the particular hospitals. The problem with this program is that the hospital's emphasis switches from care to efficiency thereby getting rid of services which are thought to be economically inefficient or unneeded. Furthermore, to maintain a profitable balance sheet hospitals get rid of undesirable patients in a process known as dumping. As Enthoven and Noll point out, the prospective payment system only controls costs per case of admission. It does not touch the growth of beneficiaries, hospital admissions or inflation costs in goods and services that the hospital buys. The Enthoven-Noll answer is to encourage competitive providers (such as Health Maintenance Organizations) to follow a standard benefit package which all providers would have to give to users.[26] There would be an annual enrollment and all plans would be required to take their share of hard and costly cases. The patient would have the right to renew his or her contract each year.

The problem with the Enthoven-Noll proposal is that it does not deal with the fundamental reasons why costs are so high. This relates to two categories. One is the income of doctors and the other is the cost of medical and technical equipment.

The root question is whether there should be a wage and price control system over the medical industry which would include the entire industry from drugs to hospital costs and medical manufacturing. A regulated industry would argue for a system of yardstick firms in the medical industry which would turn out medical equipment with low profit margins. A new section of the National Institute of Health would be established. Its task would be finding reasonable administrative means to control costs and establish regulative mechanisms throughout the entire medical industry. Without this or a similar approach to control costs medicare will become a serious burden in the society and taxpayers will resent old people who use the medicare system. As Enthoven and Noll have pointed out, medicare outlays have grown from $9.5 billion in 1973 to $56.8 billion in 1983 for an annual increase of about 19 per cent.

Clearly, a person's health is no longer an intimate matter in which the person suffers in silence or seeks to find personal ways of transcending pain. It is taken for granted by most people that pain does not have to be and that while health cannot be assured suffering is unnecessary. This modern point of view is wholly different from the past, even the nineteenth century, where suffering was taken for granted and was seen either as reflective of a person's evil character or saintliness.

Once health is no longer separate from the community but is part of it in the way we deal with our ailments and pain, certain consequences flow. One is that the person comes to learn about personal fitness. But also the person becomes aware of what is in the environment that may cause personal pain. Here we become aware of the social and work environment as an instrument of stress and disease. We want to see our communities and shelters as ways to escape debilitation and disease. The person comes to think of his or her body as a shelter just as the community and housing also become shelters against pain and difficulty. They protect and ennoble persons on centering us in a world which requires us to have both protection from the elements and mediation with others and with the community. As we shall see, shelter is an extension of the person and the person's possibility for health. It is not only a space to be, and to be left alone, but a space to allow a person his or her development. Communities and shelters therefore are meant to give us satisfaction and present us with the possibilities of health through our surroundings. They are meant to help us escape a deadness without challenge and grasp a sense of freedom, happiness and potentiality all of which are necessary for good health.

Thus, communities and housing, even furnishings should increase human possibility. This is not done in the types of projects that have been developed through our architecture, through the market and through public housing. The only way it can be done is through forms of direct participation in direct democracy where people share their public and private lives and where problems of everyday life and abstract problems are considered. It is through education that such skills are developed.

Education

Just as in the reconstruction of the health system and a consciousness changed in our attitudes towards health are needed (and as I will outline in the next section a reconstruction of our housing and shelter system which would benefit public happiness and social health) so it is that certain changed attitudes towards education could result in the fulfillment of the mental and humane capacities of the person. The social health of the society, that is to say its common good, can be aided or degraded by the requirements of education which are determined in the society. If our education system is one of standards and preparation for specific tasks which define narrowly what a person is to know, if a person is taught not to ask or question, we may be sure that the sense of freedom and potentiality will be absent, that emphasis will be placed on standards and that standards will not be ones of "enablement" and personal empowerment but ones which are meant to separate out people into categories and classes of dominance and submissiveness.

For those pursuing the task of social reconstruction, however, education in a democratic society is the means for a person to become cognizant of those values which begin from the premise of extending freedom (in the sense of the power to choose), dignity and justice through the complicated dialectic of self-regulation and participation. It is the social space in which the person may learn about the limits of human beings in relation to nature and those technical functions which can be performed with and on nature.

The process of education, defined as the necessity and compulsion to learn which the society recognizes and praises, also encourages that type of social regulation which needs and demands alternative modes of thinking and living.

It is no wonder, therefore, that schools, the compulsory havens for education of the young, are battlegrounds between differing points of view. For some, like William Bennett, President Reagan's Commissioner of Education, schools are places where children are meant to learn how to internalize without question the values of domination accepting those social attributes which assert the settled, traditional nature of society where everyone learns his or her place through "standards" that are undemocratically arrived at. In the Reagan-Bennett vision schools become an alien place for children who learn that they are not their own "property" or space. They learn the limits of what they can be and they are expected to internalize (and teachers are to transmit) the hopelessness of what can be done in their communities and in their places of shelter. The social world for them, unless they happen to belong to a ruling class, is set, unchanging and incapable of reconstruction. Their social space is the world of fantasy and star wars. They learn the catechism of alienation in which their own personal health is related to their willingness to conform and accept the "realities" of the given and the settled.

There can be no social reality or future other than the one they are handed. For others, this author included, education is meant to be a means for liberation and understanding in the personal and subjective sense of *verstehen*. It becomes a way of organizing one's own perceptions as well as that of others into a means of analyzing social and "natural" situations and phenomena. It is meant to teach political and natural reality including their relationships and stimulate the imagination so that the young can frame and form liberatory possibilities for themselves and their generation. They are not relieved of the responsibility of shaping reality. The educational process, therefore, becomes the central way to bring forth value considerations in relation to actual situations in the lives of people and their institutions and in the way human beings are to relate to nature.

In this definition of education, ideas, reasonably accurate perceptions of the world and intuitive imaginings can have powerful and liberating political consequences. They explode ideology and dogma which hide different modes of domination and which are passed on from one generation to another. The schools are the ideological battleground for those with power for it is in education that class inequity is either reinforced or ameliorated and racism and sexism accepted or challenged. The school is the place where young people come to internalize limits about themselves as well as what is to be known and taught. It is here where quite mad choices around the nature of the economic system, war and peace are either praised or damned. And it is in the schools that a person will first come to grips with personal or group understanding and liberation.[27]

If society through its legislators, educators and parents does not encourage liberation and wonder, reason and reasoning itself atrophies, for one's reason is reduced to a means to justify narrow class concerns. Schools and education then abuse the morally undeveloped reasoning faculty to maintain oppression and encrusted "beliefs" that fill people's heads and hearts with fear, inadequacy or superiority. Under colonialism, for example, the educational system was the way in which the colonizers confiscated and wasted resources of people, categorizing them into useful instruments for exploitation. In neo-colonial settings education fosters attitudes of helplessness and subservience in those who they exploit and brutalize – paradoxically, even as the exploited carried out the daily technocratic work of the society. These conditions do not have to pertain in America although there are many elements that are present which conform to the colonial system. For most students a practical, concrete and non-abstract education encourages their productive and imaginative side. If schools pursued this course the society would become an existential and experiential laboratory for students. Schools would become the central place to bring one's personal experience, other people's experience and findings together with human needs.[28] The experiences themselves, the way they were described and understood could and should include the ethical ought and the nurturing of the artistic.

In all modernizing cultures it is assumed that production in the nineteenth-century sense of factories, processing of raw materials, calculation, etc., is of greater value to people than the esthetic sense or art. But the brutal fact is that human society is only alive and conscious (rather than *anesthetized*) when it can exercise and celebrate imagination attached to a moral sensibility. Esthetics helps us to escape our visible and hidden chains, that is to say, when we are "esthetized." The revolutions of the twentieth century have failed to achieve their purposes because they turned against culture and esthetics, too often surrendering this high ground to the rich and powerful or to the state bureaucrat who reflected a platonic fear of the arts. In the process an extraordinarily narrow view of reason was adopted. In the United States the social imagination of the society was left to the reactionary high priest of mass culture, Walt Disney.

While we can agree with the Marxist philosopher Roger Garaudy, who says that "Authentic esthetic education is also the cultivation of the senses that have become atrophied in our Western tradition as a result of the exclusive emphasis of logic and discursive reasoning,"[29] we may also say that our senses can give us warning against the cold, abstract madness that parades as reason and "objective reality" – the very reality of one-dimensional positivism which, unfortunately, is fostered in elite schools and now throughout the educational system. Students and children are stopped from exercising their cooperative and caring impulses in favor of destructive choices which are used as mechanisms to maintain those choices that are bound to deform civilization and people. Part of the reason why this reinforcement occurs is that knowledge is segmentized so that changes which are fundamental to the workings of the entire society are discussed, experimented with and acted upon by those very few privy to a particular discipline – plus their government and corporate patrons. The final difficulty with "objective reality" as it is explained to us is that consequences are not discussed or analyzed nor the part we play in that objective reality. Students are not given methods to change "objective reality." Instead they are offered life adjustment courses or ideological pap to reinforce the oligarchic vision of society.

Reagan's America is to be buttressed by an educational system that creates images and golden lies for the people through sentimentality (thought of as values by the purveyors), skills for production of war and technological fantasy among the technical elite as well as power for the powerful and aggressive, who in turn are expected to buy couth through universities and render obeisance to inert, fetishized principles for which others are expected to die as the few profit. Are there institutional ways to overcome this situation?

Vouchers, credits and choice

One of the great communications problems in an age of public image debate is that ideas and programs from vastly different points of view and with very different purpose, even with the substance significantly different, may end up sounding alike rhetorically. This problem is exacerbated where the idea or the social invention appears to be "neutral" in that it seems to favor anyone who uses it.

An insightful critique of voucher plans and tax credits has been offered by Apple in *Education and Power*.[30] While accepting the validity of current thinking among some radical theorists that there is an attractiveness to such proposals because they break up the hegemonic power of the state and because alternative models for schools could be generated (even "socialist alternatives" to the present character of the public school system) Apple argues that competitive schools could result in the legitimation through the state of the "bourgeois ideal of the market," a model of all social relations based on "individual calculation and the pursuit of self-interest." It is certainly true that the voucher plan ideas of the Reagan administration have this purpose rather than those put forward from the reconstructive side of the political spectrum. How to guard against this danger?

Any particular social invention or change should be analyzed according to its immediate effects. It is to be judged according to the particular social context in which it is presented to see whether by its nature, or by easy cooptation it can reinforce top down, hegemonic control. In this sense, voucher plans or plans that increase the power of participation must be presented as a link in a chain to increase the power of participation in the economy and as part of a movement of social reconstruction which seeks the extension of democracy in all areas of public life. In the context of a process of social reconstruction voucher plans and a guaranteed education insurance allotment fund becomes part of an *ensemble* of policies. For example, it is true that teachers employed by the state could be hurt by a voucher system and this may adversely effect the possibilities of new coalitions between parents and teachers for basics transformation of the schools if the voucher plan stands alone. But in the context of social reconstruction it would be possible to find new roles and new definitions of teaching once the conventional public school system is changed. Thus, programs for teachers of the community should go hand in hand with student choice and educational insurance programs. Recognition would be given to teachers as potential organizers and teachers of and in the community beyond the four walls of the school. Their task becomes that of relating and criticizing institutions, helping young people and employees initiate and continue dialogues and inquiry for their own awareness. In other words, the political task of organizers and leaders is to relate the particular limited social invention to larger changes by being clear on the importance of the social invention as it relates to more comprehensive change. They are charged with the responsibility of showing how certain changes and social inventions are meant specifically to relate to other changes, seeing within each change the need and character of more comprehensive transformation. They are responsible for linked changes, that is changes which must come together to avoid the problem of the change being regressive.

In *Being and Doing* I suggested that greater openness and experimentation in education could be achieved through the establishment of an education insurance fund which would entitle each person as a matter of right to use funds for educational objectives throughout his or her life.[31] A person could drop out of school at any time knowing that he or she still had an available fund to their credit. The fund would be available for two purposes: (a) increasing the person's skills, knowledge and creativity; and (b) fostering activities that included projects which reflected attempts to transform social decay into regeneration. In specific terms this would mean organizing education projects to rebuild cities, encouraging work groups to make music, magazines as well as inventing new machines and assembly lines. The education fund would give special consideration to projects

119

controlled by students, workers and teachers outside of already existing institutions. Teachers would be encouraged to leave their classrooms and become "teachers of the community." The fund would emphasize the various stages and social linkages in production as in film-making, airplane production, microprocessing, architectural design or agriculture. In other words, this trust would fashion interrelated grant programs between education, work and society. The National Education Insurance Fund's program would encourage people to attend school at any particular time during their lives past eighth grade with the understanding that they would receive a public stipend for this purpose.

The NEIF would be subsidized through general and assigned tax revenues at the national and state basis and administered by trustees elected through the political process. Students enrolled in schools or who received funds from the NEIF would be expected to know how the fund operated, and would be political participants in investment choices.

The expenditures in 1983 dollars for public education at the state, local and federal level is $101 billion. The revenues collected for public education are roughly calculated at $112,000,000.[32] Most states use property taxes on homes as the means of financing education. Given the exposed financial position of the middle and working class, high interest rates, the increasing age of the population and the broken connection between employment and education, individuals are less interested in the kinds of education which are now offered in the schools. Furthermore, education taxes are increasingly resented. As President Reagan's budget program shows, the ideology of the Republican party is to defeat public education. This attack requires a far more comprehensive alternative to Reagan than that presently offered by the Democratic party and the various education associations. Their programs do not adequately take into account the types of education that American society needs and that people will immediately recognize as such. Their recognition can only come where they have choice and participation in a manner that gives them the choice of how and when to be educated. The NEIF gives this type of flexibility. It would become the counterpart to the Social Security Insurance Fund. It would develop new programs, teachers and teacher training, offer subsidies and direct educational opportunities to students by establishing alternatives to high schools. With parents, teachers, students and communities it would fashion the teachers of the community program and work with unions, vocational schools and corporations in establishing worker schools. It would also present Congress with tax credits for those who contributed time to schools.

The educational experience is used in all nations as a social method for bonding individuals and groups to one another. This process is most successful where parents or adults are integrated into the teaching and learning experience. The voluntary system of time "donated" by older people to younger ones, especially by those who have skills to contribute, is of course an ancillary but nevertheless important part of the educational process. It is one means of demystifying certain types of work, particular skills and knowledges which are now hidden from the student's view until he or she is actually working. One way to encourage this activity would be through a nominal tax credit of several hundred dollars a year for services to education which the individual taxpayer would claim if he or she participated in the program. Under this proposal specialists from journalists to machinists, from doctors and lawyers to farmers, would take on apprentices or teach in apprentice situations as part of a national education system.

During the Kennedy administration I suggested a similar proposal that would give government officials released time from their work if they taught in schools or participated in some public school educational activity several hours a week.[33] I meant this proposal as an additional method to (a) improve the District of Columbia schools; (b) enrich the students' classroom time; and (c) break the barriers between school and government workers. There are skillful and intelligent government workers who are inhibited from sharing and testing ideas but are in a position to greatly increase the effectiveness of the schools.

There is no question that federal participation has greatly increased in the schools since the Second World War and my proposals follow this trend. This is viewed by the conservatives and the right as an unmitigated evil. But to the extent that federal participation generates an excitement around educating, committing the society to the process of educating, and to the extent that it is able to increase the social bonding element which will save the United States the pain of another civil war, or a race war, to that extent federal participation is a central, important element in the educational system. Federal participation does not have to mean the centralization of schools or schooling. Indeed, federal participation could – and should – mean exactly the opposite. Thus, federal participation should encourage individual schools to buy their own equipment, obtain their own supplies, buy their own books and hire their own teachers. In this altered framework teachers' unions such as the National Education Association (NEA) and the American Federation of Teachers (AFT) would continue to secure rights and protection for the teacher, insisting on greater emphasis on teachers' work over administration, the superstructure which lays on top of the activity that the society wants and seeks to perform. One change, however, would occur. Unions would also contract with school boards to operate schools much in the manner that public hospitals are run by medical schools.

Educational centralization since 1950 has resulted in a great increase in the power of administrators, a decline in the number and power of elected school boards and a decline in the teacher's authority to shape curriculum. The result is that parents and teachers are isolated from the actual operation of the schools except in communities where parents act out of fear and racial motives, or among the rich who see the schools – usually private ones – as their instrument for reproducing a national class structure. Given a conservative mood, there is a direct need to transform the schooling system in the United States. There is an administrative and tax overload while at the same time less and less real teaching goes on in the schools. The teacher is turned into an attendance monitor and social cop.

I appreciate that one must be wary of such arguments. Too often they do not sufficiently cherish what has been built. They play into the hands of a right-wing know-nothingism which merely wants to gut the public school system. Nevertheless, there are ways to take advantage of the shifts in attitude people have toward the taxation system. A concern of taxpayers is that they do not see any direct benefit from their funds. Nor do they see federal funds used in their own communities which have a generalized worth that they could directly control. For example, teachers are thought to be remote and bound to a school building so that education and teaching is seen by parents as a distant activity that is alien from the daily life of the society. But teachers have long recognized the need to liberate themselves from the constricting principle that education – and teachers – should be separate from other institutional and productive activities of the society. For reasons of economic efficiency as well as pedagogical technique the teaching process would be integrated critically into other functions of the society.

A primary task of teachers is that of going into communities and encouraging their students and themselves to formulate a continuous system of challenge and dialogue with institutions and individuals in local communities. Thus, the walls between education and work should be broken down, while production and theory, imagination and execution should be brought closer together. In this process knowledge itself is to be shared in the most public way with access being given to people outside of school settings.

Teachers of the community would operate with a reorganized national library system in which computer terminals would be located in neighborhoods, shopping centers, and other public places. The reconstituted library system would operate through computer terminals as a national self-teaching process in which people would keep track of their own progress on any particular subject of interest to them. There are two objectives to the computer library system. One is to encourage people to participate in scientific argument. After all, it is the outsider, the non-specialist, who must bear the consequences of work done by a few scientists or experts. The other is to help people judge the specialist and specialized information even to the point where outsiders participate in debates of any particular discipline. It is now obvious to a number of researchers that just because of the effects their work has that non-scientists and non-specialists must have access to the questions and the debates of any particular discipline.[34]

What might young people explore in and outside of school with teachers of the community? Not only what institutionally is but what could be. How to escape the war system, confront and end it; how to help others directly and through national governments and associations; how to create new technologies that liberate while using fewer natural resources; how to live socially without the creation of false needs; and how to live in communities the young want to generate.

Through teachers of the community, participation in the teaching process by adults, walk-in computer information libraries, student book and tool allowances to all children 12 years and older, and an education insurance fund the world of education and teaching can be placed at the center of the society's existence. Concern for such paraphernalia as accreditation would become secondary.

A society reaching for the common good must seek to be inclusive. Therefore, it endeavors to refashion or remove those accrediting and certifying systems which operate to restrain either entry into or understanding of a particular profession.[35] Since the Second World War an entire industry of certification has come into being which impedes the actual needs of the society just because of a false view of standards and merit. The Educational Testing Service and other testing systems are an example of the certifying system which groups and grades people to impede access to education and to enshrine certain types of knowledge as sacred.[36]

Higher education and the knowledge problem

When we think about higher education and the changes that should be made it is well to remember how elitist and closed the university function was prior to the Second World War. The GI bill helped to transform the university system in America as did federal research funds. More than 8 million young men and women attended the university and technical schools under the GI bill thus affording them the chance of obtaining a benefit they would not have ordinarily received. (Of course there was an important side benefit for the political economy. It limited the unemployed who otherwise would have swelled the labor market between 1945 and 1955.) American universities changed from a social elite instrument of self-appointed local and national establishments to the kind which favored a very specific definition of merit along the lines of specialization and modern corporate organizational principles.

One unfortunate change was that knowledge and organization, the type of questions considered, and the sorts of preparation needed for university life have tended to require that the young person fit within a bottle designed by national testing criteria that operated much in the manner of federal meat inspectors who stamp sirloin cuts as "prime," "choice" or "commercial." This system has caused great tension among people and a skewing of what is taught in high schools. They are seen as way stations for the university in the middle and upper classes, and places where corrupt forms of competition are nurtured among students, who come to believe that they can only be "educated" in schools. The educational system has encouraged one form of intelligence over another and played down creative potentialities among the young. To redirect the individual competitive drives of students into cooperative impulses will require the development of shared responsibility between young people for the success of each other. In the elite law schools the professors are fond of saying to the intimidated student, "Look to the right of you and look to the left of you, two out of three of you will not be here for graduation." In a society committed to the common good, the professor would say, "Look to the right and left of you. Our joint responsibility is to be sure that you are educated and your fellow students will be here for graduation."

The lifeblood of democracy is cooperative and continuous learning beyond class, race, sex and religion. It is meant to forge new understandings which will change bias and social rigidism. It is important to note that universities control "access to almost all the major institutions in the society." In political terms this is why open enrollment in universities is so crucial. Added to this social fact is that the most profound technological and value changes are being brought about through the university. Thus, the institution of higher learning is the "soft" instrument for security hardened class lines in society. One way around this situation is through a national education "pool" in which all univerisities and colleges would participate. Legislation on state and national levels would be prepared so that any university that uses public funds or tax subsidies would enroll 10 per cent of its first year students on the basis of chance with a percentage increase of 1 per cent a year to 35 per cent. This program would be initiated through a national education lottery system. Conditions for qualification into the pool should be quite flexible so that those who either graduated high school, had its equivalent in experience or passed a national examination would be eligible.

The intended effect of such a program is to foster a system of shared values between the various classes while transforming the ideology of class stratification and inequity which is increasingly dominating American life. It should be noted that once people from different classes are admitted to the leading universities in larger numbers the nature of inquiry and the questions that are to be considered will begin to shift. This does *not* mean that people's interest in creating, analysis or inquiry will be lowered. It merely means that the agenda of one group or class and the issues of knowledge which it fosters will be shifted. The political and intellectual issue of pre-focussing social and scientific inquiry has not received the attention it deserves even though it has become obvious that university research is extremely prone to follow the direction of corporate or national security funds.

In the 1980s elite universities such as Harvard and MIT actively seek partnerships with corporations such as IBM and Monsanto on profit making research projects even as they redouble their efforts to obtain defense department funding. Universities uncritically accept the tenets of "scientific capitalism" and "capitalist science" without examining whether their principles and methodologies best serve an understanding of fundamental social and scientific explanations and best addresses the value questions which will determine whether justice and freedom can be sustained in the modern world. A non-elitist, open attitude, but critical of all, is the most likely way of keeping universities alive as humanist enterprises. Professors need not fear an open enrollment system for the concerns and insights of a broader group of students will enliven the concerns of the professoriat and deepen their own inquiry. It will help them escape the present crude prefocussing mode and introduce a "moral epistemology." The question of a moral epistemology raises profound issues about the content of research in the project of science which bears on the common good.

This suggestion brings me to reflect on the *Bakke* case. The issues in the *Bakke* case were obscured by the rhetoric that the best were being turned away from medical school because this quota system was eclipsing meritocracy. According to this tale the quota was forced upon a bank of medical savants by crazed civil rights advocates who would otherwise continue their foolproof method of choosing who should go to medical school. In this little *bobbe-mysah*, medical school is the place where professors teach right answers according to science, which brooks no contradiction for what it claims. But this is a nonsensical view.

Scores on medical school entrance exams do not tell more than who will most likely do well in the first year. We do not know who will be a better doctor on the basis of test scores or whether there is any correlation between doing well in medical school and becoming a good doctor. Medical schools, in fact, use a variety of criteria for judging eligibility other than merit – i.e., whether the school will obtain funds from the parents or family; whether the parents are alumni or doctors; and the family's connections. So the question of why not special treatment for Third World applicants is hardly one to raise any hackles. Indeed, it could be argued that Bakke's complaint should have been against those who enter medical schools as a result of their parents' status, class or income.

Reconstructive knowledge

A crucial matter in a modern democracy revolves around the way we think – and teach – about science and technology. Depending on the attitude and fashion of the time, physical and social reality is conjured as either dependent or independent of "man's" wishes and needs. (As Evelyn Fox Keller has pointed out it is man struggling and conquering "nature", which is invariably described in the feminine.) Present day education usually teaches that actions taken should be related to a science which recognizes facts as independent of the observer, "his" biases and "his" personal situation. In reality "facts" learned in schools are usually of a justifying and rationalizing sort. Political leaders also now see scientific information as important not because it is "true" or "false" but because its contents create a common language which releases private jargons, collective or personal dreams and understandings to a newly shared public one. The scientific project is perceived by political leadership as an important ingredient for the myths and metaphors of politics, that is, the way people live with one another. The struggle between Bellarmine and Galileo was less a question of astronomy and more about the way authority and hierarchy were to operate in everyday life. Cardinal Bellarmine was prepared to have the Church share authority with science. That is to say, he believed science to be one proof about how reality operated, not *the* proof. The scientist Galileo wanted full reign.

While we do not ordinarily care to admit it, scientific inquiry and information are culturally derived or politically and economically framed. In 1932 the writer James Gardner Murphy conducted an instructive dialogue with Albert Einstein. At the time, Einstein was perplexed by the spirit of the Weimar Republic, then on its last legs, which exhibited decay in its government, insecurity among the people, inflation in the economy and a rudderless politics among the middle class and aristocracy. Physics was permeated with ideas of accident, free will and the end of truth. Nineteenth-century traditional rationalism was overthrown. Physicists did not believe that there was an external reality to be found and understood. Furthermore, after the First World War scientists adjusted their world view. Just as social and political structures have manifested shakiness since the First World War so our interpretations of scientific events were no longer to be shaped by the scientist's question for cause but his understanding of free will, indeterminacy and statistical relationships. Murphy said to Einstein that Einstein's view of seeing as being autonomous and finding basic causes would fall out of fashion because

> scientists live in the world just like other people. Some of them go to political meetings and the theater and mostly all that I know, at least here in Germany, are readers of current literature. They cannot escape the influence of the milieu in which they live. And that milieu is characterized by a struggle to get rid of the causal chain in which the world has entangled itself.[37]

That we eliminate cause does not mean we eliminate moral purpose. Our scientific enterprise can be criticized on scientific grounds (in the sense of full disclosure and radical objectivity) because it masks its work in narrow formulations thereby avoiding the way political and economic structures (as well as discarded experimental results) impinge on science's own experiments. It is mistaken to understand science as narrowly defined or separate from the society as a whole. It is not credible at all to believe that even Bacon thought that science and its method were autonomous. After all, Bacon had spent his life as a political and legal advisor seeking to find a way to make relevant the common law to institutional changes while seeking to rid man of the various Idols which governed his life. (Unfortunately, he did not see the problem of power, conquering, and sexism as Idols to be addressed.)

We are lost as a people if we do not fashion a moral epistemology which includes a critical analysis of society and its institutions, a critical analysis of the experimental method used, both in terms of their values and ethics, and what is being proved or demonstrated. Without such a method we will be left with the scientism of Ronald Reagan, the religious fundamentalism of Reverend Moon or the science of the National Academy of Science which careens forward with no consciousness of purpose and no moral purpose. It derives its strength from explanations, in other words myths which fit with ahistorical power.

Social scientists have their place in the present colonizing galaxy. Much social scientific work is related to the manipulation of people and to the treatment of them for purposes they do not know about or understand. Either consciously or unconsciously they champion the political idea that people should not learn from the experience of which they are objects. The corporations and the state, the indirect managers of the scientific project, stay out of view. State and corporate bureaucracies do not have to dictate directly either experiments or results to the scientists. Once there is linkage in their mind between resources, fame, acceptance and pay-off, the scientist gets the message and embraces pre-focussing. The methodologies that are employed mesh well with the mammoth organization which seeks control over basic material aspects, and then human existence itself. But it is a control that is single dimensional, without much attention paid to the immeasurable or to that which cannot be quantified in the usual ways. With this type of "science" people are meant to live out their lives as controllable objects. They are expected to surrender their own feelings and subjective understanding, not to the group of which they are a part but to impersonal authority. This is not very different from the work of Frederick Winslow Taylor, the founder of scientific management, who put his point in the following way at the beginning of the twentieth century. "In the past the man has been first, in the future, the system must be first." Scientific management, he said, was "an evolution representing survival of the fittest."

Social caring

The person was to fit into the method and function designed by others, virtually always for profit. The applied social scientist at the beginning of the twentieth century played his role in designing the new social and industrial system.

There was a specific picture of "man" which those involved in the rationalization of the social system carried with them as they did their brand of social science. Taylor stated this formulation in the following way:

> One of the very first requirements for a man who is fit to handle pig iron as a regular occupation is that he shall be stupid and phlegmatic, that he more nearly resembles the ox than any other type.[38]

The assumption that attached to this sort of social science was that man's intelligence could be quantified, as Stephen Gould has put it, on a simple scale from ape to Einstein. Productivity and profits would be greatly increased if people could be placed in the correct slots and statistically measured. (It is the hope of those concerned with "humanization of work" that the new non-hierarchic method will be the modern answer to productivity and profits.) This social science, in one form or another, sometimes cruel and blatant, other times masked and relatively benign, still remains at the heart of how we measure productivity and why we measure intelligence. Social science is a modern method for "proofs" of myths and ideology. Unfortunately, the *way* things change the more they stay the same. The "new" stage of social science is that it invents artificial intelligences and machines which frame the person into acting according to pre-planned programs of those dominant groups, now computerized which redefine the problems people have into categories acceptable to the dominant forces of the society.

Science and politics of the common good do not have to be separate from each other nor need they be separated from the reconstruction of our institutions. Therefore notions other than value free science can find their way into our understanding of the scientific project. Then we can state explicitly and have analyzed our own values, once we recognize their continuous presence. Perhaps we are called upon to invent a new language of symbols that infuse the scientific project with ethical axioms (themselves subject to analysis) and historical probabilities of consequence.

Research workers should join with the person who is being researched, acted on, as equals in the sense that each should share a common empathic sensibility, both trusting the other and sharing the truth to the extent they understand it. In this process both the actor and the acted upon may be shocked at what they find. As Paul Feyerabend has pointed out, they will learn that there are no set procedures for conducting inquiry. Indeed, the unity of people is their uniqueness shared by a common consciousness and quest. The best modern teaching starts from reaching to the empathic sensibility between teacher and taught. And even in such recondite fields of inquiry as neurophysiology, we see that an empathic principle must operate. Wilder Penfield in his work understood medicine as a joint venture between doctor and patient. He sought to break the unbalanced equation that is so common to modern politics and modern science, namely, that the dominator equals the experimenter/researcher and the dominated is the object of research. Penfield described his technique with epilepsy patients during surgery which strikes me as a model of scientific inquiry just because it starts from the direct engagement and involvement of the researcher in the "researched," and will result in aid to the patient. Penfield kept the patient awake and alert.

> These operations could be done safely, and with a reasonable chance of cure, only when the surface of one hemisphere of the brain was exposed widely for careful study and possible excision. . . . There was less danger to life and a better chance to understand each patient's problem if consciousness could be preserved throughout the procedure. Local analgesic was therefore injected into the scalp to prevent pain, and no sedative or anesthetic was given. To be successful as well as humane, it was essential for the surgeon to explain each step. Indeed, he must take time for talk before and during the operation. He must, in fact, be the patient's trusted friend.[39]

Penfield was the best sort of professional because he saw knowledge exploration and humaneness as a joint project between those who have technical skill and those who existentially need to find out for their own well-being. This reconstructive approach is one which professionals may hold up to esteem. By extension we may say that social science itself must involve the person or group studied as equals, not deceiving them. It must take them into the project as colleagues. It is then that the nature of knowledge and the learning process changes. It is also then that institutions can begin to be participatory just because the nature of the process of inquiry has changed.

In our time, both Marxists and non-Marxists have held to the view that there is a science to administration and management. And whether it is the University of Moscow or the managerial science school at Yale, such views are cherished. They believe that social and physical reality can be subjected to "statistical" control and direction through a process that is scientific, freed of class bias and personal interest. Too many socialists wrongly believed that because they wish out of existence the different classes, the dialectic of conflict over interest would cease. Lenin and other communists believed that politics would disappear as social and economic classes disappeared. They conjectured that one instrument for the disappearance of politics would be science which would carry bureaucratic administration to a new level *against* the politics of the street or of the assembly. The old Bolsheviks, good platonists that they were, believed that moral questions would disappear in the face of a concerted and "correct" way to handle a problem. There was a truth and it was known, as luck and history would have it, by the powerful who had made a revolution. They erroneously believed that there was a "right" answer out there which would end politics. This belief intensified the internecine struggles of the revolutionaries. The horror was not realizing that politics could not be made into science and their correct answers were not everyone's correct answers, especially between the revolutionaries themselves.[40]

In our society it is impossible to separate science, modern technological methods, bureaucratic administration and politics from each other. There is no way that these elements are not intertwined in social relationships and institutions.

In this sense the Marxists have been correct, just as John Dewey was correct when he said that science itself must be consciously related to ethical purpose. It is already a human enterprise. It is to be demystified and not treated as autonomous. That the Russians saw science as non-autonomous does not mean that they were opposed to scientific mystification. Further, they were prepared to abuse the direction of science for ends which themselves could only be questioned. Surely this is the story in the Soviet Union and the United States of the nuclear arms race.

As an existential enterprise scientific investigation is centered in institutions. It is learned through imitation and experience. A young scientist is often given a "problem" and he or she is expected to solve it through a form of systematized trial and error, as well as hectoring from his or her teacher and co-workers. Scientific method is imagination and reasoning as a *social* process. Thus, it is sloppy, often petty, quite impure and it invariably involves "bureaucracy." In any case, the sciences are not abstract. They must be linked to purposes that themselves can be "cross-examined."

> When physics, chemistry, biology, medicine, contribute to the detection of concrete human woe, and to the development of plans for remedying them and relieving the human estate, they become moral; they become part of the apparatus of moral inquiry or science.[41]

Whether one may formulate a science of interests or whether social change can be made into a scientific endeavor is quite another matter. Among certain radical thinkers, Marxism is thought to be as much a science as theoretical physics. In some way there is truth to this statement if we say that both Marxists and physicists are concerned with probabilities. To put it another way, Marxist theory is like weather forecasting as a scientific instrument. What is clear is that Marxist ideas have no longer to be justified by either a working class or a middle class. They infuse us and what we are, whatever class we are in. However, Marxists have failed in comprehending the ethical dimension to political power and the role it must play. Because Marxists have not dealt directly with ethics and power, Marxism becomes nothing more than state pragmatism among those who operate the state. Too often Marxists fail in truth telling when they refuse to apply their critical faculties to those who have control of state power.

A science of politics is possible to contemplate only when everyone is part of the decision making and critical process so that the subject-object distinction which science now holds so dear is transformed. Then a human science can be imagined which will transcend the type of social science that explains passivity from the dominated and control from the dominator as the natural order of things. This is what the experience and process of democratic education can do for those parts of the process. Often matters of science, technology and education are understood as moral tools in the solution of concrete problems and issues which arise in the establishment or regeneration of a community. Communities demand that knowledges serve mankind rather than the other way around. Where people are, how they live is at once a concrete, immediate problem, but simultaneously giving life to the character of civilization itself.

If, as I have said, democratic education must be practical and experimental, concerning itself with immediate human questions and the character of how people live, education will include ways of using the city and town as the curriculum for study and how personal shelter fits into the physical environment. As I have suggested, the caring conception cannot escape what is humanly constructed and what the relationship of that work is to the environment. Consequently, the question of shelter and the way a city, town or neighborhood comes to be as it is should be made part of the educational process for it deals with the human relationship to physical materials, social relations and architectural and economic design. A proper educational process, therefore, would turn the city and the town (or the farm and the earth) into an adjunct to the school. They would be the laboratory for understanding values and conflicts in both their immediate and abstract meanings and they would help young people understand and choose, giving their values an experiential and humane dimension. This way of looking at education would restore excitement to education and give rise to a new vocation of political and social education. Educators would help people to know what to ask and how to take control of their environment in a sensible and democratic way.

Shelter and community as part of the person's guarantee to be human

To address a national shelter and city/town policy it is necessary for the citizenry in their locales to debate about the various functions of the city and town. It is for them to ask ethical and esthetic as well as economic and political questions about their town or city and the various kinds of shelters, business, and public enterprises they intend to construct and rehabilitate. Thus, public policy, as it relates to shelter and community requires that we know how we want to live and whether that way of living is collectively a good way to live. Obviously, this question cannot be answered abstractly. We need to know the consequences of large-scale highway programs on the cities, of sewage disposal, of large-scale industrial systems on the lives of people in the cities, of different energy systems on the cities, of never owning but always renting, of seeing people as if they are spectators who are planned for and about, but who do not participate in the process of transforming their social situation and existence, of being tax cows for the nuclear war system while being hostages to the national state for that purpose. Such questions are the concerns for healthy communities. They highlight the lived meaning of equity, caring and personal dignity in new ways. We have to be sure that without freezing people into gender roles that our living spaces are liberating for women and children as well as men, that they provide for sufficient joint and communal work and play areas and activities.

In the past Americans thought they were able to escape concern with such questions because of the blessings of the frontier. It is no news to even the most casual student of American history that the existence of vast amounts of land and the possibility of settling it was thought to be a means of relieving the poverty of the Atlantic states and the squalid slums caused by the expansion of nineteenth-century industrial capital. Expansion of the frontier was the most important system of urban and community planning which American statesmen devised through federal legislation. As Charles Beard believed, the Homestead Act had the effect of downgrading trade unions and postponing any successful schemes for social revolution.[42] Whatever its putative negative effects the Homestead Act caught the imagination of the urban masses. It was in the mainstream of thought laid out by the founding fathers, especially Thomas Jefferson who claimed that overcrowded cities such as the kind he saw in Europe were anathema to establishing a republic for a free people seeking public happiness. A connection to nature through the land was thought to be necessary to fill out human nature. And a nation could fill out its nature or destiny only if it settled the land.

It took the Civil War to make the principle of homesteading a reality. While to some, President Buchanan for one, the Homestead Act and its underlying principle was seen as a form of socialism and radical land reform more in keeping with Europe than the United States, to others it became the means of shrinking the power of the state and public control over the American land, and, therefore, over individual choices, entrepreneurial and otherwise, that Americans made about their land and the nature of their towns and cities. There was of course a contrary mind. Throughout the latter part of the nineteenth and beginning of the twentieth century progressives such as Henry George sought to act as mediators on the question of land and private ownership of capital. His single tax proposal meant that land would be owned and collectively provided for. A public responsibility and trusteeship would always be present in the way buildings were built and how they were laid out just because the land remained collectively owned. The assumption of the single taxers was that since nothing is added to the land, there was no reason why any private person should gain from appreciation or depreciation of its value. Thus, the community would control the building market by holding on to the land. Single taxers believed that as a result everyone would be housed well in an aesthetically decent environment.

Had George's conception been implemented at the beginning of the twentieth century more careful urban planning would have occurred, the mortgagee's and banker's role in the housing market would not have been as great as it is and homeowning independence with a shared community interest would have been sustained. It would have been easier to reassert certain, traditional, Lockean notions of land and production in our cities: that legal rights follow use and that rights in property are determined through the relatively objective standard of use and taking care.

The question which we are now called upon to answer is whether present lending activities of banks add to the common good and provide the necessary shelter for people or whether a wholly new approach is necessary. While most people look to the private housing market to fulfill their needs it is not likely that the future housing market will be able to supply decent shelter at a modest price. The average cost of a new home as of 1980 is $70,000. Given high interest rates, unemployment and inflation, as well as increased costs for services that are usually collectively paid for in most societies, it is unlikely that people will be able to afford high prices for houses.[43]

In capitalist societies where basic needs are not met collectively, loans become the single most important means for the debtor to meet his or her needs and wants. But where a society becomes *dependent* on the lender to fulfill needs and wants, it is then obvious that the society is running its social and public institutions "backwards" under a trickle down theory of capital formation. Banking as the private instrument to control the number of shelters is not a conscionable way of operating a democratic society. On the other hand, we cannot be very pleased when we come to think about the nature of public housing even though we know that if we wanted to the United States could "finance the construction of all new housing and rehabilitation of old housing through direct government spending rather than a debt system, which mortgages the future."[44] Unfortunately, the motivation for public housing and the way it has been administered is more worthy of Dickens' Scrooge than of a nation committed to the common good.

Congress passed public housing legislation as a mechanism of social control over poor people. Like so many other government social assistance programs, it was *meant* to fail. For example, black congressmen have complained that the federal government handles integration regulations in such a manner as to assure that inner cities which have a preponderance of black people will not receive housing aid. While there is liberal-minded talk about shelter for the poor, there is little understanding of shelter as a fundamental, inalienable right, which includes the type of participatory freedom to control, make social rules and maintain property. So long as those who use public housing are stigmatized with the badge of economic failure and people with middle-class incomes are forbidden access, public housing will remain a depressed and depressing area of American life. Is there any urban planner in 1986 who would live in public housing? Nevertheless, the problems of public housing notwithstanding, shelter should be thought of as a collective good guaranteed to all people in the society. The shelter market would operate for the purpose of efficiency, ensuring varying tastes and securing more expensive shelter for those who can afford it. The only way to ensure decent shelter for the next generation is to change our value emphasis. Decent shelter must now be thought of as an individual right, a collective good, and last, as a commodity. If we politically came to the conclusion that shelter is a fundamental right, that is to say, not a throw-away commodity open to the vagaries of the market place, the entire nature of the city would change as shelter shifted to an inalienable good. What are the contours of such a program?

Suppose we begin from an updated version of Henry George's project and say that shelter is a joint right and obligation which can be best fulfilled through ownership or co-ownership with the community. Is it too radical to say that we are only trustees for each other of things made and therefore a person who cannot care for a thing, or a house or land could lose it because he or she has abandoned trusteeship and that which is in his or her care? On the other hand, to the extent that people join with others in caring and making a thing, they acquire it, as for example, where a family might improve on their shelter in a public housing project thereby obtaining joint title for what they have produced. (I would even say that where governments, and certain corporations, have abandoned old property their use falls to those prepared to operate them thereby achieving joint title with the public.) In general, if shelter is an economic right then it must become a shared social cost and therefore a concern which should be provided much in the manner that we have come to assume that education is a basic right through high school. Several specific mechanisms should be created which would change our attitudes toward shelter, the most important being the establishment of a land and shelter trust. Its primary purpose is to implement the principle that shelter is a right with its cost shared socially. The operational effect is to remove the speculative character of the present American housing market as government policies would emphasize the public housing system and encourage cooperative and non-profit housing associations to enter the building, management and joint owner market.

The housing mortgage debt of the nation is some $900 billion. Ninety per cent of this debt is held by savings and loans and banks.[45] These debts should be purchased or converted from the Federal National Mortgage Association (FNMA) and the Federal Housing Administration (FHA) debts into trust instruments held by a federally instituted Lands and Shelter Trust.

The Lands and Shelter Trust would operate at local levels and have the power to buy mortgages, land and buildings. The Trust itself would not be a private bureaucratic agency. Instead, it would operate as a public elected body.

Under this plan, members of precincts no larger than 50,000, and depending on the geographic distance, would be elected to carry out the terms of acquisition of land and houses (predicated on a negotiated price), protect individuals and families against any undue hardship, and assure that shelter is provided for and maintained in each respective community. The local trusts would purchase savings and loan banks, an industry by the mid-1980s in distress. In the process the trust would formulate rules in which mortgage payments would be forgiven in exchange for ownership through the renter's or mortgagor's sweat equity. The Lands and Shelter Trust would devise instruments for joint ownership or life tenancy. The land on which houses or apartments were already built would be bought and held by the Lands and Shelter Trust for a seventy-five-year period. The fair value of property would be set by local trust board members who would be chosen through a procedure similar to that followed by the Selective Service system. Trust board members would apply a system of compensation which might be the computation of a five-year historical average of executed sales of properties in the community.

Obviously, certain subjective judgments will enter into the equation. One such issue is how to treat landlords or banks that invested unwisely, or did not invest in the local communities. Should they be penalized by the Trust as against those who invested wisely and in the local community? This problem could be dealt with most judiciously by Congress if it set forth a federal compensation act which outlined the steps of repayment to banks and individual owners. Individual owners who cared to sell their property would be remunerated for work which they performed on their places of residence. And they would receive payment for mortgage expenses such as closing costs. Compensation to homeowners would be computed either at current market value or mortgage payments plus equity.

The Lands and Shelter Trust, or its "agents," non-profit institutions including churches, unions, universities would promulgate a joint ownership between itself and occupants of houses and apartments. Thus, tenants would be given a chance to co-own property with the Trust which they inhabited. However, if an occupant cared to move, he or she would be able to sell only to the Trust on the basis of a fixed rate of return for the equity that was accumulated in the property. Family houses could be inherited by children as long as the house remained part of the family estate. Within city limits all land would be purchased by local land and housing trusts or taken through eminent domain.

A private housing market should exist, indeed, thrive. However, the scope of it would be limited because shelter as a necessity would be offered free or at the most minimal cost. Under such pressure the character of the housing market would change. It would now encourage personal refurbishing as a major part of the housing business. Local shelter trusts would become the major customer of builders, even though trusts would encourage and grant technical assistance through offering architects, artists and others skilled in crafts to those who wanted to work on refurbishing and building their own home.

As part of the community trust system national cooperatives and non-profit shelter and town associations would be established and would receive grants for building towns. Such funds would be made available through the Social Security Trust and the Land and Shelter Trust. Funds would be made available to a number of people (from 3,000 to 25,000) who were organized as groups. The group would organize and incorporate as a voluntary land trust to establish a "new" town with the proviso that the petitioners would have to follow democratic and constitutional requirements on race and sex. Incorporation would qualify the new town to receive capital from the federal Lands and Shelter Trust, as well as technical assistance through universities and labor unions. The groups that gave such assistance would be recompensed from the Land and Shelter fund which in turn would sell or deed these lands to the new towns. Each respective town would either keep in perpetuity the ownership of the land or share title with the Lands and Shelter Trust. The land would be acquired either through eminent domain, or sale by the Lands and Shelter Trust and then assigned locally.

The new towns would continue the decentralist tradition. They would be encouraged to build and control their own local industry, commerce, schools and cultural activities. However, they would be expected to meet certain congressionally mandated criteria such as the development over time of local industry, an efficient energy plan for the town, locally controlled combination office buildings and apartments, a school and community college system, commercial stores, public health clinics, amusement centers, theaters, local public access media, parks, private spaces for lovemaking and meeting, library, craft centers, scientific experimental terminals and artists' quarters.[46]

In the new towns program special attempts would be made to integrate the cultural worker into the social, economic and esthetic life of the town. Thus, the Social Security Trust (discussed in Chapter 4) and the Lands and Shelter Trust would dispense grants and loans for aspects of public life which recreate the public good. Each new town would be expected to ensure that participatory rights of control over the neighborhood, local investment policies and apartment and shelter decisions could be made by those who live in the cooperative or public housing system. Where the new town is developed outside the city the communities would follow the greenbelt concept. They would be self-contained, separated by town-owned agricultural lands used for raising crops and animals. Farming methods would be integrated into the education of young people. To the extent possible, such communities should expand, but only to a modest size. Towns inside cities could also be incorporated as neighborhood governments. In the 1970s Senator Mark Hatfield of Oregon introduced neighborhood government legislation to stimulate neighborhood economic growth and culture at the grassroots. There is much to be admired in his proposals.

Since the Second World War attempts have been made to assemble large blocks of capital and construction organizations which could build towns and subdivisions anywhere in the United States. Proponents of developing the housing industry as a rational and big business (such as James Rouse) sought a market situation in which several corporations would have the resources (usually obtained through insurance companies) to build whole towns. Except in a few cases this process has failed. The reason for this failure is wholly consistent with the fact that people subjectively experience shelter and community as something more than a process of commodity exchange. Building entrepreneurs who hoped to rationalize the housing industry have only been moderately successful even though the structure of capitalism and the mortgage market has tended to push builders to see their houses as commodities. This is why any national effort such as the suggested national Lands and Shelter Trust must have strong local roots among small builders and unions. It would make great sense, therefore, to establish skills training, courses and programs at the local level under master craftsmen. Their responsibility would be to teach workers in the building and construction trades. The program itself would be jointly run by the Lands and Shelter Trust and labor unions. The Lands and Shelter Trust would encourage towns to employ film makers, writers, architects and musicians who would be given space to work in and to create public art. As part of its program all builders would be offered courses on the history of the city, the various types of shelter which can be built, the types of problems caused by wretched housing to families, the problem of sexually segregated spaces and alternatives followed in other nations. Builders and workers would be instructed in planning cities and communities which establish spaces for people and which by their nature encourage interdependence and access between people. For example, suppose they were granted funds to build cooperative kitchens and eating facilities. The modern liberty is privacy but this liberty defeats responsibility and obligation to others where no proper public spaces are present for debate, conversation, hand holding and other shared activities. Through the tax deduction for homeowners government sponsored mortgages, and hyper-individualization through appliance technology, the automobile and television, the public space was emptied.

Reagan's public policies start from the assumption of the private space. It is no wonder, then, that when services are eliminated in narrowly framed public policies the first to be cut are those that deal with public spaces such as playgrounds, parks and the arts. The result, if not its purpose, is to hide people by getting them out of public view and in front of their television sets. However, in social reconstruction the task of any housing and shelter program is to encourage and provide for the development of public space. Such space must be of use to people in their capacity as walking, running, talking, active and affective people. It must be "free" in the sense that it should not be of individual concern at the time of use. It would encourage speech, drama, sports, hanging out, the arts and other joint activity, even cooking through the establishment of public cooking and eating facilities. Beyond the guarantee in the leisurely and participatory sense, the various social security and Lands and Shelter Trusts would find ways of providing or stimulating services which the commercial market no longer provides. In our older cities, stores, medical services and various other services have fled from poor neighborhoods while real estate speculators await or promote the gentrification of the center city. The result is massive abandonment of most cities to upper and middle income couples who help to inflate prices in the rental and real estate market.

The gentrification of American cities since the 1960s brought another tension which seems less explosive than it did when it was first noticed. The city became the public place of liberation for gay people. Because they had significant funds to spend and were at the center of much of the refurbishing of the American city, they tended to increase real estate speculation which had a negative effect on poor and black people. Protection of sexual liberation through civil rights laws does not mean protection of high rents against the poor. Thus the complex task of federal activity is to champion public housing, protect civil rights and generate the refurbishing of communities. However, government officials can only act accordingly if they see shelter as a basic right, one mandated as such by Congress. Once "shelter as right" permeated the national consciousness certain questions which are now answered only by vested building materials interests or entrenched bureaucracies would become available. For example, a constant complaint of small builders is that government regulations at the local level operate in harsh and foolish ways against builders and occupants of apartments and houses. They prevent the use of different types of materials, initiative and enterprise in the building business. Part of this difficulty can be corrected through a system of regional "enablements" which would be modified by local trusts to meet local circumstances. A rational system of "enablements" would encourage the use of new equipment and procedures to create new housing. Building regulations do not have to be impediments to development of community or to civil rights. In this sense zoning codes meant to protect the "substantial" people of communities are by their nature not predicated on equity or community but on privatism and selfishness. Zoning became the way of enforcing collective uncaring against the Other. One should be careful about judging too harshly. The middle and working class that have attained some equity in homes fear neighborhood changes and integration because their savings are in their houses. Once their savings are protected and rewarded, a great deal of pressure against integrated neighborhoods will disappear.

Beyond the question of economic tension between the middle class and the poor, city government officials must also face the seemingly intractable problem of the high cost of subsidy to the automobile. The costs of maintaining roads, police, parking, etc., make the automobile the single most important hidden cost in the budget of cities. Once acknowledging this fact, land and shelter trusts must take precedence over transportation departments in planning the revitalization of the cities. Cities are not launching pads for highways. In other words, transportation is a means to an end. As Elliot Sclar has said,

> The purpose of transportation is to move people and goods between one location and another. If the supply of service between the points is not adequate to meet the demand, there are two approaches to a solution. The first is to supply more service between the two points; the second is to relocate activity to obviate the need for the service. Although the former approach has been more popular in the last ten years or so, the latter has been the dominant approach for much of human history.[47]

The city should speak collectively on matters of transportation. Accordingly, it should control commerce and transportation by controlling the number and kinds of automobiles, trucks and other vehicles that are used in the cities. For example, suppose New Yorkers might only buy new cars through a city in which the city council would decide on the number to be purchased from an automobile manufacturer each year. Obviously, besides controlling numbers and increasing revenue a city could begin to influence the manufacturer in the type of car to be produced. The city would shed its role as passive consumer or tax gatherer, recipient of motor vehicle fumes for the auto industry and instead would begin to generate income through production, sale and control of the product. It would become active in the productive process, participating in the ownership and sale of auto manufacturing facilities. "Productive" cities already exist in some limited way in different areas of the United States. For example, Milwaukee, Wisconsin sells Milorganite, a fertilizer, to farmers. Waste materials can now be analyzed into their component parts for the purpose of detailing whether municipal solid wastes can be recycled. Cities will then be able to convert the process of generating, chemically treating and then selling the waste materials as reused minerals. As David Morris, an eminent commentator on appropriate technology has written,

> the capital expenditure required to establish a recycling smelter is far less than to establish a mine, permitting cities not only to collect their raw materials, but to partially process them as well.
> Of course, cities are not really "mines" in the traditional sense. However, the more times a city recycles its raw materials stock the greater it becomes like a mine, which, after all, does not regenerate its raw materials either.[48]

An urban land and shelter development program which champions cities as productive economic units will also have a positive effect on the citizenry who will change themselves (ourselves) from consumers, dependent on the whims of corporations, or decisions made elsewhere, to producers who have the technical understanding and possibility of direct participation in the basic productive processes of the society. A national shelter and building program will emphasize self-reliance in the context of mutual aid. And it will emphasize the public and "voluntary" sector as a critical productive element of the society. For such notions to become operative educational and political processes must promote values that can be integrated in daily practice.

When we study the question of commercial buildings certain other criteria must enter. Office buildings by their nature are often wasteful because they are not used at night. Often whole sections of cities become ghost towns after 6pm and stay that way until the following morning. The alternative is to concentrate on designs of buildings that are multipurpose, include public space and have energy efficient apartments.

This use of space is followed in Europe with success. It appears to decrease the instances of crime because it tends to integrate people's work and home life more closely, with the attendant effect of causing lighted buildings, streets, etc. after dark.

To the extent possible light industrial plants should not be separate from residential areas. What should be separated, and this can be enforced through health and ecological standards, are dangerous procedures from factory work which might cause harm and difficulty to workers and people

140

in the local communities. Comprehensive research and teaching programs should be generated by OSHA to empower consumers, and especially workers, in regulating the health hazards of factories.

As Paul and Percival Goodman pointed out in their important work *Communitas*, urban planning cannot be very successful unless we are to raise the question of what ends we have in mind. In other words, what type of society and physical plant do we intend to have? Community intention can be determined concretely through congressional juries and town meetings, which emphasize decentralization and autonomous towns and cities that are locally planned. The end of this activity is attending and caring for the needs of human beings in cities where people have concrete problems. But such attention requires that the city or town be seen as an organic unit, aesthetically, economically and socially. Democratic participatory planning allows people to get control over their own environment and situation. This will, as I suggest in Chapter 4, require a reconsideration of the system of national markets which makes the city and its citizens easy prey to the commercial system. That burdens on commerce need to be placed may be startling; that the federal government must do so for the common good is undeniable, and necessary. It is not worthwhile to cavil over whether economic questions are the "base" of a "superstructure." It is enough to recognize the centrality of the economy and therefore economic policies. In modern societies they are inextricably linked to our individual well-being and the common good.

4

Economy for the common good

The economy of a democracy is grounded on the political proposition that people have collective responsibility for one another. The means which we use to reflect that responsibility are social, beyond the family. They are adopted through voluntary associations and governmental programs to secure people's mutual needs and obligations. I have suggested that people's natural predilections are cooperative ones. I do not accept the psychological assumption of capitalist economies that people must be mobilized to work through the market system because they are inherently lazy and disdain work.[1] Once economic questions are rooted in collective responsibility the nature of the answer should permeate the laws, policies, social and productive arrangements which are made between people, economic functions and government. As I suggest, what is collective and what is private changes with each generation. For the individual, economic pre-eminence must always remain in the social sphere between workers and consumers.

In all modern, political systems governments play *the* key role in setting economic arrangements. For example, *laissez-faire* advocates expect the government to protect and set the terms of the monetary system. They insist that the state should set the "rule of law" to protect contracts, stability for investment and private property. Property would have no meaning without legal sanctions as enforced by the state. These legal sanctions require an enforcement mechanism and a military police system which is used to assure standards *against* the exploited or deprived. Investors and the middle class seek government guarantees against inflation.

Laissez-faire economists believe that government must build the "infrastructure" such as roads, air and sea ports and all transport systems claiming that these should be commonly held. Keynesian economists suggest that governments themselves should compete in capital producing activities to set a standard for private firms. Even under the present "free enterprise" economic system, according to the Congressional Budget office,

The Budget contains approximately 200 accounts that are revolving funds. These funds are for business-type enterprises operated by the federal government.[2]

In other words, what is true of *laissez-faire* theory is of course true of the government interventionist system as practiced or promulgated in its different forms by such capitalists of democracy as Roosevelt and Keynes and the capitalists of fascism, Mussolini and Hitler. Modern political leaders believe that they are required to intervene in the economy to relieve unemployment, secure the capitalist system and consolidate internal, political power. If necessary they are prepared to mobilize for war as one means of solving their internal economic crises. Even President Reagan's economic policies are grounded in a build-up of the military. Reagan's planners overruled the assumptions of a generation of war planners who did not believe that a non-nuclear war could be fought with the Soviet Union. This doctrinal assumption was changed when Reagan's planners embraced the dogma of fighting a non-nuclear war with the Soviet Union on an extraordinarily large scale, along the lines of the Second World War, and for a long duration, as well as opening up a new arms race in space. Preparing for war on this scale is labor and capital intensive, and of course, deficit producing if taxes are not raised. The Reagan administration, like its liberal predecessors, put themselves in the dilemma of seeking internal "class" peace or preparing war with other nations.

Those committed to capitalism as an end unto itself seek ways in which the state will protect the private entrepreneur or capitalist's call on the future without creating in the sovereign a superior power over private capitalists to control the future. In the United States capitalism has sought to protect its power against the state while using the state's coercive instruments by:

(1) Manufacturing a currency which can be guided by the state and the banks. The Federal Reserve system operates fairly independently of Congress and the President and is, of course, very close if not representative of the largest banking interests. The Federal Reserve maintains its aura of legitimacy by appearing to operate in the public interest and under public control although it is primarily an instrument by law and practice of the large banks; in other words, the banks act out of their private needs ostensibly for the public interest.
(2) Finding a means to assure that the state does not interfere in the corporation or market except to ensure that labor and social costs can be passed on to a consuming public. Such costs are to be absorbed by the state – in this case the state means the people; they are not added into the cost of the individual items, but paid for through the taxing mechanism.

(3) Assuring a climate for investment. Investment in this framework means setting up that machinery of governing which allows the capitalist to forego risking his or her present holdings by using the state as a guarantee collateral system. This method shifts the burden of loss from the private firm to the state.
(4) Developing a civil service and policy making group which assumes that corporate power is "private" with rights of citizenship under the Fourteenth Amendment. In a democratic or liberal administration the civil service is given the power of regulators in an authoritative way where the particular industry is unstable or new. Here the civil service is used as an instrument to secure stable corporate control over the future. In a conservative administration planning and regulation devolves directly to the corporation. And the government and management of the corporation are attuned to the same goals. Modern corporations seek "high managerial income, good profits, a strong competitive position, and growth." This goal, of course, is the modern definition of "busy-ness" and power for its own sake, as it is manifested in control over other operations and parts of the social system. There is no interest on the manager's part in the common good. Thus, the position taken by the economists, Baran and Sweezy, is quite correct when they criticize such ideas as "soulful" corporations. By their nature and purpose the corporations represent only money and assets. Their function is profit for those in the corporation, and not for the society as a whole.

Most socialist movements start from the assumption that state power is to be used as the primary instrument to nationalize the means of production, distribution and exchange so that social justice and equity can be achieved. Until recently, most socialists believed in centralizing political power as a means to formulate a comprehensive economic plan, which would yield the reallocation of investment and the redistribution of wealth and power.

Various conservative commentators, for example Hayek, have said that the difference between various brands of socialists was one of method but that all believed the state is the prize to capture because it is the most powerful single instrument to organize investment and bring about change in the whole society. Through its command of coercive power it was thought that the state could redirect recalcitrants if not through education, then through the use of subtle or overt force. Thus, the Fabianism of the Webbs of Great Britain, the parliamentary gradualism of Western European socialists and the direct revolutionary actions of Lenin in East Europe were merely different tactics to the same set of objectives.

In reality, socialists are invariably uncomfortable with the state's coercive powers. Perhaps hearing the wailing of the anarchists, or of those who did not appreciate the abstract distinctions between state socialist violence or

144

bourgeois violence, socialists have devoutly believed that the very process of transforming society would cause the state apparatus to self-destruct. The idea of the state withering away was as important a principle to Marxist socialists before they had power as it is to a von Mises or Friedman. Whether thought of in Fabian gradualist terms or in terms of the chiliasm of certain infantile leftists, for most of the twentieth century, the state's self-destruction represented another of the goals of the socialist project.

Like most concepts and purposes which are tempered through the harsh and dialectical realities of history, insufficient attention was paid to means-ends relationships. The state became an end in itself and its governors had no intention of "self-destructing" their institutional power or their own reason for existence. Power is the continuous problematic of relations among people. It does not disappear with revolutions although it can be diverted for good ends. In some socialist nations the growth of state power has merely meant the burgeoning of bureaucratic power without yielding social justice or equity. And in day to day activities government bureaucracies, whether in China, Russia or Poland, have found it difficult to choose wisely for the people because of their top down, enforced, participatory nature.[3]

There is another reason for the state socialist failure. Public control as mediated through the state cannot be an end in itself. As Bertrand Russell pointed out in his essay on individual liberty:

> The reason a society wishes to control the selfish impulses of men is because liberty is to be increased both by the prevention of private tyranny and by the liberation of creative impulses. If public control is not to do more harm than good, it must be so exercised as to leave the utmost freedom of private initiative in all those ways that do not involve the private use of force.[4]

Thus, according to this view and I am fully in accord with it, bureaucrats and politicians can best understand their purpose in the economic sphere when they seek to enable the workers and groups most directly involved in the productive and consuming process to fashion creative possibilities for production, work division and participatory control. Control through bureaucracy is stifling and keeps people from being subject-actors of history and maintains them as client objects. In other words, the economic system in a society committed to the common good is aimed at changing the passive character of workers in the economy and increasing consumer control in the public space and lessening wasteful consumption patterns. This reconstructive objective can only begin through a political process. It requires a direct commitment to public education and dialogue at the plant and small business level, in the bureaucracy, the schools, custodial institutions and welfare lines. It seeks changes in and through the culture and it seeks to rally groups inside and outside the present political parties. Economic transformation is a cultural activity. And because it is a cultural activity initiated organically the likelihood is that a reasonable, non-violent strategy will emerge to bring about economic reconstruction.

A fundamental purpose of this cultural-political process is to press for discussions of how self-management, worker community and consumer councils would operate before formal political action would be taken. Self-created units within communities and the largest industries would be encouraged to take on those actions that would allow such councils to be important decision making bodies in a particular industry. Each union within particular industries should establish worker-community control discussions, planning mechanisms within the industry, worker community schools for accounting and management, etc.

There is no longer sense to the argument that communities of 500 people – villages – are "public" and economic organizations of thousands of people that set the investment and consumption patterns of millions of people, who often encourage and frame the decision of governments to stay at peace or go to war, are the private sector. The argument that the great corporations are passive suppliers of goods and services because they do not control the violent power of the society and cannot exercise it, turns out to be hopelessly naive. The everyday life of people is framed by economic "market," and industrial decisions that are made by corporate bodies that are called private, and which structure coercion in their daily activities.

This is not to say, however, that the public realm is *identical* to that of the state. It is to recognize that by their nature economic activities fall within the public realm.[5] The major political question is where the line should be drawn between what is to be privately or publicly controlled. Activities in the public realm may include both the state's activities and those of voluntary associations, cooperatives, guilds, even city-owned enterprises which operate without the coercive power of the state. This area is an important one to defend *against* the state and the commercial market. The public realm is not a cover for private activities which seek to amass an accumulation of capital against the community. On the whole, except in national security and defense activities, this has not occurred. It may be noted that since the Second World War the fastest single area of growth of the American economy has been the public sector which for purposes of analysis includes education, culture, museums, galleries, symphonies, training, health and caring services.[6] These are public interest oriented work activities subsidized by the government and public with profoundly positive effects for the development of human capital.

A vast array of positive alternatives can be found and developed through worker-community discussion groups to assure the public nature of the economy and the accountability of its participants. Such worker-citizen groups would study the different types of public service and business enterprises in the United States which tend to distort the use value of production and invert that which is valued and valuable to that which is dangerous and socially costly. Whether public or private sector activities it is the workers on the line and the communities directly affected who have an interest and existential understanding of how to improve conditions. It is through analysis and discussion about production and its consequences by such groups that a new kind of market can be constituted.

As part of social reconstruction and once the Congressional-political party apparatus accepted the economic reconstruction, a national deliberative process[7] through the Congressional juries (town meetings) could be organized to operate as a grassroots information network for learning about needs and problems of the community, including the best ways of organizing the productive capacities of each community. (This method seeks to find ways of restoring active, cultural forms – talk and deliberation – rather than consumer ones as manifested in polling or advertising techniques where questions asked are of interest to the pollsters, not necessarily to those being polled.) As the political process matured, collective bargaining would begin to reflect the worker-community control concept. It would not be impossible for the American Federation of Labor-Congress & Industrial Organizations (AFL-CIO) to insist that the largest firms in particular industries (especially where unions had leverage through pension funds) would be expected to plan publicly and cooperatively with other industries, deliberative assemblies within firms would be organized to relate directly to the work of deliberative assemblies in allied industries as well as industries indirectly involved in the production process. A system of deliberative assemblies could be initiated by unions in major industries with or without sanction of management. The political space is there for such actions. Such voluntary actions initiated by workers and unions would serve as a model for participation and decision making. The results of their deliberations and actions would be legitimated through legislation and government actions as well as contracts with management.

At present, capital accumulation and investment decisions are made privately and primarily to guarantee short-term return on investment even at the expense of industrial innovation. Very little attention is paid to social costs in allied industries or to the general public. Accounting methods need to be developed at universities, business and accounting schools that begin from the assumption that social costs are to be computed so that the public has a far more exact understanding of what any particular item or process costs the society as a whole. Surely this could be organized at our universities by enterprising business school professors.

Trade unions share some responsibility with business in the investment of pension funds. But the fact is that under present rules and custom it is business which controls the direction of these funds. They are thought to

147

be, by business, indeed, they are, a primary source of investment in private industry. There is little reason that workers should not totally direct pension funds and decide where they are to be invested. The purpose of such a policy is to decrease the dependence of the worker on decisions made by centralized authority, whether the state or the corporation, wherever this is feasible.

Numerous empirical studies show that shared ownership among workers yields participatory decision making. There is strong evidence that participation results in more humane working conditions, increased production and better products.[8] *But even if shared participatory ownership did not result in improved efficiency, it would still remain a primary value of a modern democracy*. The reason is obvious. The productive system (plant facilities, assembly lines, etc.) must fulfill humane working conditions along the lines specified by the workers and community. I assume, therefore, a political aspect to the productive process. Consequently, what should be made can be changed and modified through public referendum as well as market boycotts or demands as time and needs of the society change.

While productive organization (worker assemblies) may decide their methods and hours of work, the prices which they charge should be open to continuous public scrutiny since price is a matter concerning the relations of the firm to the rest of the community, but in recent times communities have ceded their sovereign power to control or set prices to the marketplace. It is important to remember, however, that in virtually all organized nations the power to set prices rests with the community, if it so chooses. Prices for basic commodities would be set through worker-community assemblies.

In a period of transition, federal price controls should be placed on certain basic items. Selective controls should be accompanied with a means of withdrawing a certain amount of purchasing power into a national savings program for rebuilding our cities. A comprehensive or permanent wage price control system assumes a very heavy planning role by the government and the replacement of the market by central economic mechanisms. The authority for this possibility already exists in the Humphrey-Hawkins Act and if the selective wage price and national savings program is unsuccessful it would be necessary to adopt wage price controls. These issues will become even more essential as the Reagan administration finds that it is unable to control the structural unemployment spiral. This situation will of course lead to greater turbulence in the cities. The Republican policy of justifying large profits belies the actual weakness of business in relation to stable long-term profits related to higher production rather than speculation in, for example, real estate and merger acquisition.

Reorganizing the public sector for a productive economy: some models and problems

There are various political means for transforming the American economy to one which assumes greater public control by worker community associations, public boards and duly constituted governments in the federal system. Each has problems and will tend to emphasize different values during transformation and therefore in result. None of these is mutually exclusive and the dynamics of history – given what is already in place institutionally and ideologically – will result in an amalgam of these methods being tried. The initial thrust for the changes I have outlined here will originate from the same feelings of fear and frustration which gave rise to the nuclear freeze movement. In other words, town and city councils, as well as state legislatures, would be called upon to debate and pass economic reconstruction resolutions. These resolutions would be supported by documents that outline how each local and state industry would be transformed and democratized as a way of saving American industry. Such a grassroots movement would probably give rise to these linked models of social reconstruction, each having its own difficulties and advantages.

(1) The first political model is that of bureaucratic institutional reconstruction brought about by technocrats and members of Congress who are part of a Progressive Caucus connected to public interest groups and labor unions that have pressed for economic reconstruction on an industry basis because of the strength of consumer movements. The plan itself would be written into the party platforms of the state and national Democratic party. On the assumption that the Democratic party controlled both houses it would adopt a multi-year authorizing and appropriations cycle. Tendencies in this direction began in 1979 under pressure from the Congressional Budget Office. In this model a proposed Budget Committee on Planning would present corporate and industrial reorganization and planning goals which would be developed with the Office of Management and Budget of the Executive Office of the President, again on the assumption of a Democratic President. These government bodies would jointly set out a timetable of planning and action, including the criteria to determine which firms are to be nationalized or reorganized through worker-community participation.

Through this public intervention system Congress and the President would assume direct but accountable intervention in particular segments of the economy, as noted in the *Four Zone Political Economy*. This model would include the establishment of a national economic council where industries with a clear public interest to be determined through national and local hearings would be represented. Industries represented on the

Council would be those which have a direct effect on the lives of people (for example the drug industry), the shape of cities and the costs and use of energy, automobiles (transportation), the use and distribution of energy, such as the oil, coal and atomic energy industry. New industries, such as robotics, telecommunications and microprocessing would also be included.

The Economic Council would include members of Congress, the executive branch, and elected members of the various public industries. In the course of a twenty-five-year period this Council would initiate the establishment of publicly owned or "yardstick" industries in transportation, energy, basic metals, agriculture, telecommunications, lumber, utilities, housing and banking. It would also encourage the formation of assemblies of workers and managers in major industries who would choose, in turn, their representatives to sit on the Economic Council. A new role would be given to anti-trust. The anti-trust system which was written into the Sherman Anti-Trust Act was demanded by an aroused citizenry led by the Populists who denounced the trusts and the "annual tribute levied by the trusts upon the people of the country." Of course under present conditions the anti-trust case system has no bite. Often such cases drag on for years. They are lost in a maze of technical legal language which creates work for lawyers.

There are two alternatives. One is a review of anti-trust procedures to shorten the time of trial and evidence taking, including the possibility of establishing special economic courts. The alternative is direct oversight by Congress of each industry. It would set standards and determine legislatively which industries are to be broken up according to criteria publicly arrived at.

Thus, in "Year One" of a national reorganization a particular sector would be transformed or nationalized depending on the decision of the Council and the various constituent groups of that industry. In Year Two, another sector would be targeted for public and cooperative ownership and so on for a twenty-five-year period. It should be noted that the cycle could be reversed for a particular industry so that it would be designated as one without direct, public involvement. In other words an industry could be deregulated or "depublicized."

There are certain shortcomings in moving to a public sector productive economy in the planned incremental way. A capital strike might ensue and credit might grind to a halt in those areas which require long-term investment and planning decisions in sectors not already nationalized. Consequently, what may appear to be an orderly procedure in fact could result in chaos because the managers of the corporations are attuned to old patterns and do not see how investment can be anything but private, or at least privately controlled.

If Congress and the federal government *slowly* move to the public control of those major corporate firms which define the national economy, great social and economic dislocations might result because the managers at the top of these corporations do not necessarily share a consciousness beyond that of profits for their individual firms. They would support a "capital strike" feeling that they are not in control of corporations whose legal status and method of operation were changed by government intervention. Owners would most likely balk if they felt that they were expected to invest capital or borrow for industries which would be taken over by public bodies, or indeed, that "their" corporate enterprise would be turned into a public body. On the other hand, they would be quick to transfer failing firms to the public sector. In Western Europe nationalized industries were those which the private sector no longer wanted because of their unprofitable nature. Nevertheless, this method of nationalizing has been the preferred one for several generations among pragmatic socialists who believe that socialist change cannot and should not come out of armed struggle; that there is a scientific and rational means to bring about economic and social justice.

(2) The second method to be considered as a way to organize the business economy calls for stronger regulation in the short term and the sharing of power between labor, management, the "public" interest community sector and government through boards similar to the War Labor and War Production boards devised in the Second World War. At that time management was required to surrender some of its control over the assembly line as a *quid pro quo* for a no strike pledge. In the present context a series of "social contracts" between capital and labor would be entered into and regulation from the government would be welcomed. These are the ideas reflected in the work of advisors to the United Auto Workers. Various public interest groups including Ralph Nader's organization have struggled for public regulation. However, American methods of regulation are costly.

The twentieth-century American history of regulation is that the regulator is coopted by the regulated, and that the small or micro-businessman suffers the most under regulations since he (sometimes she) is unable to pay the bureaucratic costs necessary to meet the controls pressed on to small business. Further, small business is almost never represented on public boards. It is hardly surprising that large corporate enterprises are able to shape regulation in such a way as to penalize small entrepreneurs and cause difficulty for those attempting to enter a particular economic sector. Micro-businesses are unable to obtain surety bonds, contracts from the government, or undertake the social contacts which generate contracts from the government. Furthermore, interest groups supposedly representative of small business are pawns for big business. The Chamber of Commerce, for example, is dominated politically by the great corporations to the detriment of small and micro-business.

Where the entrepreneur and small business are penalized just by virtue of their size and the fact that they can't control or compete in the market a

151

type of syndical fascism could emerge in which the largest industrial and financial units of the society would control the regulations and laws of public bodies for their own individual advantage. We see this operating in the relationship between, say, General Motors and other automobile manufacturers. In the Carter administration the federal government's efforts to shape a more balanced transportation policy, even according to principles which would help in the rationalization of the capitalist system, were thwarted. It is not clear that a social movement can be built out of a need for regulations. It may be useful for issue specific activities, but it is not useful as a broad alternative for the economy.

(3) In the 1930s another method was put forward by Oscar Lange as a way to change the capitalist economy. He called for a swift nationalization of industries on the basis of a plan where there was a clarity of purpose, familiarity with the industrial and financial operations of particular industries and absolute guarantees to those industries which were to remain in private hands.[9] But swift nationalization is the direct result of a mass movement that understands the modern production line and has skills of administrative leadership which can transform the old property relationships to a more equitable and public form quickly and with a minimum of disruption. (Disruption in this context means interruption of the assembly line which would be no greater than that of an economic strike.) The financial and accounting side of business enterprise is not well known by the labor and consumer movement, although it is true that this talent can be hired and learned by union and consumer groups. The third position assumes a working people's party which would control or emerge from the present Democratic party. It would aim its political and economic message to those who earned less than $30,000 a year for a family of four. It would not be a "Vanguard" party where its members would think of themselves as guardians for the people. Vanguard parties become fossilized, as one can discern by examining the communist parties in Eastern Europe and their relationship to their respective economies.[10]

One might imagine that those on welfare grants, pensions, and those industries such as defense and railroads which are heavily subsidized by federal contract might favor swift nationalization if it meant that they could retain their private power and high salary scales. For the most part public workers and old people would support swift nationalization in such areas as health care. Those elements of the Democratic party which had been most adversely effected by inflation and depression, and who needed more benefits and transfer payments might favor an immediate strategy of democratization and nationalization of major industries especially where a crisis of the proportions of 1929-32 were to reoccur.

Those institutions and people that have been dependent on federal government intervention for employment would, after wide-ranging discussions, favor the emegence of a national planning process and different forms of community and federal government nationalization. It is not likely that without a well-articulated program which is logically compelling, and which is based on agreement among those who have been supported by government intervention since the New Deal, there would be much possibility of translating such claims into legislative action. The political likelihood is that in the long run such a program could emerge from the AFL-CIO (because of its broad worker base). The AFL-CIO is dominated, to a great extent, by the theories of Jay Lovestone who believed that American capitalism was an exceptional case in Marxist theory and that it was possible to work with American capitalists.

The Reagan administration's onslaught on organized labor plus the actual changed conditions of the labor market within the United States will no doubt cause a serious debate within the labor movement as to its next steps since capital has made clear that it has little interest in assuring the continuation of the labor movement, even a pliant one. Whether the AFL-CIO will therefore seek its allies through organizing in the secondary labor markets is not clear. The place where some sort of *modus vivendi* could be worked out is within the Democratic party, except for divisions raised over defense and national security between progressives and the labor movement. However, the attitudes of the AFL-CIO could change as it becomes clear that the economic benefits of the defense budget are subject to greater scrutiny. Also, it is clear that the ideological assumptions upon which the organized labor unions based their acceptance of the national security state are being systematically undercut by conservative and reactionary Republicans who use the labor movement and its allies to mask their own reactionary economic activity.

It should be noted that this method assumes that fundamental change does not occur without governmental authority and a strong party commitment – a commitment which seems to be stronger on the right than the left. Most important, it does not encourage people to undertake their own cooperative forms or to transform enterprises through their own efforts. It does not help people initiate, understand or feel confident about activities which they undertake. It is too dependent on top-down controls, and government as provider rather than enabler of freely chosen actions.

(4) The fourth method is that of increasing power and participation in the economy by the public and the government through a combination of grassroots and federal activity. It means expanding the public sector and redrawing the zones of public and private responsibility.

In the United States of the 1980s there is anger – fueled by the Reagan administration – among those who think of themselves as producers and taxpayers as against those who are thought to exist on transfer payments and subsidies. In my view there is no mediating way for these antagonistic groups to work together for common political purposes except through such devices as redefining the nature of meaningful work, and securing full

153

employment. To achieve a coherent and agreed upon program a national political party will have to redefine and clarify the meaning of work, employment, democracy, participation, and adopt a far more equitable distribution of the benefits and burdens of work and taxation.

Workers, businesspeople and consumers should, with governmental and university people, begin the debate on the present efficiency of American corporations with specific reference to their purpose, size and the quality of product. *As was earlier stated, where a particular industry affects the general welfare, governments, whether on the state, local, federal or even neighborhood level cannot be stopped from undertaking public enterprise.* Both the power and the authority are present for this purpose. But two questions have also to be debated once this direction is taken. There is little to suggest that the state will be more efficient than the methods of American Telephone and Telegraph, for example. What public intervention can do is make clear that the public sector will be represented and that investment patterns of "natural monopolies" favor the public's interest and public service rather than private profit. To insure this direction the citizenry should involve itself in the participatory planning process through public hearings, membership on committees of industries and on boards, even including public election of major posts in industry. In this regard, the Securities and Exchange Commission (SEC) should begin studies of the great corporations to ascertain the market and actual worth of corporations. Public bodies, such as cities, states, neighborhood governments and unions, would be encouraged to acquire the stock of major corporations which affect the public interest, whether or not they are profitable. There should be no limit placed on this acquisition process.

As Derek Shearer has said in an important article in *Working Papers*, "The party should advocate a pluralist society in which...workers, consumers, and citizens have access to, and control over, institutions around them."[11] This requires a mix of economic institutions, "from co-ops and neighborhoods corporations and municipal industries and local land trusts – to state corporations, bank insurance corporations, etc..." all of which would operate within the democratic planning framework.

To ensure this direction, the citizenry and workers would participate in the planning process of the economic sector through public hearings, membership on committees of industries and on boards. Thus, for example, it is time the head of General Motors and Exxon were elected through the political process. Public bodies such as cities, states, neighborhoods, governments and unions would, in the first stage of the transition process, be encouraged to buy stock in major corporations which affect the public interest so the corporate investment direction and policies could be democratically and publicly determined.

Zone One – The oligopoly and public interest sector

Zone One of the economy is composed of "natural monopolies." They are the utilities and energy industries, the largest banks as well as those industries organized for the most part along oligopolistic lines. The boundary of the zones would be delineated by Congress with special attention paid to Zone One enterprises.

Three tests should be used to determine the public character of industries and whether they fall into the Zone One category. (a) That private industries use substantial resources already determined to be owned by the public as in the case of air waves or public lands. (b) That by their size the respective industries exercise investment and social cost decisions which shape decisions that are unaccountable and may be contradictory to the common good as determined through public deliberation. (Such industries as energy, weapons, communications, transportation, banks and insurance of a particular size and magnitude may fall into this category.) (c) The third test is applied to those industries of the economy which can cause great damage to the public health of the society. (This category includes drugs and certain aspects of agriculture and chemical industries.) They are to be reorganized in their daily operations to include (1) workers participation of those directly working in the particular industry; (2) consumer participation by those directly or indirectly affected by the work of the particular industry; (3) public representation of communities where the plants are located; or (4) federal participation, either through appointment or national election. In other words, Zone One corporations would be Congressionally mandated to constitutionalize and to organize worker-community assemblies.

Congress's task is that of adjusting the proper representation between the various groups through legislation. It would also retain its oversight responsibilities and would assert a public trust through partial legal title. To guard against tokenism, worker-employee representation of the firm should never be less than 40 per cent of the boards of directors of firms. Elections for membership on such boards would be held in worker-consumer assemblies and through appointment by Congress and the President.[12]

As I have suggested, it is not necessary to wait for Congressional action or legitimation. Groups of workers, technicians and junior managers within the largest one thousand corporations, once the aura of public legitimacy exists for such actions, can organize discussions of alternate modes of operation in production, administration, marketing and quality of the work place. Labor unions should not be reticent in taking the lead in this effort. They should *organize* managers into seminars and discussions that are framed according to the principles laid out by workers and public interest groups.

While the top corporations may call themselves part of the private sector, they are not entitled to rights of privacy granted to individuals or fourteenth amendment rights. A direct legal onslaught needs to be made on the privileged status granted to corporations through the metaphysics of capitalist constitutional law. Where a particular industry can affect the direction of the society, economically and politically different ways should be found to open the management and assumptions of that organization to workers and the community at large through the political process. Thus, as one example, we may think of ways to apply first amendment rights to the work place. This right should become an almost automatic one as the productive and technical process changes so that workers can relate their needs and that of the community to the production line.

Part of the reorganized federal relationship to the economy necessitates the formation of central information banks which will generate public planning mechanisms and methods for sharing information. Congress would develop and own its own econometric models rather than relying on Chase bank, other private economic entrepreneurs or the University of Pennsylvania as is presently the case. Public boards would be responsible for inventing those forms of advertising and information sharing that would emphasize production and its consequences, consumer education, skills to repair machinery, goods. They would seek to end the present sales methods predicated on consumer envy, and products as if they were panaceas to obtain happiness, love, etc.

Obviously, one of the major questions to consider in the transition of the economy is the political method to be used to pay off present owners of stock. Those who directly work in Zone One public corporations as well as communities (cities, towns and villages), eleemosynary institutions (schools, universities and hospitals) and worker associations (unions, cooperatives) would own shares. Those who work in Zone One corporations would be limited in the amount of stock they could own. Their stock would be dividend bearing. They would not be voting shares since the task of the direction of the firm would now fall to worker community assemblies.

The next stage of American life is rich in possibilities and could result, even for the largest firms (Zone One) in a profoundly creative period in the productive process. But to fulfill their potential corporate firms will have to be legitimated, constitutionalized, through the political process. Historically, corporations received charters from the state only if they were thought to "advantage" the common good of the society. They were chips off the sovereignty of the society. Charters were not immutable.[13] Thus, it should hardly be seen as revolutionary for Congress to assert its authority to control the operations of major corporations through a legitimating, constitutionalizing and chartering process. In our time the constitutional charge of Congress is to manage or charge the property and productive relationships of the society as it seeks to simultaneously define the common good and guide the direction of a modern democracy.

There are several legislative ways to reorganize the industrial and financial firms in Zone One. One such means is through the appointment of a group of commissioners by Congress and the President who present to Congress a comprehensive bill which cannot be amended from the floor of either the House or Senate. It is to be accepted or rejected as a whole. This method was used in reorganizing the Amtrak railroad system.

Another parliamentary means can be fashioned which is intended to increase the likelihood that proposals on economic reorganization would be passed and implemented. (It should be noted that such proposals would be fashioned and discussed in the plants and through town meetings prior to Congressional debate.) Economic reorganization for Zone One industries would begin through the initiation of two-thirds of both houses of Congress, or on the initiation of the President. If there is no positive objection by a majority of both Houses after sixty days that particular firm or industry will have been reorganized. This legislative method follows the procedure prescribed by the Atomic Energy Act for transferring atomic materials outside the United States.

The industries touched would be those that had already been studied by the SEC and deemed oligopolistic or monopolistic, which by their nature could not compete,[14] and which by the products made or mined were critical to the public welfare. Prior to Congressional or Presidential action the Securities and Exchange Commission would present Congress with a method for the orderly purchase of stocks by public bodies, such as cities, unions, worker community associations and individual worker-employees in Zone One industries. The SEC would be charged with formulating a plan according to publicly debated and Congressionally accepted principles of the common good. The fair value of the stock would be determined by its average market value over a seven-year period so that the stocks would not increase unduly because of governmental interest. The various relevant departments of the federal government would coordinate their activities and receive worker-community reorganization plans for those industries designated by Congress as necessary for reorganization and public intervention.

In the present period of economic turbulence, capital and industry are fleeing communities like some convicts trying to escape prison. Needless to say, one of the worst fears of workers and communities is the runaway plant. Communities are threatened by businesses which say that unless a "friendly" climate is given to them in the form of tax credits and other incentives they will leave and set up shop elsewhere. The long-term effect of giving in to corporations this way results in the destruction of the tax base and therefore of necessary public services to the community. The community is expected to pay for the effects which are caused by the industry, while private enterprise is supposed to reap the profits. The entire Northeast and Middle West regions of the United States are the victims of this type of "free" enterprise. What can be done? If a substantial number of workers are to be laid off in a community by corporations, corporations should be required to file justification claims for doing so. The federal government, in consultation with cities and states, would be empowered to review corporate books and plans to ascertain the effect of layoffs on the community immediately involved. A new system of societal insurance called "unemployment bonds" would have to be paid by corporations to local communities in the event a particular corporation laid off a substantial number of workers. Such bonds would be credited to increased costs of social services as a result of layoffs.

Another bond should also be required. It may be called the "runaway corporations" bond. Prior to a substantial-sized corporation leaving an area it would be expected to "make whole" or give restitution to the community for what it used in basic resources and other hidden costs paid for by the community. Corporations in Zone Three might also have to post such bonds with communities where it was determined that they were substantial employers or beneficiaries and users of a community. One example would be a corporation that took the use of local rivers for its sewage disposition.

Zone Two – The public service sector

The second zone of the economy concerns the public service sector by which I mean teachers, the armed forces, social workers, sanitation workers, conservationists and all those who are employed directly by the state, universities, non-profit cultural and economic institutions.

The actual numbers of workers on the federal government payroll has stayed remarkably constant since 1947 when taken against population increases and size of government program although the number of public workers on the state and local level has increased greatly. On the other hand, the number of workers who operated in the private sector and in fact are virtually totally dependent on public funds through contracts for their income has very greatly increased. The payments made by the federal government directly to federal employees is $73,219,898 a year, while payments in benefits is $10,692,617 a year.[15] The fact that the government is the single most powerful "actor" in the economic system poses an important political legal question. Is there a means of holding workers and government policy makers publicly accountable without subjecting them to harassment?

One of the most interesting economic/legal principles developed in law is the majority-minority position among judges at the appellate level. This decision making system could be used in virtually all areas of the bureaucracy and major industrial enterprises as a means of presenting arguments to the public about decisions. Thus, for example, on any particular issue a majority/minority position would be made public by any particular agency of the government in forms similar to legal cases so that the arguments are publicly made. The Secretary of each department would be required to sign off on one side or the other. In each case, the names of bureaucrats would be publicly announced under their decisions and arguments. Although this procedure may appear to be an unrelated and relatively minor administrative detail, it is in fact a critical principle of political economy because it means that allocation decisions are publicly debated, arguments are made publicly and stated in ways that make clear the reasoning of the various factions of government. In this way, public workers can be criticized fairly and openly. The curtain of bureaucratic anonymity must be raised and the play of public responsibility must go forward.

A word should be said about the invidious distinction which is often made between government workers such as teachers, food and drug inspectors, mining inspectors, or government officials, and those who work for "private industry." Some analysts make distinctions on the basis of productive and derivative work. It is assumed that the work of government officials is derivative and work in the private sector is productive. This argument is used by conservatives in the two major parties to split government and non-government workers from each other. Those who work in the private sector (so-called) are told that they are paying for non-essential services. This invidious distinction against government workers adds to the deplorably low state of morale among government workers. There is an alarming ideological fashion which governs the media, the "private sector" and even political leaders who operate the government. It is that government workers are thought of as "parasitical." Milton Friedman talks about the American bureaucracy in a way that conjures up images of the nineteenth-century Spanish bureaucracy which wrecked Spain and kept it out of modern industrialism. The American reality is quite different. As Eli Ginzberg has pointed out, the spurt in American economic well being since 1945 is directly related to the emergence of the non-industrial and govermental sector as a powerful organizing, catalytic and institutional element in American life.

This is not to say that there are not unnecessary governmental tasks which may be excised when we forge a politics of the common good. The history of government, after all, is that it causes problems of a serious social nature. Such activities would include surveillance, police and dubious social controls that are masked by claims of national security. These activities, including surveillance, police and prison controls need to be evaluated in terms of their purpose and usefulness. (See Chapter 6 on citizenship.) The government in certain cases impedes innovation and substitutes the government's judgment for that of a person or group without any tangible gain or aid to the common good. Democratic government should act as a catalyst for the creative, positive impulses of society,[16] not its oppressor.

Once particular activities are scrutinized and found to serve a public purpose, to the extent possible, the government's role should be less coercive/regulative and more mediationist/pedagogic. In other words, government should help to organize and perform the enabling function in the economy. When it acts for the society as a whole government must also protect what should be held commonly.

Government's secondary task is to develop yardstick industries which would have an experimental and innovative character to them. Government workers would formulate alternative efficiency and work patterns, including experimentation with new types of machinery and industrial processes which would be specifically designed to encourage a more humane and politically active population. The Departments of Commerce, Labor and Transportation would reorganize the infrastructure system by rebuilding everything from harbors to railroad beds, schools and environmental anti-pollution stations. Each state would submit to Congress a needs assessment plan for review which would outline the problems and needs that were not met through private enterprise actions or present governmental policy. Startling clues about the internal needs of the society were given by the 98th Congress. According to the Committee on Public Works it will take our $700 billion "to maintain a decent highway and bridge system through the year 2000." For example, nearly 45 per cent of the bridges are thought to be obsolete. Congressional juries would hold hearings for Congress on the feasibility of governmental actions and enterprises to meet the local needs of the states.

Zone Three – Competitive and small business

The third zone of the economy concerns small and micro-business. The question of what a "small business" is in the latter part of the twentieth century is not easily defined. I define small business enterprises as those that do not control a particular market, exercise price fixing power over services or a product, or have fewer than 500 employees. A small business cannot control the price of others, the supply of the market, but it still maintains independence in its decision making. (The latter can be guaranteed through small business entry loans and rigorous enforcement of the anti-trust laws, a condition which is impossible to obtain under present economic rules.) It should be noted that a significant number of firms in the United States are competitive and by their nature perform in such a manner that services are given adequately and carefully. Even so, we must be careful about giving a blanket endorsement to competition among small firms. To increase sales and profits, firms may drastically lower the quality of their product.

160

At the present rate of large corporate takeover, small business, defined according to the parameters set out above, and without government intervention to intercede for it will contribute less than a quarter of the GNP by 1990. After the Second World War small business accounted for more than half of the GNP. By 1980 it was 36 per cent. "That meant that 97 per cent of the business establishments (12 million) in the country accounted for little more than a third of the GNP." Under the Reagan tax and anti-trust policies which directly subsidize big business, small business is losing its independence and government support.[17] Contrary to the conventional wisdom of the right this obnoxious trend can only be interrupted through direct government intervention and worker-community participation in Zone One of the economy. Between 1960 and 1976, 37,500 firms were merged and acquired by big firms outside of transportation, communications and banking.

Through legislation Congress would guarantee that small business will not be interfered with in the third zone of the economy either through investment control, takeover, or regulatory harassment. Instead, a policy of social reconstruction would favor small business, entrepreneurs and their workers through strong support of union organizing, tax breaks and subsidies. It is widely accepted that small business needs to be guaranteed the power to make investment decisions with a sense of security. One means of guaranteeing this security is by fashioning investment opportunities banks which would help small businesses maintain themselves and compete efficiently. But workers do not have to be penalized with low wages and non-unionization. Where small or micro-businesses are in the public interest, for example, laundries, they should be subsidized and aided to ensure decent working conditions and pay.[18]

The common good must include human enterprise and initiative. However, it should not create social privileges which the majority of the people must bear with adverse consequences to them. There is no cogent, economic reason why small and micro-business should not be aided even as Congress would move to a stance of direct public control and democratization of the largest corporate and banking units in the society. Congress's role is to assure that the third zone would operate according to a national planning process organized from the grassroots.

Zone Four – Non-profit, small-scale, worker control activities

The critical fourth zone of the economy should be protected, aided and encouraged through law and regulation at all governmental levels. The fourth zone concerns small-scale activities which are worker controlled or are established as non-profit activities. Throughout its history the United

States has had many examples of small-scale enterprises. In the past, these collective enterprises have had a profoundly religious character as in the case of the Shakers. Since the 1960s the current manifestation of this sentiment is found in cooperative auto repair and maintenance shops, small newspapers, research groups or fiercely independent people who have sought another way. An Albuquerque communard indelicately said, "Why should I work 30 or 40 hours a week for someone or something that doesn't give a shit about me so I can get money to buy things I don't give a shit about owning?" There are now numerous attempts by workers to buy out management and they are supported by federal programs that favor employee buyout and ownership. In the context of transformation of the economic system buyouts of this kind should be encouraged. Where workers are stuck with poor machinery or unsecured markets such buyouts might be questionable. Thus, governments must be prepared to underwrite specific infrastructural aids to worker-owned establishments. Worker ownership should be understood as part of the changed consciousness which propels us to an economic system that includes public participation. It states clearly the need for productive work which is humane and shared in the most democratic sense, and it cries out for a redefinition of both need and the products people are induced to consume. Presently, post-industrialized schooling favors the development of workers for Zone One and Zone Two activities. Zone Four economic enterprises should be favored in the schools. (High technology activities will fall in Zones Three and Four.)

As part of its task publicly-funded, vocational education would emphasize skills, cooperative modes of management, and autonomy for its success. All interested workers should be given retraining options that would encourage them to establish worker-run activities. Special transportation, technical assistance and loans would be made available to small-scale, worker-run enterprises and worker-community enterprises. Workers would be taught entrepreneurial and service skills. Such programs – and the Comprehensive Employment and Training Act (CETA) is not their model – are meant to initiate a "chain of creativity" which is already there in the communities. People skilled in a craft, such as plumbers and electricians, retired skilled people and members of technical schools (for example, art, engineering and architecture), would organize projects with communities, unions, neighborhood groups and local governments. These projects should be transformed into locally controlled economic enterprises which have a teaching and productive function. Needless to say, carrying out this economic reorganization would require the support and active participation of a political party that debated such matters internally, held "town meetings" about them and made them part of its electoral program.

The Democratic party is the most likely one to consider these questions because it is predicated on reaching all sections of American life It should renounce any predilection to become an upper class based party in which its electoral politicians struggle for support from the dwindling upper middle classes.

Carrying out this program administratively would require a significantly changed relationship between the Executive and Legislative. Instead of a stalemate system, both branches would organize a Joint Cabinet-Congressional body to coordinate the economic planning process that would emerge at the grassroots in the Congressional districts. This process would uncover fundamental questions as they related to the role of economic policy and its moral purpose.

The citizenry would become conscious of the fact that the economic system answers moral questions by what it does or does not address, what it holds constant and changes. Thus, the following questions are both moral and economic ones. Since national economic systems by their nature are linked to state power even in market economics, the question of where and for whom state power is to be used is never far from center stage in economic policy. A moral economic system must ask what needs are and who is to pay for fulfilling them.

The moral economic questions are what is to be held in common? What should be made and how is this to be determined? What is the work to be shared and how is productive work determined? What if any spread of income or inherited wealth should exist in private hands of individuals and families? What is the economic and moral meaning of money and credit? How are we to guard against inflation, ensure full employment and protect the environment?

In a modern democracy these questions are almost wholly political by which I mean that they are to be answered through dialogue in the entire society, both in the neighborhood (dwelling), the work place and the legislative body. In other words, political deliberation defines the nature of market choices by expanding the "grassroots" public space for concern over economic matters.

Once we understand such questions as a collective and cooperative concern we will be able to fashion a different kind of economics. One that is:

> neither capitalistic, socialistic or communistic, but will transcend all these nineteenth-century ideologies. It will need to incorporate both the knowledge of how to design regenerative productive systems based on renewable resources, and the knowledge developed by humanistic psychologists on the almost unlimited potential of human beings as our greatest natural resource in which our investments will yield the largest returns.[19]

Such questions cannot be decided in any simple discipline of knowledge according to a belief in an abstraction called "economic laws." They are, instead, questions for continuous dialogue between the people that economic "laws" can be shaped according to principles of equity and fairness. In other words, economic questions are *political* questions which have embedded within themselves the issues of value. Each one of the policies proposed has distinct value determinants to it and should be judged accordingly. The reader would be in error if he or she thought that these difficulties were limited to the United States.

An economic distribution in a modern democracy

Every nation has the power to limit the present use of resources for the benefit of future generations. Consequently, *each successive generation must participate in making a stark and necessary social contract with the unborn*. Needs are determined by the society on a continuous basis through deliberation and public dialogue. Once so determined the need is to be fulfilled through a system of free goods. That is, goods collectively paid for. In a modern society they include decent shelter, security, education, food and health care. These obligations of the nation to the individual are meant to foster individual dignity. It is the task of government to assure equity and dignity and to examine any specific economic program from this perspective.

In public policy terms, there are two somewhat different ways to achieve this dignity. One is by ascertaining decent standards which are applicable to all and are accepted as necessary and automatic for all citizens. This standard is to be enforced *prior* to any allowable economic and social differences which exist between individuals and groups. The second method sets a more pragmatic standard for seeking well-being. It accepts the class system and simultaneously seeks to devise various means of economic growth which will assure improvement for all classes.

The first method is usually seen as unattainable and it is thought to contradict the operations of society in the case where a revolutionary process is initiated. Thus, liberals and socialists accept the second mechanism as the way of bringing out change. It is predicated on a theory of growth and progress which is necessarily and infinitely expansive without taking cognizance of who is used or how many real resources are used. (Resources are assumed to be unending or substitutable.)

Scientific and technological progress which leads to economic growth is often thought to be the way to solve competing political claims between classes. This is why twentieth-century political leaders have linked governing to technical progress. But our experience tells us that technical progress and the common good are not necessarily compatible. Researchers have brought:

"New" controversies . . . over bans on saccharin and cyclamates, over fluoridation, weather modification programs, research on the XYY chromosomes, the swine-flu vaccine, the use of pesticides, genetic screening techniques and the study of sociobiology . . .[20]

It is virtually undisputed that major technological and scientific advances can be problem causing and repressive. It does not seem to close economic gaps, but increases them between the bottom 95 per cent of the population and its top 5 per cent.

The facts seem to contradict the growth and technology recipe for society which twentieth-century capitalists adopted in rhetorical terms. Less, rather than more, economic and social disparity has been the result. According to liberals, narrowing the income and social gap was to occur by giving people rights of opportunity (which failed). Because of its individualist assumptions, traditional liberal thought did not contemplate rights to social equity, that is, redistribution of income, wealth and power on the sole basis of being human. Paradoxically, however, individual opportunities and liberty can only occur by transcending capitalism, an insight discovered by Bertrand Russell at the beginning of the twentieth century. In any case, the attempt of capitalist states to reach the goals of social peace and individual opportunity through technology and/or economic growth has not been successful. Capitalism's own political goals and choices, when they are humane, cannot be achieved inside the capitalist system. We are confronted, therefore, with a technical and philosophic question that can only be resolved in political practice. It centers around the question of what type of guarantees people want from each other which promote their security and well-being prior to recognition of natural differences between them, or prior to a preference system which emerges either from the market or from collective political decision making.

The standard which is usually pointed to as either humanity's aspirations or its minimum needs is embodied in the various convenants on human rights or in socialist and social democratic programs.

Economic programs for the common good start from the assumption that a natural affection among people can be found and that there is an inelastic demand with little interest among people in denying others their conditions of decency. Consequently, coming to self-consciousness is not contradictory to another's entrance into history (his or her self-consciousness) because people want to encourage the creative impulses of others. It is only in moments of extreme fear or neurosis that an anal retentive or possessory sense emerges to captivate the individual and the political debate.

In the United States "real world" differences, fixed by social and legal rules of pyramidal authority, inheritance laws and capitalist accumulation, inhibit reaching collective aspirations of decency. But these rules are not inherent in the American constitution being, as it is, based on eighteenth-century conceptions of sentimental affections and common bonds or, indeed, in the undeformed aspects of the twentieth-century American project. This project, stimulated by Andrew Jackson's democratic impulses, took hold with the Civil War.

If modern democracy's project is equity, caring and human creativity each person recognizes (and is taught to recognize) that he and she have an economic (productive) attribute in the world which is a function of two conditions: their existence and their willingness to produce. In the case of the first, each society which concerns itself with caring and dignity is prepared to take care of and provide all people with an economic basis for creativity. The person acquires a maturing political or participatory right to decide the direction of the society as he or she takes on another aspect of existence, that of creative and productive activity.

Once there is willingness on the part of the person to participate in the productive and creative aspect of society, that person acquires a democratic right in the daily life of the community to decide what is to be made and how much is to be made. "He is seen and can see others." This right is one which includes access, participation, deliberation and implementation, attributes of democracy which are discussed elsewhere in this inquiry. What is true, as well, is that the second right matures with the age of the person. The older person is now credited with having learned and given, with being a "national treasure" or resource. (This has meaning in terms of what the person knows and can return to others through the sharing of his or her experience and understanding. This will help people begin the evaluation of their own experiences in their lives because they will know that their lives are socially important to others.)

In a period where "enlightened self-interest and self-awareness" abounds, pernicious but telling phrases, not unlike those expressed by the Ik people, are commonly used among the middle and professional classes such as "it's your problem." This statement is of course the social reflection of the economic principle of competitive individualism. Such principles are harmful to the young who fail to see the important cooperative and collective aspects which define human existence and those aspects of the American project which are bound by equity, caring, and cooperation.

As a result of failing consciously to understand the types of cooperation which are necessary to human existence, those committed to progress invent and then sustain deformed organizations. These inventions result in the destruction of the fundamental human capacity to cooperate because they organize the cooperative effort for individual gain. They emphasize man's capacity for envy and accumulation over caring, empathy and sharing. They emphasize possession, and the importance of possession and property as an end unto itself. Where political or economic monopoly in either the public or private sphere becomes the framework of society, no social space

166

exists for autonomous changes which people can make or seek to regulate from the base of the work place. Consequently, it is of great importance that autonomous, democratic reorganization *within* factories and other institutions of the civil society be encouraged by Congress to counteract any top-down bureaucratic or monopoly tendencies. These concerns should be kept in mind when judging the transformation of a political economy.[21]

Economic proposals for the transition to democracy

The world's economies are all suffering but in different degrees from the same set of political economic diseases. They are inflation, unemployment, community dissolution as a result of technical advance, worker dissatisfaction, and worker alienation, the marginalization of the labor force, attempts at restoring order through a corporate state, a greater income/ wealth disparity which is not solved through economic growth, an emphasis on material goods which turn out to be shoddy, industrial decline as a result of stiff competition, poor management, high energy prices and an unskilled labor force. These problems will not go away. They may be engulfed by others in the future although for the rest of the twentieth century these problems will remain with most of the world's nations. They take on an especially acute form in the United States because each is thought of as separate from another problem, and each is thought to be manageable without changing the organizational and problem solving method we use to address them. Even with a Rightist belief in private enterprise it is increasingly clear that government, not the market, is looked to for help in solving economic problems. The market can never be more than a mechanism for exchange. It cannot correct social imbalances, income or wealth maldistribution. Under the proposals I have made the federal government's role will increase as it acts under Congressional authority to ensure fairness and smooth functioning between and within the four zones of the economy.

The problems that I have mentioned do have either partial or complete solutions although with each solution will come another difficulty, hopefully less virulent than the problem one is attempting to solve. This is why it is of the utmost importance to consider problems beyond themselves as part of a comprehensive political strategy to stimulate discussions of the means and goals of the economy.

The programmatic solutions to particular questions should be dealt with in the context of national dialogue. The short-term policy proposals which I have made are part of an attempt to move the economy from a system in which invisible hands control it to one which can be understood and democratized as well as publicly guided. Each of these proposals can be initiated pragmatically and incrementally. However, all of them require the widest discussion before they are implemented in practice.

Inflation and full employment

Among conservatives and some liberals it is taken for granted that governments are the chief cause of inflation and therefore should not be trusted with control over the money supply.[22] But an analysis of this question yields certain ambiguous conclusions. Sharp increases in defense expenditure have an inflationary effect because "income is generated without any corresponding increase in the aggregate supply of goods and services for which that income will bid in the marketplace."[23] There are other reasons for inflation. One is that the federal government must borrow from the richer classes to pay off its current indebtedness rather than tax them adequately to pay for social and defense programs. Borrowing rather than taxing creates inflation. Another reason for inflation is that in those sectors of the economy which are oligopolistic the tendency is to pre-emptively raise prices. These prices are not adjusted or discounted later even if labor or resource costs do not increase.

The second area which causes inflation is the commercial banking and the credit system. Bankers create near money such as credit cards in the "private sector." A related issue is interest costs. In 1983 interest payments owed to banks and other loan operations were approximately 958 billion dollars.[24] In fact personal debts are often symbolic statements of profound psychological insecurity. Crime, fear and other forms of anomie are often the result of indebtedness of individuals to institutions. The conservative claim that debt arrangements are a drag on future generations has much validity to it once we include private as well as state obligations. In both cases people find themselves confronted with arrangements and a social system protecting those arrangements to assure that such debts are either continued or paid off even though they might not have been contracted by the person. The result is that future productive activity is already mortgaged for past activities which have little value. Wars and defense expenditures are the obvious example. This is, of course, another reason for having the lowest possible defense budget.

It is also true that large debts cause inflation and that inflation adds to debts which are then to be paid for through higher interest rates. The collateral behind loans increases and when that collateral is not present the common bonds of amity between people are invoked to continue the ballooning system. When ballooning fails the tendency is for business and government to resort to manipulative accounting schemes which give the appearance of solvency and positive productivity when neither is present. The manipulations of David Stockman and Donald Regan are examples of self-deluding accounting. Such activities on the art of the system's manipulators are misplaced because they avoid the value choices which democracy must make about the nature of its economic system. The traditional way to end inflation is to decrease governmental expenditure and increase unemployment. These two methods are ostensibly being used by the Reagan administration to decrease inflation. The alternative method is selective wage and price controls, cutting the defense budget and simultaneously changing the obligations of the US under the alliance system, reinvesting defense cuts either in public enterprises or social services. The latter is the method I prefer.

The full employment economy

The nation has both the wisdom and material resources to develop itself into a productive, humane and creative society allowing its citizens to be relatively free of civil strife and economic insecurity. To do so the nation needs a program of full employment of meaningful work for the common good. Under the general welfare clause of the Constitution, it is the responsibility of modern government to guarantee a meaningful job to anyone willing and able to work. It is humane, productive work that should be guaranteed, not a status known as "employment."

A full employment economy is not a "free enterprise" economy. The Right's theory of capital formation which in practical terms does nothing but subsidize the rich, has had a disastrous effect on the poor and working class of the society. No one should have been surprised that the present oligopoly system thrives on unemployment as well as a deprived social class that must take any jobs offered to it. This is the fundamental reason that social programs were cut. The Reagan administration plan, like that of Thatcher and Pinochet, was aimed at cutting those programs which had given the poorer groups in the society some independence and skills. These programs were flawed but necessary ones such as education, student aid, and manpower retraining as well as CETA training.

With Reagan's 1982 federal budget, the direction begun under President Carter for induced unemployment as a way to cope with inflation and a working class which supposedly had too many benefits was embraced by Congress. The private enterprise budget of 1982 guaranteed an unemployment rate of at least 8 per cent. In fact, the unemployment rate by the summer of 1982 reached 10 per cent. By 1985, as a result of huge deficits and stunningly high military budgets, the unemployment rate was reduced to 7.3 per cent. These rates of unemployment indicated a profound fallacy with the principle that government should only be an employer of last resort, if at all.

What can be done? There are five interlinked lines of economic policy that should become the basis of an alternative in the short term that serves the common good. (a) The capitalization of communities through federal loans and grants so that communities can operate public enterprises and develop public controlled surplus producing activities; (b) the development of new definitions of work which are far broader than those defined as work in the present oligopoly market system; (c) the regeneration of towns, communities and cities directly, which would be formed into local participatory governing units to receive public funds for rebuilding and maintaining services (any 2,000 people should be able to define projects of a community nature which would receive automatic support where the income of the group was less than $25,000 a year on the average per family); (d) the development of price and credit guidelines policed by consumer groups. The purpose of this move is to control inflation; (e) the development of an understanding that the great corporations are not "private" but use public funds and affect the way people live in the United States as well as a good part of the world. Thus, they are to be seen in the framework of a democracy of the common good. It is not enough to seek full employment. It is necessary to seek the control of capital and credit allocations for the public sector which would enable municipalities, towns and states to initiate public enterprises and buy private enterprises. These local entities would be in a position to purchase and control plants, machinery and raw materials. If such a credit allocation system is not followed, the industrial base of the United States will continue to decline as business seeks cheaper labor and higher profits in non-unionized industries or the Third World.

The Humphrey-Hawkins Act, while insufficient because it does not include capital investments, is nevertheless an opening wedge to obtain full employment and reassess the priorities of the nation.[25] One of its most important aspects is that it lists needs and specifies categories of programs that would meet those needs. Its major difficulty is that it assumes that the employment problems of the economy are temporary. This was an error of the New Deal and it should not be repeated. Furthermore, a full employment system requires continuous attention to the needs of the communities of the United States. Needs must be decided locally by communities as part of democratic planning processes.

The responsibility for full employment and meaningful work with decent pay should be shared on all levels of government. It can only be meaningful when the governments themselves develop projects and ongoing enterprises that are more than bureaucratic in nature. In conjunction with communities, they must be prepared to undertake the development and sponsorship through loans and subsidy of local transportation industries and small-scale, publicly controlled community technology firms that invent hardware and software which are more in keeping with the ongoing needs of the society. Too often the type of scientific and technological innovations which the federal government has encouraged are irrelevant and even counterproductive to the needs of communities and people. (It is also shocking that where once innovations such as work on semi-conductors and micro-processing were encouraged by the federal government such activity is now inhibited by the policies of the Reagan administration. The result is that the United States is ceding another market to the Japanese.)

Full employment at decent pay raises the moral issue of minimum compensation for those not in a position to be entrepreneurs. Minimum decent compensation should be linked to three considerations. One is need, the second is equity and the third is the volatility of the labor market. Minimum compensation should be derived as well from the number of services that are collectively paid for in the society and are, therefore, not directly paid for by the individual. By increasing the amount of free goods in the society compensation could be kept at a relatively stable rate. Where the basic needs of the society can only be purchased through the market and are not the basic minimum of what people are to *have* as a group, a democratic society should expect constantly increasing demands for higher minimum compensation individually or through groups. Even among those employed, the wage disparities are too great and obviously inequitable. The enormous disparity in salary between the President of General Motors and workers on the assembly line is not obviously justified. Where such profound disparities are present, and given the extraordinarily skewed wealth distribution curves, there is little chance that people will accept the fundamental premise of American life, namely, that rich and poor citizens are citizens of the same nation. Beyond setting upward limits on wealth and income through taxation, there are two other ways of assuring that different economic classes of citizens feel themselves to be citizens of the same nation. One is a cost of living escalator in equal dollar terms rather than percentage terms. Such an escalator would be continuous and mandatory for those who live on fixed incomes, are on public welfare, or who are unable to achieve sufficient funds – a minimum wage through the market system (for example, artists, musicians and writers).

The second method is by the federal government taking as its task assuring price stability, to the point of setting prices. This political action would be necessary to guard against inflation as new public investment decisions would be made through an increase in free goods.

Stabilization could be enforced through Congressional juries and other consumer groups subsidized as public watchdogs for price watching.

Under the present American economic system credit controls are lax. In itself this is not bad since production will expand on the basis of trust. However, certain distortions occur when credit cards and demand deposits are used to lend money by banks. Money is no longer a measure. With advertising it encourages consumer spending for items that steer people into the program of impulse buying. Furthermore, money becomes a commodity to be bought and sold. It loses its neutral measuring stick quality and does not help consumers and producers choose between products or understand real rather than inflated wages and prices. To be a "measuring stick" money must remain stable. Stable prices are only partially the reflection of the market. Money retains a stable characteristic where there is a cultural and political underpinning for achieving stable prices.

Free goods

The economic and political assumption behind free goods is that at any one historical moment it is relatively easy to determine people's needs and the order of priorities in which they want to fill them. The further assumption is that the easiest way to fill such needs is to take their costs out of the market system and make them "price free" to the individual. There may be cases where the historical moment does not adequately teach us about real needs. For example, it is taken for granted that defense is a "free good" even though it may have deleterious consequences, or that only one class wants or benefits from an imperial defense with world "responsibilities." As defense costs continue to climb we may find that particular communities might opt for a regional or local system of defense which it would "purchase" from the federal government because it reflects a more economic or humane way. The extraordinary costs of defense will cause taxpayers to weigh the relative merit of, say, an MX missile system to a health care system for the aged – especially as the population grows older. (Some states have already sought a veto on the kinds of weapons to be put in place in their territory. For example, the Mormon church effectively stopped the MX from being built in Utah thus implicitly stating that it wanted to decide what kind of defense it should have or could afford.) There are obvious benefits to rethinking what should be collectively paid for so that a changed list of priorities is determined by the citizens.

After a period of study and national public dialogue it would not be too difficult to imagine that medical care, shelter and education would be "voted" as free goods. They would be removed from the market system in which each person received credits up to a certain amount for their necessities. (This is not to say that a market system would not also operate in the "sale" of these goods and services.) It should be assumed, however, that after a period of time virtually the entire society would avail itself of these necessities as a matter of right. The present distribution systems, namely, hospitals and schools, would be fully utilized. It is obvious that a guarantee of free goods would require careful planning. Furthermore, it could only occur after weighing the difficulties inherent in bringing such a system into the United States. There are problems of a technical nature in initiating such a program too quickly.

In any increase of "free goods" it is necessary to assure that no great economic disruption will occur because of unplanned demand, and therefore shortages in other industries. This can be accomplished by initiating the program of free goods in the first instance in those consumer areas where demand will not greatly increase, as a result of making goods free. If, for example, eye glasses were given away they could be made in a more standardized way without the likelihood of enormously increased demand. The question of shelter, medical care, education, as well as other "free" goods, could be discussed in multiple hook up television debates from neighborhood and factory assembly groups to Congress. Congress's task in this process would be to set broad outlines of investment expenditure into free goods. Technical advice coupled with citizen hearings through the Congressional jury system[26] would need to be held on the likely social effect of a massive increase in free goods, as well as social changes if certain goods were deemed free.

While it cannot be demonstrated conclusively that proper collective attention to improving the material conditions of life will stimulate "good" aspects or "bad" aspects of people, it is demonstrable that the common good cannot be either approached or taken as a serious concern until there is much greater income equality, greater distribution of economic and political power and interruption of those institutional barriers which result in economic maldistribution.

A change in the price and goods system will make possible the path which leads to fulfilling certain of the constituent parts of the common good, fairness, dignity and caring. Where basic necessities are "provided" in the sense that people know that they are to work with others so that the community has these necessities, the emotions of acquisitiveness and envy can be modulated and reduced thereby limiting distortion of individuals or the society as a whole. It is not likely that these aspects will become dominant in man's life as they often do in an oligopoly market system.

There are those who argue with some justification that prices are necessary to determine how much of each good should be produced. Through the use of modelling input-output analysis and the further development of econometrics it should be easier to rationally calculate outputs and needs on the basis of "as if" demand curves and stochastic modelling. Such methods are already used by oligopoly corporations. It should be used by public groups, states, cities and the federal government but with the added dimension of including likely direct and indirect benefits and costs to communities and individuals for the manufacture and consumption of particular goods. As a check, however, against the "as if" method others should now be devised and funded. Research groups with access to information and materials as well as computers should be publicly funded at all levels.

Free goods and need

The issue of free goods goes to the determination of need. Need as a concept grows out of our own historical situation, the economic potentialities and obligations we have beyond ourselves to protect the unborn and replenish the earth. Thus, for example, what may appear at one particular period as a common need the costs of which should be shared, at another historical period may appear to be a product or service which should be borne individually.

When we consider what is to be shared and held in common, we are asking which costs should be borne by the society as a whole. Often certain services are thought of as "free" in the sense that direct payment is not made by the immediate user. In the modern state, for example, the education system in the lower grades is considered a "free system" and the parks likewise fall in that category. But as these "free" services develop under capitalism or state socialism the reason for their being collectively paid for is often tied to ideas and values long since declared questionable or inexplicable. Perhaps after extended public debate it may no longer be quite so obvious why education should be shared by a community as a cost and therefore "free" to the user while food should be paid for by the individual through the marketplace.

This question rings true in a population which grows older and which sees its needs defined in terms other than schooling.[27] It may not be altogether clear why fire protection should be paid by the community and shelter should remain an individual market enterprise. Nor is it quite so obvious that cities, persons and states should embrace the costs of a collective defense through a national state when that "defense" is veiled genocide. Indeed, it may be inexplicable why needs such as transportation, food and health care should be paid for by individuals rather than communities or that "defense" (the hostage system) should be collective.

We should not forget that need has powerful psychological and time-bound attributes that shape an economic definition at any one time. Need is that condition which we seek to escape. But what we seek to escape at one time may be that which we wish to keep at another. Often what we escape multiplies our needs. Because of the limits of resources we should be careful that we do not come to believe that the multiplication of commodities or specializations in knowledge or skill in fact represent what we "need." Nor should one assume that what is put before us in a market is what we "need."

Social security investment trusts

As part of a new economic program for social reconstruction trust funds would have an active role in the daily life of the society. The most important example of a change in role for public investment would be in how social security funds are handled. Presently, the social security fund's operations go unnoticed as investment funds. They are internal government book transactions of the Department of Treasury. Virtually no investments are made by the fund except in government bonds. But there is no reason why the system has to stay passive rather than be used as a public instrument for certain types of reindustrialization and rebuilding of towns, while assuring that a full and decent life is given for those on social security.

A participatory aspect should parallel the new uses of social security. It is possible to transform the recipients and claimants of social security into an active citizenry who participate in decision making, administration and control over the Fund. This would answer an argument of conservatives that an element of liberty is taken away by the social security system. They have argued that people should learn to save for their own futures, but that social security has interrupted the self-help (self-reliance) process. According to conservatives, people in the middle, working and poor classes have the power to insure themselves and to save for a future which they then control. However, there is nothing to suggest that given the distribution of political and economic power any of these classes would be able to "control" their future through individual efforts. While it is better that most people participate in defining the future, because that is how civilizations are nurtured and become great, there is nothing to suggest that this can be accomplished through individual "savings."

In modern Western societies where state bureaucracies and big corporations control large aggregates of wealth and big corporations seek to capture even more capital for their view of investment and control over the future, it seems obvious that out of defense the vast majority of people require associations of their own making which are a collective and communal way of saving and insuring so that they might control their respective futures. Associations of this kind can be forged politically and people who contribute to social security could be made responsible for investment.

The management of social insurance and security funds should be directly reflective of citizens' decisions and participation through committees chosen off jury rolls, or census data. The investment policies of these funds could be organized and elaborated through citizen decision and implementation.[28]

In other words, the second public purpose of a national social insurance fund is that its income through general revenue and payroll taxation should be reinvested in public services, rebuilding cities and public enterprises, either controlled municipally or through other public, voluntary associations. These purposes will require an altering of the current cost financing principles in which revenues "are almost immediately paid out to beneficiaries" so that revenues at best only equal expenditures. It is time for a comprehensive national insurance system to be integral to public economic investment and services.

In various nations pension funds are used for investment purposes. Sweden's National Pension Insurance Fund is the major source of funds for the capital market. "It exceeds the combined funds of the commercial banking sector," according to a study by the Social Security Administration. As of the end of 1978, the Swedish Fund divided its investments: 39 per cent housing, 27 per cent business and 26 per cent government. The investments of the fund are channelled through the banking sector. In Canada excess reserve funds are lent to Canadian provinces and then allocated for the province's respective needs. The provinces use these funds for projects such as schools, hospitals and road construction. The Quebec province invests its "surplus" funds in financial markets. The Quebec fund operates on the principle of "protection of capital, the achievement of a return compatible with the risks taken, and sound diversity in investments," which are meant to promote Quebec's growth. In Switzerland there has been a cutback in public and private investment because of the decline in the size of the fund due to an increase in the number of beneficiaries. However, even with this decline and even though since 1977 the fund is not large enough to finance a single year's expenditure, the fund continues its investments in confederations, cantons, communes, mortgage bond institutions, banks and public undertakings.

These policies are followed throughout the world and are a major source of capital allocation and investment. The question raised by my suggestion is whether investment can be local, public and responsible through participatory boards. The answer is obvious. There is no reason to think that a group of elected citizens chosen for the purpose of investment will be any less responsible than a church's investment committee, the board of AT & T, or for that matter the Secretary of the Treasury. In other words, the US social security system should be changed from a passive and indirect system, which continues the pretension that it does not affect the economic decisions of the society and is apolitical, to one which is not hidden and which becomes a source of well-being that is public, productive and participatory. It should be predicated on local controls and investment procedures for local production purposes which would be part of an overall productive investment program that could be debated and approved through locally elected social insurance planning councils.

This political mechanism is meant to increase public participation and accountability, provide more humane service, and integrate older people into the society more directly by having them perform investment and social services activities in public enterprises that affect not only themselves but the entire character of the community.

The administrative challenge is fashioning a national social insurance fund which will operate openly and democratically in setting standards for public health, pollution control, types of food to be grown, productive processes best able to assure the health of the worker and the community. One way of achieving this end is through public election of social insurance fund board members. Such elections would be held for local, regional and national office. Because of constitutional constraints such elections would be "advisory" although a strong presumption would be carried with election that the president would appoint those elected to the social insurance fund boards. Those eligible to vote would be both beneficiaries and contributors. A regenerated social insurance fund would coordinate its investment activities with local communities in developing and maintaining the cultural, economic and health standards of each community. It would also investigate how to play an active role in communities beyond that of check dispenser.

A social insurance fund creatively managed by donors and beneficiaries could fashion non-monetary activities that would have powerful and positive effects on the lives of communities and fund beneficiaries. For example, in city neighborhoods and small towns the social insurance fund would purchase land, buildings, machinery and tools jointly with old people and the very young. These purchases could be established on a "sound businesslike basis." The public policy purpose is to recapture the skills and the services that are being lost in many communities, and through joint ownership to assure that they will continue in the future.

National social insurance could be organized locally and regionally to ensure community social and economic creativity. Social insurance funds could also be used to establish new marketing, transportation and distribution arrangements which would be shared between the various geographic regions, individual firms and cooperatives. Firms and associations that fall in Zones Three and Four would seek loans from this fund. The social insurance fund could be especially effective as a planning and stabilizing mechanism in small towns and rural areas for it would be authorized by Congress to buy farms outright or act as co-owners with farmers. They would be further authorized to lend funds for equipment and rebuilding. In all such endeavors the Fund is to be endowed with the spirit and technical capability of showing individuals and communities how to develop and maintain humane local cultures. Often this sensibility is already present. It merely needs some catalyst, capital, public acknowledgment and legitimation.

Social security and social insurance cannot be predicated on the idea that values and the stability of the money and banking system are inured from political shocks. Social security funds are required to take into account the problems of fluctuation of monetary worth and continuously assess social programs through public participation, taking as their question whether their programs and allocations increase people's dignity and well-being. Nevertheless, social insurance investments are implicitly linked to a full employment policy. Social investments are also integrally connected to the value of money as a measuring instrument and to the nature and credibility of the national banking system.

Money and banking

The political question to be confronted about money and banking is whether a single national institution such as a central bank or the Federal Reserve should be entrusted with control over the money supply and credit. Conservative economists argue that such a banking institution should be kept separate from democratic government because a banking institution, being elitist, is better able to withstand popular pressures to inflate the currency. I reject this argument for two reasons. There is nothing to suggest that central banks have sounder judgments than popular governments. Institutions, once demystified, often yield the same motives of trust, despair, disinterestedness, envy, as well as purposes shaped by the usual mixture of whim and pressure. But more important than the question of banks as pristine enterprises is that the common good requires that the share of the national income which the society will use collectively will climb substantially rather than shrink. As a result of this collective use, closer coordinative mechanisms have to exist between the financial outlays of the government and the control of money in the long term. This coordinative effort can best be achieved if the federal government sets up banks that have lending power for industrial enterprise.

It should be noted that the largest American lending institutions now invest more abroad than they do in the United States. Thus, it becomes more important than ever for the sake of redevelopment of industry to generate new lending systems through government. For example, a way of strengthening and protecting communities and neighborhoods is to extend the role of credit unions by transforming them into local neighborhood banks for development. Their major task would be to invest in Zone Three and Four, neighborhood services such as laundromats, small shops and publicly controlled companies. Credit unions would become another instrument for regenerating neighborhoods through local investment and initiative. One way to begin this process is through investment of government employees' pensions into public banks which would be lent to new public enterprises and small business at the local level. Pension funds used for this purpose would be secured by federal guarantees, similar to the kind given by the Federal National Mortgage Association and Home Owners Loan Insurance. As it did in the 1930s in agriculture, the federal government should again actively encourage a banking system which would serve low and moderate income families. With the passage of national cooperative bank legislation, a community and public banking system is legitimated. The Consumer Coop Banking Act, signed into law by President Carter, could have been an important step towards the development of a public banking system competitive with the private or commercial interest system although it has not fulfilled this role.

While the Federal Reserve banks appear to be a public banking system the reality is otherwise. It is a banker's club using the federal government's legitimating power. On the other hand, the Cooperative Bank raises the possibility of a new banking system with responsibility to invest directly in local communities and neighborhoods. Such banks could act as agents of local communities and city wards with citizens being elected to investment and loan boards by their neighbors. Those eligible for such election would be people whose names appear on jury lists.

Legislation should now be drafted to change the charters of consumer credit unions so that neighborhood groups and community organizations could apply for aid. Under present custom and rules the credit union operates as a subsidy to the department stores and banks by making available small amounts of money for a short term to individuals who are engulfed in consumer debts. A democratically organized local banking system would generate local capital and savings into projects which were aimed at refurbishing neighborhoods, establishing worker cooperatives, and small businesses. These banks would formulate services that commercial banks have found too risky. For example, in Washington, D.C., the richest bank, Riggs Bank, has given only four loans in a recent four-year period for housing to the poor area of Anacostia.[29]

The community cooperative bank would not operate as "pure money lender." It would mobilize public and private resources inside and outside the community for those projects which met with community approval and where the community offered to participate in its execution. Cooperative banks would operate under locally elected boards much in the manner that local school boards were once elected. The second step in transforming the banking system of the United States would be accomplished by amending charters of state banks, savings and loans, as well as credit unions. Amendment of these charters on the state and federal level should begin with discussions in communities of the new role of banks. After such discussion, publicly elected bank directors would be expected to participate in the presentation of a development plan for local communities which would formulate how local capital, labor and technical skill could be mobilized for local projects. They would be expected to show how the plans and loans they made fit with full employment, continuous education,

179

participation, rebuilding, maintenance, innovation and esthetic decency.

The success of such a banking system is dependent on national approval and federal participation to enable local communities to act according to nationally understood and developed standards. Accordingly, the banking system would be reorganized through a federal comprehensive banking act that would spell out loan procedures to respective enterprises in the four economic zones. Changes in the banking system will occur just because of the crisis that persists in the economy. As savings and loans merge and collapse because of low deposits, legislative and charter restrictions and high interest rates paid in money markets, the tendency will be to see the banking problem as one of banking rather than one of economic and social development. This would be a tragic error.

Under a comprehensive program, the Federal Reserve system would be rechartered as a public banking system, and all banks would be required to join. (Presently, this is not a mandatory requirement. Twenty per cent of its membership have dropped out since 1976 in order to escape credit limitations.) On the national level, Federal Reserve governors would be elected according to particular classes of activity or occupation. This was the original legislative intention of Congress when it first established the Federal Reserve system. In practice, however, only the most powerful corporate units in the nation are represented on the Federal Reserve boards. In virtually all cases "public" participation in the Federal Reserve is represented by a thin elite of university presidents or professors who usually double as consultants to corporations.

Shaky capitalism

While the debate on public or cooperative ownership ebbs and flows with the "crisis of capitalism" as reflected in plant closings, budget deficits, inflation and unemployment figures, it is clear that the long-term prognosis for the conservative brand of capitalism is about as viable as it was in November 1929.

The signs of crisis are clear and they are of the kind which will deepen rather than go away. The first is unstable basic costs in energy which are caused by international corporations and small nation-states. The second is increased competition from European and Japanese corporations in areas once thought of as dominated by the United States. The third is declining skills base among the American population as industry moves away, and finally, wretched judgments made by corporate managers that favor profit over production and in the process are guilty of profound errors in misallocation of capital. To remedy these problems corporations have now turned to the government (the nursing home of capitalism) for aid. Chrysler, International Harvester and Lockheed are all examples of what we can expect from the "smallest of the large corporations" in each oligopoly market. As they mouth the pater nosters of free enterprise there will be a stream of managers and capitalists coming to Washington for public subsidy and they will use the unions and workers as their trump card argument for receiving aid. Other corporations will seek foreign owners, while the "healthy" group of corporations will seek tax incentives, environmental abatement assistance, and other bribes to keep their profits high. How particular corporations attempt to save their profit margins, whether through moving their most expensive labor facilities abroad or through insisting on tax incentives, is not the central issue of our economy. These activities are merely indicative of a far more important issue.

The problem for the political economy, defined as its productive system, is how it is to serve the common good, and how workers will retain their present skills as they add others to their capabilities. The shocking situation in American life is that we have switched from a productive to a consumer society without any increase in the quantum of happiness. The result is that we are losing our collective skills at making and doing things. Emphasis must be placed on production for use and the teaching of skills which match this purpose. But just as the productive system should have this purpose, it must also have the purpose of publicly debating what should be made.

Budgeting and taxation

To the extent possible the government should strive for a balanced budget. But saying this merely opens up the debate of how this is to be obtained. There are several ways. The first is through a progressive federal taxation system which is aimed at paying for all federal programs. This does not mean that people cannot allocate a portion of their taxes to different funds and authorities. It does mean, however, that through progressive taxation the society would distribute to its members what it needs as a whole-living within its income. The unbalanced budget is a mechanism to *hide* costs and to quiet class conflict in the society. And the result is seen in the unwillingness of people to accept the unbalanced budget. We should not forget that the unbalanced budget requires borrowing for programs from the richest groups, corporations and individuals, who instead should be taxed. The US tax expenditure budget is well over $400 billion.

The second way to balance the budget is through budget cutting. The most obvious programs at present are in the military system, in the development of nuclear power and in interest payments on the national debt. The third way for budget balancing is for the federal government to initiate direct public enterprises which, over time, would be surplus producing and would augment the taxation system.

Finally, the entire budget system should be understood in terms of the values we believe are to be reflected in the nation's various programs. Thus, strict budgeting and democratic planning should be integrally related. Since there is a common belief that the federal government has the responsibility for a prosperous economy, it needs more "technical" economic tools and economic data at its disposal. A system of national budgeting needs to be developed which incorporates states and local budgeting. Because of their profound influence on the economy, national and international corporations in the Fortune 500 category should be required to open their books for national budgetary planning purposes, credit and investment allocation. To deal with the budget deficit without surrendering the assumptions of modern capitalist states we may expect that a value added tax will be recommended by "reform minded" economists. This tax will of course penalize those at the lower end of the income scale reinforcing the regressive nature of the tax system and the continuing subsidization by the poor of the rich in terms of social programs, tax expenditures and defense.

Reconstructive economic reforms

The question of tax cuts

A tax cut would not go into the pockets of the citizenry directly or immediately. Instead, it would become part of a national savings bond program in which people would be given bonds in lieu of the tax cut.[30] Taxpayers would be asked to give an equivalent amount to their tax savings from their own pockets for which they would receive interest payments computed at 9 per cent a year. A substantial portion of the funds obtained would be lent through the national cooperative bank which would be earmarked specifically for those areas of the country which had high unemployment rates. Those eligible for the funds would be neighborhoods, cooperatives, unions and cities.

Voting by taxes

In *Being and Doing* I outlined a proposal to increase democratic participation, deliberation and choice by allowing taxpayers within limits to vote their taxes.[31] This proposal would enable citizens to debate, contemplate, and effect the character and cost of their national security and social programs. Citizens could choose directly between Tridents and education, medicine as a "free good" or tax expenditure. Taxpayers should be given the right to assign and divide a sum, up to $150, to the twelve functions of the federal government. Alternatively, the taxpayer would be given the right to pay this $150 either to the city, state, neighborhood or the federal government.

The twelve functions of the federal budget would be explained in some detail with a discussion of the programs that are covered by each one on a special tax form. Giving the individual choice of which political authority to pay taxes is a more efficient and democratic mode than that of the revenue sharing system which Congress has used over the last decade and the Reagan method of block grants to the states. Revenue sharing increases rather than decreases bureaucracy – and further alienates the citizens – while the block grant approach increases local bureaucratic and oligarchic control as it decreases expenditures for the poorest groups within society.

The question of regulation

Conservatives have made a fetish of deregulation. Their argument is that regulation adversely effects the operation of a free market which would otherwise be in equilibrium. We must distinguish two types of regulation. One type concerns the question of the health and safety of the workers in a particular industry and the consumers of the products of that industry. The consumer may of course not realize that he or she is consuming the product or its effects. The other type goes to the competitive situation of the particular firm in which the government seeks to control the economic activity of the firm by limiting access or controlling prices. While these distinctions may overlap in certain cases, it is possible to draw certain general rules. The terrifying nuclear disaster at Three Mile Island in Pennsylvania should cause even the most devoted advocate of free enterprise to champion standards, regulation and stiff penalties for those who work in the nuclear industry whether it is operated by the government or by private industry. This is also true in the case of the drug industry and the asbestos industry. The notion that industrial or consumer health should suffer because of primitive ideas about workers and consumers proceeding at their own risk may have a certain late eighteenth-century charm but it is hardly relevant in the age of meltdowns or industrially and chemically caused cancer. (Some have made the argument that government regulation is "inflationary" and that the consumer is paying a "hidden tax" for regulation. But the reason that most costs are passed on to the consumer is that the firms are not competitive with each other in terms of price, only in advertising.) *It is advertising that is a "hidden" and unnecessary tax which the consumer is paying.*

An argument can be made for relieving smaller firms of the burden of regulation, government forms, etc. where the health and safety of the people are not involved. In the past the health argument was used as a means of controlling industry in favor of the larger firms and against the smaller firms that could not compete. This situation does not have to obtain, however, where there is policing of environmental conditions in smaller firms by the workers themselves who would then be charged with the responsibility of setting health and safety standards for themselves. Worker/union courses of study should be established so that the workers and consumers themselves can be aware of toxic materials and dangerous processes that can be controlled or ended.

Transportation system

For the rest of the twentieth century, the government will have to work with transportation, energy, engineering and agricultural groups to undo what the automotive industry has done to the American transportation system.

The federal government does have the responsibility of facing up to the great transportation corporations and the effects they have had on the physical face of the United States. According to an Institute for Policy Studies Federal Budget study, "The United States presently has one mile of road for every square mile of land area in the nation. We have so many trucks that on any given day, 30 per cent of them haul empty. On any given day 50 per cent of all trucks are idle."[32] Forty per cent of our energy goes directly or indirectly to transportation. It is no wonder that the first five corporations on the Fortune 500 are energy and transportation corporations.

None of this happened without forethought. It should be remembered that the modern American transportation industry is to a large extent the product of the private plans of General Motors. Testimony before the US Senate Antitrust Subcommittee showed how GM destroyed more than 100 electric, rail and electric bus systems in forty-five cities. From New York to Los Angeles, General Motors accomplished its objective: the automobile became king and our cities were conquered. This situation will change by force of circumstances and new felt needs. It is also changing as a result of high interest rates and competition from Japanese auto manufacturers.) Nevertheless, the past choices of a few in transportation have dictated the physical landscape of the nation, its towns and cities.

Design of towns and cities/an ecological economics

A further word needs to be said about the design of towns and cities in relation to political and economic questions. It is not news that in American society banks often dictate the shape of communities, their architectural and esthetic texture while in socialist states or highly centralized bureaucratic ones architectural and artistic designs are shaped by central authority. Both tendencies should be resisted. Architectural and artistic design can be the

184

sum total of local attitudes and beliefs. They reflect the continuously changing participation of people who live, work and directly define their towns and cities as living organisms. While architects and designers should be encouraged to be on their guard against their personal hubris, they should be prepared to confront centralizing authority which may seek to set patterns on cities that have nothing to do with the natural habitat of those settlements or the organizational needs and purposes defined by the people who live and work in the towns and cities.

In a society which pursues the common good there is no meaning to the notion of the "neutral" authority in architecture and design. What has meaning is the need of artists and architects to merge their understanding of how to organize the subjective feelings of others and themselves with the process of openness and to discover ways of using physical space in the public realm in a humane, cooperative and efficient way. The public can use spaces and artistic-architectural design as an objective, "physical" means to exercise their rights and their task of pursuing the common good. Such design would internalize in its process and goals the primary sentiment of caring and personal dignity while building within the physical manifestations of design the attributes of modern democracy, access, participation and deliberating space. Artists and architects would present alternatives and competing physical options which could be debated and judged by the community in terms of their continuing needs. (Our present public architectural method emphasizes remoteness, police security, energy inefficiency and zoo-keeper characteristics.)

The wasteland of gas stations, fast food chains, honky tonks and motels in suburbia and exurbia is a question to be directly addressed by architects, artists, unions, small business firms, social entrepreneurs and local communities. American architectural and artistic design should result in a more vibrant esthetics which is participatory, and reflective of a new democratic spirit. This spirit can take concrete form as it transforms institutional sexism and racism.

Let us take the case of sexism: one important way that sexism is buttressed comes through the physical separation of the household space from the public space and the "economic separation of the domestic economy from the political economy." What is necessary is to make women's lives visible by transforming the definition of public's space. In the early years of the twentieth century, according to Delores Hayden, some women sought exactly this objective. As a result, "they developed new forms of neighborhood organizations including housewives' cooperatives, as well as new building types, including the kitchenless house, the day care center, the public kitchen and community dining club. They also proposed ideal, feminist cities."[33] Such ideas redefined the entire conception of the city, shelter and even the definitions of work for now household labor and child care could easily qualify as labor. The definition of the esthetic and the functional changes once we rearrange our social space.

In considering space and labor we need to reformulate our thinking not only about the design and protection of physical spaces, namely cities, shelters and nation, but the question of importing products that are not from one's own environment. This issue raises the question of tariffs.

Protective tariffs

President Washington enunciated a policy that held that Congress should help the United States be "independent of others for essential, particularly for military, supplies." It should be noted that in the latter case the US has now undertaken co-production of basic weapons systems with the NATO nations, outside of the United States.

Historically, the United States has been split between the manufacturing states that believed they needed government subsidy and relatively high tariffs to keep American industry competitive with European industry. And the other side, represented by the Southern and Southwest states, which believed in low tariffs so that their farmers could sell their produce abroad at low prices, because no or few markets could be found in the United States. This situation has existed in the US in one form or another since 1830. The question is somewhat hidden by special legislation meant to help those who might suffer from international competition and the Tariff Commission which adjusts rates. The present national means of helping American corporations is to allow them, indeed encourage them, to set up export platforms outside the United States and then sell to the US market. This greatly reduces our own technical and industrial base without necessarily helping the nation's people where multinational corporations are located such as Brazil, South Korea or Taiwan. The protective tariff should now take the form of assuring that the skills base of American industrial firms are protected consonant with a review of American industry to assure that it is reasonably competitive with other developed nations. Some have complained that labor costs are too high in the United States and that this is "fast" pricing the US out of the international market. This question can only be answered accurately in terms of each particular industry. Suffice to say that workers, through pensions and other means, hedge in a capitalist framework and correctly so through pay and duplicative jobs in some cases. If workers indeed participated and felt that the firms which they were involved in were directly owned by them (at least to some extent), it is likely that American industrial firms would be more successful in international competition. In this context protective tariffs could be phased out with the consequence that farmers would be aided in their international sales. However, a new vision about rural life is necessary to help farmers and the small town.

Agriculture and rural life

When we lose sight of the land, the food that is grown on it, the animals to be cared for and exchange it for our belief in the type of "progress" which totally centers us in the national state and in absentee corporate entities that control the agricultural markets we lose the richness and the powerful symbolic relationship which human beings need with their limits and their roots. One way that these relationships can be expressed by the nation as a whole is by recognizing the importance of rural communities and agriculture.

The destruction of farm and rural life in America is virtually complete for it has been absorbed into a national and international economy. The attack upon rural life has been relentless and it has come from a fundamental belief that people no longer needed a relationship to the land or to crops, that farming could be mechanized and then automated, that village and town life was "idiotic" and that the efficiency of the farmer was now defined in terms of modern methods of accounting and the use of highly sophisticated farm machinery, fertilizers, pesticides and other chemicals half understood and totally controlled by non-farming people.

Since the Second World War it has been the unwritten assumption of those who have attempted to aid the small farmer and rural America that it is subservient to the cities in terms of cultural potentiality and of being suppliers to the city. This point of view crossed ideological lines for rural America has been understood by liberals and conservatives alike as being an area over which to exercise outside control. Thus, business corporations saw farming as an instrument of their expansion. "Today's agriculture is controlled by such corporate empires as Tenneco, Boeing, Del Monte, Ling-Temco-Vought, General Foods and Cargill."[34]

Former Senator Fred Harris pointed out correctly that "a few corporate directors have more to say about agriculture than do the millions of people who live and work on the farm." Liberals as well have sought market standards of efficiency for farms, attempting to cushion the farmer with price supports but doubting that anything could or should be done to generate or protect a rural culture (really rural cultures) that are not appendages of metropolitan areas with dependence on international capital and government aid to non-indigenous firms.

As a 1938 report on Southern economic conditions made clear:

The paradox of the South is that while it is blessed by Nature with immense wealth, its people as a whole are the poorest in the country. Lacking industries, the South has been forced to trade the richness of its soil, its minerals and forests, and the labor of its people for goods manufactured elsewhere.[35]

The same may be said of the Appalachian region where the natural resources of coal, gas and timberland have not resulted in economic development for the region.

It is not surprising, as Sher has pointed out, that rural America feels colonized directly by corporations, banks and metropolitan areas. They have not been able to develop organically, that is, find internal means and economic strength in their own culture. Food and mineral extraction do not bring adequate prices to the primary producers because of the secondary, dependent role which producers and small towns now have in American society. Those concerned with the common good and social reconstruction should be aware that exploitation of the Third World, at home and abroad, follows the same script, the same attempts at the internationalizing of markets and the rationalizing of top-down control away from the locale by national and international corporate elites.

It is of course true that farmers have sought to find international markets thereby increasing their hostage situation. In the process they became dependent on international markets which are volatile and uncertain. Thus, farmers become prisoners of government policies, the weather of other nations and agricultural production elsewhere. Furthermore, farmers are put into a position of competing against the farmers of other nations who themselves find that they are in an exploited condition. As farmers sought international markets, they became more dependent on the metropole and large-scale capital even as their power as a bloc in Congress declined.

What is the answer to declining towns and the marginalization of farmers? The first consideration is to recognize that rural life is an important set of separate cultures which need to be protected and enabled to reach their own potential. The problem with liberal notions of economic development is that bringing in national or international corporations into the rural area did not result in much local hiring except in relatively unskilled work. Although funds might have been borrowed locally (thereby causing a shortage of capital for small business), larger corporations invariably repatriated their profits outside of the region. Activities of governments have been "sectoral" without attention given to community and regional participation or planning. Little attention is given to finding means of maximizing participation for common plans which could be drawn locally with the understanding that they were to cohere with other local plans. (Again the work of Congressional juries is to present to Congress local community plans which fit the fundamental premise that a new and better balance between urban, small town communities and farms must now be generated throughout the society.) Rather than continue the situation in which people leave rural areas for urban slums, programs for rural development would seek to end the ghost character of our rural areas.

One way is through direct federal investment in economic, social and cultural development of towns where the townspeople, including people in surrounding areas, were able to present a plan for development. Part of the fund could come from social security trust investments (see p. 173 ff.). Special attention would have to be paid to education of the young and to educational programs. Education and schooling would have, as part of their curriculum, rebuilding the locale, studying and learning new modes of conservation. Thus, educators and teachers should formulate curricula which emphasize physical construction, geographic, political and economic conditions. They would explore the importance of rootedness. Vocational education and skills training, even more abstract forms of thought, can and should be related to the project of social reconstruction in rural areas. In this context schools become the local, catalytic force to bring about a new consciousness among young people who would be more likely to stay in the rural area once they had a hand in rebuilding their communities.

In the early 1970s legislation was introduced by former Senator James Abourezk of South Dakota to encourage young people to return to farming. Government would actively purchase farms which it would then resell to young farmers. Abourezk's bill called for a five-year period of working the farm which would be bought from the government for a minimal sum.[36] An amendment to Abourezk's legislation would be to assure that farms were given on a life tenancy basis to small farmers. Farmers' savings in the past were thought to be their equity in land. Under the suggested plan equity could be secured for farmers by direct farm pension grants which would vest upon their retirement.

To stop the continued centralization of farming toward agribusiness (1.9 per cent of all farms accounted for over 33 per cent of total US farm sales), non-farm corporations should be required to divest their farm operations. The purpose is to call a halt to the control of rural areas by banks, energy and real estate corporations.

Finally, the federal government should seek to buy from firms and coops in the third and fourth sector of the economy. The federal government is the single largest buyer of food in the United States. Its procedures should emphasize buying from coops and smaller farms as a means of helping community coops and non-profit stores. Public grants and low-cost loans should be made available to trucking and food enterprises in cities and farms which work out cooperative arrangements between them. This program would do much to generate a balance between urban and rural areas, farmers and workers.

Workers and the common good

There is a serious question as to the nineteenth- and twentieth- century applicability of what production means in relation to our modern methods and needs. Modern technology changes the definition of worker and

189

production. The phrase "dictatorship of the proletariat" does not adequately describe the productive process in the United States, does not comprehend the American commitment to citizenship within the nation or to the importance of celebrating humanism over production and control by the category known as "workers." This recognition, therefore, requires a new emphasis on participation which avoids any roots in authoritarianism or dictatorship. Furthermore, the question of "dictatorship over whom?" needs to be answered. In the early stages of the Russian revolution, actually through the 1930s, proletarian dictatorship meant dictatorship over the peasantry. A working-class dictatorship within the United States would be no better, for it would be aimed at the poor and the helpless.

The participatory system contradicts the dictatorship system for it extends to deliberation for all at all levels of production – experiment, inquiry and human relations. In practical terms dictatorship is changed into cooperation, and discipline arises out of self and group willingness to act or perform rather than prepare or hope for domination from outsiders.

When we think of the common good we look to two groups of people: those on the margins who often present the yearnings of a new society (they have surplus consciousness by which I mean those with the self-controlled time, awareness and capacity to experience through the abstract, concrete problems) but who do not know how to systematize the changes they put forward into practice; and those workers and the marginalized who are the very center of society, who are trapped by it and who cannot easily express their ideals in daily actions. (They have a surplus of pain and anguish.) Workers become alienated where there is no way to deal with these psycho-political sentiments. Often workers are prevented in their occupations from doing craftsmanlike work by virtue of economic constraints laid on them. Thus, plumbers cannot do a first-class job because of the kinds of piping that are made, the types of fixtures that are sold, or the foolish licensing laws they must follow. Engineers cannot design reasonable safety features because they are informed by the administrative hierarchy that the product would be uncompetitive or government administrators are not clear about whom they serve or why, or workers, as the saying goes, feel themselves to be cogs in a machine. They are without knowledge or control over the productive process, because of division of labor and specialization.

Ideas of people in work situations are usually constrained because they are concerned with the sources of livelihood. As Alice and Staughton Lynd said, "Those who are in a position to decide what others will do, when, where, and how they will do it and how much they'll get paid, have tremendous power over the lives of the people who work under them."[37] Women are in an especially precarious position at the work place. They are invariably in the subservient station. According to Wright, Costello, Hachen and Sprague "women are more proletarianized than men." They further point out that

190

while women are underrepresented in all categories of managers and supervisors . . . the most striking underrepresentation of women is in the capitalist class. While women and men are almost equally represented among petty bourgeois producers, among employers of over ten employees, men are nearly 3.4 times overrepresented relative to women.[38]

Those who do the work are thought of as replaceable, and when necessary, as I have said, dead wood. Except in TV commercials for product hustling the entire purpose of the industrial and automated revolution is to hide workers from the public. They are thought of as extraneous, lazy, unnecessary and somehow reprehensible. Who is "responsible" for the work produced and its quality is now lost. The capitalist and the stockholder also escape personal responsibility for the products of the corporation through legal principles of limited liability.

The historical shift to anonymous responsibility may appear to be a progressive advantage to the worker because the owner becomes responsible for defective products or malfunctioning. But another view should be taken into account. The worker cannot be freed from a submissive position unless the public as a whole and the worker as well sees herself or himself as integral to the product and in control of the productive process. Thus, where the individual worker puts his or her imprint on the product in some way, the public should know it. Anonymity should pass away and personal responsibility should emerge. Perhaps one could require a Hippocratic oath for workers who are then held responsible for the worthiness of their products. The common good demands personal responsibility from the individual worker so that trust among consumers can be restored and participating control over the production process can be exercised.

The public would recognize how marginal the capitalist or the stockholder is to the making of the product. Stockholders, of course, do everything in their power to escape personal financial responsibility for the corporation's products through principles of limited legal liability. Obviously I am not saying that the worker must bear the brunt of the malfunctioning of the product except in this sense. A national social and product insurance fund should be established which would sue or be sued in the name of workers or the injured people in the public. Each worker would be insured through a national fund so that defects caused by this or her work would be compensated through the fund. One can imagine different divisions of this fund for each industry. Workers who consistently made bad products would be required to improve or leave their jobs. The fund could subsidize work training programs in worker-run schools. Even in football there is a measure of personal accountability. When a player commits a foul the team is penalized and the infraction is announced publicly by the umpire and the player who committed the infraction is publicly named.

There is of course a serious danger with this approach because it can easily be ripped out of context and made into a regressive social instrument. This would happen if workers were granted public recognition by being encumbered with obligations for the productive process *prior* to the time there is worker-community ownership. Obligations without ownership are exactly the situation in which workers find themselves. And the strategic question of how to arrange obligation and power for workers is utterly dependent on the balance of political forces at any one moment in the society. Workers must begin from the sense of solidarity of class as well as human solidarity. If individual workers lose their identification with this type of solidarity, they will not know who and with whom to bring about the changes which they perceive as necessary to accomplish. Consequently, the worker, by what he or she does, should not be considered as an isolated atom independent of the group. Cultural concentration on individuality may also lead to turning the person into a reified object which is as much for sale as anything that the worker makes. This may be hard to see in mass markets and mass industries where "individuality" is both prized and serves as the mask for the objectification of and thingness of labor.[39]

Nevertheless, there are individualistic occupations that need to be controlled by laws and regulations. The independent truckdriver who is a necessitous and competitive small businessman must increase his speed to shorten the time of his trip. Truckdrivers are pressed to act against laws because the laws and regulations undercut their economic position. Where there is no economic problem for them, it would mean that there would be less reason for them to go faster, or take chances, etc. There is nothing to suggest that truckdrivers fancy themselves as risk-taking heroes acting out of an instinct for adventure and fear of boredom. But these are concerns which could best be decided by truckdrivers and local communities themselves once the "discipline" of economic profit was taken out of the driver's seat and once the truckers were part of an ongoing dialogue for developing a new type of transportation industry. In other words, transportation workers would participate in defining their segment of the common good.

The economic policies that I have outlined in this chapter reflect the idea that the extension of government makes sense only where there is active citizen participation and oversight. As we shall see in Chapter 6 the extension of governmental benefits and democracy also includes the extension of personal rights as a fence of protection for the individual. In economic terms, however, there is no way for the modern state to disaggregate itself from the operations of the economy. To think otherwise is a pipedream.

5
Securing the nation: an alternative foreign and defense policy

Overview

A great nation living through the continuous experiment of democracy is not fenced off from the rest of the world without relevance or relationship to it. Thus, the citizens of a democracy are required to formulate international policies which relate to the needs of the nation and the requirements of a world made up of actors having their own interests, needs and aspirations. Over the course of the last generation the United States has played down its interest in international institutions and activities which would concentrate the nations of the world on solutions for common problems and common needs. While conflict about value is surely present in the world and no amount of emphasis on cooperation will transform that conflict, there are institutions which can be generated, activities undertaken, ideas developed and arrangements made which reflect our awareness that we are part of a humanity which is struggling with problems attendant to liberation, tradition, self-determination and economic sustenance. What I argue in this chapter is that by continuing our own experiment in democracy we will comprehend more clearly what other people are striving for. And by reintroducing into our own policy and fundamental thinking about foreign and national security affairs principles which are not unknown in international affairs we will generate a mutually reinforcing dynamic that could allow nations to turn away from the course of continuous world-wide disasters or international war.

The foreign policy that I describe in this chapter is based on the recognition that new actors in international politics must now appear since states themselves are caught in the vise of military parochialism. These actors will operate transnationally and will seek and offer answers to questions that states are not yet ready to provide.

A foreign policy for a democracy may be thought of in terms of a triad[1] of themes which resonate with each other. They are in my view central to the fashioning of specific international and national security policies.

The first theme of the triad is that there must be more citizen and people action in international and national security affairs. Once we assert that people are the subject actors of modern history they become more than the objects of nations or the nuclear hostages of leaders. They come to articulate human rights against states and rights against war. They organize resistance to madcap schemes of states and participate in the redirection of common purposes. How we as a people, a citizenry, can redirect ourselves to a definition of human rights that protects us and generates greater freedom and security should be the central task of those whose lives are given over to diplomacy, politics and law. They would help us recognize, after they *hear* and *listen* to the problems of modern society, a general principle of distributive defense and security. The Mississippi tenant farmer, a Rockefeller or Scaife, a Kansas schoolteacher, a Detroit auto worker or a Los Angeles communard are all entitled to the same protection. If a particular group is overrepresented in terms of committing us to what should be defended, then the common defense and national security that is embraced retains a skewed, elitist bias. And if defense is related to profit and waste, indeed coincident with it, the *common wealth* of people through their taxes is being used as a subsidy to the few with the state, through its coercive taxing mechanism, acting as the fig leaf for plunder. The second theme of the triad is that a strong UN is a necessary and central organizational social invention which should not be degraded by alliances or groups of nations that scoff at an international social, economic and legal order.[2] A revitalized UN can serve as the authorizer of international action and the way to limit dangerous conflicts of nations. As the third theme, the United States needs to operate out of a fundamental understanding of itself. It must not assert unbridgeable, adversarial status towards any other nations and be "threat-oriented" in its analysis of world affairs. Its leadership should recall the sage advice of George Washington and conduct its day to day relations without passionate attachment to any specific alliance or cabal. American leaders will have to be aware of massive changes from a religious turning in which women seek to redefine the biblical tradition and therefore the world's religions to serious attempts at establishing human communities in space.

Such themes may appear to be irrelevant in a world of nation-states where, at best, sovereigns or governments define their responsibility to their own people, not to others, and where the currency of political leadership is power and force; where nations are bedeviled by modern weapons and alliances that have long since lost their relevance. However, even leaders of nations cannot deny certain facts of interrelationship. Each nation is increasingly dependent on every other nation for satisfying its needs. (The more developed a nation is the more it is dependent on other nations.) Every nation is hostage to the decisions of other nations' military and political leaders. Every part of the globe is a microphone and TV relay station for another culture. Transportation, communications, technological and aesthetic creations fill the world's spaces. In other words, material and spiritual conditions drive every nation and ideology to be part of the same world historical process. Each person and nation seeks subject actor status not to be determined as objects of others, but as subjects with others. This is why a truly international framework must be celebrated rather than savaged, for it speaks to this need by including all the world's people, why hostile military alliances have only pathological relevance, and exhausted ideologies are laughed at, East and West. Nevertheless, certain guides to international relations remain.

It has taken close to five centuries for the world to catch up with the insights of Grotius, namely, that the basic premise of modern international relations and law must be predicated upon the bonds of community and natural law. The law of the universal community of humankind was meant to govern the actions of states. But this law has to be created and forged through the ill-fitting crucible of pluralist ideologies and cultures.

The technological facts of the twentieth century and the horrors of world war as well as regional war, the genocidal nature of governments stricken with misguided purpose or even governments single-mindedly committed to just causes, mandate every nation's populace to demand that governments restrict themselves to universal principles of equity and caring in international relations. As we shall see shortly, such an application is not as pollyanna as one might think.

In the physical sciences it is thought that two seemingly opposite explanations or methods may have the same relevance in bringing about understanding and scientific progress. In this regard the principles of non-intervention, or what George Washington called "no passionate attachments," is a non-contradictory but in fact complementary road to a new international order of peace and equity. If those directly concerned with foreign policy accept the nation-state's limits, then its practitioners must be prepared to foreswear certain types of behavior as violative of international decency and the principles of internal equity and stability within the United States. The three themes I have mentioned contradict the practice of foreign policy as a thin sheath to mask the nuclear sword or an instrument that is to save the United States the trouble of coming to grips either with its internal contradictions, its consuming habits, or its unwillingness to directly defend itself against attack except through nuclear weapons. But having made this argument we must remember the complementary argument and set of principles that go along with it.

If we assert that the common good *must* seek passionate attachments as the means to bond the peoples of the world to one another, but not as masters and slaves or colonizers and colonized, we must now also prescribe a practical international politics in which such a bonding can occur but which takes account of the meaning of Washington's words. The

195

drafters of the UN Charter hoped that it would be the UN organization which would work out in practice the complementary nature of non-intervention and internationalism.

To state their hopes and clasp them to our own bosoms will no doubt bring smiles to the lips of the reader who can immediately detail six instances of UN impotence (as if its impotence is not reflective of the wishes of the Great Powers). But the fastening of legal forms on human activity takes generations. These forms, and the politics attendant to them, tame force and violence through mediation, conciliation or activities which in turn sublimate human tendencies to force and violence. Perhaps at no other time has it been so necessary to build up legal forms or an international need to decrease and end the massive use of violence in international affairs.

There is a spirit reflecting this world need which we find in greater communications, greater trade, and a far greater consciousness of others in vastly different cultures. They are now seen by people as having rights and participatory ones at that – in the project of world civilization. The skeptical reader may rightly ask how we are to know what "world civilization" is calling for. Who keeps that spirit and causes the rest of us to pursue it?[3]

The spirit is there in those qualities and attributes of people, their moral impulse and then in their attenuated form in the frozen aspirations of basic international documents of freedom and justice. They are what some in each generation recognize as being the undiluted underpinning, the *ought*, of what we intend which we reflect first in how we "see" and "listen" to each other and then in the way people seek to come to their individual and collective conscience. This "ought" can be found and made our practice. When we seek the common good we must identify with this impulse even in international affairs by those means which do not threaten, or posture, which do not contradict certain universal moral principles, admittedly diverse in application but more noticed than ever when they are not practiced.[4] In its multifarious struggles the world's human rights movement builds on these universal moral principles, and their presence within us. It develops international solidarity. There are solid reasons for this popular attention.

Prior to modern scientific discovery, our moral ability to identify with the suffering of others was indeed limited, mediated only through the sufferings of a Christ and other prophets. But modern communication has universalized moral struggles. It raises moral sentiment and empathy to a prominent place in international power politics.[5] From the Nuremberg trials forward and in Article I of the UN Charter people have had the chance of becoming the subjects of international affairs. These documents raised people's pain and deprivation to a central concern and with modern communication the conditions for this pain had to be noticed. That is to say, the conditions are now present for the consciousness of passionate attachment to each other, a consciousness that can drive and discipline social institutions and states.

How can the precepts of caring, bonding, and empathy be applied by American policy workers in the harsh world of international politics? The answer to this question is found in the phrase "less is more." In practical terms it means that the American foreign and national security policy is to promote a new international political and economic order by avoiding the creation of insecurities and dependencies in other nations and people. Economic dependency destroys the possibility of self-development or subject-actor status for other nations. (It even adversely affects our own chance at internal, social transformation.)

The American system of dependencies takes different forms. It may be mercantile capitalist as in the case of Puerto Rico. Or it may be military as in the case of Latin America and the Middle East. Military dependency increases local and regional military tensions between historic rivals, as for example, in South Korea. It decreases the possibility of peaceful change internally and invariably builds a national security state whose constituency will only extend to the top 5-10 per cent of the nation in terms of wealth. To maintain power it must guide dissidence and when that fails repression is used. Because of these effects – obviously – American politicians and policy makers should not use armaments as the coin to pledge allegiance among various nations as we did in the former Shah's Iran, having given his government over $20 billion in grants and loans in the last few years of his reign. It is not unlikely that the US will be embroiled in the same set of problems in the Philippines.

American economic power should not be used to distort or control world markets, or otherwise seek to develop or sustain modes of imperial domination, as American policy makers attempted to do at the end of the Second World War and as it does under Reagan with an artificially high value to the dollar. It must not make commitments in defense of particular groups or states through "special relationships" derived from ethnic, class, bureaucratic attachments or ideological fervor. The costs are too great, as the British anti-imperialist Norman Angell pointed out at the beginning of the twentieth century.

These precepts do not have to be written off as a headlong jump into isolation. Rather they are based on the classic definition of internationalism in which an emerging standard of world principle, new and clearly identifiable humane norms, are brought forward and internalized by national groups and national bodies into their respective domestic laws and mores. The identification of one nation with another – especially where agreements are involved – is best mediated through international organizations. Through international organizations a continuous political process would operate to generate and reinforce the most clearly humane ideas in the world consciousness with those ideas becoming the legitimating and reinforcing system within nations.

Humane ideas have a chance in practical terms if the UN and its resolutions are given policy and legal priority in the internal affairs of nations so that they are taken seriously and become the basis of actions of states and their governments in day to day activities. Without sacrificing any of its "vital interests" (which body in our nation should decide the meaning of this mystical phrase?) there is no reason why the United States cannot adopt and champion a foreign policy which accepts most UN resolutions as American policy, and accordingly accepts liberation movements, proposes and accepts plans for world economic development, disarmament and anti-apartheid. Indeed, it should not take too much to show that embedded in these concerns are vital interests of most Americans.[6] And they can be staked out as a system of world law with other states.[7]

The human rights covenants and charter could become the rallying point for rights detailed in that document, but not effected in practice in the United States. In other words, international rules can legitimate domestic behavior of nationals and their willingness or need to confront injustice in their own land. Basic international treaties, the human rights covenants and many of the UN resolutions can give sustenance to groups seeking to secure their rights. In the US, actions around anti-apartheid, disarmament and world economic development by pressure groups would find support for their activities from UN statements, resolutions and rules internalized into American law. For his own reasons President Carter embraced this legitimating process by signing the Covenants on Economic and Social Rights in February 1977 and sending them to the Senate for ratification. Liberals and the left in the United States were unaware of the profound effects these covenants could have had on American politics had the Senate ratified them. The right has understood the power of the human rights covenants in far more realistic terms than either the liberals or the left.

Since the 1950s, conservatives have feared their adoption, and for good reason. The leaders of the conservative movement after the Second World War, Senator Bricker and Senator Taft, were unalterably opposed to the legitimation of international rules that influenced the American social system. Their fear was that the United States would be changed from a republic to a democracy. They feared that American courts and legislatures would use the international rules as the basis of changing American law, property and race relations. Property oriented conservatives believed that this trend would lead to an excitation of the poor classes within the United States, an erosion of sovereignty and the introduction of socialist ideas which would also excite the passions of those who favored or needed domestic civil rights. This "dangerous" process began with a California Court of Appeals case which held against racial discrimination in California land law on the grounds of Article 56 of the UN Charter and that the Charter was self-executing in American law. Conservatives such as Robert Taft, and then John Foster Dulles, were successful in interrupting American interest in the UN and interest in the convenants.[8]

UN delegitimation among the nationalist right has quickened its tempo in the Reagan administration with the scuttling of the law of the sea treaty which attempted to work out certain definitions of common owner trusteeship of the mineral rights in the context of a sovereign state system, the withdrawal from UNESCO on the grounds that it was "politicizing" its studies and the withdrawal of jurisdiction on the Nicaraguan matter from the International Court of Justice. The nationalist right has sought to undercut any international law that is not a clear justification for unilateral action and intervention. This point of view is quite different from that of the conservative, Robert Taft, whose critique of intervention retains a current relevance. It applies whether that intervention is unilateral or multilateral. For example, liberals who champion a pluralistic world civilization can serve a bald colonizing or imperial purpose not too different from the French mission of spreading its culture and class system to Indo-China and parts of Africa, or the Italian fascist movement which sought to bring its "culture" to Ethiopia through military invasion, or the Soviet communist crusade into Afghanistan to save the modernizing attempts of a left cabal. As Hedley Bull has said,

> If a right of intervention is proclaimed for the purpose of enforcing standards of conduct, and yet no consensus exists in the international community governing its use, then the door is open to interventions by particular states using such a right as a pretext, and the principal of territorial sovereignty is placed in jeopardy.[9]

Those seized of the idea of world civilization are prone to practice justice mongering, asserting standards for others but not their own nation. Such triumphalism and asymmetric behavior can best be controlled in the context of a world body where pluralism and divergence as well as a special sensitivity against imperialism and colonization can be found and organized to confront those who would threaten the peace. To their surprise the Soviets found this sentiment operating among nations after their intervention in Afghanistan. It was the world reaction against Soviet intervention in Afghanistan which emboldened the Polish workers to confront the workers' party of Poland and the state apparatus. The Soviets feared the world's collective response to intervention as well as their concern that even the Polish military and the communist party would stand united against Soviet aggression.

There is a second problem that Republican isolationists noted and to which attention must be paid. In each nation, especially representative ones, there are groups that favor one nation or clique over another. Often this favoritism is bureaucratically, ethnically, ideologically or class based. And just as often it is for quite indiscriminate or unfathomable reasons. Thus, in 1985, it is more fashionable in Washington to favor the Chinese over the Soviets as others in another time might favor the Soviets over, say, the Japanese or the Germans. How can such tendencies be overcome? For the US a change will occur as the ethnic demography of our people changes. The US will be less Europe-oriented as Chicano, Black and Third World populations rise in the US. Further, the tendency to identify interests with a narrow-based oligarchy will end as it becomes clear that democracy is more than a form but a process which is fundamentally antagonistic to the national security state.

The core question is what should the role of a Great Power be in international affairs? Ideally each Great Power should play a minimal role outside the United Nations and an exemplary role within the UN. For the United States this requires the exercise of great restraint by refusing to intervene directly or indirectly in the regional or ideological differences of other nations, even where requested, unless there is unanimity in the Security Council.[10]

By sending military assistance to any nation without positive agreement from the UN Security Council or the General Assembly, or to act independently of these bodies, is to continue the deterioration of reasonable world arrangements and increase the likelihood of autarchic policies leading to local, regional or even world war. When nations act unilaterally outside of the UN framework, they destroy the possibility of building a world law system and they fail in working out those joint efforts which are most likely to avoid war and misery.

When a superpower militarily intervenes to protect its international class position and prevents an equitable distribution of the world's resources it flies in the face of the emerging consensus of values which transnational groups, the UN, diplomats, churches and even most political leaders at least rhetorically embrace. The homage which even establishment leaders pay to law and equitable distribution should tell us that there is slumbering within men (to use Kant's phrase) a moral disposition which seeks to foster behavior and institutions that support a moral sensibility. The sentiment of moral invariance, weak as it is, can be strengthened in international affairs through a system of multilayered relationships of a "social," non-official nature. Such relationships deepen interdependence among individuals and groups to the point that they might be able to stalemate action – especially if the media system can be brought to play on the side of such pacific efforts.

The US should lead in fashioning joint projects on a state level which go directly to the source of difference among the antagonistic nations. Thus, for example, in a modest, incremental way the SALT II arrangements between the Soviet Union and the United States were meant to reflect a joint arms planning process in which both sides would play poker with all cards showing. It was an attempt to control excesses in either bureaucracy and in the same process generate confidence-building relationships between the two nations.

Can the arms race and armaments be understood by government officials as a *mutual problem* rather than as instruments for national power and defense? The tragedy for humankind is that the existence of nuclear weapons is mediated through nation-state bureaucracies that see advantages to be gained by the existence of mass murder weapons.

The assumption of armament discussions by states is that the arms race is a problem of political bargaining to maintain advantage. But the reality is that the armaments race is not a problem of bargaining, it is a *joint* problem of humanity beyond the nation-state system. Problems between states are often transitory, as George Kennan has said; the effects of nuclear war are not. Americans especially will have to relinquish certain encrusted assumptions of national security which we have held on the basis of fairly unique experience.

Do Americans find it difficult to understand the horrendous nature of war because American war involvement has been on the soil of others? While Americans have suffered from such wars, it was not until the Indo-China war that the United States as a world power could have been thought to lose from war in either economic or political terms. The United States has not known an invader since the American-British war of 1812. Although the American Civil War was one of the bloodiest in nineteenth-century history it was not caused by "outsiders" but by our own view of interest, purpose and justice. In the aggregate Americans not of Mexican or Indian descent have not had an understanding of the horrors of war brought through invasion on their soil.[11]

In recent times, strategists, American Congressional leaders and presidents have believed that American security and independence from war and invasion is best maintained by denying the three themes of foreign policy I have mentioned. Instead, Americans have fashioned a forward strategy since the Second World War which would continue American luck with war by fighting on someone else's territory. In the rest of this century the forward strategy will be an economically costly one for it asserts a military force "second to none" and a willingness to intervene militarily as we constantly expand our international commitments. For example, it requires the United States to have first strike (objectively unattainable) capacity and nuclear war fighting capability now to be accompanied by a "strategic defense initiative." The US is to be in a position to dictate its terms after a nuclear war exchange or to formulate a preemptive strike through the operation of its satellite surveillance system. Ronald Reagan has committed the United States to a three-ocean navy, the capacity to fight a major nuclear or non-nuclear war in Europe, a half-war in Asia, a rapid war in the Persian Gulf as well as the capacity to intervene in local "brushfire" insurgencies at a time and place of US choosing. To quote one of the guiding lights of the Committee on the Present Danger, a former Undersecretary of State and Reagan's Director of the Arms Control and Disarmament Agency: "We have permanent interests in Western Europe, Canada, Mexico, Japan and other allied nations and many places can become critically important depending upon circumstance."[12] The covert and overt war in Central America which engages Reagan's attention and US military involvement is further evidence of our "permanent interests." Because of our armed might, other nations, to reverse John Kennedy's phrase, are to fear to negotiate and negotiate out of fear. In practice this stance courts continuous engagement in the daily affairs of other nations and societies. Hysterical and unpredictable action also accompanies such a posture causing adversaries and friends alike to fear but not respect us. Nevertheless, this foreign policy is justified as the best means the US has to avert war on its own soil, prosecute its own world interests and set the framework for conflict among others without any cost to the institutions or people of the United States. Such ideas enjoy bipartisan support.

Unfortunately, there are some radical publicists and liberal political leaders who in their own way hold to this triumphal position. They believe, as did Woodrow Wilson, that the salvation for the United States, in the sense of avoiding deep conflicts at home, is found by making the entire world "safe" for American democracy. As Congressman Ron Dellums has put it, "If one person is not free, then no one is free." Those who fly this banner believe that the United States has a purchase on goodness and justice which it is required to press on the rest of the world. President Kennedy in his foreign and national security policy represented both of these strands of triumphalism. They are now stitched together by missiles, nuclear weapons as well as idealistic hopes (some would say pretension). American clients and allies are to fit under a nuclear umbrella. (Of course a number of other nations want their own umbrellas.) The Soviet Union has had its own version of ideological triumphalism which addresses the world with nuclear destruction, communist homilectics and forward defense.[13]

The modern system of great power security is tainted with fatal flaws and contradictions. It fails on moral, political and security grounds for it assumes that genocide of one's own population and that of others is a viable military strategy and "defense" – a principle of government which defies all logic and politics. It also directly contradicts the statements, resolutions, charter of the UN and the covenants against genocide. Second, it assumes that one's own population, as well as that of other nations, surrenders its right and power to say "no" to an irrational system of defense. This cannot be the path which world civilization seeks to travel as the preferred road, for that road leads only to the world of armed camps and militarism. Third, it leads to world defense budgets of $900 billion a year with the correlative need to silence internal voices who press an alternative political view.

General Maxwell Taylor understood this when he called for repression of an American minority which opposes the reinvigoration of the national security state. How ironic it is that at the beginning of the twentieth century it was the anti-militarist view that was the dominant strand of American statecraft. In 1913 William Jennings Bryan, then Secretary of State, formulated treaties which employed conciliation as the prime method of resolving disputes. After the First World War Secretary of State Francis Kellog followed Bryan's lead by pressing for the position of outlawing war, seeing preparation for it and war making as antithetical to the interests of humanity or the march of world progress based on reason.

In 1938, before the Second World War, President Roosevelt pointed out the fallacy of the militarist vision. "You cannot organize civilization around the core of militarism and at the same time expect reason to control human destiny."[14] Roosevelt's argument before the Second World War became even more compelling after the devastation of the Second World War and the invention of nuclear missiles. Nevertheless, when we preach against or prove by reason and ethics that imperialism, triumphalism and nuclear war preparation are not legitimate modes of defense, we are left with the painful fact that no major world power is prepared to follow alternatives which flatly contradict irrationality and madness in international affairs.

Admittedly the question of alternative diplomatic strategies has become more complex, even more bedevilling since the end of the Indo-China war for it is obvious to everyone that no nation or ideology is free of the type of irrationality which would set civilization towards a regressive course. Those who believed that the world could be divided neatly along bipolar lines have been rudely awakened by the independent moves of nation-states in recent years as well as other international actors, namely, churches, multinational corporations and Islamic movements. States professing socialism now stand in confrontation with one another and those analysts, notably Hans Morgenthau, who believed that interests of states do not shift with ideological changes have proved (at least for this period) to be more accurate than those who believed that, for example, China and the Soviet Union were as one because they flew the flag of socialism. (Yet, it may still be that China, the Soviet Union and Japan will forge closer ties along the lines of "peaceful co-existence.")

I am not aware of any Western analyst or leader in world politics who predicted that the antagonistic conflict between, say, the Khmer Rouge and the Vietnamese would have occurred with such virulence at the end of the American withdrawal from Indo-China. Nor are there many analysts of world affairs who would have predicted the resurgence of the Catholic Church as an important political instrument in psychologically reintegrating Eastern Europe with the Western nations as a result of the election of a Polish pope. Nor would many American analysts have guessed at the development in Western Europe around social democracy and later the legitimation of Eurocommunism. Nor would any but the most zealous advocates have predicted success for the liberation struggles – as in Nicaragua – which were waged with the support no less than some segments of the Catholic Church in Latin America, or a successful workers' strike in Poland which brought down the Polish government thereby forcing the communist party to cede governmental power to the military for the purpose of keeping some semblance of control.

These very shifts, changes and "surprises" can cause us to act in one of three ways: to allow such changes to occur, realizing that our capacity for controlling historical forces is limited; to run on the nationalist track which would place great emphasis on armaments for symbolic as well as war fighting purposes (Weinberger and Reagan); or to realize the destructive course American national security has pursued over a generation and to change the values and assumptions of the American relationship to the world along the lines of the three themes I suggested. This latter course will require changing the mission of the American military who since 1940 have been given world-wide responsibilities and tasks by civilians which are justified as defense. The changes in military missions abroad also reflect a need to secure military support or neutrality for major political changes in the United States. To change the assumption of the military and national security officers of the American state at a time when their power approaches that of a military oligarchy is no small feat. And the changes in attitude there are reflective of events outside of their own military culture.

. In 1977, over lunch in the dining room of the Joint Chiefs of Staff, I asked a senior general whether if a movement or party gained wide support for a program of democratic reconstruction, the military leadership would attempt to stop such a movement by entering into politics directly as the instrument of the right. He said that attitudes had changed in the military and that a number of young generals were far less enamored of an anti-left position since the Indo-China war. According to him, the American military is "constitutional" in that it would not intervene in American politics against such a movement. It was above politics. He also pointed out that the military around the world has greatly changed, using the example of Portugal where officers themselves had turned to the left. This conversation took place at the beginning of Carter's term when the military was still adjusting to its defeat in Vietnam.

Within four years it found itself to be the object of amorous affections from the right. On its own the military intensively organized politically in electoral campaigns. One example is in the state of Virginia where no candidate can be elected without the direct support or neutrality of a well-organized retired officers corps. Rightist tendencies notwithstanding, the military has undergone substantial changes in the last fifteen years. The commanders at the highest level are primarily bureaucratic technicians who are at home in seminar and situation rooms, and whose innate conservatism is disturbed by sabre-rattling or "off the wall" statements by right-wing

204

politicians or junior officers.

Whether officers on active duty will in the future attempt to stop a program of social and international reconstruction depends on the meaning of the military leadership's phrase "above politics." Morris Janowitz pointed out that to be above politics in authoritarian societies meant that the military favored the status quo.[15] In our society he thought that it meant not to be overtly involved in political parties or partisanship. Of course one could say that even most big businessmen are "non-partisan" for they see the political parties as subservient to their economic purpose. They identify civilian control over the military as big business control. Generals and admirals are to pay obeisance to the pecking order.

Until the late 1970s retired officers faded very quickly once they were out of power, melding into such groups as the American Security Council and finding institutional jobs with great corporations. Some general officers continued government service as police or social welfare controllers in local bureaucracies. The military officer's cast of mind is usually anti-political and often moves to principles of obedience and authority. Their attitudes toward business are often tinged with class doubts since those who are not sons of generals are usually from the lower middle class. They see capitalists as primarily interested in personal financial gain and patriotism second.[16] The international investment speculations of large banks and corporations against the dollar would seem to support their view. Nevertheless, military leadership is committed to constantly expanding defense budgets. If citizens committed to the common good attack these budgets, and successfully organize against them *without changing* the imperial mission of the military, a movement for social reconstruction can be sure that it will earn the enmity of the military leadership.[17]

The military in American life is not an independent variable acting in the political sphere according to its own values. To be an element in stopping a shift to democracy it would have to be seduced and captured by the right and then used by it. The New Right would have to confront their own conservative allies, the culture of individuality and democracy which has emerged over this generation as well as make common cause with the military. The military leadership would have to love its imperial missions, be enamored of fighting aggressive war and reflect a revanchist streak. This may happen although even under Reagan these arrangements and connections have not been made. The military retains a cautious attitude and is far less bellicose than Reagan's civilian ideologues. One reason is the military's awareness of objective constraints. The sheer costs of carrying out the military's hopelessly gargantuan imperial mission, the possibility of internal instability (riots, unemployment, and inflation), as well as a new economic competition between the allies could enable the program of reconstruction to receive a fair hearing from many retired and active military even during a period of right resurgence.

This hearing might fall on receptive ears because the enlisted armed forces are predominantly working class. Even within the National Security State the officer class remains a dependent variable, reluctant to undertake direct political actions to undercut the usual play of politics. But one should not be overly optimistic. Recent events show that where the question of legitimacy is involved the American military will not shrink from taking an activist role in determining outcomes. This is surely the lesson of the Watergate controversy where General Haig, on advice from the Joint Chiefs and Secretary of Defense, pressed President Nixon to resign rather than face impeachment. The American military has been caught in the rhetoric of democracy. They are aware of the volatility of American politics and of the acceptance by Americans of at least the rhetoric of democratic principles as part of their political covenant with each other.

There is another matter which commands realism about our present "perplexing" situation and which must be overcome. There is no agreement in practice that the arms race is an evil, or that having nuclear weapons is an evil no matter the number of times statesmen say so, or United Nations resolutions declaim it. In idealistic terms the battle against nuclear weapons and the arms race was won by the survivors and dead of Hiroshima and Nagasaki. It would take no Clarence Darrow to argue successfully before a jury of world opinion that the employment of nuclear weapons in a war violates the Charter of Nuremberg which states that mass bombing against innocent populations is a war crime, or that counterforce strategy falls within the context of planning and preparation for aggressive war. Yet in terms of military reality nothing could be further from the consciousness of leaders and military officers, including those who profess socialism.

The reason for this is not that there is anything inherently evil in human nature or inevitable in history. It is that people will hug old structures and reassert their old ways because there are no others, no ways prepared that are practical, that are alternatives which assert the power of people doing things in concert once they learn again that they know how to do things. As I have suggested elsewhere, ideas precede practice. They allow us to open the window to air out social structures that are wormy or outmoded. Surely there is no area of public life where this has more truth than in national security: a field of activity which creates greater insecurity and hardship by the assumptions and practice of its practitioners.

There are clear alternatives and they involve our attitudes to the international economic order as well as the political order. What follows is based on the themes of national self-restraint, realization that equity, dignity and wisdom do not stop at the shores of California and New York, greater involvement and use of international organization to replace alliance systems, greater security through disarmament and the realization that interests and needs shift. No nation is an implacable enemy or friend through eternity. Yet all must find a way together to build a new international political order.

206

US national security and world arms limitation

The United States has made a number of serious national security blunders since the Second World War. It is merely enough to see how they revolve around armaments and the governing view of their importance in world affairs.[18]

It is true that these national security blunders have cost American society dearly. And the likelihood is that if we continue to accept those blunders as successes and the assumptions that led to those blunders we may be sure that the United States will decline precipitously as a nation and miss the chance of building a very great civilization. Let me just mention those errors and blunders.

The first was the use of the atomic bomb. Whether it was dropped to scare the Soviets or to keep them from being a full partner in Asia is beside the point.[19] The way it was used opened up a period of fear and madness in policy making in which all nations are now caught and no national leadership has recovered.

The second error concerned manipulating and misusing the UN once the Cold War began.[20] This meant that there was no effective international organization in which nations would be able to relate law, power and politics in such a manner as to control the irrationality of the world's leaders. Downgrading the Security Council by American leaders was related to the belief that the United States could act as the sole arbiter through its military power.

The third error related to the US intervention in Korea. This war was justified on the grounds that the Soviets ordered the invasion of North Korea into South Korea. There is almost no credible evidence that supports this view.[21] The American involvement in Korea was used as an occasion to increase the American commitment to Western Europe in the form of NATO. After a quarter of a million US casualties, and 50,000 American deaths in Korea, including a needless war with China, the United States found itself committed to a continuous military involvement in Asia through war and alliance. It is not surprising that military casualties create interests and commitments. It also stimulated McCarthyism at home.

The next blunder related to the military buildup for the protection and patrolling of Western Europe.[22] The "protection," while incredibly costly to the United States, was of minimal value to it. Its major purpose was political, namely, the control over West Germany which became the strongest power in Europe, save the Soviet Union, by not building up its own military. The fact was that the unwillingness on the part of the United States and the Soviet Union to find a formula to end the Second World War around Germany caused the military buildup in NATO. The US presence in Europe has cost over a trillion dollars since the end of the Second World War. It should be noted that the GNP of the West European nations is greater than that of the United States. The people of Western and Eastern Europe would like to transcend the military bloc systems. But they are stymied by lack of will and vision.

The next error of American national security policy makers was the decision to make the hydrogen bomb. This decision, pressed so avidly by a handful of scientists and the military, created a weapon of such mass destruction as to destroy any meaning of defense, any meaning of morality in the use of armaments, and any notion of prudence in relation to arms production. The United States, as Herbert York and Jerome Wiesner have pointed out, ran an arms race with itself in the nuclear field and in weapons launchers well into the 1970s.[23] Throughout the Cold War negotiations could have led to interrupting, or at least slowing, the direction of the arms race. But each step of the way the decision to do so was interrupted, or sabotaged. Thus, for example, Harold Stassen in the 1950s worked out an arrangement with Valerian Zorin for missile and arms reduction in Europe. This was sabotaged by John Foster Dulles who believed in the importance of NATO and believed that the American military, technological capability could force the Soviets to surrender.[24] What it meant to surrender no one quite knew.

Another blunder was the Cuban missile crisis for it caused Americans and especially the military to believe that the US military was invincible, that the Soviets would stay only in their own sphere of influence, that the United States would be able to do with force what it proved unable to do such as fighting a land war in Asia. The missile crisis has had the most profound effects on policy making and most importantly made clear that the entire world was hostage to the whims and transient interests of a few.[25] They could decide whether the world would be or be nothing.

The Vietnam war was the next blunder. It related to the American willingness to take on, first with some hesitation and then with alacrity, the French sphere of influence. The result was a civil "war" conflict within the United States of great magnitude and the loss of the American military in a war which did not have to be. The ideas of Robert McNamara and Maxwell Taylor – to be able to fight brushfire wars and strategic nuclear wars simultaneously – were the doctrinal basis for the American tragedy in Vietnam.[26]

These failings are the results of the refusal to generate a policy of realism, that is, one which starts from the premise that ends can be achieved in international politics which serve a common good if judgment is used and if experiences are used as the basis to discern meaning, pattern and new directions. Each of these errors was taken by a relatively small number of policy makers, often in secret and without wide-ranging support. They were, for all practical purposes, oligarchic decisions, or decisions where the few coopted the institutional leaders of the Republic, the members of the

House and Senate. In no case were these decisions taken democratically. When the citizenry became aware of them, and their costs, as in Vietnam, they rebelled. As President Reagan discovered with regard to his Central American military policies, to keep the involvement of Congress is to open one's security policies to blocking. It seems that there is a clear antagonism between Republic constitutional forms and the use of the American military in continuous war.

For a nation seeking the common good through democracy, foreign policy begins from the assumption that the real interests which divide the United States, especially the American people, from other nations and peoples cannot be resolved through war or preparation for it. It should be clear to anyone who cares to look that the present arms policy will serve only as the means to develop a state of military oligarchy.

Since the agreement in 1963 which banned nuclear tests in the atmosphere, arms control and arms discussions have been fragmented to the point that the people of the various nations, and especially Americans, cannot follow the growth of the weapons system and the commitments which all nations are making to weapons and war. No country appears to have an overall disarmament strategy although the Great Powers follow a public propaganda campaign around disarmament. Discussions are meant to give the appearance of real caring for arms control or disarmament. In fact these activities are for the most part symbolic. No nation or group of nations, no national leaders, seek the fullness of vision which would strive for what is so patently necessary: namely a world security arrangement.

Because there is no alternative vision and no will on the part of the Great Powers to press for that vision no nation appears willing to accept armament reduction because military strategists and political leaders assume that any change undercuts their respective arsenal, their interests or strategic possibilities for the future. No nation which feels itself ahead militarily will cut back unless there is enormous internal and international pressure to do so. There is little likelihood that nuclear weapons proliferation will be interrupted unless the Great Powers begin their own independent process of nuclear disarmament.

The problem of nuclear proliferation is of course not only a problem between nations but *within* nations as well. It becomes that much more serious with every passing day. The US manufactures ten nuclear weapons per day. As of 1985 the United States had over 30,000 nuclear weapons. We may assume that those who manage the Soviet arsenal are also expanding the size of their armamentarium. It is foolish to think that revolutions or civil wars can never occur in nations that have nuclear weapons. After all, all of them have had such conflicts in their past.

Nevertheless, no nation will foreswear nuclear weapons unless the context for them has changed and their value is diminished and ended in the power politics game. To accomplish this objective it is necessary to change the framework in which nuclear weapons and launchers are considered by states. The only way to change the framework of defense which the military, national security advisors and defense industrialists champion is through popular direct action. Thus, for example, the nuclear freeze movement in the United States penetrated the concrete doors of the Pentagon and the White House because it included popular action at the local level, involving city councils, and a substantial number in Congress. But the freeze movement and any citizen action must now go much further. It cannot depend on the military and the national security managers to devise programs of disarmament. Their vested interests are too great. While they are important to bring along as a constituency they cannot be the engines that fuel the ship of state to safe harbors. Thus, out of self-defense, the citizens movements must put forward proposals on a world-wide scale. They must develop world security plans which are then pressed by demonstrations and then through governments at the state, local and federal level within the United States and elsewhere. Perhaps other nations such as Denmark and Norway will take the leadership within the General Assembly in pressing for a world security arrangement. If this occurred and it was passed in the General Assembly as a comprehensive plan and charter on disarmament and security, this program/charter would become the document to organize around locally, through state legislatures, cities and town councils. If carefully drawn, these resolutions might even be translated into statute law. What we might find is that local law, buttressed by international law would be used to break the arms race system just as federal law was used to break local segregation practices in the 1960s. Practical steps toward a security system can only be taken where there is a consciousness among organized groups in major arms spending nations that the cause of ending the arms system is at least as important as ending slavery was to the nineteenth-century abolitionists.

We will find that there are two groups who must work together to end the arms system. The first group we may refer to as the abolitionists. They take the view that the use, and preparation for use, of nuclear weapons, and other weapons of mass destruction is a war crime. Therefore, to contemplate their use at any time is to mistake crime for defense. The second group, the prudentialists, begin from the perception that our technologically sophisticated weapons systems are almost unmanageable and incomprehensible to most of our military, and that the military's weapons are not proportional to the objectives which a people may wish to achieve or defeat. These two groups must now seek a new framework for disarmament and security. This can be done through a series of continued discussions on world security and disarmament which indeed could be conducted excluding those who use arms control as a cover for arming (see pp. 219–54).

As part of their purpose prudentialists and abolitionists could work together to challenge defense leaderships in local city councils and state assemblies to explain how the present or future defense plans of the US are meant to defend world civilization and any geographic area of the United States from external attack. They would challenge government to work out new modes of disarmament and security so that the bureaucracy itself would shift its concerns and gaze.

A proposal and a policy

In the last twenty years certain proposals for comprehensive disarmament were put forward within the Arms Control and Disarmament Agency and by members of the Kennedy White House Staff, this author included. The most ingenious proposal was advanced by Louis Sohn in which disarmament by the United States and the Soviet Union was to proceed by geographic zones of each nation.[27] And each nation would inspect only the particular zone under consideration. This proposal continues to have merit with some variations. Any proposal of a comprehensive sort must combine elements of graduated, reciprocal reduction of weapons and abort practices which are most threatening to adversaries. Thus, to fulfill this condition, in the first stage of an agreement preliminary to any inspection, the two superpowers would independently remove weapons from their respective arsenals that they intended to junk.

Each nation would perform such disarmament independently except that the right of citizens' inspection from one's respective nationals is to be granted and guaranteed through the UN, unless the "host" nation preferred outside inspection either from the UN or an agreed-upon third party. During this preliminary stage, joint arrangements would be made so that inspection techniques and collateral forms of inspection through technical means would be operated as part of an international satellite system operated in the UN organizational family. The likely reason for superpowers junking particular weapons is either beause they are thought to be outmoded, pressure from their own people because of economic, legal or moral reasons, or a realization that a new form of security must be found.

These reasons would operate within the United States. The American military would be challenged to formulate a non-mass destruction defense system which was in direct defense of the United States. It would reject the use and buildup of weapons of mass destruction under the Nuremberg and UN Charter principles because they violate the laws of war.

Presently, the military and technological development of modern statecraft does not take into account the legal nature of the weaponry designed and produced. But nations should and there is enough law wrought through the crucible of war and international politics to make such statements more than the pollyanna pretensions of utopians. Thus, under

211

the language of the Charter of Nuremberg, strategies such as counterforce, or so-called second strike deterrent strategies aimed at population centers, could be classified either as crimes against humanity or crimes against peace.[28] Individuals and groups who involve themselves in the planning, production and implementation of such strategies are in mortal danger of being categorized as criminal *per se* under the framework of the Nuremberg Charter.

As crucial as the question of what a legal and moral national defense is, is the question of what is to be defended, in what manner and by whom. Less than one-third of the defense budget can be thought to relate to the defense of the United States. The rest of the budget may be assigned, as Earl Ravenal has pointed out, to the defense of Europe, Asia and Latin America.[29] Our defense and hardware system is linked conceptually to our alliance system which supposedly is the seamless, circular web of defense for "the free world." In this seamless web one segment justifies another segment. In practical terms this means that the national security bureaucracy obtains bases and alliances for the defense of our weapons and surveillance system, which in turn are needed for the defense of our bases and alliances. The cost of this mode of defense in financial year 1986 is $330 billion of which $100 billion could be pegged for US defense. If the United States changed its nationalist strategy to one of world security it would be in a position to reduce its defense budget by one half in the very earliest stages of the new security process. Indeed, it would be able to free many more resources for civilian·reconstruction than the Soviet Union just because the Soviet Union is land-locked and fears invasion through Siberia and Europe.

In the second stage of the process each antagonist would have the right to choose from its adversary those weapons which it thought of as a threat to its security. Where the adversary refused to dismantle weapons chosen by the opponent the process would be interrupted but it would not end. Each side would then choose a second, third or fourth choice for what is to be junked. Alongside this process the UN would encourage the establishment of a self-executing organization like Amnesty International. It would initiate an international registry of scientists and others involved in weapons and arms research who would sign an international public oath that the terms of the security arrangement would be carried out and that they would participate in no research work which would contradict the spirit or letter of a world-wide military security agreement.

In the third year of the security arrangement more general disarmament negotiations would be conducted including establishment of a fifteen-year time limit for the reduction and abolition of weapons of mass destruction. This part of the arrangement is to be premised on an agreement in the military committee of the UN on the contours and operations of a new world-wide security arrangement. Past comprehensive plans for disarmament have called for the staged and balanced reduction of armaments in which the Great Powers would be the first to reduce their forces in the context of a world-wide disarmament arrangement. Less heavily armed nations would then be more likely to follow suit and accept the trend including inspection provisions. A major reason for their likely acquiescence will be that armaments sytems are dependent on the technology, spare parts and contractual obligations made with the superpowers. (The longer it takes for the superpowers to come to grips with signing a comprehensive security arrangement, the less validity this reasoning has.) Weapons would not be bought or sold for export; mutual non-aggression arrangements would be made and conciliation teams in the context of the security arrangement would be established.

Since the initiation of the SALT discussions in the 1960s the assumption among the nations of the world, and especially the United States and the Soviet Union, has been that because the two superpowers were the driving engines of the arms race they had to compose their differences on armaments. Both sides have refused to have the "company" of other nations. This is an error for it does not take account of the political and security realities. That is to say, other nations will be damaged or grievously destroyed in any nuclear exchange between the United States or the Soviet Union. Furthermore, other nations are involved in the production, storing, or basing of weapons and launchers. Thus, it is necessary to move beyond the bilateral negotiation if each event and negotiation is to be used as the cumulative means to build international order. This is not likely to happen if the discussions remain bilateral. The following changes are called for in disarmament negotiations:

(1) The SALT agreement provides for a joint commission to review complaints of both sides. This commission merely represents both parties. Instead of this arrangement there should be an international commission that is an agent of the International Court of Justice which would sit continuously as judge and mediator on compliance to a world security for any more limited arms control arrangements.

(2) A special agency of the UN Security Council should be organized for the purpose of studying movements of troops, missiles, nuclear chemical and bacteriological production. This agency would report its findings to the International Court, the Security Council and the UN General Assembly with suggestions about any remedial action which should be taken. For example, a range of penalties must be devised beyond that of merely breaching treaties. Such notions from the domestic law such as surety bonds which are forfeited for repeated violations or trade embargoes are examples of pressure short of treaty abrogation.

(3) The technological aspects of the arms race and the creation of a wide variety of weaponry make ascertaining the commensurability of "rival" weapons systems virtually impossible among the Great Powers. This is why a combination zonal/fear approach is necessary. Under these terms each

213

nation would be divided into a security geographic grid. Each side would choose weapons which, within particular regions, the opposing side feared the most.

If the zonal approach to disarmament were pursued between the United States and the Soviet Union a prudent national security policy would encourage cities and regions to forge international compacts of peace and arms limitations within the context of a world security arrangement, or barring the conclusion of such a pact one could imagine bilateral arrangements with different areas and zones *within* each nation. In practice this policy would mean a virtual 180 degree turn from our present direction. In the American case it would mean that locales and states would have a part to play in the negotiation of disarmament. Compacts would be presented to Congress for ratification, thus ensuring their constitutionality and empowering the states and regions of the US to unhook from the arms race.[30]

It will be argued by some that "decentralization" in foreign and national security policy as well as efforts at democratizing the issues involved will have a reverse effect than that which is intended. Cities and local populations might seek to acquire their own nuclear weapons and missiles. Obviously, if this were to occur the likelihood is that such proliferation would *increase tensions* in the world. But the weaponry – to the extent it is now – would continue to be controlled nationally.

In the United States a revised national defense structure should be erected on four participatory mechanisms, *the conclusion of an international security arrangement notwithstanding*: (a) a participatory tax system in which each taxpayer within limits would "vote" his or her preference according to the function of the government; (b) a defense banking system in which regions of the US would be allocated weaponry and armed force for defense of themselves on the basis of regional defense plans but would remain under centralized control; (c) an agreement on a regular basis between state governors and regional planners as to the needs and costs of defense. These arrangements would be carried out as a corollary to international negotiations to end the arms race with the understanding that all defense activities at the local and national level would be performed in the context of international security and disarmament agreements once such agreements are signed; (d) passage of a constitutional amendment that no American government can surrender to another nation which invades the United States. *And that any government which does so is traitorous.*

It is of some importance to spell out this last point. A constitutional amendment on the common defense would make it clear that no other nation could occupy the United States. In practical terms this amendment would be understood as part of a solemn declaration of continuous guerilla war against invading forces, its occupiers and collaborators. Such a provision would be one that should be incorporated into international agreements, for example, the suggested international security agreement and the UN Charter itself.

A similar provision is found in the Yugoslavian constitution where it is meant to secure the Yugoslavian people from any invader or collaborator. If such a provision were enacted into American law and would be the new pledge of allegiance in the schools, Americans would discover that they had significant and *direct* responsibility to resist invasion or collaboration with enemies if war occurred on US soil.[31] It would help us resist the antiseptic system of believing that wars could be exclusively fought on the soil of other nations. Although the strategy I suggest is a defensive one it is totally unyielding in nature. Its effectiveness is greatest in the context of an international security arrangement where the assumption of international politics switches from aggressive action in military affairs to a clearly defined strategy of self-defense. It specifically means that no nation can be a world military power except in the context of internationally accepted security arrangements.

When we consider the physical security of the society and the forward strategy the US has pursued we should recognize an astonishing fact. The more funds that are spent on the military the less secure as a nation Americans become. And correlatively, the more the United States participates in the arms race, or leads it, the more other nations find it necessary to do the same. There is general agreement between left and right opinion in the United States that the Soviets are developing an extraordinarily large arsenal of nuclear weapons, missiles, submarines and armed forces which, thanks to its intervention in Afghanistan, is shown to be as aggressive and beyond any "rational" measure of defense. The Soviets conclude that the entire system of forces which the United States has fashioned is *not* geared to defense but to imperial intervention, first nuclear strike, or a second strike capable of destroying the cities of opponents as well as remaining military targets.[32] But neither antagonist feels secure. The present American security system downplays the need for a democratically oriented armed force, and therefore armed forces are inherently less useful than we think – as Vietnam showed.

The history of twentieth-century armed struggle suggests that to be successful, armed forces have to be relatively democratic and participatory, reflecting a cooperative spirit and the group feeling of having been wronged. As Western powers have learned, the technology which combatants employ is secondary in importance to the spiritual, daily, democratic practice that they follow. The success of the formidable Israeli forces is related primarily to their democratic spirit and only secondarily to technology. The American defense system confuses means/ends purposes and overcommits the US to undertaking tasks that are not in the interests of the American people and cannot pass the muster of a war declaration by Congress.

215

Securing the nation

By transforming the emphasis of American war making from weapons technology to our common defense I mean to recognize the entitlement of the armed forces in the context of international legal standards. The military's task becomes more prudent and less pathological. It is to provide protection for the land, people and institutions within the US as it passes through major social changes. The military's economic entitlement is decent living conditions, civil liberties, pay for the non-officer class at the level of skilled workers *with participatory rights*. Consequently, a democratic reconstruction in defense will mean the extension of labor unions to include the armed forces necessitating a revision of the Thurmond law which prohibits the labor movement from organizing a union in the armed forces.[33] As part of their negotiated labor position members of the armed services would underscore their allegiance to the judgments at Nuremberg, their refusal to use nuclear weapons (they open officers and armed forces personnel to charges of genocide and war crimes under international law and the 1977 Geneava protocols, initiated by the US and 115 other nations), their commitment to the constitutional procedures necessary before armed conflict can be undertaken and their support of a no-surrender pledge.

A modern democracy requires its military and defense organizations to formulate plans of actual defense of the United States. These plans would have to be consistent with principles of personal courage and respect for non-combatants, which means refusal to resort to weapons of mass murder, and acceptance of a joint planning process of government which acceded to the implementation of a world system of security. The planning process should be initiated in study groups on all levels of the national security bureaucracy and in the war and defense colleges. Attempts at consciousness raising in the military and national security groups are meant to begin the double process of transforming and rebuilding in the way that will allow civilization to step back from the precipice of militarism and nuclear war. The choices are now more stark than ever: either they are counter-force, deterrence, and a forward base strategy coupled with a strategic defense initiative which commits the United States to an ever more costly world imperial role ($330 billion by Financial Year 1986), with no returns to a depleted American society, or an international security and defense system that grounds our thinking in a prudent realistic view of the transient nature of human disputes and a belief in the common good of humanity.

The perplexing public policy problem for those concerned with preventing war is whether war and war preparation can be turned into a question which is understood by the leaders of states as having moral and legal importance beyond that of geopolitical gaming. By viewing war and conflict in moral and legal terms, the transient, and often trivial, causes for war could be dealt with through mediation, arbitration and other legal and peaceful proceedings. War should be susceptible to the same mode of analysis\that we use to assay individual wrong-doing in a nation's criminal

216

law. Nuclear war and its preparation can be understood as a strategic and diplomatic fact. But it would be far more useful to comprehend this fact as a set of interlinked actions which is criminal in nature, and which can be changed by a new, deeper sensitivity to justice and caring.

In the history of civilization's development, slavery was once recognized as a "fact" until it was seen as immoral and a political blight on humanity. Like slavery, nuclear war falls into the category of moral abhorrence. This means unilaterally forswearing the use of weapons which would terrorize innocent populations and which could only be of use in aggressive wars. The Geneva protocols on non-combatants in war, a document which the US initialed in 1977, is the basis upon which a change could be made in international affairs, and, indeed, in the types of weapons stockpiled by the military. It forswears the mass bombing of civilian populations. By implication this agreement could proscribe the use of nuclear weapons.

Most strategic thinking in the field of arms control, arms strategy and disarmament starts from pre-Second World War assumptions that the greater the number of armaments the less likely a respective nation will be attacked and the more likely that, if necessary, the nation will be in a position to attack others. This habit of mind continues to guide most of those who think about arms control in the Soviet Union and the United States. Any attempts at quantitative reductions in armaments, either on the basis of budgetary cuts, as has been proposed by the Soviets, or proportionate cuts which has been proposed by the United States, proves to cause great fears in the national security bureaucracies of each nation. The likelihood of stability emerging from an arms race of "small wars," let alone a measure of security and justice for the mass of humankind, is almost non-existent. There is a direct correlation between an increase in the world's arms expenditures ($900 billions in 1986) and a consistent decrease in international economic aid for poor nations.

When we examine the behavior of nations, we find that fear of national destruction has not served as a deterrent against war. While the arms race appears to hold off wars at the highest level of violence, it allows and encourages regional wars as in Indo-China, the Middle East and Africa. The types of weaponry deployed, such as missiles, nuclear and thermonuclear weapons, chemical and biological weapons, have changed the nature of civilization. Millions of people in their daily lives are involved in making instruments of destruction which, if ever used, would mark the end of civilization. What does it mean that the most sophisticated minds are given over to earning their keep in the world through destructive activity?

There is a general recognition of this dire situation among the world's leaders, but they are trapped in those assumptions and institutional structures which gave rise to habits that magnify fears and impede us from overthrowing the slavery of the arms race. Part of the fear is a material one: that to begin such a process is to cause almost certain, profound, internal social and economic dislocation. In the United States this is experienced as more real than the "slim" possibility that a thermonuclear war would be fought on American soil.[34]

This latter conclusion is not without its rejoinders. One is that the pathological nature of the arms race aborts social reconstruction because the type of state structure which the arms system engenders (the national security state) has nothing to do either with the common good or the common defense. Because of the misuse of intellectual and material resources and lack of public participation there is virtually no channel for the common good to be achieved through the national security state. Second, the internal economic and social prosperity which is achieved through the arms race and arms acquisition is applicable to a very few indeed.

The effects of the arms system on the United States have been very costly when measured against other nations whose military burden was less substantial. (This lesson was understood in the first half of the twentieth century by such conservatives as Robert Taft and Herbert Hoover.) This can be seen most clearly when we compare Japanese economic recovery and growth to that of the US over the last twenty years. While Japan has a favorable cultural fabric for economic growth most of its success can be best explained in terms of Japan's small expenditure on defense. Until 1977 Japan's military expenditures amounted to less than 1 per cent of its gross national product whereas its average annual investment in fixed capital amounted to about 33 per cent of its gross national product. The result was that the growth rate of Japan's economy was exceptionally high. The United States has spent between 6-11 per cent of its gross national product since 1941 on direct military spending. On the other hand investments in fixed capital in the United States amounted on average to about half of the share of gross national product channeled into fixed capital in Japan. The average annual economic growth rate in the United States was lower by half of Japan's growth rate. Whereas Japan's industrial output grew by 322 per cent during the period from 1960-71, in the United States it grew by only 74 per cent, i.e., four times slower.[35] In recent years the strategem of American administrators has been to put considerable emphasis on the Japanese to rearm. While the purpose of this strategy is unclear, its consequences are potentially very dangerous. Japanese rearmament will, over time, strengthen revanchist forces in Japan, make formerly occupied Asian nations insecure, and increase military tensions in Asia with China and the Soviet Union. Those traders and government officials who believe that the US can gain from such a policy are shortsighted.

The growth rates of nations with small defense forces are especially upsetting when we realize that present military preparations have little or nothing to do with protecting or directly defending American society. Whereas the Reagan administration committed itself to a forward offense position in which engagement and military intervention is seen as crucial to American interests, a defense system that seeks to reflect the common good calls for an entirely different set of assumptions. The doctrines of launch on warning, preemptive first strike, and unilateral military intervention must move to the scrapheap of history.

General principles for security

What then are the general principles which should undergird the foreign policy of the United States, especially as it enters its own rejuvenation? Are there rules which would bind bureaucracies, diplomats and politicians in the period of reconstruction?

(1) It is clear that the policies of non-interference in states or symmetric interference in their affairs is the most difficult to achieve during a period of fast communications, technology transfer, imperial ambition, human rights pretension and especially because of the character of American and Soviet foreign policy since 1945. Since 1648 the principle of non-interference has been a relatively important one which determined limits and operated as the way in which states intended to deal with each other. The UN Charter is the culmination of this principle. It starts from the assumption of peaceful co-existence and cooperation of sovereign states. The Charter offers protection for individual and group human rights to be achieved through peaceful processes of international law. There can be no intervention in the territory of another state by the UN or any other state except where the offending state is the aggressor, threatens the use of force or has violated its obligations under the Charter. If collective action were to occur, as for example, in South Africa, it could only occur with the affirmative vote and authority of the Security Council. Under the Charter military actions, boycotts, etc., can only be undertaken by a nation where such actions are supported by the UN Security Council, or where the General Assembly has so sanctioned their use, and they must be done for obviously accepted and humane practices. Unless the world has gone utterly mad UN collective responsibility would not champion apartheid or genocide. *But even in the most seemingly noble cases the United States must preserve its option not to join a peace-keeping force. Great Powers should be the last to militarily intervene if at all in any situation even where the action is collective.*

The same principle must apply to unilateral covert activities. Covert activities are merely another name for the intrusion of one nation into the life of another, violating the laws of the host nation. They are almost invariably criminal activities from bribery to murder and theft. Such modes of intrusion increase instability in the host country, and then in the intruding nation as well.[36] It is for both reasons that nations attempted to fashion an international law that accepted the principles of non-intervention.

The rule of comity, as it was called, is even more important during a period of international social transformation. Observing this rule and recognizing its importance as an instrument to keep the peace will be especially difficult in a period where newly emerging rules which require action opposing genocide, apartheid, and protection of human rights become the norm.

There will be well-meaning statesmen who may want to intervene militarily in another country on the "just" side of a struggle. For example, there are some committed to social reconstruction who would favor a United States intervention in South Africa to overthrow this benighted racist regime just as there were American liberals at the end of the nineteenth century who saw intervention as a way to save the people of Puerto Rico from Spanish imperialism. If direct intervention is proscribed in what may be an obvious just cause, what is the way that "the decent opinions and actions of humankind" can make an impact on those nations which systematically practice racism, or war and repression on their own people? This question is often raised in regard to South Africa. But in the case of South Africa the path is relatively clear. There is a right and duty under UN resolutions for governments and citizens to confront American corporations that do not boycott racist regimes. This confrontation should be carried out by American citizens *within* the United States just as there is a right and duty through the direct action of demonstration and civil disobedience to support the anti-apartheid movement of South Africa in the United States. The attitudes and actions of American citizens to the intervention and engagement of global corporations is a matter of internal American politics. Accordingly, groups have the constitutional and legal right to boycott US-based global corporations and apply pressure to transform the activities of corporations especially given the added force of UN resolutions. On the other hand, little attention should be paid to groups that seek official state or governmental involvement in other nations' internal struggles where there is no international consensus.

The alternative to this view is an unhappy one. It is the perpetuation of a "left" imperial system which will not be any more attractive than the status quo systems the United States organized and sustained for thirty-five years after the Second World War. In this regard, it is likely that the Soviet-Cuban activities in Africa will be no more successful than interventions tried by the United States for its clients, nor will the Soviets look any more noble or rooted to the wretched people of Afghanistan or the frightened people of Eastern Europe than the Napoleonic attempts to spread the ideals of the French revolution at the beginning of the nineteenth century in Spain, Russia or Egypt.

Spreading an imperial system has negative effects on the intervening nation's body politic. Early twentieth-century British writers showed that states which sought colonies deprived their own populace for the elixir of empire. While particular segments of the commercial classes might have gained from British imperialism, by the First World War it was clear to most politicians in Britain that imperialism was a wasteful enterprise which stopped it from coming to grips with its own need to reindustrialize itself. Cuba's involvement in a two-front war in Ethiopia and Angola has had grave economic and social consequences on its people.

There has been an exception to this rule. At the inception of the Cold War the United States began to change its official stance on domestic apartheid because of its world competition with the Soviet Union. But the ugly underbelly to imperial involvement has been more important. The imperial system is a means to deny one's sense of law and justice for it treats the Other or the enemy as objects not part of the common law of civilization. And in this treatment those who operate an imperial system find themselves hiring and encouraging thugs to undertake all manner of degradation from assassination to wiretapping to bribery or other deformations of statecraft. This form of pacification and containment was first used in the United States on the poor and the outsider domestically, and then exported abroad and used on other nations to teach or tame them. (In this we have been no different than other empires.) But the methods used on those we did not see soon came home. They were applied more widely on all segments of the society, even those who for a time held state power. It was not long before those who held power within the state competed with each other, and used that power on each other.

The shift from shock at this behavior by the end of the Indo-China war and Watergate to justification of it through legislation is truly an astounding turnaround. This justification as laid out in the new orders for the FBI and CIA mock our own public, legitimate structures such as Congress and the courts. When the intelligence apparatus is able to deceive the public constitutional forms, when false budgets are submitted to Congress (not a selected few), when agents and informers are to remain "nameless" under penalty of law, and when activities are conducted that are in the service of small cliques, we know that we are passing into the rule of the national security state which knows only its own rules and those of its leadership, which sees constitutional forms as ornamental to the real purpose of arranging power for imperial purpose.

While the process of dismantling the national security state is necessary for the common good *it should be understood that this process is linked to the development of a more rational national security system*. This is a complex but necessary political feat to accomplish. It will require working with members of the armed forces, retired officers and veterans organizations who will help in defining national defense as an activity to be performed in the context of personal accountability standards as laid out in the UN Charter, the Nuremberg and Tokyo trials, and the genocide treaty.

(2) There are modes of engagement and joint interference which I would construe as "positive" peacekeeping. They fall into two categories.

The first is that of joint accountability systems where, for example, the US and China checked on the minorities problem in the Soviet Union, and the Soviets, Latin Americans and Africans did likewise for the United States, with all attempting to find ways to take into account the critiques of the other. (This issue will become more important politically over the next generation in each nation as the Soviet-Asian population continues to increase at a faster rate than its Soviet-European population while the Chicano and Black population within the United States also increases at a faster rate than its Caucasian population.) The second category concerns areas of joint enterprise where economic aid is given to a third group or nation under rules laid out by the host nation and that of the Security Council. As part of a joint system of *interference-non-interference* accountability, UN conciliation and mediation should be greatly expanded. Individuals and groups would fulfill this function on the international scene both as advocates of internationally accepted standards, but also as those who would seek to mediate and conciliate disputes. Through the recently formed UN university the United Nations would be mandated to train teams of regional conciliators who would prepare plans and take over conciliation functions in disputes referred to them by the UN General Assembly or the disputing parties. The conciliation service would operate under the Secretary General according to resolutions of the Security Council and the General Assembly. The UN university should now take on the obligation of teaching and setting out certain types of curriculum materials and problem questions which would become courses of study in universities and schools of diplomacy and international relations *within* member states. The purpose is *to denationalize* diplomatic problems to the extent possible in order to generate a transnational consciousness among practitioners of diplomacy and elites.

(3) Under Article 43 of the Charter the Security Council was mandated to establish a military committee which was to produce an international security plan. This work was interrupted by the Cold War. International rules concerning intervention and disarmament security are utterly necessary if we are to escape a major war. One should note that it is not only the Soviet Union that has practiced intervention since the end of the Second World War. Given a dozen interventions and wars since 1975 it is more necessary than ever that we alter our international system which has broken into one of international military autarchy. Either the UN Security Council, with agreement from the General Assembly, or the Secretary General should independently call for the reconvening of the military committee. It would review various international arms limitation arrangements and treaties that are meant to change, then limit and finally proscribe war as a means other than that of defense of one's own territory. The military committee would explore the feasibility of UN border detachments slowly replacing national armed forces on borders.

Consonant with such changes is the requirement that the US and other major powers transform the present alliance systems by independently withdrawing troops and naval forces from different parts of the world as an international security and disarmament plan is implemented through the UN. As an international security agreement was negotiated the United States would take the leadership in proposing that the NATO and Warsaw Pact nations would pursue regional arrangements in arms control and disarmament within the context of the international security plan. NATO and Warsaw Pact nations would become a joint disarmament entente.

Is it naive to think that the Security Council and the General Assembly may be brought to play in managing and transforming the alliance system so that it becomes part of collective self-defense and international security rather than the reflection of world confrontation and tension? This naivete has a realistic basis to it in the costs of the arms race and the fact that the alliance system, in the sense that Dean Acheson and Jean Monnet or Molotov and Ulbricht formulated it, is coming apart. Thus, there is no question that Poland, France and West Germany pursue foreign policies toward each other which cross and undercut the traditional, confrontational lines of alliance systems.

In the quiet of their offices, Kremlin and State Department diplomats are concerned that Germany (both parts) may pursue their own foreign policies and cut loose from their own sponsors. And European nations know that tactical limited modern war means their utter destruction. Their very survival is dependent on finding a course that steers them from the alliance system and nuclear confrontation just as the Soviet Union must continue to find a way to demilitarize Germany. This feat can only be accomplished in a world-wide security arrangement. The question which goes begging for an answer is whether the bureaucratic structure of the alliance system in NATO, Warsaw or Comecon and OECD could be used to perform joint activities of development and disarmament. International civil servants and the bureaucracies they serve could become important actors for peaceful transformation if they would reflect a transnational consciousness that is tied to an emergent, pluralist world culture and which would be rooted in both stated and unstated acts to forward the building of world community.

On a regional basis Western Europe appears to be relatively successful in controlling West European animosities toward one another through joint democratic planning and international intercourse reflected in cultural activities such as communications, food, music and travel. This conscious- ness is spreading to all of Europe. Consequently, it is anachronistic and self- defeating for American policy to hinder this natural flow either in Europe or elsewhere.

From the point of view of American security the issue is whether alliances which were initiated in the post Second World War period and which sought to determine or stop social transformation both abroad and in the United States have any value in a time where the United States begins its own transformation. The policy of *bipolarism* and the cordon sanitaire relationship to the Soviet Union and East European states is peculiarly inapposite. The so-called *real politik* merit to this policy is even less obvious given cultural and communications changes which have occurred in Europe. Had the US accepted the Rapicki and Kennan plan of disengagement a generation ago, Poland and Eastern Europe would not be continually on the edge of repression and the West would not feel impotent.

There is nothing to be gained from any policy which attempts to isolate another nation except where there is general agreement among all the nations of the world. It is merely recognizing reality that the American foreign policy task during transformation will keep friendly relations through the UN system with all nations and help them adjust as we pursue our own internal agenda. In this international adjustment period ideas and analyses which are tied to the explication of values and practical manifestations of human dignity and shared purpose are the ones which need to be exchanged. These can best be championed through the UN rather than any particular military alliance system just because an alliance is predicated on a we-they conflict model.

World economy and arms race

A revitalized UN is an integral part of a transformed US national security and foreign policy. This is true to the extent American political leaders see themselves helping other nations and peoples achieve subject-actor status in world history. In practical terms this means that a nation which seeks equity in its internal activities as well as its foreign policy is to forge transnational interdependence which would unhitch national and international economics from the arms race.

The purpose of the "unhitching" policy is to remove the excuse of leaders and groups who pursue arms races for economic reasons either in their inception, or because they fear economic dislocation if they are interrupted. Such concerns are often hidden or unstated ones. But they become paramount at any moment where a nation's leadership may seek arms limitations and seek to confront those vested interests that are tied to armaments production, distribution and development.

It is likely that international decoupling from the arms race will cause problems of economic dislocation. Just as some areas of the United States are integrally related to the weapons and mobilization industry, Connecticut, Texas, California, New York, Georgia, and South Carolina, so it is that other nations have developed themselves and their raw materials base in terms of the American requirements for exquisite raw materials used in military manufacturing, or in buying, leasing and receiving gifts of American

224

weaponry.[37] (Thus, the lesson of the former Shah in Iran.) Once the United States seeks to free itself from the arms race it will become less dependent on other nations for raw materials since the raw materials base the US presently requires is directly related to its defense mobilization structure. Its arms sales system is based on a world of conflict that exists within and between nations which US strategists believe can be managed with arms sales.

In some cases it is likely that without arms supply from the US the regime in power would fall. In the first case alternative international programs are necessary to enable poor nations committed to the production of raw materials for US defense purposes to redirect their economies. Plans for this eventuality should be drawn through regional conversion authorities under the aegis of the UN. These authorities would help nations change their industrial and exporting base and intensify a system of regional common markets. In the second case, where arms sales would be interrupted, as in Egypt, Formosa, Israel, Saudi Arabia and South Korea, it is likely that except in the case of Israel, the character of the regime would change and would result in one that favored demilitarization and democracy. Compared to other nations in the Middle East, Israel has a strong democracy which is tied to a triumphal foreign policy. The policies of the Israeli government have not been cost-free. Nations which import large-scale armaments match those increases with a great tax and military burden on their own nations. Israel is no exception, for the more military aid Israel receives the more it must tax internally or sell to military Third World regimes, and they will end up – as they have – regrettably selling to the most reactionary and tottering regimes themselves becoming a military state.[38]

Since a changed military assistance and armaments program would cause certain regimes to feel endangered, the question to consider is whether alternate international arms limitation systems can be formulated and implemented to eliminate regional conflict between states which would limit the chances for bloody regional civil war as, for example, in Lebanon and Korea. This question is not the sole or necessarily a paramount responsibility of the United States.

The reader will recall from our first principle that American foreign policy should not start from passionate attachments to particular groups or leaders especially where loyalty from their own people is weak or non-existent. This element of *realpolitik* is to be balanced by the passionate attachment we muster in favor of arms limitation and disarmament, international moves to equity and caring, and the fostering of root principles of the UN Charter and convenants. In practice such legal principles mean that where certain regimes have been protected and foisted on their people through armaments, the US will no longer be party to such actions. Instead what it will do is lead the world in ending the arms race

225

through an international disarmament agreement. This will give dependent nations and their leaders time to change their internal policies. As part of a world-wide disarmament arrangement regional economic mutual aid discussions should be encouraged which would signal a deep change in American foreign policy and would avert unnecessary instability and conflict.

The question of arms control

I do not deprecate the attempts of arms strategists and scientists who have sought a measure of sanity in the arms race and who have labored hard to work out an arms control system which would limit the arms race or its consequences. The nuclear test ban agreement in the atmosphere, the SALT I agreement, the US-USSR hotlines are examples of limited arrangements that have some positive value. However, strategists and scientists would be the first to admit the narrow character of these agreements.

They have not changed the intensity of the arms race. But while there has been a tranquilizing effect on the world's populations because they were told that arms control could be achieved, it has masked the real character of our situation. This has happened because of the use arms control has been put to over the last two decades. In one model it was an instrument of the arms race itself, of weapons acquisition and allegiance to specific strategic models. According to this view, arms control did not have to result in reducing numbers of weapons, launchers and size of conventional forces. It could be a system of tacit and explicit agreement between the superpowers to arm together and to assure that the mandarins on both sides of the Atlantic pursued similar goals, methods and acceptable "codes" of arming behavior. This position came to be identified with Professors Schelling, Doty and Huntington of Harvard.

While the Soviet Union might be able to sustain this form of international atomic diplomacy because of its governing and decision-making process, since the experience and revelations around Watergate and the Indo-China war the United States is less able to accommodate a closed, mandarinate system of arms discussions such as the kind preferred by the mandarin arms controller. Decisions on MX, cruise missiles or ABM can no longer be made in the vacuum of national security secrecy. Indeed, SALT II foundered on its close identification with experts who had little political support.

National security decisions made at the top of a bureaucracy or with weapons experts require wide political acceptance and, indeed, cultural legitimation. This legitimation is no longer forthcoming for arms control. The Reagan and Carter versions of arms control had no independent political energy, while the nuclear freeze movement, an existential wail which said "Enough is enough," has had mass support. Any arms proposal, if it is to make political sense, must be detached from the arms race and from the institutional centers of power which accept the conceptual blinders of deterrence as an end in itself, counterforce, MAD and belief in first and second strike weaponry and now the strategic defense initiative, so-called, Star Wars. Instead of adapting itself to arms strategies, arms controllers must adjust themselves to working in an overall framework of disarmament paralleling an alternative security system.

Only a few advisors in the Kennedy administration realized in 1961 that arms control and disarmament had to be related to one another. Without arms control being part of an overall framework of comprehensive disarmament arms control by itself would be nothing more than a Sisyphean task in which each tortuous step forward for arms limitation would be accompanied by several quick steps backward into the arms race. Why? Reaching partial arms control agreement for one weapon system is even more complex and difficult than getting agreement on a comprehensive arrangement because a partial arms control agreement seeks to fit within standards and assumptions of security that are reflected in the military arms race. Partial agreements in arms control are not designed to take into account or change international organization, reach for fundamental military transformations or disturb institutional alliances within nations. They are not meant to renounce the paradigm of the arms race as the inescapable reality of international political behavior. Consequently, the tragic reality of arms control and the search for it has not decreased tensions in the world caused by armaments.

The nature of the arms race today is that it has an autonomous character exacerbating political tensions. Nations arm not to fall behind; if they think they are behind they arm to catch up, if they think they are ahead, their leaders believe that they do not need to have disarmament.[39] But meanwhile, real problems of nations grow worse and the likelihood of major war grows greater because of the arms competition. President Kennedy sought an answer to untying the gordian knot in his speech to the UN General Assembly when he introduced the McCloy-Zorin Agreement:

> The program to be presented to this Assembly – for general and complete disarmament under effective and international control – moves to bridge the gap between those who insist on a gradual approach and those who talk only of a final and total achievement. It would create machinery to keep the peace even as it destroys the machine of war. It would proceed through balanced and safeguarded stages designed to give no state a military advantage over another. It would give the final responsibility for verification and control where it belongs – not with the big powers alone, not with one's adversary or one's self, but in an international organization within the framework of the United Nations.[40]

227

Arms control needs to *compete* with military strategies and frameworks, not complement them. Consequently, arms controllers need to work with those who seek a new international and national security system.

Perhaps arms controllers hoped that they could keep stability in the context of international political bedlam. But there is no way to isolate arms control arrangements from other questions of politics. The harsh fact is that any political issue in the American political context can be used as a reason to scuttle an arms control arrangement. Policy makers see specific issues through a strategic geopolitical screen. This is especially true when antagonists are involved. Each "irritation" is proof of an affront, which is further proof of an overall strategy by the major antagonist to harm and destroy its adversary. In other words, issues and difficulties which separate one nation from another when they are antagonists are aggregated together by the policy makers of each rival nation or bloc. They are seen as symbolically related to other issues. On the other hand, where there are differences between nations that are not antagonists the dynamic of disaggregation operates. For example, policy makers see problems between the United States and France as ones which can be handled separately or on a problematic basis. Disaggregation does not operate where the protagonists in a mirror image way see themselves as fighting a battle of good against evil.

Indeed the great power protagonists have implanted their struggles on other nations or intensified the enmities that were already present. Great power confrontations in the Middle East, Africa, Latin America and Asia have added immeasurably to the instability of these regions and the wretched and insecure condition of the people. Military assistance, increasing reliance on armaments in these areas (supplied by the Soviet Union and the West) add to regional conflict and the aura of continuous war. The arms race defines most other regional conflict and the aura of continuous war. The arms race defines most other regional questions. The single most important *political* action to solve other questions is to develop local and regional disarmament arrangements which would include the staged ending of military assistance. Setting conflicts between states in security and disarmament terms will transform these conflicts and dampen them. Rivalries will appear less threatening and peaceful, mediating machinery would take the place of arms as the means of resolving disputes.

The arms control diplomacy of incrementalism and disaggregation as a strategy is ineffective against the mind-set created by comprehensive antagonism. What is needed therefore is a different framework which fits with the possibilities of a new global conception of how disputes can be handled and how antagonists might change their conceptions and actions toward each other. This is what is attempted through a comprehensive disarmament program; one which could be linked to a world security arrangement that has the support of the citizenry. Such general support is there in the populace – if ways could be found to reach these audiences through the media and through transnational discussions of groups.

Arms controllers have argued that given institutional constraints in each nation comprehensive disarmament endeavors are not feasible. They also argue that in the United States the realities of political power are such that Congress would not even countenance a limited arms control agreement. Some have also argued that it is "too late" for comprehensive disarmament because other national players in world politics are not likely to follow the lead of the United States and the Soviet Union no matter what they agree, that the problem of matching an opponent's weaponry and forces with one's own is now so complex that only experts can understand the issues. They are aware of the paradox that the experts are part of the arms system and therefore they are part of a vested interest to perpetuate it. These analysts hold that because good is the enemy of the best, all we can attain is the application of self-interest rationality to an irrational situation. Furthermore, to seek more is to court failure in a world that is now inherently volatile and unstable.

These points are real and cannot be wished away. What might have been possible a generation ago in terms of disarmament will be harder to attain today. The ability of the US and the Soviet Union to set the framework for disarmament on their own initiative was much greater in 1961-2 than it was in 1985. Then there were fewer nuclear actors, fewer missiles and weapons as stage props (or Golem!). *Nevertheless, for the foreseeable future the US and the USSR will continue to set the framework for nuclear weapons development, in terms of numbers, as well as delivery vehicles and conventional forces.* Between them, they have created the coin of nuclear and missiles currency as valuable. Just because this is so, it is also possible for them to debase that currency by taking the lead in *changing* the concepts, attitudes and assumptions which undergird the arms race. This can occur by including citizens as well as officials in the disarming process. Nuclear age citizens are less prone to accept the idea that nations are able to offer security either to their citizens or their allies.

The populations of each nation will have to participate in saving their own situation. One way they can begin the task of saving themselves is by recognizing the modern character of sovereignty. In the modern world sovereignty is linked to the decisions made by other states. State A may either directly or indirectly frame the existence of State B in terms of national survival, economic or social well-being.

The Great Powers will have to realize that military superiority, or belief in economic superiority, pressing the fruits of their respective military and economic system on to reluctant nations, is an obsession that should be surrendered, to be replaced by real security.

Such feelings on both sides are now deeply rooted in each society. They represent different parts of the triumphal and expansive nature of modern ideologies. Both may be traced to the least attractive elements of the enlightenment. Neither comes near to helping us out of humankind's tragic situation. Yet, both systems claim their allegiance to sustaining humanity. The Great Powers can prove their case by jointly beginning and continuing the McCloy-Zorin disarmament process.

Any new paradigm of international relations must (a) be credible to the contending nations and those nations and people who are passive but could be mobilized in its favor; (b) be committed to a future beyond war, in other words it must show that there are social and political inventions and new institutions which can sustain humanity; and (c) it must present a political and social path which makes the proposal credible. It must recognize power as the given and problematic of human history. Institutes, universities, foundations and the peace movement have special obligations to make such a proposal the *cultural* framework from which governments cannot escape. In states such as the Soviet Union and China the new security and peace race challenge to their society may come from increasing international contacts, unilateral steps and making concrete (that is, insisting on putting into practice) prior statements of disarmament, nuclear free zones and disengagement which their nations have rhetorically espoused.

A word should be said about the next stage of the arms race. We encapsulated ourselves in nuclear missiles, weaponry, and war fighting capability at all levels of violence. We have indoctrinated ourselves with strategic rationalizations from MAD, to NUTS, and now with the space race, DEAD; that is, a launch on warning system which surrenders the power and judgment of making war in space, or from space platforms on to earth with lasers to computers. Is it not obvious that the old security system is collapsing and that in the process humanity is going to be ground under?

An alternative to the arms control-arms race system is a program for common security and general disarmament which is detailed in the next section. (For those readers interested in pursuing the legal precedents and authorities of a general disarmament treaty program write the Institute for Policy Studies, 1901 Q Street, N.W. Washington, D.C. 20009 for "Common Security and General Disarmament.")

Program treaty for security and general disarmament

Chapter I

Foundation

ARTICLE 1
(1) Upon signing this Program Treaty each signatory continues its commitment to the purposes and principles of the United Nations as set

230

forth in the Charter of the United Nations.

(2) Each Party to the Program Treaty commits itself to use the machinery of the United Nations for the peaceful resolution of disputes and will follow Articles 41-7 and Chapter Seven of the Charter in carrying out the purposes of the proposed Treaty for Security and General Disarmament.

(3) Each Party to this Program Treaty agrees not to initiate the use of nuclear weapons, nor to use them against any non-nuclear nations.

(4) Each Party agrees to a comprehensive test ban treaty.

Chapter II

General principles

ARTICLE 2

(1) By the year 2005 the Parties to this Agreement intend to achieve security and general disarmament. The Program is divided into three stages of five years each, to commence in 1990.

(2) The purpose of this Program is to secure the peace by eliminating all weapons of mass destruction, offensive weapons, chemical and biological weapons, and military forces (except those that may be required to keep internal order or those which may be required pursuant to Chapter Seven of the UN Charter).

(3) All collective self-defense alliances such as the NATO-Warsaw Pact as well as bilateral arrangements shall be changed to reflect the terms of a Security and General Disarmament Program.

(4) Each stage of the disarmament process will include assurance, inspection and verification. The disarmament process shall move automatically from stage one to stage two to stage three unless two-thirds of the Parties to this Program (including one of the permanent members of the UN Security Council) object.

ARTICLE 3

(1) The Program for Security and General Disarmament between the US and the Soviet Union shall, in stage one, achieve a reduction of 30 per cent of strategic, tractical and conventional forces. The reductions will proceed on the basis of a zonal system of inspection. Stage two shall achieve a further reduction of 40 per cent in the period of five years, on a zonal basis. Stage three shall achieve a further reduction of 30 per cent and shall be completed in the remaining time, until the year 2005.

(2) While the United States and the Soviet Union will initiate the disarming process, all other nations shall enter into the Program on Security and General Disarmament according to their category of weaponry in the first stage. All alliance arrangements such as the Warsaw Pact and NATO

and the nations party to them will begin their reduction of weaponry in the first stage.

(3) Within each stage, the reductions shall proceed on the basis of quantitative measures. The categories for the disarming process shall be space delivery vehicles and space objects, including lasers, ballistic delivery vehicles under 20-mile range, ballistic delivery vehicles greater than 20-mile range, airplanes with speed above 1,000 MPH, airplanes less than 1,000 MPH, nuclear warheads under 20KT, nuclear warheads over 20KT, naval vessels, munitions, uniformed military personnel (full-time), chemical, biological and radiological weapons. (Note Article 64 for list of initial declarations.)

ARTICLE 4

(1) Upon the recommendation of the Secretary-General of the Disarmament Organization, the Board of Inquirers, comprising eighteen members from the International Disarmament Organization, including the permanent members of the UN Security Council, will issue yearly reports on the disarmament process with comments and recommendations on how the process is to be carried out. It shall issue reports on technical aspects of verification, inspection and assurance.

(2) The Disarmament Organization's Board of Inquirers shall involve non-governmental groups such as scientists, technologists, peace and disarmament groups, military staffs, women's groups, labor unions, church groups and political parties to secure their active involvement in the disarming process. The Board will draw on special researchers on matters pertaining to the disarming process which are commissioned by the IDO, UN, Non-Governmental Organizations and other bodies committed to the success of the disarming process.

(3) The International Disarmament Organization will ascertain the effects on the program and process of disarmament of any nation or territory that declines to enter into an International Program for Security and General Disarmament. It will submit reports on this question to the Security Council, the General Assembly, and the Parties to the Treaty.

ARTICLE 5

(1) As preparation for entry into the Treaty each nation will deposit X billion dollars in gold bullion into an escrow fund. These funds will be forfeited where a Party to the Program opts out of the Program. In cases of violation as determined by the International Court of Justice or three referees appointed by the Court, the offending nation will be penalized financially according to a system of fines drawn up by the ICJ. The fine schedule shall be submitted to the UN General Assembly and the Security Council for final acceptance.

(2) Revenue from fines – if any – will be used for international aid and

development through the specialized agencies of the United Nations as well as costs of operating the International Disarmament Organization.

ARTICLE 6

(1) Sanctions for violations of this agreement may be applied to non-signatories as well as signatories.
(2) Sanctions may be applied by the Disarmament Organization or the UN Security Council upon recommendation of the General Assembly.
(3) In some cases, the sanctions called for will be those found in the UN Charter, specifically, Articles 41-7. Sanctions stated in the UN Charter are incorporated into this disarmament process.

ARTICLE 7

(1) Each Party shall cease all research on new weapons, or the improvement of old weapon systems, upon the signing of this Program.
(2) The UN, through its specialized agencies and then through the International Disarmament Organization, will establish an international registry of scientists, technologists, laboratory and factory workers. The internal law of the respective parties shall be amended to include an oath by scientific workers which abjures them from doing research, development, and experimental work on weapons of mass destruction; this includes strategic delivery vehicles (and other offensive vehicles or weapons) and military space and laser research. The oath shall be either the following or a variant of it: "I will not use my scientific, educational or technical training for any purpose which I believe is intended to harm human beings. I shall not work on weapons which, if used, would result in mass destruction. I shall in my work strive for peace, justice and the betterment of the human condition."
(3) Each Party to the Agreement shall cease manufacture, production and experimental development of conventional armaments upon the operative date of this Treaty Program. The manufacture of spare parts may continue for no more than one year from the date of signature of the Program.
(4) Definitions of "research," "experimental," "development," "manufacture" and "weapons of mass destruction" shall be determined through normal uses in international law, scientific inquiry and commercial manufacture.

ARTICLE 8

(1) Parties to the Treaty solemnly undertake to uphold the Treaty and perform its terms in the required time.
(2) Where performing the disarming and dismantling process may not fit the time allotted for a particular stage, the Inquirers shall be immediately informed so that an alternative technical procedure may be found to accomplish the objectives of the disarmament program.

Chapter III

International disarmament organization and the UN Military Committee

ARTICLE 9

(1) The Parties to this Program establish an International Disarmament Organization. It shall be staffed by competent individuals from all nations. The International Disarmament Organization shall conduct training, education and research activities as part of the disarming process for its staff, inquirers and inspectors.

(2) The International Disarmament Organization shall operate according to the objectives of the United Nations Charter.

(3) It will operate in close association with the specialized agencies and will seek advice, counsel and staff – where needed – from other international agencies.

(4) It will negotiate an Agreement with, and where necessary, employ the services of, the International Atomic Energy Agency.

(5) The United Nations will appoint an Undersecretary-General who will serve as liaison with the International Disarmament Organization.

AARTICLE 10

(1) Notwithstanding that the primary responsibility for the arms race rests with the militarily significant states, the International Disarmament Organization shall operate as the world's principal agency to end the arms race and create international security. The IDO shall work closely with all non-governmental organizations in seeking non-state support for carrying out the terms of the Program.

(2) In the initial stages of organizing the IDO, the Parties to the Program and the UN are not relieved of the responsibility for carrying out the objective of ending world insecurity caused by the arms race.

(3) The IDO will seek ways of assuring that the terms of the Program are carried out fairly, without military advantage being given to any nation or group of nations.

(4) The IDO will assure that the quantum of armaments and military forces in the world are continuously reduced to enhance the security of the world's nations.

ARTICLE 11

(1) The Military Committee of the United Nations Security Council shall meet on a continuous basis with the Parties to the Agreement and the International Disarmament Organization to fulfill its obligation of preparing a world security arrangement. The Military Committee shall begin and continue work on the Security Agreement as the process for

implementing a Security and General Disarmament Treaty continues.

(2) At the end of each stage of the Treaty Program elements of a world security arrangement shall be presented to the Security Council and the General Assembly for debate, assent and implementation.

ARTICLE 12

(1) The Board of Inquiry shall be made up of the permanent members of the UN Security Council. The General Assembly will vote on thirteen other members from those that are signatories to a Treaty.

(2) Each member of the Board of Inquiry shall be elected for a term of four years. Terms shall be staggered.

(3) The Board of Inquiry shall be responsible for the administration of the Treaty Program.

ARTICLE 13

The Board of Inquiry

(1) shall appoint the Secretary-General of the Organization;

(2) shall also appoint regional Undersecretary-Generals of the International Disarmament Organization;

(3) shall have the power to recommend to the UN Security Council and General Assembly fines on nations and other punishments as prescribed in this Treaty and the United Nations Charter, excepting the direct use of force;

(4) shall fix the assessments and contributions of the Parties to the Agreement;

(5) shall initiate, formulate and approve all agreements with members of the UN, international institutions and specialized agencies of the UN in carrying out the objectives and terms of this Program;

(6) shall follow the same rules of election and rotation for Chair of the International Disarmament Organization as are followed in electing the Chair of the Security Council;

(7) shall meet in places other than where it is permanently domiciled if the disarming and security process would be facilitated;

(8) may establish committees comprising consultants, specialists and members of non-governmental organizations to facilitate the disarming and security process;

(9) shall supply interim reports to Parties of the Program, the UN Security Council and the General Assembly;

(10) shall regularly use television, film, radio, and other means of communication to report to the world's people on the status of the disarmament process;

(11) shall report on current research in the disarming and security process to the Parties to the Treaty, the UN, and the international public at large.

Chapter IV

Integrity of the staff of the International Disarmament Organization

ARTICLE 14

(1) A Secretary-General of the IDO shall be chosen by the Board of Inquirers for a tenure of seven years.

(2) The staff of the IDO shall be supervised by a Secretary-General.

ARTICLE 15

(1) The Secretary-General shall be assisted by Undersecretary-Generals who will be expert in diplomacy, disarmament, or other fields of endeavor that will facilitate carrying out the objectives of the Program.

(2) The Secretary-General and the Undersecretary-Generals shall be entrusted with the appointment of staff and administration of the IDO.

ARTICLE 16

(1) The staff of the International Disarmament Organization shall owe its primary loyalty to no government. It shall be independent and will, in its conditions of service, hold to the highest standards of integrity and technical skill. It shall specialize in settling disputes or conflicts over technical data or disagreements caused by language or cultural misperception. The staff will be chosen without regard to race, sex or age and will reflect, to the extent possible, wide geographical composition.

(2) The staff shall be instructed in procedures of verification, assurance and inspection for at least six months prior to acting as independent investigators. Contracts for professional staff shall be five years.

ARTICLE 17

(1) The staff of the International Disarmament Organization, including the Secretary-General and the Undersecretaries, shall not receive or seek instructions from any Party to the Program. All discussions between the Secretary-General, deputies and staff with government officials shall be deemed official discussions when they concern the disarming and security process.

(2) As part of the Security and General Disarmament (SGD) Treaty each nation solemnly agrees to protect the integrity of the disarming process by respecting the quasi-judicial functions of the Secretary-General and the staff of the IDO. The right of citizenship may be offered by signatories to the Program to staff members of the IDO and their immediate families.

(3) Governments which seek special favor with the IDO through bribery or

suborning staff may be penalized by the ICJ or its appointed referees in ways proportionate to the transgression. The use of force or the interruption of the disarming and security process will not constitute a penalty for subornation.

(4) Where possible, the IDO will seek to determine whether there are difficulties in the procedures of the disarming and security process which caused a Party to a Treaty to act irresponsibly or to seek undue influence.

ARTICLE 18

(1) The International Disarmament Organization shall have the power to hire consultants, call on research institutes, award contracts for specific work and seek advice and counsel from non-governmental organizations.
(2) All such discussions are to be considered official discussions with records kept of them.
(3) No individual, institute or other organizational body shall seek to corrupt the disarming process or the staff of the IDO.
(4) Where such occurs the IDO will inform the authorities of the nation in which the citizen lives for any legal action that they may take.

Chapter V

Forces and arsenals to be retained at the end of the disarmament process

ARTICLE 19

(1) By the end of stage three the Parties to this Program shall retain only those weapons, forces, and industrial capacity for military purposes which may be viewed under the UN Charter as that type of defense needed to keep internal order.
(2) At the beginning of stage one of the disarmament process the Parties to the process shall seek to write into their domestic laws the Asian and Nuremberg Tribunal standards so that the destruction of innocent populations, the preparation for aggressive war, the use of terror weapons, or the use of force in international relations outside of those actions prescribed in the UN Charter shall qualify as a crime against internal domestic law.
(3) This body of doctrine shall be written into the domestic law of nations by the end of the third stage of the disarming process.
(4) The military of each nation shall internalize these standards in their respective regulations and codes of behavior.
(5) No international organization or peacekeeping force shall retain, develop or contract to be developed weapons of mass destruction and terror weapons, nor shall it secure the peace through plans and

237

programs of terror, mass bombing or other means that would violate the principles of the Red Cross Convention of 1977 to protect noncombatants, or the Nuremberg and Asian War Crimes Tribunals standards.

(6) The UN and the IDO will encourage universities, law schools, institutes and governments in preparing research materials to facilitate the implementation of Article 19.

ARTICLE 20

(1) Each nation Party to the Program shall internalize in its respective laws a no-surrender clause which makes it a domestic crime to surrender against an aggressor nation. Legislation to this end should be internalized in domestic law by the end of the first stage of the SGD Agreement.

(2) The Board of Inquiry shall report to the UN Security Council any breach of the peace and shall recommend to it whether Chapter Seven of the UN Charter should be applied by the world community.

(3) The Military Staff Committee in conjunction with the staff of the International Disarmament Organization shall prepare a world security arrangement including rules governing ways to handle border incidents and plans for securing armed forces upon short notice from member states, where called for.

(4) The Military Staff Committee under Article 43 of the Charter shall retain a modest number of armed forces not dependent on contingents from member states.

(5) As Parties to the Treaty disarm, the IDO and the Military Staff Committee will, upon request, instruct national military forces and others on the use of non-violent techniques as a primary way of encouraging non-compliance against a potential aggressor nation.

ARTICLE 21

From time to time, but at least every five years, the Parties to a Treaty shall meet to discuss whether further reductions in forces may be made after the end of the third stage. They shall also discuss the results of the world security arrangement as a primary way of keeping the peace.

ARTICLE 22

(1) The Parties shall retain only the armed forces and armaments agreed to at each stage of the Program.

(2) Prior to the first stage of the Program, but no later than the end of the first stage of the disarming process, the Parties to the Treaty shall file interim but comprehensive official inventories of all military equipment, as well as industrial plants which engage in the making of military equipment in substantial amounts. Parties to the Agreement shall also supply contract data or requisition data to the IDO. Military

and personnel lists shall also be supplied to the IDO. The inventories and lists shall not include the location of these weapons and forces. Such disclosure is left to the zonal disarmament procedure.

(3) Signatories to the treaty program shall have a choice of one of two methods of carrying out the disarming process. They may choose (a) percentage disarmament by zone or (b) overall percentage cutback with each particular zone being cleared of the agreed-upon categories of armaments and manpower referred to in Article 3, Section 3. In method (a) the inspection process conducted either by the IDO or an adversary shall assure that there is a diminution of weapons and forces in a particular zone according to the schedule of reductions for that year, with a complete accounting being given for the weaponry that is left in that particular zone. In method (b) the signatory shall completely eliminate all categories of weapons and manpower in a selected sequence. The parties to the Agreement cannot change methods without the express consent of two-thirds of the signatories including either the United States or the Soviet Union.

(4) All Parties to the Program may mend the inventory and personnel lists throughout the first stage. In the second stage the inventory and personnel lists may be amended twice. In the third stage the inventory and personnel lists (members of the armed forces including paramilitary and intelligence personnel) may be amended once.

(5) In the first two stages of the disarming process the nation under inspection shall have the choice of deciding whether it is to be inspected by the IDO or those states commonly thought to be its adversaries.

(6) In the first stage of the disarming process, assurance, inspection and verification shall be attained *three ways*:

(a) checking against inventory and personnel lists and ascertaining that what has been dismantled and destroyed or disbanded has in fact been destroyed or disbanded. One method of verification shall be through direct on-site inspection at specified depots;

(b) an independent satellite capacity under the control of the International Disarmament Organization which will ascertain, through photography and sensor technology, the character and place of the Parties' forces;

(c) assurances through non-governmental organizations, scientists, testimony and other means of public testimony which state whether the Agreement is being adhered to.

(7) The IDO will encourage joint and multilateral satellite inspection systems among adversaries. Information gathered from such means or through unilateral satellite inspection may be made available to the IDO for examination.

(8) With the presence of representatives of the United Nations the IDO will

inspect the destruction and dismantling of weapons of mass destruction, strategic delivery vehicles and other offensive weapons.

(9) The Parties to this Program encourage the creation of citizen inspection and assurance groups whose task will be publicizing all manner of information on the disarmament process including the publication of violations.

(10) The Parties agree that the armed forces and armaments remaining after each stage shall be determined by the provisions of the Program.

(11) The Parties further agree that the remaining forces shall be found in particular zones designated at the beginning of each stage of the Program.

(12) The states party to the Treaty Program will develop a system of assurance and verification by challenge and explanation.

ARTICLE 23

The Parties agree to reduce the personnel of their armed forces according to the terms of this Program.

ARTICLE 24

The Parties agree, that for the purposes of this Program, "Military personnel" shall mean the armed forces of a nation including its civilians employed by the armed forces who serve a military purpose. Paramilitary, police forces, border and custom guards who have been issued machine guns or other heavy weapons are also included in the terms of this section.

ARTICLE 25

Each Party agrees that it will eliminate its organized reserve forces by the end of the third stage of this Program. Full-time cadre for the training and absorption of reserve forces shall be counted as part of the armed forces. All obligations of reservists will be eliminated by the end of the third stage of the Program.

ARTICLE 26

Parties to the Agreement shall reduce and eliminate all naval ships, except those specifically excluded for defensive purposes under the terms of this Program. Fleets shall be divided into two categories. Those that are

(a) in storage as of the commencement of this Treaty and
(b) those that are deployable battle forces.

ARTICLE 27

Each Party to the Treaty agrees that all ships other than those specifically allowed at the end of stage three shall be destroyed under the supervision of the International Disarmament Organization. The Secretary-General may allow the acquisition for peaceful commercial use individual ships where military equipment has been removed and destroyed from the vessel. The Board of Inquiry must certify that the ship is no longer capable of military attack use.

ARTICLE 28

(1) Parties to the Agreement may invite signatories or others to witness the destruction and dismantling of the ships and hulks.
(2) Inspectors from the International Disarmament Organization shall be authorized to board ships and cruise with Parties to the Agreement.
(3) In the third stage of the Agreement the International Disarmament Organization is authorized to appoint one or more inspectors per vessel, but no more than six per vessel. On board, the inspector shall have inspection rights, diplomatic immunity and access at appointed times to the ship's crew and officers.

ARTICLE 29

Nuclear units shall be removed from nuclear-powered ships. They shall either be destroyed or placed in safe custody of the International Disarmament Organization.

ARTICLE 30

During the period of disarming Parties to the Program shall refrain from activities at sea which may engage nations in war or in forward strategies beyond their own sea lanes.

ARTICLES 31

As part of a world security arrangement the Military Committee of the UN and the International Disarmament Organization will be encouraged to address the question of border patrols in the Middle East, between China and Vietnam, the Soviet Union and the People's Republic of China, North Korea and South Korea, Cambodia and Vietnam, the Republic of South Africa and its neighboring states. The Military Committee will recommend ways to assure the non-engagement of troops beyond each nation's borders.

ARTICLE 32

In the first stage of the disarming process all Parties to the Agreement, either individually or as part of alliances, will withdraw their forces, including their artillery, rockets, airplanes and ground forces from areas considered as direct engagement with an adversary. Wherever direct engagement exists between opposing sides a process of "back-off" shall be completed in the first fifteen months of the first stage.

ARTICLE 33

The Parties to the Program shall designate depots at which weaponry and

Securing the nation

war material would be destroyed before inspectors of the IDO and invited nations. Citizen inspection through non-governmental organizations and citizen groups will be encouraged.

ARTICLE 34
The Parties agree that they will reduce during stages one, two and three military aircraft in all categories. In the first stage by 30 per cent of the inventory as of 1995, in the second stage by 40 per cent and in the third stage by 30 per cent.

ARTICLE 35
For the purposes of this Program signatories may, after the third stage, retain short-range fighter planes with a maximum speed of 2.1 Mach per hour. They may also retain helicopters at a maximum speed of 250 miles per hour and maritime aircraft at a speed of 2 Mach per hour. No aircraft will be fitted with air-to-surface missiles with limited range.

ARTICLE 36
Airplanes, guidance and navigational systems will be destroyed physically at depots assigned for that purpose. The International Disarmament Organiz- ation, citizen groups and invited representatives of other nations will witness the destruction of airplanes and other military instruments attendant to air warfare.

ARTICLE 37
(1) Each nation Party to the Program will contribute armed forces to a United Nations Force.
(2) The primary military emphasis of such forces will be highly techno- logical and non-lethal. It shall explore sub-lethal methods for maintain- ing the peace. UN forces will be used for aid in handling natural disasters and in securing humanitarian rights only under order of the UN Security Council.
(3) Other uses of the United Nations Force shall be in conformance with the decisions of the Military Committee of the UN Security Council.

ARTICLE 38
Over the course of the three stages of the disarming process all weapons, vehicles and armaments shall be destroyed if they are listed in the schedule contained in a Program for disarmament.

Signatory nations in the last stage of the disarming process may apply a percentage of the percentage to be destroyed to a United Nations force, if so agreed to by the Military Committee of the UN Security Council.

242

ARTICLE 39

Bases retained for the purpose of maintenance, repair and manufacture shall be disbanded in the last stage of the disarming process. An exception is made for the repair, maintenance and manufacture of defense weapons allowed in this Treaty.

ARTICLE 40

Industrial training and educational activities which are part of the maintenance, testing and development of a prohibited weapon are prohibited.

ARTICLE 41

A Treaty for Security and General Disarmament incorporates the following treaties:
(1) Protocol for the Prohibition of the Use of Poisonous Gases and Bacteriological Methods of Warfare (1925);
(2) Treaty forbidding the military use of Antarctica; (1959);
(3) Treaty Banning Nuclear Tests in the Atmosphere, in Outer Space and Under Water (1963);
(4) Treaty on Principles Governing the Activities of States in the Exploration of Outer Space, including the Moon and Other Celestial Bodies (1967);
(5) Treaty on Non-proliferation of Nuclear Weapons of 1968;
(6) Treaty on the Prohibition of the Emplacement of Nuclear Weapons and Other Weapons of Mass Destruction on the Seabed, on the Ocean Floor, and on the Subsoil Thereof (1971);
(7) Convention on the Prohibition of the Development, Production and Stockpiling of Bacteriological (Biological) and Toxic Weapons and their Destruction of (1972);
(8) Treaty Between the USA and the USSR on the Limitation of Anti-Ballistic Missile Systems (1972)

ARTICLE 42

Parties to the Program are deemed to have waived the power of reservation to any particular part or Article of the Program unless both the US and the USSR accept the reservation and two-thirds of the other states party to the agreement accept the reservation.

ARTICLE 43

Non-governmental institutions, such as research institutes and universities that have networks of scientists and technical personnel throughout the world, will be asked to join in a public system of assurance, inspection and verification. They are requested to make public their data to the Parties to the Program, the International Disarmament Organization and the media.

ARTICLE 44

(1) Leaders of militarily significant powers shall report to their own nations on the importance of continuing the disarmament process. They shall report at least twice a year. This report shall have maximum media coverage.
(2) On a twice-a-year basis, through the media, and in official proclamation, leaders of nations who are Party to this Program shall encourage the citizenry to cooperate in the inspection, verification and assurance process.

ARTICLE 45

Parties to the Program recognize that the Security and General Disarmament Program is an overall framing system for ending the arms race which includes building up institutions and social relations of trust. Joint or international projects of verification, assurance and inspection, and research are encouraged between Parties to the Program.

ARTICLE 46

Nuclear weapons shall be destroyed according to the following procedures:
(1) The weapon shall be detached from its mode of delivery.
(2) Its guidance system shall be destroyed.
(3) The fissile material shall be removed from the weapon and deposited.
(4) The weapon will be physically destroyed.
(5) Inspectors from the International Disarmament Organization shall be present at the destruction of the weapon.
(6) Parties to the Treaty shall be invited to attend the process of physical destruction.

ARTICLE 47

(1) The fissile material shall be denatured as quickly as possible.
(2) It shall be placed under the custody of the International Disarmament Organization.
(3) The IDO through its Board of Inquirers and Secretary-General shall make public the stage it is in with regard to denaturing the fissile material.

ARTICLE 48

Thermonuclear weapons shall be destroyed in the following manner:
(1) The atomic trigger shall be denatured as quickly as possible after being removed from the weapon.
(2) The weapon shall be detached from its mode of delivery.
(3) Its guidance system shall be destroyed.
(4) Tritium shall be disposed of through burying at sea.
(5) The remainder of the weapon shall be physically destroyed.

244

AARTICLE 49

Ballistic missiles shall be destroyed according to the following procedures:

(1) The guidance system shall be physically destroyed.

(2) Fuel shall be removed.

(3) Toxic fuels shall be encapsulated by vitrification, concretization or other means and disposed of by the disarming nation with full concern for the environment and human safety.

(4) Where there is any scientific doubt about the harmful effects of other fuels related to the delivery vehicle it shall be destroyed or buried at sea with the highest standard of care.

(5) The remainder of the vehicle shall be physically destroyed.

ARTICLE 50

A limited number of missiles may be maintained for satellite surveillance during the disarming process. At the end of the third stage the Parties to the Treaty will ascertain whether independent satellite inspection should be continued to reinforce the satellite and onsite inspection system of the International Disarmament Organization. These missiles shall not be used without prior notification and examination by the IDO or public examination.

ARTICLE 51

(1) All launching pads, silos, underground depots and platforms, mobile and fixed launching systems which can be used for storage or blastoff and which are capable of delivering nuclear weapons or other weapons of mass destruction, shall be demolished.

(2) Launching and guidance of such vehicles, including their equipment shall also be demolished.

ARTICLE 52

Launching for peaceful purposes of satellites shall occur only after prior notification to the International Disarmament Organization. Such launchings shall be public and are to include the presence of citizen groups and journalists. Launchings shall be limited to no more than two sites.

ARTICLE 53

Maiming weapons such as napalm and other weapons which cause adverse long-term toxic effects to persons or land are prohibited.

ARTICLE 54

Destruction of chemical, biological and radiological weapons shall be carried out by agreed upon means among a panel of scientists and technologists chosen by the International Disarmament Organization or signatories to the Treaty Program.

Chapter VI

Unnatural and inhumane weapons

ARTICLE 55

(1) The Parties note with grave concern that the use of herbicides and defoliants may lead to ecocide. Weapons deliberately designed to produce changes in the environment are prohibited. Inhumane weapons such as enhanced radiation weapons are prohibited.
(2) Research, development (including testing), production, use and military planning for or in connection with possible use, are prohibited in relation to unnatural and inhumane weapons.
(3) This prohibition applies to:
    (a) herbicides and defoliants,
    (b) enhanced radiation weapons, whether involving a nuclear explosive device or the spreading of pulverized nuclear waste by air or any means whatsoever,
    (c) weather modification of any kind whether it be rain, fog, hail, lightning or severe storms,
    (d) climate modification,
    (e) electromagnetic radiation,
    (f) electrical behavior of the atmosphere,
    (g) interference with the ozone layer,
    (h) wide-area fragmentation munitions,
    (i) fuel-air explosives,
    (j) napalm-follow-on controlled fireballs,
    (k) viral or bacteriological poisoning of the food, water or atmosphere.

ARTICLE 56

The Parties agree that they will cease all research, development, manufacture, or deployment of space satellites capable of destroying other space satellites.

ARTICLE 57

(1) Parties to the Treaty Program shall in conjunction with the IDO, or the UN, undertake regional and international arms discussions to end the export or import of armaments and war materials one year after the Program takes effect. Replacement parts may be bought and sold throughout the first stage of this Program. At the end of the first stage an international arms trade conference shall be called under the joint aegis of the UN and IDO to ascertain the means needed to assure that the arms assistance and arms replacement trade system will end by a date certain.

246

(2) Each Party to the Program shall inform the IDO about all arms and material which it has exported in *the ten years prior* to this Program or which were *in transit* at the date the Treaty Program takes effect and the destination of those exports.

(3) Likewise each Party undertakes to inform the IDO of all arms imported in the ten years prior to the Treaty Program coming into force or which were in transit to it at that date and the source of export.

(4) The IDO shall encourage scientists, workers, journalists and scholars to report their information and findings on all aspects of arms trade and military assistance.

ARTICLE 58

The information to be furnished to the IDO shall include information as to licenses for the local manufacture of armaments from designs provided by an exporting country, whether the original designer or not, and the extent to which any such license makes an importing country self-sufficient in the manufacture of any particular armament. It shall also include the names of designers and management involved in the licensing or manufacturing process.

ARTICLE 59

Each Party undertakes to amend its domestic law so as to ensure that the operation of this Chapter shall give no right in jurisdiction to damages or other remedy for international breach of contract.

Chapter VII

Prohibitions on industrial plants and economic conversion

ARTICLE 60

(1) For the purposes of inspection and verification industrial plants that produce armaments as well as transportion centers (whether by rail, land, air or sea) shall be detailed for the International Disarmament Organization and for Parties to the Program at the commencement of the disarming process.

(2) The plant facilities include those
  (a) devoted to the production of armaments,
  (b) plants and bases wholly or partly engaged in their repair and maintenance,
  (c) plants, bases or arsenals engaged in the testing or experimental operation of armaments.
  These include either privately or publicly owned facilities.

ARTICLE 61

Each plant manager, owner, board of directors, and local labor union president shall sign an affidavit stating that military production, testing, experiment and shipping have ended according to the terms of the Program. Affidavits shall be made public and filed with the national government and the IDO.

ARTICLE 62

(1) International Disarmament inspectors shall be invited throughout the life of the Treaty to investigate on a spot-check basis the condition of the various plants to be assured that production, experimentation, storing and weapons testing is in accordance with the terms of the Program and that such "production and development" has ended.
(2) Journalists and others are encouraged to write about the disarming process as it relates to the prohibited plants or prohibited military facilities.

ARTICLE 63

(1) The internal laws of the Parties to this Program shall be adjusted so that each industry wholly or in part involved with military contracts will file an economic conversion plan.
(2) The Parties to the Program are aware that dislocations may occur as a result of the disarming process, and therefore each Party to the Program shall find ways, consonant with its own economic system to develop an economic, industrial, community, and worker conversion program.
(3) The International Disarmament Organization shall establish a special unit of the IDO and the UN will be encouraged to do likewise in order to assist any nation with economic data and advice for economic conversion.

ARTICLE 64

(1) The Parties agree that all plants wholly or partially involved in military construction shall follow the terms and stages of this Program.
(2) Machine tools and equipment designed for the production and maintenance of armaments shall be destroyed by the end of the third stage.

ARTICLE 65

Military academies may be maintained subject to the terms of this Program. Their respective course of study would include training and participation in non-military techniques as well as joint exercises through the United Nations peacekeeping force.

ARTICLE 66

(1) Each Party shall furnish full details of its military and paramilitary budget and appropriations to the IDO. It shall give IDO inspectors, specifically appointed for financial verification, access to financial and budgetary records.

(2) Parties shall reduce their arms and armed strength simultaneous to a reduction in military budgets and appropriations for military and paramilitary purposes.

ARTICLE 67

(1) The Board of Inquirers shall submit an annual report to both the Security Council and the General Assembly of the United Nations on the reductions of national expenditures which have been achieved, as well as the expenses of dismantling, destroying or converting to civilian use arms, armaments, plants, equipment and other military items.

(2) Parties shall submit defense budgetary planning documents concerned with military procurement, weapons, acquisitions, and personnel projections.

(3) The report shall make recommendations as to the use to which the resulting savings could be put in providing economic and technical aid to the developing countries, stimulating world trade and aiding national economies.

Chapter VIII

Initial declarations

ARTICLE 68

(1) To facilitate inspection and verification a Party shall deposit an official Declaration on the state of its armed forces at the time of ratification.

(2) The United States and the Soviet Union will deposit their lists with the IDO at the same time. These lists shall include personnel strengths, arms and equipment, plants, facilities, bases, establishments and all other information which is relevant to the duty of inspection and verification.

(3) Without limiting the generality of the preceding paragraph, the Declaration shall include:

  (a) the personnel strengths of naval, land and air forces and auxiliary forces,

  (b) the number of conscripts, the Party's intention with regard to its draft law.

  (c) the number of reservists liable to be recalled for full-time or part-time service,

  (d) the number of single atomic and thermonuclear weapons with their yield in kilotons, as of date of signature,

(e) the number of multiple warheads and individual guidance systems, with their kiloton range,

(f) the number of vehicles of delivery capable of delivering atomic or thermonuclear weapons at a range greater than 100 kilometers,

(g) the number of locations of sites for launching those vehicles of delivery,

(h) rocket launching sites for peaceful purposes,

(i) naval bases,

(j) shipyards for building and servicing ships of war,

(k) the number of ships of war, by categories and types, including fleet auxiliary vessels,

(l) the number of aircraft by categories and types,

(m) the number of airfields and air bases with locations,

(n) plants and facilities producing or servicing any military arms or equipment,

(o) training establishments and their location,

(p) the numbers of weapons for land forces by categories and types,

(q) proving grounds and firing ranges and their locations,

(r) the locations of stockpiles for weapon production,

(s) laboratories engaged in research and development for military purposes,

(t) the location of chemical, biological and radiological weapons.

ARTICLE 69

Any declaration under this Chapter shall clearly indicate where any listed item is located outside the territory of the Party making the declaration.

ARTICLE 70

The Parties to the Program shall provide the IDO and invited members of the UN with the locations and times it will discharge members of its armed forces as required by the Program.

Chapter IX

Verification

ARTICLE 71

(1) The Parties to the Treaty and the IDO, to the extent possible, will rely on technical means of verification from satellite and other non-intrusive monitoring devices.

(2) Each Party agrees that effective verification of this Treaty is necessary to achieve Security and General Disarmament and undertakes to cooperate

for this purpose with the IDO.

(3) Any failure to comply with the obligations of the agreed upon Program for Security and General Disarmament shall be presented to the Board of Inquirers and reported to the Security Council for required action.

ARTICLE 72

(1) The Secretary-General of the IDO and Parties to the Treaty Program shall establish Verification Agency Committees to assist with all questions relating to verification of disarmament and in particular to deal with:

(a) the procedures for verification in each category of weaponry and military forces,

(b) the technical means of making those procedures effective and credible and facilitating their application,

(c) the areas and subjects of research necessary for ensuring that verification procedures are both effective and credible, and

(d) the perfecting of verification by challenge and satisfaction.

(2) Parties to the Agreement shall encourage universities, research institutes and others to carry out studies, discussions and transnational contacts to assure that the inspection and verification process is effective and does not lead to either an unwieldy, ineffective or intrusive policing system.

(3) The institutions mentioned in Article 72, Section 2 will work together as part of a transnational network, sharing information and research.

ARTICLE 73

(1) For purposes of assurance, inspection and verification the IDO shall have the following rights and responsibilities:

(a) to require the maintenance and production of operating records concerning matters relevant to this Program;

(b) to call for and receive progress reports from Parties to the Program, and until technical inspection and verification satellite systems are perfected it shall have the power to send inspectors into any area,

(c) to send inspectors into, or station inspectors, in the territory of any Party as directed by the IDO during the life of the Treaty Program. They shall have access at all times to all places within designated zones, according to the particular stage of the Program. They will have continuous and permanent access to the seat of government. They shall have data and access to any person who by reason of his/her occupation or special knowledge works with materials, equipment, facilities, personnel, financial expenditure, or any other matter bearing on the successful outcome of the disarmament Program.

(2) Parties to the Agreement shall direct its government officials to cooperate fully with the inspectors. They shall indicate the exact location of, and identify, all materials, equipment, facilities, records and data.

251

ARTICLE 74

(1) The Secretary-General shall inform the Party in writing of the name, nationality and background of each inspector proposed and shall transmit a written certification of his or her relevant qualifications. The Party shall inform the Secretary-General with ten days of receipt of such a proposal whether it accepts the designation of the inspector. If so, the inspector is then designated as one of the Organization's inspectors for that Party and the Secretary-General shall notify the Party concerned of such designation.

(2) If a Party at any time objects to the designation of an inspector for that Party, it shall inform the Secretary-General of its objection. In this event, the Secretary-General shall propose to the Party an alternative designation or designations. The Secretary-General shall immediately report to the Board, for its appropriate action, any repeated refusal to accept the designation of an inspector where such refusal would impede the inspection and verification process, and where technical satellite inspection is deemed impossible.

ARTICLE 75

(1) The visits and activities of inspectors shall be so arranged as to ensure the effective discharge of their functions with the minimum possible inconvenience to the host and disturbance to the facilities inspected.

(2) Transportation, lodging and other services shall be provided by the Party under inspection.

(3) The Parties agree that the IDO shall have full rights to install sensing recording and communications instruments in zones where inspection is or has taken place. These may be installed – where necessary – inside plants.

(4) Consistent with the effective discharge of their functions the activities of inspectors will be conducted in harmony with the laws and regulations existing in the state.

(5) No inspector or other staff member of the Organization shall disclose to any person whatsoever any industrial secret or other similar confidential information coming to his knowledge by virtue of his official duties.

(6) Inspectors shall be granted the privileges and immunities necessary for the performance of their functions.

ARTICLE 76

(1) The Secretary-General shall determine upon the basis of the IDO's inspection whether

   (a) the Party has performed all its current obligations under this Treaty,

   (b) the Party has seriously failed or omitted to perform those obligations, or

   (c) the Party while in arrears in the performance of those obligations is seriously and sincerely striving to complete their performance.

(2) He or she shall recommend to the Board of Inquiry what remediable steps if any should be taken to carry out the terms of the Program.

ARTICLE 77

(1) Any Party which suspects that some activity in contravention of the Treaty Program has been carried out or is about to be carried out, may lodge a formal objection to the Board of Inquirers. A Party against whom suspicions have been reported may also lodge an objection.

(2) Non-governmental organizations and other groups may file with the Secretary-General information which shows non-compliance with the terms of the Program. The Party against whom an objection is raised may respond and offer explanations.

ARTICLE 78

(1) Objections under either of the last two preceding Articles shall immediately be investigated by a special committee of inquiry comprising five persons chosen by the Secretary-General from a list prepared by the President of the International Court of Justice.

(2) The Committee's report shall be reported to the Board of Inquiry for special remedial action. It shall also provide a method to disprove the complaint of necessary.

ARTICLE 79

(1) The International Court of Justice may give advisory opinions on any legal question arising under the Disarmament Program which is brought to its attention by the International Disarmament Organization. Its advisory opinions shall be public and made available within three months of filing.

(2) Any question or dispute concerning the interpretation or application of this Program shall be referred to the International Court of Justice by Parties to the Program in conformity with the Statute of the Court, unless the Parties concerned agree to another mode of settlement. The time limit for decision by the International Court of Justice shall be no more than six months from filing.

(3) Each Party undertakes to propose to its legislative authorities during Stage III that it should accept the compulsory jurisdiction of the International Court of Justice in all legal disputes to which it is a party.

Chapter X

Miscellaneous

ARTICLE 80
(1) The Parties encourage independent measures of disarmament announced and executed by any Party able to do so.
(2) Any Party may act, either individually or together with other Parties, to
reduce its armed forces and armaments in advance of the stages of the
Disarmament Program. It shall not, however, be subject to inspection
and on the ground verification until the time and period called for in the
Disarmament Program.

ARTICLE 81
Each Party undertakes that it will make available to the International
Disarmament Organization all information relevant to the obligations of this
Treaty and the disarming process. Where the information is not forthcoming
on specific dates, the Board of Inquiry may assess fines against the late Party.

ARTICLE 82
Each Party agrees to appoint a senior national official and give him or her
the power of direct communication with the Secretary-General of the
Internaional Disarmament Organization on technical matters.

ARTICLE 83
(1) This Program shall be subject to ratification by the Parties in accordance
with their respective constitutional processes. Instruments of ratification
shall be deposited with the Secretary-General of the United Nations who
shall notify each ratification to all its members and to non-members who
have signed the Treaty.
(2) Where a conflict exists between the Security and Disarmament Program
and other Treaties, the Program will take precedence.

ARTICLE 84
Each nation will be assessed for the work of the IDO according to a
percentage contribution formula based on defense expenditure for the
calendar year prior to the initiation of the Program.

The draft treaty program on common security and general disarmament
seeks to take account of the complex dialectic in international affairs
between law, sovereignty and peace as they relate to the centralization and
decentralization of power among nations. These questions also relate, but

only partly, to a group of problems in the international economic sphere. National economics are clearly interdependent. Whether or not this is a preferred consequence of trade, communications and technological development may be questioned. What is clear, however, is that the internal economic changes of national states, especially those of the US, have an important effect on other nations.

The international economy and social reconstruction

Because the US is the leading actor in the international economy it is useful to look at how its own social reconstruction will affect the world economic system and what foreign economic policy changes it would put forward.

It is the only feasible way we will be able to escape the further deterioration of the world economic system and the desperate situation in which the Third World now finds itself.[41]

The three areas where changes in the world economic system must be made are: (a) the international money market; (b) international assistance through aid and trade; and (c) control over international and domestic corporations through domestic and international law.

International money market

Since 1946 the dollar has functioned as the basic standard of monetary exchange in the world. Thirty-two per cent of all world transactions are carried out in American dollars. It has continued to hold its preeminence because as President Carter's Undersecretary of State once put it, "there is at present no feasible alternative."[42] Other nations have accepted the dollar's position and therefore America's preeminence as part of the belief that the US would guarantee protection and stability through economic and military assistance to what we choose to call the "free world." In exchange for its economic and military services the US was accorded a variety of privileges which other nations did not share. As the US seemed to need its special position because of its own internal problems other nations sought to deny the US economic hegemony. The French government, for example, argued that the growth of international reserves should not be controlled by fluctuations in the US balance of payments because this control implies that the US can unilaterally determine world-wide monetary expansion or contraction. Nevertheless, America's capacity to act in this way is likely to continue so long as the United States is able to control, or lay off, inflation on other nations, and peg unemployment at substantial levels without endangering the operations of its economy.

It should be noted that the inflation rates of other capitalist nations have been higher than those of the US, in part because the US pays its balance of payments deficit in dollars rather than goods. The US has had this luxury because of its military preeminence. But this military preeminence is costly and adds greatly to the inflationary situation within the US controlled by the Reagan administration through the "strong" dollar which depresses American farmers and exporting industries. US policy makers also have pursued the course of curbing inflation by cutting domestic programs – rather than curbing military commitments. The result of both policies is predictable. They increased internal class conflict. Our present economic situation is linked to an international economic struggle wherein the losers and aggressors of the Second World War, Germany and Japan, increase their industrial export production under the military umbrella of the US. The Reagan high interest policy is meant to balance off US military costs in Asia and Europe by attracting capital to the US which supposedly would be used for reindustrialization purposes in American society. An aggressive US monetary policy is also used in other nations.

Until the mid-1970s when the dollar was used as exchange currency for transactions inside other nations, the value of the "host" country's currency was adversely affected. In other words, "good money drove out bad money," although in this case it happened to be the currency of the host country. Galloping inflation then resulted for the host country because more local currency was needed to equal American dollars. But the costs of imported oil, of keeping up an alliance system, of banks and international corporations trading against the dollar,[43] and the US government's policy of encouraging US corporations to invest abroad contributed greatly to the loss of value of the dollar during the Carter period. As I have said, high interest rates, which penalize virtually anyone except big business, were used to attract European capital as a way to stabilize the dollar against other currencies.

More than any other single reason, American international policies have been the most likely cause of American inflation. Beginning with President Eisenhower's administration, no American government has been able to easily pursue US well-being with plans for internal economic development, distribution of equity or protection of American products. The US "starved" its poorest groups for its military doctrine and alliance system that was outmoded at its creation. The US generated a so-called forward line method of defense at the cost of decay of its urban areas and destruction of its non-agribusiness farming population. It used economic gimmicks as a way of continuing its imperial errors.

In the course of the Cold War and the Indo-China war the United States sought to cure its balance of payments deficit by calling for a flexibility of exchange rates after having ended the convertibility of dollars into gold.

The strain and the drain on the dollar had become too great; and

256

President Nixon threw all previously orthodox economic theory and policy overboard on 15 August 1971, declaring the dollar no longer convertible against gold. He forced other major currencies, especially the German mark and the Japanese yen, to revalue upward in relation to the dollar in effect devaluing the dollar without wishing to say so.[44]

This was a direct onslaught on the 1944 Bretton Woods agreement, an international concordat that was meant to hold dollars to a fixed rate of exchange. The dollar's value was defined in terms of gold (and convertible into gold) and all the other currencies were fixed in relation to the dollar. The International Monetary Fund, which grew out of the Bretton Woods agreement, was meant to promote international monetary and exchange rate stability.

> It was anticipated that short-term balance of payments deficits and surpluses would be adjusted by using international reserves or by borrowing from the IMF, while long-term surpluses and deficits were to be adjusted by changing the par value of a country's currency (devaluation or revaluation) and by deflating the domestic economy.[45]

The tendency of leaders of all nations to praise joint stability as an end unto itself is especially powerful in the sphere of international monetary activity where it is taken for granted that the world depression of the 1930s was partly caused by the American reluctance to exercise coordinated responsibilities for monetary and economic policies through the League of Nations or some other international mechanism. Government officials who would otherwise favor liberal or even radical policies such as full employment and price stability are tied to the international balance of payments system because they fear even greater world-wide depression or inflation. As a result of a confluence of concerns there is interest among academics and even some Wall Street bankers in "inventing" a currency which is backed by the nations of the world and which acts as an independent or neutral medium of exchange for official transactions that cannot be converted into local currencies. Indeed, an international common good calls for just such a social invention.

During the Second World War Lord Keynes suggested the establishment of an international "clearing union" with "Bancor" as its unit of exchange. Creditor nations would give initial large credits and the union itself would build its assets without a ceiling with substantial obligations upon creditor as well as upon debtor countries, with a leadership role for America and Britain, and with the right of any country to devalue its currency up to 5 per cent a year without prior permission. In recent years international bankers and analysts, for example E.M. Bernstein and Robert Roosa, have put forward proposals for reserve assets that would be created in industrial nations through deposits of their own currency with the IMF.

While it is infinitely easier to get a changed monetary system after a war, it is not inevitable that rational changes can only come after traumatic events. Establishing a separate currency for official transactions would have an extraordinarily stabilizing effect on world affairs. It would allow each nation, from Jamaica to the United States, to generate the currency that each needed for internal development free of excessive concern with the financial judgments of private bankers, the political judgments of other nations or of international lending agencies. In the United States liberals would not have had to champion high interest rates or recession as they did in the 1979-82 period during the Carter-Volcker-Reagan induced recession.

International development

When we discuss monetary reforms which will be free of the foreign and domestic policies of any single nation we are aware that we have dealt with but one side of the economic equation. The actual productive side and the means by which the American nation can help others during its own period of readjustment looms important.

Throughout the post-Second World War period, we have had much discussion and activity around "development" of other nations. Missing from this discussion is the question of what we really mean by development. Surely it cannot be as self-serving as locating markets for American or European consumer goods hustled at the expense of Third World communities that are then broken by a new import market system. And surely it cannot mean finding a way to turn peasants into factory workers at highly specialized tasks which are soon replaced by machines, less tired workers or unemployment as the international corporation moves its plants to even more hospitable nations. Surely it must mean something more than the US giving a present of two-tenths of 1 per cent of its gross national income to the Third World mostly in military related aid. Surely development must be cognizant of humanity whose old ways have been tampered with but who have not found a way to a practical and operational definition of international equity, empathy and justice. In other words development must mean overcoming a shocking disparity between rich and poor nations in which

> Thirty developed countries with less than 30 per cent of the world's population now, and foreseeably only 20 per cent of the population in the year 2000, account for approximately 90 per cent of world income, financial reserves, and steel production, and 95 per cent of the world's scientific and technological production.[46]

There must be awareness that development has deteriorated into over-populated cities unable to provide services even as agricultural communities and towns also are depleted. No wonder one should question whether the issue of the international economic order is to be couched in terms of "development."

Charles Bettelheim aptly pointed out that underdevelopment has been a mode of development pushed on Third World nations which distorted and degraded them as the Western colonizing nations attempted to make them their appendages. There is a touch of absurdity about old cultures being "developed" by the United States. Is it not patently foolish and arrogant to think of developing the Indians and the Chinese whose culture is so rich, varied and powerful? Can we say that the US is to develop, with its earth machinery, pills and nuclear energy in Africa so that Africans may become the US? So where should we look for a definition of development?

The answer to international development is found in the collective and individual attributes of caring and equity; concerns which are meant to yield dignity for the world's people. They are found in natural, non-market activities of human beings: play, sex, creative work, thinking, ritual, politics and then in requirements for shelter, food, health and human dignity. Such ideas cannot be made manifest through nationalism and bogus assistance programs which are "used to justify and defend class domination at home and economic imperialism abroad."[47] So long as inequity and a money system co-exist special care should be given to overcoming the assumption that the hallowed metaphor, "market forces," will benefit the poor nations. If this eighteenth-century hope, which lingers into the twenty-first century, is not so, what then is the political method for achieving equity among the rich and poor nations?

There are two fundamental economic trends of international existence which, if there is no world war, will govern the nations well into the twenty-first century. Curiously even as US indebtedness increases it will remain the richest large nation in the world and it will continue to be the single largest user of the world's resources. Second, those nations which are dependent on a single commodity that is not oil will continue to grow poorer as developed nations grow richer. Various proposals have been advanced over the past decade to rectify this condition, one in which well over a billion people hang on to their human condition of starvation.

The question of how to deal with the power and affluence of modern nations as against the wretched condition of the Third World, those areas which were once dominated by the colonial power of the rich, was first formulated at the end of the Second World War at a 1948 UN Conference on Trade and Employment which met in Havana. The participants called for the establishment of an International Trade Organization that would frame code rules "to regulate international trade in the post-war period." Its charter elaborated organizational plans that would operate according to principles which accepted income transfers from the rich to poor nations. This charter was scuttled by the United States because of isolationist members of Congress who feared that the establishment of such an organization would limit American sovereignty.

The conceptual framework laid out in the Havana Charter did not die. It found its way into the first meeting of the UN Conference on Trade and Development which became a permanent organ of the UN General Assembly. UNCTAD, as it is known, remains the world-wide instrument for seeking equity and fairness in the international trading and marketplace. In this body the US has continued to find itself a minority, often of one. While other nations, notably European nations, seek an orderly and secure supply of commodities, the US continues to champion free world markets and the "open door" under the theory that the open door policy fits best with its own views of competition and finally dominance over certain markets.

After the success of the 1973 oil boycott by the OPEC nations all nations were aware that a new element had occurred in international politics. It caused leaders, especially in developed nations, to reinvestigate and reconsider their own position *vis-à-vis* producer nations. Conversely, pressures in the Third World built up for the reformulation of international trade and equity systems which were first made at the sixth special session of the United Nations General Assembly. A group of seventy-seven Third World nations called for a new international economic order. The concept of the seventy-seven was the child of the original Havana Charter of 1948. The Third World began confronting the developing nations as a bloc within an international framework irrespective of Marxist or capitalist tendencies.

The seventy-seven called for a common fund in eighteen basic commodities. This fund was to provide for buffer stocks in order to stabilize prices. It would do so by integrating the commodities so that the developing nations could band together and generate agreements that would be mutually supporting to their interests. It was not until President Carter's administration that the United States was prepared to change the American emphasis on free markets and overcome its suspicion of buffer stocks. The Carter administration purpose was to fashion a program of commodity supports and agreements that would effect the following purpose:

(1) reduction of disruptive fluctuations in export earnings of developing countries;
(2) assurance to the United States that there would be an adequate supply of commodities by improving the climate for investment; and
(3) distribution in a more equitable way of the burdens which agreements on particular commodities have historically been spread between major producers and consumers.

While this was thought of by Third World leaders as glacial progress, progress it was. Other similar arrangements were made through the efforts of the European Economic Community with African, Caribbean and Asian states in a program called STABEX (Stabilization of Export Earnings). This is a system of financial compensation which was established between the EEC and African, Caribbean and Asian states in 1975. The ACP countries have import access into Europe without giving trading concessions to the EEC.

The major innovation which the producing nations favor and to which American economic diplomats have given some economic credence is the establishment of a common fund first proposed by the seventy-seven nation group. The fund was to accumulate some $6 billion dollars of buffer stocks for the eighteen UNCTAD commodities in order to stabilize exports and earnings for single export countries during difficult economic periods. While the creation of such a program would probably increase the cost of individual commodities, there would be a "steady supply of materials to the consuming countries" without causing them to turn to substitutes. This system of price stabilization, however, only tangentially touches the question of development. The plan, as it is being conceived under the Reagan administration, if it is supported at all through the Senate, is not meant to deal with the question of equity through income transfers. In other words, it retains a limited scope, that of keeping the world economic pyramid where it is. At best it is an insurance and grant work against disaster. Nevertheless, the common fund's enactment will allow the poorest nations to have some protection in cases of drought or surplus.

The Third World has made the common fund the *sine qua non* for bringing in a new international economic order. In doing so they are trying to break with the belief that the market system can dictate or should dictate their own situation of development. In the period of American reconstruction, as we come to grips with the limits of the market system, we will also need to do the same critical work in international economic affairs. This is little more than recognizing reality, according to former Assistant Secretary of State, Julius Katz. He pointed out to Congress that there are very few free markets in the basic UNCTAD commodities since they are controlled and operated through state trading organizations. In this sense a dose of realism with justice will change the nature of our debates on international economic trade and development.

An early task for an international economic order is to explore a pricing system which is explicitly political and which takes account of the principles of justice and caring in economic arrangements. In practice this will mean (a) fashioning a two-track pricing system for raw materials and (b) creating an indicator system to determine whether a particular nation is meeting the needs or attempting to meet the needs of its people. The first track would operate along present lines in which prices are negotiated binationally and multilaterally. This would be accomplished through the present administered market system with longer-term commodity agreements being drawn between the producer and the consumer.

A second track should be introduced for poor nations. Where it is determined by a vote in UNCTAD (which would meet continuously) that fluctuations in the price of commodities are adversely affecting the poor nations and where a poor nation can demonstrate that its social services and capital investment budgets are *not* being slighted through inequitable tax and fiscal policies, then the US and other nations as well as international agencies would contribute to a fund which would subsidize the difference between the market price and the price that would be fair to the poor nation, given its needs. This grant would be given under the auspices of the UN by the common fund. The fund would, of course, not be restricted to price stabilization, but would include an expanded role through a UN Development Fund. The common fund, over time, would move to become an international UN social and development agency similar to SUNFED, a proposal that had much currency in the 1950s. However, this fund would start from new understandings. For example, schooling in traditional forms developed in the US and Europe may be wasteful, even disastrous, that top-down development projects which are based on the value assumptions of the great power often turn out to be conspicuous waste in the Third World, and that capital intensive activities destroy communities where there are large populations. Development should no longer mean the replication of the West and its technology around the world.

Ideally, popular assent in the US for a world development program should come through a national referendum. This would be a way to give maximum play within the United States to participation on foreign economic matters, allowing citizens the opportunity of debating the level of aid which they intend to give others. It is a means for individuals to directly express economic motives of caring and equity through politics.[48]

Obviously, implementation of the second tier subsidy should not have to wait for internal participatory changes within the United States. A more traditional method is to arrive at a shared subsidy amount based upon political negotiations within UNCTAD. There is a *quid pro quo* which all the industrial nations will seek from Third and Fourth World nations especially where the industrialized need critical raw materials for their societies. Because there are fears of resource shortages in industrialized nations, an international plan between the industrialized and non-industrialized world could be forged if it would take into account long-term needs of all sectors of the world after first assuring the non-aligned nations that their primary responsibility was to find ways among themselves to meet minimum needs. Thus, for example, oil-producing states would be encouraged to invest in other Third World nations to develop raw materials, technology and skills. They would encourage markets and finance arrangements which would strengthen national economies in the Third World without mediation through multinational corporations.

If the United States were to champion an economic magna carta for the

Third World it would result in changes in American trading and consuming habits. The US would begin to plan the use of its resources more carefully. No doubt this would result in greater discipline around resource use. As part of this internal discipline Congress would establish a new federal administrative mechanism to trade in resources necessary to the general welfare of American society. A federal trading corporation would include a council of governors and mayors that would plan long-term energy and likely commodity needs. The agency would act for the consumers in dealings with the oil producing nations. The present system of having oil corporations act as the broker between consumers and foreign producers is an anomaly on the international scene.

Reagan administration members argue from the nationalist position that the United States must maintain an interventionary force, for the purpose of maintaining current consumption practices of Americans. The example usually given by strategists and politicians concerns the need to continue oil supplies to the US at virtually any rate the American people (and oil companies) care to use foreign oil. Our geopoliticians argue that any attempt on the part of other nations to control prices or raw materials which the US "needs" should be rightly open to direct military intervention on the part of the US, and to ringing the Middle East with American military bases. (The arguments that were made by the oil interventionists, before the price of oil per barrel began falling, were similar to the ones made by the Japanese pre-Second World War cabinet with regard to the US oil blockade of Japan.)

There are four objections to this currently fashionable, geopolitical point of view.

(1) The nationalist position flies in the face of any principle of equity or need which can be justly asserted. The gap of economic and social well-being between the rich and poor nations would merely continue attitudes of selfishness and domination which statesmen reject in their more prudential moments and which are specifically proscribed by the Nuremberg Charter, the UN Charter, numerous UN resolutions and the Kellogg-Briand pact. These political documents make eminent good sense in the face of basic material considerations. The present use of the world's resources, and the distribution of income and wealth shows such a glaring and deepening disparity, that there is no legitimate national security basis for US military intervention. The ground for such intervention would have to be found in selfishness and domination, not in any principles of equity, justice or caring.

(2) The present technological system adopted by the West and especially the United States is inherently wasteful because it places great emphasis on individual ownership of many consumer goods, that should be held commonly, spends its own and the world's energy on innovations around packaging, and encourages product differentiation where none is necessary.

Present resource requirements in American life are a function of two interesting developments. One is the conscious imperative of capitalism and state bureaucracies which have not found a way to measure the cost of private profit to the society, nor have efficiency and utility been defined in ways that increase the scope of popular understanding. The unfortunate corollary is that the type of technology which is most praised is that which requires understanding by fewer and fewer people. If, as Paul Goodman argued, technology should be a branch of moral philosophy, then the technological system must serve the common good, as a whole, and people need to learn the costs and effects of technological products and tools. Scientific and technical groups would devise means to assure that technological discoveries would do minimum harm and maximum good to present and future generations.

When we make such qualitative and quantitative calculations we should be prepared to reject a nationalist security attitude which assumes that the US cannot change its own value system, or alter a technology which engenders wasteful habits.

The fear that de Tocqueville had for American society was that it would not be able to control its individualist appetite for material progress; that it would not calculate correctly the costs of such socially shared attitudes. De Tocqueville feared that the American drive for material well-being would result in collective unhappiness and that this purpose, if it ever became singular, would be America's undoing. But the direct negative effects that certain types of material progress have brought to our society have stimulated a reverse political consciousness. This consciousness calls for a halt to resource squandering protected by costly and wasteful military policies that seek to perpetuate and defend this squandering.

(3) The nationalist strategy will require a policy of continuous intervention and engagement, the re-adoption of the discredited fascist ideology of racial superiority and the sanctification of selfishness. Paradoxically, the military and human resource cost of maintaining such a system will lead to the spartanization of the American populace in defense of its raw materials flow and the embrace of military oligarchy. Such "will-stiffening" in the defense of gluttony is not a very attractive policy on any ground. For it is not likely that the combination of satiety and spartan military forces can buttress each other for very long. The likelihood is that such wars which would be initiated to mask class disparity would intensify internal class enmity and struggle. This is surely true if the war is long and drawn out, as in the case of the Vietnam war, or is one in which the US uses nuclear weapons. In the latter case, there should be little doubt on the part of the nation's leaders, especially since the 500,000 person demonstration for nuclear disarmament on 12 June 1982, that the first US use of nuclear weapons in the Third World where there was no retaliation against the US would yield massive civil disobedience and the kind of resistance which

would make it impossible for the authorities to govern. Such a public reaction should not be a source of surprise; the authorities would have lost all moral legitimacy.

The trade and tariff question as part of international development requires considerable alteration in liberal ideology. The present system of free flow of capital is causing deskilling among American workers resulting in a change in the standard of living for the mass of society without substantial positive effects redounding to other nations.[49]

The eighteenth-century belief in free trade and no tariffs was related to a rational and humane sentiment. Advocates believed that free trade would promote the common good by establishing an orderly flow of capital and skills. Under the theory of the invisible hand all nations achieve well-being and even economic development would occur. But the fact is that free trade does not work in this manner; that it often promotes uneven development and therefore greater disparity between nations and social classes. Flying the banner of free trade and technology transfer, and accomplished with the support of both political parties, capital and industrial flight from the United States has had a disastrous effect on American society, namely a depletion of skills among American workers causing decreased productivity and an increase in structural unemployment in the US. On the other hand, it is not demonstrated that capital-industrial flight to Hong Kong, Chile, Brazil or South Korea has added to a growth rate that translated into an equitable redistribution of income for their respective societies. They have led, however, to a terrifying overpopulation of cities. Thus, lowering tariff barriers for goods made abroad by US owned firms is not a favor to American society or, for that matter, the producer nation. When international capital is exported and uncontrolled the beneficiaries are a relatively invisible international class of banks and multinational corporate investors who set the framework of economic and political decisions for Third World nations with few if any national or international political controls on them. This international commercial culture, glued together by its own cosmopolitan business accounting values, creates a social corollary, namely the depoliticization of people into passive consumers and the destruction of traditional community and self-generated community action. Governments, especially in Third World areas (this may include a bankrupt New York City) are reduced to being policemen consigned only to keeping social peace as their economies are manipulated internationally by the great banks and multinational corporations; entities which since 1973 have been operating with recycled funds from oil producing states. The situation and problems are similar for Zaire and New York City as regards Chase Manhattan Bank or between Brighton, England and Fort Dearborn as regards Ford Motor Company. What might be proposed, if anything, to remedy this situation?

We need to invent concepts for rationalizing the existence of new actors on the international scene. Even if we were to embrace a positivist view of international relations we would conclude that international corporations receive their legitimacy from nation-states, or the combined will of nation-states. They do not operate without the approval of a sovereign. In other words, the global corporation's freedom of access and purpose is derivative, dependent either on the host state, the parent state or the United Nations. This being the case it is incumbent on nations, deriving their authority from people to regulate the activities of the international corporations. Furthermore, with a continued increase of total exports between nations and with the emergence of multinational corporations as instruments to maneuver technology, skills and resources, the effects of what happens in one nation are going to be very quickly felt in other nations as well. As a former deputy director of the CIA has put it:

(1) The flow of goods, funds, people and firms across borders makes states and societies increasingly sensitive and vulnerable to external events and actions. Governments will not be able to manage their national economies and the welfare state without cooperation with others to regulate the system of money, trade, and investment, and economic policy as well as the multinational corporation.

(2) Expanding demand and shortages will require joint action to assure the steady supply of raw materials, energy, food, and fertilizer, as well as efforts to foster growth in the developing nations and the control of population.

(3) Technology and the shrinking globe are producing new problems of interdependence. Pollution from one state may damage waters or atmosphere beyond its borders and harm the environment of others. And resources of the oceans, such as fish or oil deposits on the continental shelf, or minerals on the ocean floor, become matters of concern to many states as technology expands the capacity for recovery.[50]

These issues of interdependence are such as to give rise to several considerations. One is the importance of refashioning international institutions so that they have the "organized intelligence" to help in managing and characterizing relationships that affect large populations and diverse nations. But this "organized intelligence" is not disembodied. It is to be related to hearing and reflecting the voice from the grassroots and putting into practice the emerging values of equity and caring. Otherwise, international institutions will not relate to local constituencies and needs.[51]

With these considerations in mind I propose for study the following recommendations. The International Labor Organization should be charged with the responsibility of preparing a charter for the global corporation which it would present to its members, the member states and the UN bureaucracy as well as to the global corporations. Such a charter would be

266

introduced into labor-management negotiations between the corporations and the unions. The charter would be presented to the Security Council and the General Assembly for passage. It would include the establishment of an agency for international chartering as well as exercising specific legal investigative functions. What might such an ILO proposal look like?

(a) A global corporation is to be defined and determined on the basis of size, number of nations in which it operates and importance of the product. The most obvious candidates for UN corporate chartering are the energy corporations. Voting stock in the global corporation should be owned locally by the host nation where that corporation either does substantial business or has production facilities.

(b) The host country would charge a profits tax for international corporations which would be deposited with a regional development fund. The Latin American and Asian Development Funds (ECLA) and (ECFA) would be constituted as regional development fund systems under UN aegis with international corporations aiding these Funds through this regional taxing system.

(c) Through presidential and Congressional determination the US would exclude any products made by American-owned companies from entering the US domestic trading markets where such labor competes unfairly with American workers and which merely exacerbates class differences in the exporting nation. The purpose of this policy is to return capital to the US for investment in our own cities and technological plant. It is also meant to restrict the adverse effects of corporate investment on Third world societies.

(d) A UN specialized agency to monitor the operations of world-wide corporations and other economic enterprises which acted as monopolies would be established to ascertain how these enterprises fulfill or deviate from UN resolutions that are premised on the stated world goals of greater economic justice, distribution of wealth and income, promotion and protection of local cultures and human rights. Over time these reports would include critical commentary on the relationships of problems of technology, deforestation, environmental hazards and other distortions which might accompany particular forms of progress or economic involvement by international corporations.

The political consequence to emerge from such an agency is that the empty spaces of the world economy, now partially filled by global, corporate activity, would be partially checked by international legal-political controls. On the other hand, global corporations would lose their bastard status by receiving the status of legitimacy from the United Nations.

It should be noted that any profound change in foreign policy direction can only occur if there is greater clarity about the *actual* political form of the American governing system and the values it projects to itself and the rest of the world.

As we shall see in the next chapter the United States is caught in a struggle about the nature of the American system, whether it is a republic, democracy, or national security state. It does not necessarily follow that the democracy is the least imperial or expansive, although the possibilities toward progress and acceptance of the principle that justice and peace are related is most likely in democratic thought and practice. The question for democracy is to yoke justice and peace to moral limits that its people accept. This is the important task of internal law and international organization.

6
The next stage
of democracy

Since the depression, a fierce struggle has been waged in the United States around foundational questions about the nature of American government and the character of American society. At first this struggle seemed to be concerned with the role of government and whether the United States was a democracy or a republic. The struggle took on more elaborate and complex dimensions as a result of the Second World War which created the option of superpower status and the powerful impulse of world-wide American responsibility.[1] With this new superpower status the national security state system was born as an imperial necessity and rationalizer of internal order.

Because of the American aversion to foundational thinking, especially among liberals, there has been an unwillingness to recognize that protagonists for power are attempting to organize the United States around one of three forms, the republic, democracy, or national security state. Obviously, some leaders and "pragmatists" seek to broker between the different forms of government thereby thrusting on the nation a hybrid system. Indeed, liberal and conservative politicians have sought to mediate between these forms. Nevertheless, there are basic differences between them. They were sharpened by Reagan's term in office.

The first group assumes the United States to be a republic, although for practical political purposes, i.e. mass manipulation, it calls the United States a democracy. Its proponents believe strongly that there are two classes of people. One class we may think of as the citizens and the other as the associates of the state. Citizens are property holders, white, male, and not beholden to others. Associates are dependent, employed, without property, female and/or of color. Citizens have status and associates have no lien on the society or its governance. That which is given to them is given by "grace" or voluntarily. According to its proponents the government of the United States is representational, if not representative, limited in purpose. If one were to scratch most members of Congress in their less guarded and more philosophic moments this would be their fundamental belief. In practice the propertied and well born are to control the destiny of American life. Of course, one might note the Senate of the United States where at least eighty of its hundred members are millionaires and multimillionaires.

The leading proponent of the republic after the Second World War was Senator Robert Taft of Ohio, who while he believed in a housing program for the poor, more like a reservation program, also believed in a limited defense budget, and limited involvement in direct international action or alliances. Taft despaired over the foreign activism of Harry Truman and Dean Acheson, men who spoke for the spread of democracy and the rationalizing of state power.[2] He argued, for example, that the NATO alliance derogated from the UN and imperial expansion would lead to an endless arms race or worse. Taft pointed out that the fundamental conception of the UN was to guard against the reassertion of blocs and alliances. While the protagonists might subjectively think of their action as defensive, their antagonists would conclude that they would have to counter-respond with their own alliances. This view turned out to be accurate as it related to Europe and the emergence of the Warsaw Pact after NATO'S inception. There was a somewhat disingenuous character to Taft's position for he feared the UN as an instrument of social change, namely its emphasis on human rights, and its idealistic democratic and decolonizing aspirations. There was another, fundamental concern Taft and his supporters voiced. It was that military and foreign expansion would transform the republic into a strong welfare state which would increase the power of the have nots of the society and possibly destroy the market system.[3]

Democracy is the second theory of the modern American state. This framework was best reflected in the work of such liberals as Justice William O. Douglas, whose numerous books and judicial opinions championed and reflected several consistent themes.[4] He believed in greater participation of all people within the United States and intended to destroy the citizen-associate distinction of the republic. His approach to internationalism included a limited unilateral military role for the United States, a buildup of the United Nations as an instrument for the solution of disputes and the raising of economic and social standards, a system of human rights guarantees domestically and abroad within the context of a rational international legal framework. Douglas knew that democracy was not a given or finished form. It was a political process which sought the perfectibility of economic, social and political relationships based on a theory of inalienable rights which were discoverable through pain, inquiry and struggle. This view of course is the history of struggle against slavery and apartheid in the United States, and struggle for voting entitlements, welfare and minimal protection for labor.

The social struggles of the 1960s were an attempt to democratize the United States. They brought the "associates" into the public space, as it were, as they put forward new arguments and considerations for what a

270

democracy was to be. The struggle of democracy was not of course limited only to government of the state, or relations between the individual and the state. Instead, democratic struggles raised fundamental questions about the reconstitution of authority and participation in our educational and social institutions covering such issues as civil rights, equality and the transformation of seemingly "settled" forms of domination, namely white over non-white, men over women and man over nature. Inalienable or natural rights became the ground of social change. Scientific discovery emphasized similarities between all people just as, politically, property rights were to take second place to people's rights. There had been a slight attempt at income redistribution on the grounds that auto workers, Mississippi tenant farmers and oil barons could not be citizens of the same nation unless there was a floor and perhaps a ceiling to income and wealth. As Herbert Gintis has pointed out, the state was drawn on to maintain a share of the social product for the have nots through social security, health, education and welfare benefits.[5]

The democratic view had also found voice in confronting the undeclared war in Vietnam. At first liberal democrats opposed the war on pragmatic utilitarian grounds, namely that it was unwinnable.[6] However, as the war progressed, it was clear that a moral aversion, felt across classes and groups, crept into the public thinking which was soon taken over by those who believed in the democracy and the republic. Senator J. William Fulbright and other senators who were not part of the movement of the 1960s were committed to a republican form of government holding to an enlightened form of citizens and associates model. Their view was that the republican form of government was being destroyed in the swamps of Indo-China.

What became clear by the mid-1970s is that the inequitable distribution of wealth and income placed enormous strains on the welfare functions of the state.[7] Either there had to be a change in the nature of capitalism itself or the rights that were extended (which cumulatively meant that the United States would continue its own road to modern democracy) would be interrupted. Ronald Reagan saved the United States from democracy by three powerful interventions into the political process. First, he related public confidence in the future to capitalism. Whereas capitalism appeared to be suffering from impossible and irreconcilable contradictions which appeared to court crises, doom and psychological malaise, President Reagan offered the argument that our condition was only true if we extend rights to all people, i.e., guaranteed the social product to everyone. Instead of social rights he insisted that people internalize the fantasy of hyper-individualism and nationalism. Second, he organized the class of "haves" to forge a coherent will and strategy if not a coherent set of ideas. Finally, while talking "democracy," this program was to be used against democracy itself and specifically against those who intended to exercise newly won rights, namely women, blacks, and other minorities.[8] These groups had begun to

271

reshape the American ethos and purpose to the detriment of the propertied. With the labor movement they had sought to raise questions of equity.

These two conceptions of government, the democratic and republic forms (using those words in their structural rather than political party sense), were both complemented and contradicted by a third form, the national security state, although both political parties conspired to develop the national security state. Liberalism acted as the pragmatic instrument emphasizing "ways and means," "effectiveness" and "management" techniques to install the apparatus of the national security state. Liberals also supplied the rhetorical justification for it to workers, educational institutions and public minded elites. Conservatives deserted Taft. They promulgated the idea of war against all classes that did not accept the market system.

The national security state form, by its nature, is expansionist for it deals with the continuous creation of activities in all aspects of public life and has become the single most important function of millions of federal workers unions, police agencies and defense corporations, universities and scientists. The national security state's link to military technology, nationalism, limited wars for interest and institutions such as the universities uses the ideological music of the republic and the democracy as it continues its expansion abroad and transformation of American life into a garrison and launching pad for nuclear war.[9]

It is of course true that as a republic the United States indulged in far-flung assertions of military intervention: ninety-nine according to the Library of Congress, 125 according to Senator Barry Goldwater. "From the halls of Montezuma to the shores of Tripoli" and China, the United States had already made its might felt through military intervention. The change that occurred in 1947 was that the United States needed a state structure that would take over responsibilities from empires that disappeared as a result of the Second World War.[10] American leaders such as John McCloy, men who came to their own power through work in national security and military bureaucracies, believed that the United States had entered into a time of neither war nor peace, that its responsibility required the establishment of states that fit within the US sphere. The US was to be neither social democratic nor fascist, and the basic decisions of security would be taken outside of public consideration. To this end the National Security Act of 1947 was passed. It promulgated a system of loyalty which would henceforth apply to government officials and industrial workers. It was taken for granted that as a superpower the United States would be continuously involved in conflict. It therefore needed a large standing armed force for conflicts, as well as secrecy, to protect its policies and weaponry, and an advanced military technology, namely missiles and nuclear weapons to be brandished in negotiation. Because the conflicts of the United States were now continuous, covert activities, military assistance, loyalist coherence on national security (the bipartisan foreign policy), government planning of the industrial defense sector and the guiding of the universities, laboratories and labor unions where they touched on "security" questions were now necessary.

Forswearing George Washington's advice that the US should have no permanent hostile enemies, US leaders concluded that the US was in a battle not with evil leaders, but with evil itself, namely communism, which would flow to those areas where there were "power vacuums."

The national security state's purpose in its practical goal was that of being number one. It practiced selective anti-communism, the use of force to guarantee the flow of resources and markets, and a "forward defense" system. This system was rather successfully challenged in the Third World by the Chinese in the Korean War, and the Vietnamese in the Indo-China war.

The principle of number oneism became an obsession with players in the national security state for it meant the assertion of dominance and the tantalizing belief that, like laws of nature, the United States could live outside of human history.

While it is the case that the national security state appears to be the most vibrant political form because it commands the resources of the society through the twin instruments of national security budgets coupled with an ideology which borrows from the rhetoric of the republic and the democracy, the likelihood is that it can be defeated once there are clear competing claims which are organized around the principle of extension of rights and assertion of sovereignty by the people. In this context the national security state emerges as a degraded form of governing which uses republic and democratic forms but which in fact does not begin from people's sovereignty, rather only isolation from their control. Thus, the national security state can be exposed as a control mechanism *against* the people. It flies in the face of 200 years of struggle for resting the power of the nation with the people. The demise of the national security state could mean the extension of internal democracy since more resources will be made available to the society as a whole and the threat of war, the prime use of people for the interests of the few, will be far less likely.

In the American form of government, as Justice Wilson pointed out in 1793, "supreme power resides in the body of the people." Justice Wilson's notions seemed to parallel the Rhode Island Constitution which in 1641 used the word democracy. By democracy this document seemed to outline its "radical" meaning, namely that the people or a major part of them would make laws in orderly assembly with the ministers faithfully executing them.[11] It is the ongoing project of American politics to give practical substance to these ideas. Indeed, each profound event in American history is related to reinforcing and defining the power of the people. In the eighteenth century, the American form of government, according to Article 4, Section 4 of the Constitution, was called a "Republican Form of

Government" and it has long been taken for granted that Congress protects and interprets this phrase.[12] In the nineteenth century it took the Civil War to define who was a citizen-person and who could share in the power of the people. In the twentieth century, democracy became the political form to assure and define the collective and individual power of people. In other words, through social accretion and the struggle of different oppressed or silent groups, the American people sought to pass out of the stage of the Republic, which limited participation to the propertied and the few, to a representative democracy which, on a voting basis, included women. By the 1960s, with the emergence of groups who thought themselves able to govern, namely blacks, women and some hitherto silent groups, democracy seemed to be reaching toward a participatory stage, moving from its representative meaning to a new meaning of representation. This newly-emerging understanding of democracy came exactly at the time the oligarchic military system also sought pre-eminence in American society through the centralization of power in the hands of national security and business elites as they tested military technology in Indo-China. These groups believed republican institutions such as Congress to be manipulable and ornamental. After all, many members of Congress were packaged themselves as commodities to be bought and sold.

Traditional conservative elites feared democracy more then they feared the national security state because democracy brought economic and social instability as well as the reexamination of American assumptions about Third World revolution. Conservatives saw democracy as dangerous to tradition, class interest and the institutions of hierarchic power.[13] It is not too extreme to say that they continue to fear the democratic spirit and have no interest in a common good which goes beyond their own class except as a propaganda means of keeping people in a docile mood. However, those who champion democracy in its fullest and most direct sense also have a more expansive meaning to the common good. It must transcend and change class relations.

Democracy's project is the sharing of responsibility between the citizenry, finding common uses and ownership of property where that benefits the whole – while continuously recognizing the needs of the person. This is not the purpose of a republic which does not wholly trust the people or an oligarchy which trusts only cliques. A modern democracy recognizes the need to generate situations and relationships which simultaneously recognize similarity in the Other, and paradoxically, seeks uniqueness of each person. It recognizes the possibility of a metaphysical harmony between people and nature. And it moves beyond individual and group interest to hammer out shared values which can be located in the whole, the group, but which cannot be found in the individual. In practical terms, democracy can find this chord of harmony by encouraging people to see themselves beyond their social roles. If democracy is understood in this

274

way, it becomes an agency for fulfilling the person's need for egalitarian interdependence by conferring on the person legitimating power, i.e. a citizenship in which all members of the nation seek to work out individual destinies and common projects, with the latter taking precedence where there is a contradiction between the two.

Democracy is a process form which structures situations and relationships. It *cracks* class differences, social, race and gender barriers through specific projects and presents people the possibility of connecting individual needs and projects in a complementary manner. Democracy builds on the complex and ambiguous sentiment of fraternity and sorority seeking to find wisdom and authority within the group rather than through an outside force (God) or in some leader-individual. While the modern democracy has its roots in individualism, in practice its governing system is required to seek harmony between individual needs and desires through common purpose. It is in the project of common purpose that people intuitively recognize one another by seeing the Other in an historical process that accepts the human rights of self and Other to be *in* history, equally dependent on each other and equally capable of wisdom. Practically speaking, no person in our time can be part of this process if he or she is a stateless person, ward or refugee. The process of interdependence can only happen if a person has citizenship status.

The process of "changing" a person to citizen may be hazardous, for in an authoritarian time the natural person may be forgotten as she or he comes to be described in social categories rather than account being taken of the person *qua* person. This danger puts much stress on the law and its promulgators, for their task is to teach that the purpose of citizenship and democracy is to protect the person as the root of civilization at a time when many in the citizenry cry for enforcers of law to be oppressors. Herein I wish to describe the conditions of citizenship and democracy which assure that power and rights are retained by the people. Without these elements it might be asked whether present meanings to democracy can be of much value – other than ornamental – to the person.

Attributes of a modern democracy

A modern democracy aims toward the common good when its leaders and major institutions teach that a person's rights and obligations are based on individual dignity, prudence, caring and equity.[14] The modern democracy constantly evolves and therefore it is not ahistorical. Teachers, leaders and organizers have an obligation to explain to people that rights and obligations are not given but are won through past struggles. (According to Gintis[15] "Class struggle in advanced capitalism concerns both the deepening of a person's rights within the state, and the extension of these rights to the capitalist economy, where they curb the prerogatives of capital and increase the power of subordinate groups.") These struggles seek to discover politically the nature of man. Thus, a modern democracy does not shrink from the doctrine of natural rights for it is a key to personhood. Such rights, *there* even before we discover them, come to define what it means to be human. Once rights are so formulated they cannot be taken away. They become the platform on which the general will rests. It may well be that these rights can be determined and discussed through modern means of communication for modern communication allows for dialogue. It is not a fantasy to structure communications so that people will have a chance to participate in such a way as to determine the general will. Obviously, any serious definition of modern democracy must take into account questions of property as well as questions of communication.

Prior to 1848, the political concept "democracy" meant more than political participation in the sense of the right to vote. For example, it would have been thought absurd to believe that voting meant anything without having property. Voting was the way in which one represented his or her property. But once property and voting separated a new theory was formulated. The vote would obtain the property and capital that was so critical for dignity of the person and the group. Alternatively, government would act as the interlocutor with the rich. Failing the power to get the property, the government would ensure that the fruits of the property had to be shared if those who voted so decreed.

Consequently, in a modern meaning of democracy, several aspects must be kept in mind as the goal and means of day to day policies. One relates to economic rights and power, another political participation and the power of execution, and a third is the use of communications, inquiry and knowledge to define clearly the natural right that people have as a result of their being human. Unfortunately, the modern definition of politics – and of democracy – is limited (and in practice it is unsuccessful) to concern with the distribution of power and resources. This limit, which produces a narrow economics at best, does not reflect on the need for changes in "ideals" even to attain economic ends. Even if democracy were to succeed in obtaining these ends as, for example, in Sweden, not enough would have been accomplished. Ideal principles must be embedded in the mode of distribution and in the relationships which take us beyond the material ones. Such ideals/ideas must show themselves in everyday life. They are to encourage humankind to establish a chain of humanness which does not fear to identify (to see) oneself with the Other, and to pursue the Other. This is not done in sentimental ways. It is carried out through certain practices of government and principles of equity which are not dependent on the whim of the "good leader" or the benevolent despot and government as trustee. There is little, if any, room for the charismatic leader in the future, if he or she is less than God, and there is not room left for unexamined tradition whether in the form of liberalism, orthodox Hebraism, Marxism or Catholicism. And there is no room for a bureaucracy which impedes people from being actors in history by solely giving them services.

A modern democracy requires practical relationships which enoble each of us and which direct us to economic rights and power, political participation, and the acquisition and use of knowledge. Accordingly, this is why we need workers' councils for our society, worker-consumer, public councils such as Congressional juries and universal and continuous education. Among the wretched, those who are thrown away by the society, we require means for *them* to organize and help each other and for the society as a whole to help them and us. Such notions should not be viewed as pipe dreams of visionaries but as necessary political goals of literally millions of people who now find themselves simultaneously marginal to the productive system, more questioning of it and the way they live. It is through the process of politics that their needs may be fulfilled.

For process politics to be successful from the point of view of an entire society, that is, that it will embrace the common good, there must be present among the political actors a certain humility, namely, that all of us have limited knowledge and understanding with little ability to foresee the results of our actions in the future, but virtually total ability to comprehend the limits of decency which cannot be crossed in the present. Once we accept the ambiguity of process as an ally rather than see it as an evil in our political lives, we can begin to discern other general characteristics, which in a formal political sense define the democratic society. These character-istics are capable of distortion and burlesque. But each of them is critical to a modern democracy: to its functioning in the various levels of government, and in the economic sphere as well.

Democracy is more than an electoral system wherein we attempt to change our quality of feeling into arithmetic quantity as the means of deciding our collective purposes and actions. Far more important, it is the means free people use to control, defang but still use the apparent invariant of politics, namely power. It is the non-violent means we use to convince each other. The formal attributes I describe are the procedural means to obtain the support of people for a program for the common good. But they are also the substantive attributes necessary for democratic governing. Thus, there is a circular quality to what I am saying. Since democracy can stick only if it emerges from the practices of people in their daily lives it is necessary to introduce such methods in certain activities such as education and production.

The four elements of democracy which I describe are readily observable in various forms in daily life. Unfortunately, we have not brought them together as the natural next step of political organization. They could be applied from the family to the production line to citizen participation in bureaucracy. They recognize the problematic of power and seek to defuse and redirect it towards positive and rational ends to the extent this can be accomplished through political organization. The elements which will present and represent the common good are *access, participation, deliberation* and *implementation.*[16]

By *access* I mean the ability and power to *see* someone or something which allows the person to petition or address the organized group with either an idea, a complaint, a feeling or observation. It allows the person a chance to reach out to another, whether to cooperate or confront. A person's "feelings and expressions" must be stated publicly, to the group, or its representative. Often such notions are shared by others. They may be about new facts, values and truths all of which invariably need a public review. (Even truths need a public. At least they need another person besides oneself to legitimate their existence.) At its lowest level, access is no more than the formal and *informal* right to a hearing by an individual or group that holds similar views in a particular place which is not ordinarily thought of as "theirs," although it may in fact be theirs through an unrecognized, shared property right, a consumer right or political right. Thus, a child appears in a parent's bedroom to complain, or a group of truck drivers, after seeing each other, come to Washington to see their representative, or workers obtain access to computer information which they claim is theirs or about them.

Law firms and lobbyists are valued according to their ability to give access to their clients. Those who are able to point to their role in the organized society may have a better chance of access. Thus, titles which reflect a certain amount of political power aid one's access to officials, or with others who have titles. But in all of these cases, access may have nothing to do with decisions that are made by those who have power. Access is not a sufficient condition to define democratic practice even though it is to allow one the right to organize or trade needs and complaints. The process of access allows the petitioners to raise demands or issues they have no way of dealing with by themselves either individually or as a group. Thus, access is the first step which allows for the possibility of influence over the process of governing to obtain desired results. There are those who say, "I couldn't even get past the door." But even if this step is accomplished it is only a procedural one. Nevertheless, access is an important first step. It is why we may refer to the postal service and telephone book as very important elements of democratic life for they allow the possibility of access to others just as first amendment rights of association are so precious.

Because *access* is controlled by the powerful it is a relatively easy process for them to distort. Political access may be nothing but symbolic and used accordingly by the powerful. In the political sphere even petitioners are more prone to remember what they are told by the powerful, or the fact that the event is taking place or the physical place that access has been gotten to, than what is said by the powerless, what they existentially know or the nature of their request. (Most people remember the date of the death of President Kennedy but cannot remember, nor do they necessarily know, the date of the death of their parents.) But the same event in which the governors are present, if they are at all clever or articulate, gives the governors a chance to make the powerless conduits for their ideas. In this somewhat magical process citizen access is soon reduced to a means which ensures that people can *touch* leaderships who then dignify and legitimate the citizenry. But little more happens. We all know of citizens who are satisfied with attending ceremonial meetings and having their pictures taken with political officer holders. In this way they are able to demonstrate their access and involvement in events. Never mind that these events are fundraising dinners or trips to Washington for the purpose of picture taking.

Clever political leaders seek access to the people since they know that they must be "in touch," if they are to be successful. They know that providing access is the most primitive but successful means of keeping a society relatively stable and involved with its various personages and institutions. Despots as well pride themselves on keeping in touch. At the close of the *History of the Communist Party of the Soviet Union*,[17] Stalin wrote about the Greek hero who loses his strength when he loses touch with the earth. Stalin said that the same would happen to the communist party if it lost touch with the people. Even when tyrants are barricaded from the people, as Stalin was, they know they must keep in touch with them if for no other reason than this is the way to keep power. In American politics there is a phrase which describes the need to keep in touch with particular individuals and their groups that is pungent, but apposite. "It is more important to have them pissing outside the tent from the inside, than having them pissing inside the tent from the outside."[18] Getting one's foot in the door (being seen) changes the nature of relationships at least to the extent that social roles have to be redefined. Thus, it is clear that symbol manipulation which is used by those who engineer consent as the means to line up the people for an oligarchy *with* power to those who are *in* power must also take into account the dangers of access for they lead to other possibilities which can substantially shift power constellations away from those who have elective, selective or oligarchic power. One of the possibilities which may emerge from access, and it is absolutely necessary as part of democracy both as means and ends, is *participation.*

Participation is the next rung in the political ladder to achieve the common good since access on its own is a symbolic gesture. At its most primary level the common good demands that the person should be encouraged to help shape the event of which he or she is a part and to know that an event of importance is taking place and leads to shaping the person's or group's future well-being. Thus, to the extent possible, the

279

person is to be more than the object of the will of others in the event. Often, we think that it is enough that a person is there at, or part of, an event even though he or she in no way shapes that event or its purposes. Armies and crowds are at events without their ability to work out the meaning of those events and the ability to shape their purpose in a democratic fashion.

In the last several decades some people have thought that participation would mean the termination of hierarchy or top-down control. But participation in and of itself does not speak to the question of hierarchy or command. Thus, soldiers participate in a battle, having much to say about its outcome. While knowing that they are under hierarchic control, they also know that their participation is central and that the character of their participation will often decide the battle's outcome. Tolstoy teaches this to us when he talks of soldiers who throw down their guns in battle and proceed to retreat, thereby causing panic and destruction rather than the execution of the best laid plans of general staffs. (I might add that it is a hard thing to comprehend especially for planners who think that administration and execution of "plans" is a straight line to the completion of that wondrous phrase "problem solving.")

All modern states assert the right of participation. Participation is no ready guarantee to achieve the good end. It can be and often is mindless. As I have said, a soldier participates in an event but it is often the mind of another that frames it. Or, citizens are coopted into participation where decisions are made administratively by unseen others. Mass participation is used by leaders as the way to organize a common thrust and an administrative apparatus that asserts a single purpose. People embrace these tasks as the way to escape the feeling of being lost, of having to face either boredom, or dread, or those other diseases of modern time which come from being ripped asunder from either community, God, the past, or a future vision. Leaders of authoritarian nations, or those who undertake authoritarian acts or lead authoritarian sects, use this form of mass mobilization knowing that people tolerate reality imposed on them when they are given tasks that include a high level of social cohesion and individual denial. In other words, participation is a highly manipulable process by leaders at the tops of organizations when democratic dissent is not strong. Participation becomes mobilization and the citizen finds herself or himself used actively because of their otherwise laudable inclination to act in the public space.

Notwithstanding all the chances for abuse, participation remains an important step that can ensure civilization's existence. For it is in participation with large numbers of people either in a mass or as a group (where each speaks for and with the other) that leaders come to recognize that others beside themselves exist with heads and hearts that can decide processes and actions with the same fervor and abilities as the leadership may exhibit. This form of participation shows each who participates that sovereignty is shared among them. This is the way that leaders may be controlled and stopped from doing something mad, like exercising the option for nuclear war, for participation teaches that people are not supine to leadership but can evolve citizen policies that are non-statist and will protect citizens over the heads of leaders, when necessary.

The citizen's participatory right is not meant to deny self-absorptive activity. Instead, it is meant to forge paths for belonging, whatever the person's age, so that the person is not left lonely, broken and a pawn. This right asserts that humane attributes are strengthened through the group and that the participatory right attaches to the person as a protective skin. It cannot be ripped away without destroying the group. It also means that government social programs are to reflect this participatory need for the protection of the individual.

Properly construed, the constitution's ninth amendment can be used as the searchlight to discover what rights the people have that are not enumerated, which in fact define them as human beings.[19] One of them is surely the right of participation in all fundamental decisions. Unfortunately, the Supreme Court has chosen to define the ninth amendment as a privacy right. But this explanation demeans the words of the Constitution makers. "The enumeration of certain rights in the Constitution shall not be construed to deny or disparage others retained by the people." The interpretation which is most consistent with the document as a whole is as a guarantee of participation for people in their social and public space. Under the Articles of Confederation people were already seen and protected as atomistic individuals who were not to be invaded by either the government or others in the public realm. Consequently, the phrase "right retained by the people" has a dual meaning. It is to be read as a collective and individual statement which frames the citizen's role in both its social and atomic sense.[20]

The rights which the document sought to protect and which were so much on the minds of eighteenth-century thinkers and activists were of an individual nature, for it was a time in which individuals appeared out of the cocoon of history to stand for self, with and against the group. On the other hand, the power which was always there for those who were thought to be citizens by virtue of class and ownership of property was the power of participation. This class comprised competing elites which usually defined the public realm either for or against the government or sovereign. For them the participatory right meant that citizens could participate collectively and define the public space. It could mean control over property or voluntary association, neighborhood or unincorporated town as well as the factory itself. The participatory right could also include all aspects of the public space – especially those aspects which the government controls outside of the public purview such as national security matters.

The next stage of democracy

Once we understand the limits and positive attributes of individual participation and access, we are ready to recognize the next constituent element in democracy. It is deliberation, by which I mean rational discussion, and best proofs for understanding, judging and acting on what is a just choice or course of action. Access and participation are transcended at the point that citizens say they want to *think* about what they are doing, using reason, reasoning and discussions with each other. And indeed that they intend to decide the question. Participation and access may be mindless, involving only the body but no thought. They are procedural ways of acting which, likely as not, stem from felt need. In other words, the first two attributes of democracy to achieve the common good through democracy do not have to include thought much more complex than that of narrow self-interest and the willingness to acknowledge each other's pains and words. Access and participation are activities which tend to show each of us that we exist, that we are there, that we have emotions and passions. It is when we keep making the same mistakes as a group that we come to recognize that the mass or the group must change itself into a thinking and deliberative body: a congress, assembly, council or jury. It is in these social forums that consciousness, awareness and interest are concretized into reasoning. Deliberation, whether of a simple or complex sort, is often integral to everyone's life.[21] And this characteristic can be shared in the public or in political matters.

Although forums for public deliberation are crucial, in modern states there are only a few places where the person who is not an official is able to deliberate and decide public matters. The notable example is the jury system. It is here where public deliberation takes place at its most sophisticated level. One reason that juries work so well is that their members know that what they decide has effect. If juries are to be used as a means of politically involving people in daily citizenly activity they must be de-liberating, for the democracy is charged with the responsibility of finding the liberating path through a conflict or problem. In other words, deliberation means little if it is the consumer society meaning of deliberation – choice between name brands. There can be no deliberation in that case, for the person at best is nothing more than the reciprocal of the market transaction. In this sense deliberation cannot be about trivial matters, and try as much as *laissez-faire* capitalists would like, our most important concerns cannot be purchased at a market. Of course, it is true that fundamental questions are raised in "trivial" matters such as exchange relationships. But it is the unearthing of the trivial as events of importance which is a central purpose of deliberations. The market focuses deliberation of the person on the commodity, neither the process of making it or the implications of it. In a democracy the citizenry must believe that what it decides must matter and must be perceived by those who deliberate that they are deciding matters that are of use to others to consider and possibly adopt in terms of assumptions, the process of organizing and the implications of any particular action. To put it another way, access must include the answer to the question "to whom," participation the answer to the question "in what and with whom," and deliberation answers the questions "how, why and which path?"

Deliberation is important to the extent the questions which are deliberated are thought to be important ones by the participants. Thus, deliberation about the size of taxes, the character of a defense force, the nature of a constitution or civil liberties, the issue of what is productive use, of how much of the environment to transform are questions which could be deliberated fully if proper citizen forums beyond legislatures were invented.[22] These are questions of general and technical interest which are not to be reserved for decision to special interest groups, Congress or the Supreme Court. There are now practical, technical ways of encouraging dialogue for the entire body politic. Information about public policy questions could be given to people through neighborhood computer terminals where they would debate its meaning in town meetings. Deliberation would be held on issues that the whole decides, or that the body politic's nominees decide. A modern republic, such as the kind which Walter Lippmann espoused, turns over its deliberative powers to experts and specialists. But in a democracy the citizen would conclude that deliberation is distorted when questions of profound concern are given to experts who narrow the issues and mystify them so that serious discussion around consequences, methodology and results are restricted to the specialist. The consequence is that deliberation is removed from the body politic as a whole and parceled out to specialists who then invent their own jargon and operate according to their own views of deliberation. The concerns of the specialist – the scientist – do not include public deliberation, a process which asserts that the effect of a series of actions must be determined prior to undertaking the action.

It should be recognized that such deliberation may be hard for the inventor, scientist and entrepreneur. Their political natures may be either republican or oligarchic not democratic in the sense I am using this term. Spengler caught the technological interest and championed it well in *Man and Technics*, but it is not an attitude which can be tolerated for much longer.

> In reality the passion of the inventor has nothing whatever to do with its consequences. It is his personal life motive, his personal joy and sorrow. He wants to enjoy his triumph over difficult problems and the wealth and fame that it brings him for its own sake. Whether his discovery is useful or menacing, creative or distributive, he cares not a jot. . . . The effect of a 'Technical achievement of mankind' is never foreseen. Chemical discoveries like that of synthetic indigo and (what we shall

presently witness) artificial rubber upset the living conditions of whole countries. The electrical transmission of power and the discovery of the possibilities of energy from water have depreciated the old coal-areas of Europe – and their populations. Have such considerations ever caused an inventor to suppress his discovery? Anyone who imagines that knows nothing about man's bird of prey instinct. Men delight in victory. Strong men call the shots and the rest march as spectators.[23]

If non-experts are no longer spectators but active citizens they will reexamine and refocus social life and technology. They will have something to say about what discoveries should be developed and others allowed to dry up. Deliberation also has the effect of operationally narrowing questions of a particular situation through the application of laws, prudence and reason. But deliberation has little meaning unless it is accompanied by *implementation*. Implementation answers the question how and by what means decisions are to be put into effect.

In most administrative states which believe in bourgeois rights, *implementation* is left to a bureaucracy which operates in part on its own, with its clients, and according to its rules, often indecipherable and silly. To transcend those rules bureaucracy, by which I mean the government employees whose daily task is to *create* purposes, goals, limits, procedures and regulations, require continuous dialogue with the people and oversight of its work. Citizen panels would operate as a means to stimulate a closer relationship to government. The democracy for the common good would organize bureaucracies in such a way as to be responsive and responsible to a Congressional jury and town hall system.[24]

This reorganization of government would give direct, positive responsibility to citizens for oversight and implementation of programs. From 1965 through the 1970s participation clauses were written into laws from antipoverty to manpower retraining.[25] The political idea was to extend participation. But soon government bureaucracies found that people had little interest in participation. Participation in these programs was limited on the part of the poor or workers because there was no power of deliberation, or implementation power for people and virtually no funds to pay people for public activity. Implementation can also be distorted and manipulated. Since 1940 the selective service system method has been the classic means of implementation of decisions from the top. The military perfected a system in which the local citizenry served as the human collection agents for the armed forces in the neighborhoods according to quotas set by them. Implementation ended up being little more than oligarchic mobilization, showing that people at the grassroots should practice deliberation and involvement according to the military's plan of implementation. On the other hand, correctly practiced, implementation could be the daily means that citizens use to assure equity and distributive justice, that is, minimum standards prior to the exercise of privileges.[26] And it is also the means that could overcome boredom and passivity. It becomes a new form of association between communities and states with Congress acting as the enabler of this democratic process.

These four attributes of democracy continuously highlight those questions which are at the political heart of any modern society. They are the basis of a never ending dialogue that sets boundaries between the person and others. They are the basis of deciding the common good.

The first question to ask is what as a person can never be taken from me, and therefore what do I have as a minimum when I am in the world? The second is what considerations do I want to turn over to others with the understanding that if I do not like their performance I may get rid of those performing the function and the third is what powers are given to the group and which the group is able to then use to command allegiance from me. These questions are at the root of all other questions that are debated. In this sense democracy is circular – constantly shaping and reshaping these questions while being both means and ends. By its nature democracy is a system, even the system of no systems. Consequently, democracy asserts social relationships and bonds which precede any particular set of laws.

Thus, should any person have the right *not* to fight in a war? The immediate answer is yes. But having said yes, we may then be forced to go to the next level. If I view it as a fundamental right not to kill or be killed because this right defines my humanness, the logical result of such thought is that the state must forswear any defense system which makes people objects or hostages. In other words, the state cannot defend my rights with pathological weaponry, such as nuclear weaponry which may court mass extermination, my life and my right to humanness. On the other hand, does a people – a nation – not have the right to defend itself, and should the people as a whole not expect that its citizens should defend the nation? I would think that the answer is yes. But it is a complicated yes. As I state in Chapter 5, people do not have to fight wars or be dragged into them in their collective or individual capacity. On the other hand, no government can surrender the nation to an outsider, an aggressor, another. In other words, those who want to continue the struggle against an aggressor should be supported and legitimated in the law and Constitution, as well as in the soul of a nation. Such a clause is written into the Yugoslavian constitution. It makes clear to any would-be aggressor that invasion will not be an inexpensive or successful exercise. I advance this argument with some hesitation for I am attracted to Kant's view that "No state at war with another shall indulge in such hostilities as would preclude mutual confidence in the subsequent peace."[27] Kant's view would mean that we renounce nuclear weapon use. But it also means that we should be prepared to conclude hostilities.

Kant premises his belief on the view that no state would interfere by force with the constitution and government of another state. Occupation of one state by another is always illegitimate, just as it is illegitimate to assert that a state is able to totalize the person. States have the power to take away a person's dignity; they do not have the right.

Dignity of person in the nation-state

We mistake attributes critical for human existence as "rights" granted to us through the state or which reflect a social process at a particular stage of history. But these are not "rights"; they are what we *are*. They define us as being human. They define our dignity. Indeed, I would argue that we do not have a "right" to food, or speech (communication, sign language) because by their very nature they either define or point to fundamental attributes as living human beings. For the state to say that these are "rights" diminishes their importance to us in a fundamental way because they are in fact reflective of our basic needs and functions as human beings. That we discover these attributes and accord them the status of rights enshrined in our laws should not give us the belief that these are mere conveniences. In other words they are natural rights and cannot be taken away by the group even though it is the collective task of the group to assure that these rights are secured and secure.

In this sense, when we review the Human Rights declarations of 1949 the nineteenth-century character of the document emerges wherein the rights are seen as something other than the essence of humaneness.[28] It should now be obvious for all those who care to see that dignity is a fundamental quality of being human, neither a bourgeois privilege or an upper-class put-on. If a modern democracy's purpose is the common good then individual dignity is central to its fulfillment.

Modern life specializes in relieving the person of his or her dignity, in dehumanizing them. Modern torture chambers are meant as dehumanizing strategies. The torturer knows that his task is to destroy physical well-being, enforce speech, poison association and relieve the person of his or her choice to act in dignity. When dignity is not thought about by political leaders or the people in these terms they are softened up for terrible debasement. The Nazi concentration camps, through the "simple" organizational trick of letting, indeed insisting, that the inmates shit and piss on themselves, destroyed their will to resist and therefore their dignity. The Nazis blinded their own will through this abomination for it was no longer necessary to think of the inmates as human. The Nazis knew that dignity is civilization's cumulative process to make us human, and that to deny what became an attribute to the person would destroy the individual person's will to resist. Perhaps the Nazis understood that people find it hard to agree on the meaning of dignity in every case, therefore gambling that people do

286

not assign a high value to it.[29] This was Stalin's wager during the Moscow trials. Some would argue, after all, that the Marine recruit masochist, or the clown, seem to get on without dignity rather well, as does the schoolboy who passes through a hazing period. Apparently, where indignity is part of a process to leave one life and enter another, perhaps for a felt sense of greater dignity, people will withstand much abuse and inflict on themselves – or have inflicted – much punishment. This must be the dialectic within Western thought and practice which supposedly builds its purpose on individual dignity. Perhaps this conceit can be first detected in Socrates when he stated that if people would know themselves they would discover their consciousness and therefore a type of dignity which would encourage them to act differently from beasts, allowing them to "take charge" of nature. Such a consciousness expands the individual worth of the person beyond economic meaning, if you are in the upper economic classes. But this form of dignity is related to the type of rationalism that came to mean control over nature for the benefit of human beings. There is another meaning to dignity. It is recognition of our vulnerability, namely the human being as helpless, as a child, as old, always dependent. Then we are put to the test of arranging our political relationship in terms of humankind's weaknesses and needs. This meaning of dignity is not private. It recognizes our need for one another.

The political question for individuals in their vulnerability is not privacy. It is whether the person can find social and constitutional defenses to combat fears caused by the political environment while the person finds positive relationships *within* the society. This is the meaning of social dignity which a society must encourage and which a modern democracy will protect in its laws. In this sense no discussion of democracy is satisfactory without being more precise on what is to be left to the person, what is the group's and what is given to the society as a whole. What is mine as a person and what is the group's is a situational question decided on the basis of particular cases which we learn and keep track of much like we do in the common law. Property and rights to it depend on each historical situation. What may "belong" to the person at one stage of history or at a particular moment may in fact be the property of everyone, or the political right of everyone but of no particular person at another time.[30]

Thus, we must be careful about making false dichotomies. In the age of specialization particular parts of our body interact with institutions and how those institutions are built on particular parts of our body, or aspects of our lives. Such institutions start from the assumption of interacting *in* persons, in their specific organs. In this process there is little that one can define as self which makes judgments and choices. The person is a social construct as much as an individual. In other words, the person's life is sustained through the Other, and therefore, dignity is socially defined. It is true that each epoch discovers and creates its own form of interdependence. In socialist states the line between self and Other is drawn in favor of the whole with people believing that what is individual is totally derivative. Indeed, the dangerous next step is to encourage only those people who see themselves as derivative of the whole. We have seen that this brand of "socialism" is doomed to failure because of the pain that it causes and because it does not begin by asserting that the person is the social root.

Democracy and personal recognition

Democracy can no longer content itself with being the process for finding allegiance between social classes for a particular economic system, be it capitalism or socialism. It is an end in itself which presents us with an extraordinary gift. The gift we receive from democracy is the sharing of responsibility, social use and control over property; plus the recognition of self. It is not equality of opportunity which democracy grants, as some liberals would have it, but the opportunity of equality which mirrors our personhood. That is, it mirrors the recognition of person as having dignity, and being accorded the recognition of those aspects of personhood which create for us greater understanding of how social and political institutions might better fit people. In its active form, therefore, democracy is itself a means which structures situations and relationships that crack class differences and social ladders by announcing the interdependence of us to each other and the sentiment which comes with unseen friendship. The democracy I speak of embraces egalitarian principles even though they are not and should not be stated in mathematically equal terms.

The opportunity of equality (egalitarian interdependence) does not presume that people are the same physically, mentally or spiritually although it does assume that there is a range which marks people's similarity in essential attributes. We all recognize them. Our sense impressions lead us to a collective ought which is that people be treated in similar ways by each other. There are several such areas for similar treatment. One is in the area of justice where rules that are publicly made and shared are to be applied blindly and similarly to everyone. But this statement is not an arithmetical formulation. Rather, it is a statement about equality which when applied to social relations and human affairs is a formula of *intuitive recognition*. This process of recognition means the recognition of one's self through seeing the Other and vice versa. We can show this by illustration in the analysis of uniforms.

The purpose of the uniform is to define uniqueness and sameness; uniqueness as against outsiders or the Other, sameness as regards those who are authorized to wear the uniform. Toward each other the initiated are equal (or ranked) according to a value system which the initiated accept. The purpose of robes in courts is to separate the judge from recognizing the defendant as having anything to do with the judge as a person. But having attempted to define one's self by recognition through others, another concern immediately appears.

Democracy recognizes the need to generate situations of *discernment* which simultaneously recognize similarity in the Other and, paradoxically, uniqueness of each person. Democracy can do this by encouraging people to see themselves beyond their social roles. (Curiously, one reason people like war is that it allows them to escape the assigned roles of the social system, join together with others in unique and surprising ways all in the context of a different pecking order. War rewards people with new social roles.)

Once we accept the democracy of means and ends we say to people that each of them may seek and make opportunities for egalitarian interdependence which is the way they can share the democratic definition of the common good. By insisting on egalitarian interdependence, the person exercises more than an individualistic or subjective act. He or she changes the political system by integrating procedural rights with political demands. The demands are meant to get the social, legal and economic system to change so that the person forges a set of conditions that guarantees his or her egalitarian interdependence in all aspects of the society. Thus, for example, the struggle for the Equal Rights Amendment is a procedural one which, of course, is meant to change social relations and the distribution of economic power.

In the twentieth century it is relatively easy to see under what conditions a person will act against his or her inequality. The person will act in two cases: moments of extreme oppression, and periods where subjective feelings of oppression and denial can be explained in terms of inequality according to some measure (both calculative and felt) which some significant Other, who is not suffering, understands and "stands with." In such a case, the opportunity for equality is rekindled in democracy by the oppressed and their intellectual and emotional friends. While inequitable distributions of wealth do not describe adequately or totally the problem of cultural impoverishment such figures do describe satisfactorily political inequality. In the United States less than 2 per cent of the adult population owns more than 80 per cent of the stock of American corporations. Feelings of impotence and powerlessness are reflected in such egregious, distributive inequality. It is at this point that people could invoke the principle that a democracy guarantees opportunities for equality and that civil war can be averted. But this is a principle which a society has to actively practice. It is a principle that is necessary to obtain and sustain democracy.

In a modern democracy committed to the common good we should say that a person is defined by characteristics which cannot be violated and which have to be complemented through the social organization that is developed by others. Thus, for example, a person has *his* or *her* life. It is *their* respective property. Therefore it means that life is inviolable *from* the state or the group even though the person retains a bond with the group or state, at all times. Neither the group nor state has "accesss" to the life of the person without permission of the person. The person may form alliances against the state or the group where this sense of life is endangered or where the institutions and processes of the state or group seek to end – or can end – the person's life. I have called this situation *characterization* where the person ceases to exist except as the object of the group, the institutions or the state. Characterization may be directly confronted, and I would add that the person or group may – and will be expected to – go anywhere for help. The atomic fallout victims of Nevada and Utah were sold out by the state, objectified and ruined. They have more than a legal complaint. To put this another way, dignity can neither be granted nor taken away by the state. It can only defend dignity. The state is to recognize that wall even when the productive side of the society is democratized and participatory.

Democracy and constitution

Beyond continuous dialogue there are guideposts which are needed for the proper functioning of a modern democracy. These guideposts help to determine the historical and future general will beyond any one situation or event, and through time. One such guidepost is a constitution. It is a partly mystical instrument that is meant to order relationships between groups and classes while giving the individual person a reason for keeping the peace. A democratically interpreted constitution provides the social and legal arrangements for social bonding, contractual rights, and the possible harmonization of interests. It further seeks to respect and limit appetites and differing levels of consciousness which emerge out of conflicting experiences.

A constitution in a modern democracy should be interpreted in such a way as to assure that the government and the governing process will act to generate and protect those public policies which fulfill the dignity of the person. The constitution exists to protect the person as self and the association and assembly of people. Its judicial interpreters should never forget that the person is the root and strength of the nation; its property and assets are less important because they are made by people.[31] The constitution is usually read as a republican or oligarchic document by its judicial interpreters. According to conservatives the government's major function is to provide security to property, and security against "attack from the outside." Under the conservative rendering of governmental purpose its interests are primarily in the protection of wealth. In the conservative nightwatchman state of a Justice Rehnquist the state's positive functions are restricted to police activities such as an intelligence collection system on its citizenry. That is to say, it is limited to managing punishment and crime. Whether this type of security system is operated by the great corporations, the federal or local government is of little consequence. It is contrary to personhood and democratic citizenship.

Some say that the American constitution, an eighteenth-century document which grew out of whiggish concerns of the petit bourgeois[32] and their fears of both the poor and a government of oligarchs can never serve as a basis for a twenty-first-century definition of equity and dignity. Nevertheless, this incomplete document which surely does not contemplate modern civilization, but does contemplate a human being's needs expresses important guarantees in the Bill of Rights and in the Preamble. This document can serve as a twenty-first-century basis for establishing justice, defense, liberty and tranquility because it accepts the principle of the general welfare.

As a people Americans are moved by two parts of the Constitution. The Preamble and the Bill of Rights, the "extraneous" statements, join together the hearts and minds of the citizenry as "We the People," in the common "pursuit of happiness." These phrases are the basis of the American vision and purpose for Americans believe consciously and unconsciously that the history of our nation is the struggle to discover the best within people making those attributes the basis on which the society should aspire, judge and construct its restraints. Of course the Constitution, based on eighteenth-century principles, such as Montesquieu's belief in divided government, provides countless chances for ambiguity, conflict and ultimately dialectical stalemate between contending forces within the government and the society. The Madisonian construction of groups checking and countering each other was meant to hold back precipitous action or major shifts in the direction of the society. Curiously, the very stalemate may cause the growth of government for if Congress does not act then, as a former Attorney-general, Edward Levi, pointed out, the Executive will, and if neither does, then the courts will seek to deal with the felt needs of the society, usually partially and haphazardly.[33] At least one branch of government will find itself speaking for the spirit towards democracy, usually presented in history as a downtrodden, unrepresented or underprivileged group. In the process the size and scope of government grows. Parenthetically the ambiguity and openness of the Constitution also increases the power of the courts for each text needs an interpreter and it is the judicial interpreter who speaks for the document. However, neither the constitution nor the courts have been able to stop precipitous action such as undeclared wars, civil war, or major shifts determined by technology, migration or commerce.

The limited value of the judiciary on political questions has resulted in political stalemate and uncontrolled technological change. Issues and problems are not resolved. They are merely engulfed, becoming larger and taking on a new and more frightful form. As a reaction, politicians seek to further finesse issues, mute but never resolve them. Are there any ways around this constitutional failure?

One is through a constitutional convention which would rewrite the rights and obligations of the several branches of government, particular economic units such as corporations, specifying the role which individuals and groups would play as citizens. The difficulty with this suggestion is that there have not been debates among the citizenry about the fundamental political nature of the United States which would inform the drafting of a new constitution except from an oligarchic-reactionary frame of reference.

The American Constitution was written after more than a generation of serious debate and a revolution detailing the nature of the American project and how it was to be expressed constitutionally. Even so, it ended up as a document dipped in the blood of slaves. Again intense discussions need to be held for at least a decade before any serious moves toward a constitutional convention are made; even then one may wonder about its necessity. There is a less cumbersome alternative.

I favor the transformation of the political parties and citizen organizing outside of the political parties on specific issues. The more progressive of the parties would seek to rearrange forces within and outside of the executive and legislative – as well as the appointment of judges – according to a program of social reconstruction. It would champion changes in the constitutional system around which citizens organized.

 Changes in a program of reconstruction can be accomplished without constitutional amendment. There is no gainsaying that the Constitution was once a racist, apartheid document with the consequent result that the courts have "been shaped by the existence of slavery, for almost half the existence of the American republic, and the continuation of the after-effects of slavery during the republic's third century…"[34] But political struggle changed the document and its underlying racism. There is nothing presently in the Constitution, either in the commerce clause, the separation of powers section, or the Bill of Rights, which bars worker community control, public enterprise, or eminent domain. Nothing in the Constitution now contradicts activities which are meant to enact those social processes and give meaning to egalitarian interdependence and life affirmance. There is nothing in the Constitution which denies full political participation of the citizenry in the affairs of state. In other words, nothing stops the United States in moving to a democracy. Nor is there anything which would deny national referenda on public issues from war and peace, or transnational compacts of amity and peace between regions and states of the United States and other nations so long as they were presented to Congress. There is no constitutional reason why the citizenry could not vote on the size of a national budget, or reallocate taxes so that taxes are kept locally through citizens choosing their jurisdictions to pay taxes to. And there is no reason why, constitutionally, the American economy must retain its present character. There is no reason why American judges and jurisprudence cannot lead in applying the most humane participatory standards which abandon the principle of republican passivity.[35]

Just as the UN Charter is more important than a traffic law of any state, or just as the American Constitution is more important than specific pieces of legislation passed by a town council or state legislature, so it is that the person has active participatory rights which are enunciated and guaranteed through fundamental documents which bespeak the idea of a "law of humanity" without, in so many words, using Hannah Arendt's phrase. These documents have meaning only to the extent that they are used and acted on by people through participation wherein a person's rights can be turned into power to affect, change or conserve. In this sense, voting and election is a derivative act. While people have a right of passivity not to form in small groups or talk, assemble and decide, their fundamental constitutional power is their power to talk and assemble. It is part of human nature to be social and to organize their lives accordingly. It is where people could exercise their judgment and intelligence to save civilization. As Arendt said to Karl Jaspers,

> Even good and, at bottom, worthy people have, in our time, the most extraordinary fear about making judgments. This confusion about judgment can go hand in hand with fine and strong intelligence, just as good judgment can be found in those not remarkable for their intelligence.[36]

Citizen power has meaning only as it enhances the person's ability to act to judge or unmask his or herself to others, and, I might add, to unmask others.

The government's power is an extension of the citizen's power and right to act, wherein the government is to act for the nation as a whole. As the agent it has many rather noisy principals. In other words, through organized procedures citizens should have the power to intervene in government. Under the program of reconstruction governmental activities would be held accountable by citizen juries, their comments, suggestions, etc., so that the citizen occupies the public space with the government.

Citizen participation in the public space should not be confused with bureaucracy. Through active citizen participation the government's role became an enabling one; namely to assure the citizenry's rights acting like a cheerleader to urge the citizenry never to remain silent partners. Thus, a primary government role is to pursue activities which encourage full citizenship status. It can guarantee and encourage the right of speech and speech itself, for example, at the place of work, or within "closed" communities such as asylums and schools. Thus, it is just because we are one nation under one constitution that intermediate institutions such as the family do not have the power to abjure or diminish rights which are constitutionally protected. These rights are tools of everyday life for all people whatever their institutional setting, for their rights attach to them as human beings and citizens – aspects of themselves beyond any particular social role.

No doubt due consideration should be given to the vexing question of when a government should intervene for individuals and groups. I do not hold that state intervention in private activities is meant either to perfect people as in various sodomy laws or to protect the good people from the less good as in the case of vagrancy laws. Instead, government intervention is a means to assure that social roles and institutions do not deny people their natural or citizenly rights.[37]

Reorganizing the government for the common good

Where citizens are fully involved a government's means to achieve dignity will be flexible. The role of government officials is to generate a planning process to encourage public participation in alternative means of achieving agreed upon social purposes. Suppose that worker participation and control in the economic sphere becomes a social objective. It becomes the public and governmental task to put forward alternatives which will show how the economic and industrial sphere can be reorganized. These alternatives would be generated through citizen juries and plans with no belief that any one method is the only one to achieve particular ends.

Given a full generation of deprecating the functions of government and government employment, no reorganization of government which will be flexible in style and which will keep the purpose of equity, caring and social justice as its concerns will be easy to achieve.

In all cases, reorganizations of government, whether for serious purpose or for relatively frivolous reasons, cannot help but cause inefficiency, insecurity and ambiguity among its members. Agencies are downgraded, government workers are frightened about losing their jobs as charges and countercharges are made to secure the needs of particular interest groups inside and outside the government. Often links to particular interest groups are cut and others are established which are meant to show what particular interest group is to be favored over others. Counselors and lobbyists are found to "plug" particular reorganization plans from their own private agencies. But under present circumstances where there is no push for a reconstruction program which would challenge the fundamental economic and national security assumptions, or make explicit a set of values to be formulated and followed in practice, we find that no one cares to face up to the challenge necessary to transform the present power relations in the society, and indeed to choose sides against the constellation of power which government helped to create in the past and is fulfilled under conservative administrations.

The first task in a program of governmental reorganization which asserts social reconstruction and citizen participation is to rip aside the mask of concern for efficiency to determine which group or class is being served by a particular way of organizing the governmental process.[38]

The most profound questions of organization revolve around issues of political and economic power,[39] and the question of shifting social relations as a result of changes in the manner in which economic and political power is organized. Contrary to the Reagan administration's views of a government which is to service the rich but ostensibly not have a value orientation, the criteria which are used to reorganize government should be consistently and deliberately discussed according to specific value standards: equity and caring, egalitarian interdependence and cooperation. Without such standards government loses its moorings, as when it seeks to manufacture mind control apparatuses, anthrax agents, and nuclear weapons which were tested on its own "citizens," or becomes an instrument for a privileged class as when Congress returns 10 per cent of tax reductions to .02 per cent of the taxpaying population.

Once it is decided that the power of government is to be exercised according to certain principles of equity and caring, dialogically derived and continuously examined, and that it will no longer act as the agent of the privately powerful, we are still faced with the question of whether hierarchy or democratic decentralization is the best means for organizing government for a series of good ends.

It is thought that the power of the federal government should be greatly reduced in favor of local government, because local government maximizes political freedom by serving as an effective counter power to central government. It is thought that federalism curbs the "potentialities for evil inherent in power" and maximizes local government and thus promotes grassroots democracy.[40] There are serious objections to this view. Even though the Weimar Republic prided itself on being a federal system of government, Hitler was not stopped in his ascent to power. Nor for that matter did the laws stop him. Indeed, Hitler insisted during his ascent that he be legitimated through the laws. Thus, laws by themselves may not protect freedom, they merely become the code for the activities of the tyrant once he and his group pervert the constitutional intention – and use the armed forces for their purpose.

Most revolutionaries cannot take law as it exists or is presented in the constitutional democracy. As Georg Lukács pointed out, law is a matter of convenience for the revolutionary. It is to be obeyed when you are weak and transgressed when you are either strong or cannot live with the rules anymore. In other words, depending on its tactical need, the use of force is never very far away. The revolutionary justifies his or her behavior on the principle that laws are class derived by the few for the few. Therefore, it is foolish to talk about following the law. In a way, the revolutionary attitude is similar to the attitude of the imperialist in a foreign culture. The imperialist does not intend to be bound either by the foreign custom or laws except when necessary. On the other hand, reconstruction assumes the principles of constitutionalism even though they might have originally had an oligarchic basis in practice and intent. In our time, the language and the spirit of a bourgeois constitution grants the existence of political space and the potentiality in practice for people to carry out profound and comprehensive actions.

An aware citizenry from the deprived classes can take "bourgeois space" and fill it with cumulative and progressive changes, just because struggles of history are stories about battles which are won for the few and then demanded by everyone. As the co-founder of the Frankfurt School, Max Horkheimer pointed out,

> Again and again in history, ideas have cast off their swaddling clothes and struck out against the social system that bore them. The cause, in a large degree, is that spirit, language, and all the realms of the mind necessarily stake universal claims. Even ruling groups, intent above all upon defending their particular interests, must stress universal motifs in religion, morality and science. Thus originates the contradiction between the existent and ideology, and contradiction that spurs all historical progress.[41]

Political action does not offer guarantees for historical progress. But because this is so, politics must be thought about in ethical terms, that is, as social relationships and actions in themselves which are both proscribed and prescribed. *A nation and a people must know what it will not do whatever the circumstances with which it is faced*. A citizen's duty is to act to ensure that that ethical line is not crossed by the state. Citizenship is then more than an empty term or abstraction.

Citizenship

Citizenship in the body politic simultaneously decreases and increases the person's power and *persona*. It decreases power by stimulating the person to believe that institutions define his or her personhood and it increases the person's potential by allowing the person to be part of a network of participation which reaches far beyond one's self or immediate group. This network of participation and bonding should not be lost between the wretched and the outcast and the most accepted and eminent.

In its best sense, citizenship is that type of participation in the life of a

296

nation which allows the person to fulfill his or her natural attributes in social, economic and political benefit with others. It guards against what the ancient Greeks termed idiocy. They meant by idiocy a person who was without citizenship and who, therefore, had no responsibilities, rights or political power to share his or her own destiny, or that of the nation.[42] They are stopped from being practical persons because they are denied the experience and acquired wisdom of being able to make rules and laws for others as well as for themselves which are binding and which, therefore, hold the person to account because of the framework which the citizen sets with others. They cannot achieve the purpose of politics, namely the good end. In its most comprehensive sense, citizens seek public fulfillment by acting and speaking beyond individual, selfish interest. They also understand that interests, if they are to be reflective of the common good and therefore of the individual, cannot be individualistic. To have imaginative insight, to do productive work, to have economic security one must go beyond one's self. Because each person is incomplete no person can be a citizen alone. For the person it is the way to make up for individual inadequacy.

In a modern democratic society active citizenship must be constantly extended. In other words, power is to be shared so that each person may gain and the society as a whole may cumulatively move towards its fulfillment. Democratic citizenship is the political and legal construct that parlays each person's capacities into a political system that yields well-being and good judgment. For the nation and nations as a whole it is the way to order social, economic and legal relationships between people without bloodshed. Under this definition of citizenship no one is to be left out. When any person is left out of being a citizen, or a person accepts colonized status, the common good recedes that much further from our grasp, for we are denied what that person knows, or his or her potential for knowing and feeling.

It is the citizen's participation with its attendant attributes of deliberation and implementation which helps us to achieve the beginnings of any common purpose and the shared wisdom which is indisputably needed in a world which lurches forward into international civil war. Citizenship spans the public and private realm of a person's life. It allows the person to comprehend in concrete terms the way each aspect of life is related and interdependent. The process of citizenship is not abstract and it is more than the pursuit of copybook principles. In a democracy it takes real work on the part of the individual as well as the reorganization of collective work institutionally controlled. It includes the principle of social caring. Professor Michael Apple has proposed that the

> separation of public and private lives could be lessened by plans that would offer all employees at least two days a month of paid leave to

297

work in schools, welfare, health or other community agencies. This would establish the principle of business and government recognition of the right of its workers to engage in community building as part of their economic and political lives. It would also enable citizens of all classes to learn the "skills" of participation and democratic deliberation.[43]

Apple's proposal is valuable although it should be extended to give workers the choice of developing their own definition of how to help others. Such alternatives would enable workers to use their work time in creative activities which go beyond the types of activities offered by large institutions. The skill of democratic participation can also be experienced by organizing and forging new projects that are not likely to be undertaken by any community program or service that already exists. (Imagine, for example, the group of workers who use their two days a month to begin a museum of cartoons.)

The right of participation includes the whiggish right to say no and "no" includes civil disobedience. It is not only a whiggish purpose that citizenship must now have, namely ways to control the destructive elements of state power or dangers institutionally caused. The right of civil disobedience should be incorporated as a fundamental protection and means of communicating. Indeed, civil disobedience may be (from time to time and on certain fundamental issues) the highest level of citizen affirmation.

Civil disobedience

Civil disobedience is a critical political mechanism for justice to make its will known against class domination, a dogmatist bureaucracy and the dead hand of the past when it is on our shoulders.[44] Because political systems and ideologies may appear one way but are really quite different as lived experience, especially during a period of profound transformation (note the horrifying Stalinist period), a nation's protection of the individual is attained by incorporating the right of civil disobedience as an inherent right to be protected constitutionally.

Once we assert fundamental rights which adhere to a person prior to his or her being part of an organized state, civil disobedience must be introduced as a constitutionally protected mechanism of personal communication and defense. Civil disobedience is the only way for the individual to confront grievous wrongs such as apartheid or aggressive war without losing a common bond with the rest of society. In the United States the alternative, terrorism or civil war, has no other result but the destruction of a highly vulnerable technological civilization.

The civilly disobedient recognize that certain issues cannot be resolved in a marketplace of ideas where minds unattached to bodies and floating in space compete with one another. In a democracy where the idea of the common good has full voice the passions and minds of people come together either through dialogic relationship or through the confrontation of civil disobedience. The confrontation of competing persons need not be one of armed struggle which breaks the bonds among people – so long as there is the right of exodus and the right of civil disobedience. Living through the horrors of the twentieth century, people would be foolish to be without the right of civil disobedience. As Barrington Moore said:

> The demands of the new militant opposition on both sides of a
> corroding iron curtain share themes that may eventually become part of
> a redefinition of the past, the present, and the future, a new conception
> of foe and friend. Some of the themes have a very old-fashioned, almost
> Whiggish ring; resistance to tyranny and oppression in all its forms;
> suspicion of established authority and bureaucracy; outrage at cruelty;
> the demand for due process against arbitrary injustice; freedom of
> speech and artistic creation; and individual autonomy.[45]

The Polish experience of 1980-1 shows the wisdom of this view. Where do rights of civil disobedience come from? There are bonds and agreements between people in a society which take precedence over an individual's oath to the state, its law and those ideologies which justify such arrangements. Such natural arrangements cannot be broken. There is no way to be disobedient to them except as a person might lie to himself or herself. What manner of bad faith is such a lie? Persons lie when they refuse to credit others with recognizing their conscience as the basis for their political action. The person might hide his or her conscience because he or she does not trust others, telling one thing and feeling another. The outsider is left wondering whether the spoken word or the unspoken inner voice is what should be credited as being authentic.

Modern political systems and especially those which have gone sour seek to separate the person from himself or herself, wherein the person must start either from a lie or not credit his or her own feelings. This system of "false citizenship" yields bad faith and therefore is dependent on oppressive law and power as the means of getting people to do what they "ought to do."

Whenever a group moves beyond the face-to-face relationship, i.e. a situation in which conscience is not experienced as eccentric, but indeed natural, it is necessary to work out legal relationships. But such relationships must always be within the framework of social bonding which consciously recognizes the similarity of all people. Thus, we may have a statement in which we say that "all people are created equally," or that "all people have inalienable rights" which cannot be undercut by any kind of contractual arrangement. Once we give credence to such words, civil disobedience becomes the method which asserts the primary social bond among people. It also adds to one's sense of personal security, for it means that the methods used to participate and to express will and reason are varied and sanctioned.

The character of twentieth- and twenty-first century states underscores the need for civil disobedience as an accepted form of political participation.[46] This is especially necessary given the manner in which even socialism was perverted in practice. Its name was used by the Nazis to justify their bestial political formations while the communists used "socialist legality" to devour their own revolutionaries. Even in those nations that could honestly be called socialist, certain basic questions arise.

Socialism, a concept which referred to the potential for everyone's liberation, does not take into account the freedom to say "no" without the fear of terrible retribution, as illustrated by Castro's powerful phrase, Inside the revolution one can say and do everything. Outside of it, nothing. But who is to decide what is revolutionary? Is it the same old state authority system that has governed for hundreds of years, but now with a revolutionary overlay? The result of not having the right to say no, or of having it in an atrophied or truncated form is to decrease the possibility of vital debate and differences, mixing fear, truthful statements, power and cowardice together in an eclipse of the common good. This failure of socialism, therefore, requires a clearly defined and recognized corrective. Hence, civil disobedience. Given the character of the struggle between the three forms of the state that stand in American society each of which defines rights and citizenship in different ways, it is not surprising that civil disobedience is a major way of forcing issues into an agenda. It combines action, passion and reason thereby changing the state itself. Needless to say, civil disobedience frightens those who uphold internal order and security.

Internal security

Earlier in this chapter, I alluded to the conservative means of attaining personal security. It is through the night watchman asserting strong authority – and sometimes Draconian measures (authoritarianism) – to maintain order, especially against those who challenge the economic and social pecking order. For example, in the course of one month, the Reagan administration asserted the powers of the strong state by breaking the air controllers union (PATCO), shooting down two Libyan planes which sought to defend Libyan air space, cutting various social welfare job and education programs against those who are not "truly needy," and talking about the need to mobilize for war. The reader might take a moment to ponder whether such policies added to or detracted from personal security.

Within the nation itself, the social symptoms of personal insecurity can be seen everywhere. They are detailed in the lives of the broken-spirited drug addict and alcoholic, the children of broken homes and the fears of old people who see their social security allotments being cut in favor of more missiles. It can also be seen in the incidence of high crime. Murders, rapes, robberies, suicides, and other forms of striking out have become the standard method of "making do" in a system which removes psychological and social supports from the person. This is happening as dreams of opportunity end up in a social darwinist nightmare.

The philosophy in which the modern nightwatchmen ground their policies is that people are more evil than good; that their sense of greed and envy can be harnessed to the modern capitalist system, and that those who are criminal should be "put away," taken out of sight. With this point of view the society falls back on old methods of governing. The citizenry is told by conservatives, including President Reagan and his first Attorney-General, William French Smith, that their personal security will increase if tools of repression are added. Thus, the number of prisons, surveillance, police control and defense budget greatly increases. The hope of the watchmen is that by heightening the appearance of awesome and forbidding strength, malcontents and criminals will shake and tremble about disturbing the peace. But this objective is a shared one. What the watchmen also want is an increase of police forces as social supports are withdrawn from people.

None of what I have said is to suggest that personal security is not a serious problem in American life. High crime rates in our society are associated with anger and frustration at the dominant social system. Usually society's values are in need or reexamination when they are not lived or internalized by an increasing number of people and when those seeking to uphold the value and power of dominant groups enforce their will without respect to the opinion or needs of others. It is at this point that a new belief system will take the place of an old one and laws end up in hopeless conflict with this transformation. Change in the belief system may stem from a new consciousness of class or ethnic difference. This is what is invariably experienced in major cities where there is looting in stores owned by the middle class. Looting is usually performed by poor people who have little allegiance to laws which they perceive as made against them and which begin first from principles of private property rather than collective need.

On an administrative level, we have an inordinate number of laws which cover virtually every bit of human behavior. This makes it almost impossible for a person not to be guilty of a crime. Because the law is remote from people, as their adversary rather than any reflection of what people want or need, people feel a double alienation; what laws are passed are the wrong ones and the law seems never to work for them. Most Americans have long ago concluded that laws favor the economically powerful who shape them through their lobbyists and who are able to shape the administrative interpretation which is used against their enemies. Law increases rather than decreases personal insecurity. It is this problem that any law revision must correct. Law revision must be predicated on ways of increasing personal security. Laws are to recognize that a person's subjective and individual sense of security can only come from a complex bonding relationship with other people. Thus, social bonding arrangements are not to be tampered with for frivolous reasons. If a person is unable to take part in or appreciate the value of the bonding arrangement that he or she is in, it is likely that there are deformations in the arrangement as, for example, in master-slave relations, or serious psychoneurotic problems that the person may have. In undeformed arrangements, social relationships and activities create the psychological and physical climate to decrease anxiety or the paranoid terror of one against others or everyone. Decreasing this anxiety does not remove pain and risk from a person's life. In this sense, there is no public or institutional way to provide a wall of cushions to protect the person. On the other hand, it is not fated that people's lives have to be made more miserable by social arrangements, institutions and foolish or cruel judgments of political leaders. While the dread of one's mortality can never be removed, the anxiety caused by institutional and social deformations can be corrected through the humanistic use of the law and the creation of social space where bonding may exist.

To be sure, the legal process is often little more than the presentation of the winner's definition of right and wrong, criminality and honored legitimacy. And law itself as it is practiced by courts and lawyers is the direct reflection of the dominant ideology and class's value system. We may take as one powerful but central example the criminal law.

Crime in a modern democracy

Prior to the American revolution, according to such leaders as John Winthrop and Cotton Mather, if the accused was guilty of the religious error of heresy he or she was guilty of crime.[47] Questions of property – who owned what – were adjudicated on the basis of fairness and compromise, modes which were meant to strengthen the bonding system to the community. On the other hand, religious heresy was accepted as the fundamental crime among the citizenry and the leaders because it broke the convenant with God. No doubt religious leaders interpreted their own role as being God's representatives and any attack on their authority was an attack on God. It is no wonder that kings and prelates believed that any set of punishments could be used to command "truth" and loyalty. Torture was not held in disrepute as it is now, for it was taken for granted that sinners, women, children and slaves needed to feel the whip and the rack from male authority so that all understood roles and hierarchy, namely, their place.

302

As I have suggested in this chapter, we must remember that our own constitutional law after the American revolution integrated into itself those principles of torture and slavery until the Civil War. It took seventy-five or more years after the Civil War – and a liberal administration in Washington – to get the courts to apply the most minimum standards as guaranteed under the fourteenth amendment to the operations of local and state officials. One should not forget that it was not until the Supreme Court ruled in 1936 in *Brown v. Mississippi*[48] that confessions could not be beaten out of the accused.

Liberalism in its best sense, as reflected in the work of a Justice Douglas or Justice Black, or in the politics of Senator Wayne Morse and Congressman Robert Kastenmeier, started from a rather simple assumption – that if nothing else, official authority should not participate in crime or in those activities that will make people's lives that much more miserable.[49] Indeed, I suppose many liberals have hoped that governmental intervention would enhance people's lives although examples abound where the reverse is true. While liberals and conservatives believe in keeping the social peace, although in different ways, the most profound public policy differences between them have to do with new responsibilities for government in the context of what I would call *crimes of indirection*.

By this category, I mean the poisoning of the air, or the manufacture of products which slowly poison the user, the improper disposal of dangerous chemical materials, or dangerous and unfit working conditions. Crimes of *indirection* usually affect an entire class or the society as a whole. Criminal intent is hidden by the market system which holds sellers to the standard of profit as the highest, even the sole good. Crimes of indirection go "unnoticed" until there is a systemic break or epidemic. Complex technological societies have little choice but to consider crimes of indirection as more important than direct crimes of personal physical violence, for it is not impossible that crimes of indirection and omission are causes for direct physical violence as, for example, in the effects certain economic policies have which increase destitution and therefore thievery.

In the late 1960s and early 1970s beginning attempts were made to confront corporate and governmental power on causing pain to the citizenry. Laws were passed which were calculated to change the attitudes and consciousness over what should be considered criminal behavior. The Federal Water Pollution Control Act, the Clean Air Act, the Noise Control Act of 1972 and the Solid Waste Disposal Act all carried penalties for their violation. Under these acts the

> penalty for a first offense of up to one year in prison and a fine of not
> more than 25,000 dollars per day of violation. For a second or
> subsequent violation, these penalties rise to a maximum of two years'
> imprisonment and a per day fine of 50,000 dollars respectively.[50]

303

I would add to these punishments. If a corporation continues to violate these acts, the criminal penalty should escalate to confiscation and reassignment of the property to the community. This is justifiable under the theory that corporate charters are in fact licenses from the state which can be revoked where there is abuse of privilege. The inclusion of such matters as befouling the air or water under the heading of criminal law should not be considered as novel.[51]

These standards must also apply to the state itself. Because of traditional notions of sovereign immunity, what might be considered novel is that criminal penalties should apply against the state's representatives where they have intentionally created such conditions. Thus, for example, if a government on any level in the federal system allows polluting waste in rivers from government facilities or is the source of the pollution, there is no reason that the criminal law should not apply to its officials. This is accomplished through laws and regulations which could be enforced either by the administrators of the government against themselves, or by the citizenry against the administrators by bringing class actions and mandamus proceedings against administrators.

Most important, to make this level of participation function well, it is necessary to define governmental secrecy very narrowly so that ordinary citizens and "busybodies" can bring actions to hold the bureaucratic apparatus in check.[52] Since our physical security also must include protection of the environment for present and future time government cannot act passively.

Security also concerns vigilance against various attempts at mind manipulation or control and the use and generation of knowledges and technologies which in fact further enslave a person. We may think about this phenomenon as a criminal tort called *social maiming*. Social maiming is a conscious intention and action by economic and social groups that frame the education of the young. The group explicitly or through negligence arranges social existence in such a way that the person cannot overcome this socially caused condition. This may appear to be a problem of only slight importance, but the issue of advertising and subtle modes of persuasion is no longer a matter of slight importance. While the appearance is that important first amendment questions are raised by any move to question advertising we should be aware of the hypnotic effect such commercial propaganda has on the more passive parts of a person's brain.[53] In other words, the person is allowing himself or herself to be violated without consciously knowing what is happening to them. A second kind of social maiming can be found in the present unemployment system where 52 per cent of blacks between the ages of 16 and 28 would lead one to believe that criminal behavior is present on the part of those who frame the policies in the society. Women are obvious victims of social maiming through dead end jobs and by socially defined incapacity.

One way of counteracting social maiming is by providing basic educational and social minimums for the person. (See Chapter 3.) This becomes part of the American covenant which all people accept and know they owe to one another. In this context basic minimums include skills and material provisioning to assure people of their *active* role in setting relations in the productive and political sphere, and the exercise of limits over activities which diminish or destroy their personhood. These considerations are the ground upon which the defense and criminal justice system should be based in the United States.

A criminal code for the national security state

Since 1965, law professionals have attempted to protect personal security and the power of the state by writing a comprehensive criminal code which, through practice, would define a philosophy of citizenship and government through the criminal law. In effect, the elite bar sought ways of bringing "order" to a seemingly subjective and states' rights oriented area of the law. Its claim has been that too much discretion was left to judges in sentencing and flagrant contradictions exist between various criminal law statutes which grant too much discretion to prosecutors and judges.

After ten years of argument the criminal code passed the Senate in 1976 with the joint initiative and leadership of Senator Kennedy and Senator Thurmond. The code itself was bottled up in the House Judiciary Committee although several years later pieces of the legislation, especially the concern about uniform sentencing, was incorporated in the Comprehensive Crime Control Act of 1984. In separate pieces of legislation a number of other recommendations which stemmed from the work of the Bell-Thompson Commission also found their way into the law including the use of the armed forces, specifically the navy, in helping on drug raids, as well as the need to build new prisons.

The Comprehensive Crime Control Act of 1984 continued the direction of the state's contest with potential defendants and· "outsiders." For example, it provides for pretrial detention and, effectively, underwrites the idea of house arrest. The act also legitimates warrantless taps in matters of national security. This means that internal national security activities of the state will be placed beyond the control of the courts. Any person or group involved in any activity or project with people from other nations (scholars, business executives, ministers, and publishers) can be tapped with warrant. The act also legitimates warrantless taps in cases involving organized crime and danger of immediate death and bodily injury. Earlier versions of the senate bill legitimated para-legal standards, that is, standards which reflected administrative necessity as defined by administrators of internal security and intelligence agencies. S1, the crime bill, treated internal security matters, for all practical purposes, as beyond the control of the courts. Although this notion is not present in the 1984 act there still lurk such ideas in the hearts of the conservative Senate Judiciary Committee. One such notion is an attempt to circumscribe limits.

The various activities of anti-war demonstrators as, for example, during the Vietnam war would, under various of the versions of S1, be open to substantial penalty. The possibility of a movement of non-violent civil disobedience either of the character of the civil rights movement or anti-war demonstrations that confronted actions of the state's bureaucrats in national security matters would be virtually eliminated as a legitimate activity sanctioned by law.

The Crime Control Act of 1984 ends the American penological flirtation with rehabilitation theory and appears to accept the view that punishment is and should be a form of vengeance or retribution against offenders who are to remain out of sight, in prison. While it sets limits to sentencing by eliminating the indeterminate sentence, a mechanism hailed in the 1950s as an important liberal reform, there is no rehabilitative way propounded for dealing with offenders and miscreants. Punishment is to border on vengeance. It is predicated on human nature as inextricably intertwined with evil – the poor – being that the poor are either evil or more prone to it than the more well to do. The act seeks to nationalize ways of dealing with crime and moves directly to an end to diversity on criminal questions among states and localities through the adoption of a grid system for sentencing. The act of 1984 established a United States Sentencing Commission which is intended to avoid "unwarranted sentencing disparities among defendants with similar records who have been found guilty of similar criminal conduct..."[54]

What then is the likely direction of the criminal law given the present distribution of power among the courts and legislature? The likely result of a federal crime act which nationalizes criminal law will tend to make the state courts an instrument for applying federal standards, although this result will not be accepted quickly by state courts and legislatures.

Attempts were made in the 1970s to mandate an administrative *redrafting* of laws passed by Congress on the theory that this delegation of legislative responsibility could be made because elite drafting committees would deal only with linguistic niceties. There is no precedent in legal history which would bear out the contention that such a comprehensive rewrite of law is possible without other conceptions being added by the drafters of "merely technical" legal language. Nevertheless, it is likely that this method will be used in the future if the sentencing commission proves to be unobtrusive. It should be noted that the neutral school of legal philosophy, when connected to conservative interpretation and enforcement, projects the following outcomes:

306

(a) A strong national security state which operates according to its own purposes without oversight from the courts or Congress.

(b) Control of the legal system by laywer elites whose work is to be legitimated by public bodies.

(c) A new emphasis on punishment which rejects either the theory of rehabilitation or a joint societal responsibility. In its stead heavy emphasis is placed on vengeance, people storing and pain as a mode of punishment and deterrence. Prisoners are to be put "out of sight."

(d) Limited or limp involvement from political bodies or the citizenry at large on public issues to the point that any sort of mass demonstration may be defused by the federal government on the ground that official business is being interrupted.

Needless to say, these implications reject as romantic or dangerous the need to make law an instrument of people in their everyday life which they discuss, apply, question and revise. It further rejects the idea of finding ways of restoring the convicted person to the community and continues the principle of isolation and punishment as a means of handling the criminal offender. It stands in conflict with a democratic system of law for that law is predicated on inclusion.

The democratic system is a greedy system for it cannot leave anyone out of being part of it, even the convicted or the accused. But it is also the most generous system for it assures that power always rests with those who are included – namely, the people.

Democratic law revision and punishment for crime

The limits to be enforced through law start from what we would never do either as individuals or collectively. In other words, we must be collectively and individually prepared to run risks for principles that define who or what we are as a nation. Those principles do not have to be positive in their formulation. They may be limited or negative prescriptions, like the ten commandments. For they state clearly what we will not do because we believe that to act otherwise is to become inhumane and to distort us either as people or as a nation. We will have been tranformed into something other than what we are or intend. For example, a solution for street crime might be a curfew coupled with the police's right to shoot on sight any curfew violator. But such methods, even if they brought crime rates down, would be odious. They would lack either proportionality or social bonding between the people. To recognize that oaths are often violated, that laws are broken and that there are reprehensible and venal aspects to people does not mean that we are to incorporate these aspects as the unconscious foundations of democratic public policy. A nation in its collective or governmental behavior does not have the right to violate limits which through a semantic sleight of hand may be called something else. Capital punishment is still murder and killing, detention is still a form of kidnapping and putting people in prisons where they can be raped is an institutional conspiracy to encourage pimping, procuring and violent sexual abuse.[55]

If a nation cannot do collectively what it will not abide in an individual, then the nation must be prepared to run a different set of risks than we presently care to accept. Such risks can be decreased in a highly developed society if certain conditions are socially accepted. Citizens are more likely to accept them where there is a social and political commitment to full employment and continuous education, a free goods system along the lines I have described. In other words, risks decrease and people are more willing to run those risks where a new social fabric of community is knitted which is not dependent on a myth system of domination-submission, or capitalist, sexist and racist plunder and foolish bureaucratic schemes. In any case the Republican-oligarchic system of justice does not work for the common good. Crimes of murder, rape, drug abuse, burglary and robbery can no longer be treated symptomatically by adding police or involving the armed forces in quasi-martial law situations. These methods breed their own forms of social repression and do not touch the immediate or underlying reasons for crime. It would be far more accurate to see crime as a failing of a social system.

According to a 1966 Presidential report on manpower, there is a direct causal correlation between crime and unemployment. This study gives us a clue to the more general attitude that a modern society should have toward sentencing and punishment.[56]

Re-bonding

A repressive-totalitarian system starts from the assumption that only what is authorized is permitted. This notion is deeply engrained among statists who embrace this principle in their application of law to crime. However, a society which aspires to the common good requires a criminal justice system that emphasizes a rebonding process between the guilty party and the community at large. The rebonding process is not the same as rehabilitation. When society seeks to rehabilitate someone the assumption is that the "guilty" party has to change his or her ways in relation to the dominant society. It exempts the society from any wrongdoing. Instead of this premise the re-bonding system is based upon the notion that criminal penalties should include within them the method by which society can reconsider its own habits, economic and social structure. In other words it must accept the need to revise critically its own institutional methods and activities. This process has begun, as I have said, where the courts intervene in various social institutions when they become obviously deformed. Judges are now being asked by claimants to serve as social bankruptcy masters to change conditions in schools, prisons, and mental asylums.

Since the Enlightenment some reforming penologists have sought to find the "correct proportionality" between the punishment and the crime. But this goal is inadequate for it does not strike the fundamental question of how to create a sense of belonging and respect for justice in a society comprising different classes and races, whose individual values and needs are so different. An important responsibility of judges is to sustain a communal belonging and assure that a penalty system is not used as an instrument of the group against the individual. Judges and legislatures should act as the society's agents to transform the present system of punishments into one wherein a mutual exchange of gifts is made between the person and the society. In this context, the criminal is expected to acknowledge his or her social being to the society and the society must find ways of showing its dependence on the individual person who has committed misdeeds. By giving a gift of service, work, or property, the defendant is reflecting a communal belief that he or she has worth, is to share that worth with others, and that the community at large will accept his or her gift. As part of the re-bonding system the community itself must then also obligate itself to find gifts and acknowledge obligations that it has to the person. It must lay itself bare and show what it is and has done to cause the situation of alienation between the person and the collective other. It must be prepared to change the economic structure. Such an attitude would allow for a wholly different view of punitive action. Imagine if the judge at the time of sentencing would call on the prosecutor to state what society had done *wrong to the offender* and how it intended to correct that wrong, the offender would no longer be seen as an outsider and the present foolish and wasteful prison system would be changed and finally eliminated.

It is at least debatable whether the "economic costs" of such interventions will be more than the present system. In New York, for example, the costs of incarcerations, prisons and infliction of pain run to $26,000 a year per prison inmate. During the nineteenth and part of the twentieth century, there was a sadistic economic logic to prisons for the prisoner was contracted out for service to business. Now the state merely houses the convicted without much economic return. The purpose of justice and punishment is to assert necessary standards for the existence of society. Government does not exist for the purpose of punishing deviants. Its role in society is to tie justice and punishment to social modes of reintegration, actions which set standards but allow for the process of banishment and exodus. For example, there is a Talmudic law that those convicted of crimes should be afforded the opportunity of leaving the city or town in which they committed the crime, if they are able to find another community to accept them. Where they are not accepted by other communities, it is then that incarceration occurs. It may well be that as part of the re-bonding process those convicted should participate in deciding their own punishment. This method has been tried with success by some local courts in Minnesota. The victims of crime should also participate in the punishment process of the wrongdoer for such a process personalizes the law and allows for the re-bonding and interdependence process to operate as part of the judicial system. In practical terms, this would mean that the courts would take into account the wishes of the victim, the victim's family and community in deciding punishment for the criminal. There is no inherent advantage in using the impersonal method of handing out punishment. It may well be that the guilty party and the victim of his or her family would prefer the criminal to perform tasks for the aggrieved rather than have the convicted stay in jail. There is a public responsibility to victims which goes well beyond that of apprehending a criminal. This responsibility derives from the constitutional purpose of ensuring domestic tranquility. It should be noted that the Reagan administration and the Democratic House included a federal victim's rights statute which states financial compensation to the victim, as well as medical aid. This is an important and hopeful sign, even though the program is partial and modest.

The process of re-bonding and integration can do much to change the outsider or deviant perception that individuals may have of themselves, since often people believe that there is no alternative for them but that of the status of alienated outsider: so too the fear and embitterment of the victim must also be addressed in a therapeutic and financial manner.

A revision of the laws for a democracy must be less an expert activity and more a *common* endeavor performed publicly which people formulate in their daily lives. People need experience for this purpose, where their judgment may be honed and exercised. One way this can be accomplished is through a neighborhood court system. Neighborhood courts, organized by citizens in their own neighborhoods outside of the "downtown" courts, would do much to generate a non-abstract, vibrant form of law that is shaped by the people as they work through everyday problems. This court system would resolve simple, civil and criminal disputes and would not be courts of record. To the extent they are kept, records would be of a much more simple nature than those kept in the downtown courts. The courts might become adjuncts of schools and young people would become aware of the life of their communities through the method of conflict resolution, community conciliation and binding which the neighborhood courts would practice. Disputes would be dealt with expeditiously by three-person juries who should be drawn from local precinct lists. The strength of such courts would be found in their conciliating and mediating activities and in their power to assign the wrongdoer tasks for the community, where they would be paid the national, minimum wage.

310

There is a danger to a neighborhood court system which should be noted. If the courts become "courts of record," there will be a tendency to include the decisions and the alleged wrongdoers as part of a national crime identification system, or a system of local control through the police. This would hinder the purpose of the neighborhood court which is to settle disputes amicably and not to aid in the centralization of police control. It is not an instrument to assert punishment. The federal government would encourage the formation of the neighborhood court system through grants paid to neighborhoods to organize and continue this system on a regular basis.

Ersatz social bonding

It is not likely that the citizenry can shape the law as an educational activity in a state which is an oligarchy but with republican trappings because law enforcement and administrative programs are used to divide the society into the watchers and the watched, investigators and investigated. The state corporate surveillance apparatus, and record-keeping system tend to change the presumption that the rule of law favors the citizen (of whatever class) to the presumption that the state's coercive power is necessary to orderly society: that without the coercive power exercised by the government with vigor, the Hobbesian state of nature would reign over human relations and property rights would become unsettled and subject to continuous conflict. This is of course the premise of the preventive detention statute passed by Congress in 1984. The unstated assumption is that as a matter of daily activity the government seeks to stay within the constraints of the republic-oligarchic framework by creating processes and relations intended to limit the life and liberty of those thought as "threats" to the community. Patterns of control and surveillance come to be thought of as "ordered liberty," "due process" and "wise constraints" in the courts. Their practical purpose is to mask problems which are generated and caused by present property relations and the power of the government to create problems.

The computerization of government and industry has resulted in successful attempts to accumulate information about people, synchronize and coordinate that information with the police, intelligence agencies, banks, credit bureaus, the military, university and corporations. We see the emergence of an ersatz bonding coercively fashioned, often through technology. The result is that there is little room left for the person who is now followed by the paper identity created for him or her. This mechanism of coordination helps the state apparatus use paper terror as its primary instrument.

The most subtle form of terror and humiliation comes through the "paper" identity of people which they must fulfill. This "paper identity"

311

becomes the state's reconstruction of the person which is then used to track and channel the individual. Records of school, military, employment, financial and credit profiles are not innocent documents. While numerous arguments can be made that record-keeping is necessary for a modern society and that it can be carried out without harsh consequences, it is time that limits on record-keeping be introduced.[57]

This limitation is best achieved if the society recognizes that each person has a fundamental property right in his or her name. This right is far more important than the person's rights of opportunity for it recognizes the person in reality, not only in potentiality. Once a person's property right to his or her name is recognized, certain powerful effects will flow. Any time that a record is kept about a person without the permission of the person a legal claim against the government or corporate body might attach.

We may note several difficulties with the theory that persons have a property right in their name. The first difficulty is that criminal suspects could have a chilling effect on the government because prosecutors and the police would not be able to keep records about the suspect without opening *themselves* to prosecution or civil damages. But even in this case, I would argue that the government is required to inform the potential defendant that he or she is being "watched" or that a file has been opened on them for specific, suspected crimes. Where there is no specific crime charged or about to be charged, the government would have no choice but to drop its surveillance. Such concerns would be written into law as the modern understanding of due process.[58]

The reader will correctly conclude that I believe in shifting the power of the state and the police system to favor the individual citizen. This shift will increase concern on the part of the citizenry with the issue of conduct and will cause people to rethink the present criminal law system. Consonant with such a shift is our need to formulate a far more realistic veiw of citizen obligations. There are many obligations to which the mass of the citizenry did not agree. In a democracy why should a citizen accept an obligation that he or she did not make? There is only one obvious answer. Every political system has many obligations. We are born into obligations. If an individual citizen consciously refuses all obligations, he or she should be carried by the community. Where enough people refuse virtually all obligations, it is likely that the political system is in – or about to be in – a time of profound and probably convulsive change. Demanding that people take on more obligations where they are already unable or unwilling to perform their present ones is a foolish and unworkable political strategy.

Police obligations

The process of changing obligations also means a shift in the obligations of the police forces. The first point to be made is that the police cannot be expected to carry the burdens of socially and economically caused ills. If a society does not commit itself to elementary standards of economic justice and assure equity and caring, it is absurd to believe that the police will be able to keep the society together either through surveillance or intimidation. Police departments are most likely to serve the common good when (a) their purposes are limited; (b) they act on the basis of public accountability from the neighborhood level; and (c) they act without using the paraphernalia of an occupying force. Crime is not reduced by giving the police tanks, troop carriers, machine guns and helicopters. Of course the consequences of introducing such technological paraphernalia is to increase oligarchic power. It is also probable that martial law effectively lowers the crime rate for a period of time. Using military force in the apprehension of the accused and criminals is a way of nudging the American form of government to one of direct authoritarianism. Recommendations that the armed forces be used in drug raids are obvious means of centralizing governmental power. Paradoxically, an increase of armaments to the police will have the effect of limiting the power of the police to act in ordinary ways with people because the police are then required, by the nature of their technology and organizational structure to maintain a separate stance from the community, as for example, in the case of the specially trained, so-called SWAT teams. In the best of circumstances, once such separateness is acquired, where police, like samurai, have their own code, they become organized strangers in the communities they patrol. They may be called upon to give allegiance to constituted authority, but because of the special role in which they are placed, and in which they perpetuate themselves institutionally, they are invariably in danger of becoming *the* constituted authority for the community, especially where they work with those who wield economic power. Often the poor experience them as occupiers, as in the case of Miami prior to the riots of 1980.

On the national level, we are faced with police agencies which have been relatively isolated from American life and organized along samurai lines. Because of violations in people's rights of citizenship and the creation of massive surveillance systems the FBI and the CIA were under intense attack in Congress and the media during the Nixon-Ford years. The charters of these agencies are rather obscure, emanating from the requirements of political and military oligarchy. The FBI's authority for investigation in political cases, for example, stemmed from a series of oral communications and written memoranda between President Roosevelt and FBI Director Hoover. The FBI used the catch-all to "detect . . . crimes against the United States." Presidents and other government officials have used the FBI to settle scores of a personal nature. Under J. Edgar Hoover the FBI acted as a pied piper to move dissenters into the class of conspirators. Its own activities included the commission of crimes such as wiretapping, bugging, entrapment, arson, frame-ups and fraud. These methods have been used by other agencies of the government with a few others supplemented by the CIA. Indeed, at least nineteen other federal agencies have police powers to intimidate, bug, or otherwise entrap people. The breadth of illegal activities by official agencies has been enormous.

The following is quoted from "Preventing Improper Influence on Federal Law Enforcement Agencies":[59]

1 40 per cent of COINTELPRO* activities created dissension and caused disruption within various groups by the sending of anonymous or fictitious materials to the members of the groups.
2 20 per cent of the activities involved dissemination of publicly available information to friendly media representatives to expose the aims and activities of various groups.
3 Investigative materials based on non-public information were leaked to friendly media sources to expose nature, aims and membership of groups.
4 8 per cent of the activities involved advising local, state and federal authorities of civil and criminal violations by group members.
5 About 2 per cent of the activities involved having informants sow dissension and exploit disputes to cause disruption in the organization.
6 A program was instituted under which employers, credit bureaus, and creditors were informed of illegal, immoral, radical and Communist Party activities in order to affect adversely their credit standing or employment status.
7 To adversely affect the economic interests of members of these groups the FBI informed or contacted businesses and persons with whom members had economic dealings of the members' activities.
8 Members were interviewed or contacted by the FBI to let the members know the FBI was aware and then attempted to develop informants out of these people.
9 Information was furnished to leaders of religious and civil organizations to gain the support of such leaders and persuade them to exert pressure on the government, employers and landlords to the detriment of the various groups.
10 In less than half of 1 per cent of the activities, described as "among the most troubling in all of the COINTELPRO efforts," a variety of incidents related to the political or judicial process. Following are the details:

> Tipping off the press that a write-in candidate for Congress would be attending a group meeting at a specific time and place; leaking information to the press that a group official was actively campaign- ing for a person running for public office; furnishing the arrest and

*A counter-intelligence and propaganda program started by the US Government to infiltrate various activist movements in the late 1960s and early 1970s.

314

conviction record of a member of a group who was candidate for a
local public office to a friendly newspaper which published the
information; sending an anonymous letter to a political candidate
alerting him that a group's members were active in his campaign and
asking that he not be a tool of the group; sending an anonymous
letter to a local school board official, purporting to be from a
concerned parent, alerting him that candidates for the school board
were members of a group; mailing an anonymous letter to a member
of a group who was a mayoralty candidate in order to create distrust
toward his comrades; furnishing background of a man who was a
candidate for public office, including arrests and questionable
marital status, to news media contact; furnishing public source data
on a group to a local grand jury chairman who had requested it in
connection with the grand jury's probe concerning arrests of an
individual to a court that had earlier given this individual a
suspended sentence and also furnishing this same information to his
employer who later discharged the individual; making an anonymous
telephone call to a defense attorney, after a federal prosecution had
resulted in a mistrial, advising him (apparently falsely) that one of
the defendants and another well-known group individual were FBI
informants.

11 Material was sent out indicating that sham organizations had been
established (for disruptive purposes).
12 In less than 1 per cent of COINTELPRO activities anonymous
communications were sent to family members or groups on immoral
radical activities on the part of various individuals.

Does a national police force contradict a democracy committed to the
common good? Is there a way for such an organization, whether unified or
broken into separate agency fiefdoms, to operate under a clearly delineated
and democratic accountability structure? Police powers, when used by
governments, are more than exemplary of symbolic power.[60] In any time of
crisis, turbulence or radical change, whatever the political "tilt," there will
be a tendency to call for repressive measures, to increase the size of police,
increase investigations, and entrapment situations to assure allegiance of the
mass of the citizenry or the discontented, and isolate others by setting them
off as criminals. Every safeguard should be invented to assure that such a
tendency is not allowed to occur. All groups that contest for power are
prone to use and strengthen the police for their purposes when under
question and attack. In 1967, for example, during the civil rights and anti-
war movements, the Bureau was requested by the liberal Attorney-General
Ramsey Clark to "use the maximum available resources" to collect
intelligence about plans "by any group of whatever size, effectiveness or
affiliation . . ." This instruction of a civil libertarian in power, Ramsey Clark,

is hardly surprising. It does not seem that ideological tendencies, whether left, right or center, when cloaked in the shield of the state act very differently. After the Russian revolution, the Bolsheviks took over the state bureaucracy and the Tsarist police apparatus, deepening their activities in the control of both revolutionary and anti-revolutionary groups. Both groups in their original form disappeared, but the police remained, as did the bureaucracy. So it has been with all modern states where political and social turbulence occurred. The reason for an action may have long since disappeared, but the habit of mind and the police structure remains, and is usually strengthened. This is why the common good requires that limits be set on state power. In this regard, some attention should be paid to prosecutorial power because it is so easily abused. During turbulent times political leaders will use the prosecutor and police as "short cuts to persuasion" of an opposition. When such "short cuts" are taken they invariably strengthen the elements of the political process which are paranoid and which tend to see all politics as that of conflict and power for their own sake. Governing is then reduced to the threat of organized personal terror of individuals and groups in such a way that conflict and power for its own sake become the basis upon which a politics is conducted. The politics of paranoia is not easily correctable. One way is through the mass participation of people in the public space, through the performance of public tasks, to democratizing the decisions of investment of the economy, in other words to making real decisions over questions that matter. It is in this way, through the continuous honing of the citizen's faculty of judgment, that half-baked fears and inhumane reactions can be challenged and answered. It would be, for example, through such dialogue in the public space that defense could be debated as a humane purpose rather than as a specialty of war crimes. Through citizen participation in the public space at the neighborhood level, equity, dignity, egalitarian interdependence and caring can be given rich meanings applicable to the group and the individual at the same time. If such conceptions inform our interpretation of law and the constitution we will be able to have a democracy which generates liberation among the people and yet recognizes individual uniqueness. We will be able to move to a system of governance which includes all people as actors rather than objects.

7
Progress and the common good

The character of politics in a society which seeks to perfect its democracy and which simultaneously seeks to find answers to the problems of modern life that would allow people a greater measure of happiness must of necessity turn to the question of progress; how it is to be attained and how individually and collectively the liberatory impulse of human beings and the need for social bonding and community can be part of a program for the common good.

It was the strength of the flowering of liberation movements around the world in the 1960s that they saw themselves reacting against what Marcuse called "pain, cruelty, injustice and stupidity." It was the weakness of those movements that they did not sustain their attempts at liberation with a program which showed the direction that could be moved peacefully and the possibilities that could be achieved through the application of principles of caring and justice, egalitarian interdependence and individual dignity.[1] It remains the yearning of humankind to find the paths and programs which link to and reflect the fundamental attribute of human freedom which follows men and women. Freedom is their shadow; part of them, always there. The question is how can a yearning which is invariant be expressed in people's actions and decisions? There are those who argue that this yearning can never be fulfilled and therefore to attempt anything, to change one's actual situation, to reformulate relationships, or social structure, or to struggle for greater democracy as the instrument of liberation and community is a colossal waste of time and energy. But such views of pessimism miss the point. Once possibility links to need, actions will be taken and the oppressor, left, right or center is at risk. While the oppressor will of course put the Other at risk, the oppressed feel the sense of rightness in their search for liberation. It may be badly expressed, or it may be poorly carried out. But this consequence is the result of not knowing rationally and pragmatically how to bring about social change and sustain freedom.

Once this is understood, and there are many clues from past revolutions

317

including the American revolution and the Civil War, we will be able to avoid the terrifying syndrome where the victim becomes the executioner.

Actors in history seek to set the compass of history and often they are disappointed for the consequences of their acts may turn out to be negative and disastrous. Revolutionary change, especially when one forgets the root of revolution as humaneness, disintegrates into a dubious enterprise. This is why I favor social reconstruction for it assumes terrible errors, blunders and surprises just because of our fallibility. Political actors are often caught up in their own will and they lose sight of the inherent limits of political action which all people must contend with:

> One human being may possess the noblest intentions, but his deeds may result in evil; on the other hand, another's evil intentions will result in some good. Two persons with the same intention can do the same thing, but the action of one of them may remain without consequences while the other may provoke a series of reactions.[2]

It is only recently that Marxists have underlined the limits and unpredictability of human action. They have not been sufficiently aware that there are very few, if any, human actions that are not linked to the actions of others. This social linkage does not cumulatively add up to certainty. Why is this so? No person is a clean slate. Each has his and her own history and intention which is then brought together with others who are then linked by the actions of each other. Not even Christ could escape the actions of others or escape being subject to their whims and greed. Once God revealed himself to the man Christ, God soon learned that even He entered history. He accepted, as Mircea Eliade said, "the historical condition of the people in whose midst he chose to be born."[3] Therefore he was subjected to the sins of others, and, incidentally, his own mistaken judgments about people that he had no power to control or correct. He could not save himself from history or others in it. And so too it is with heroes. Heroes who attach themselves to movements or seek to bring about change are unable to save either themselves from the whims of others or from the fate of the situation which they enter.

When Che Guevara went to Bolivia and was turned in by the peasants, he suffered from lack of political judgment about those who ultimately determined his fate. Gods, heroes, and tyrants are no bettter at escaping history than the rest of us. Those who practice politics know that their intentions and actions are linked to others who have their own "agenda" and needs. The Bolivian peasants had *present* problems. They could not save, struggle, or plan for a future. For their only surplus was that of individual pain. To have progress there must be, at least for some, life slack, awareness beyond·the immediate, and the type of capital we may think of as a surplus of consciousness. Humanity lives in a cyclical framework of life

318

tied to necessity. Without a surplus of consciousness it is hard to accept the claims of those who argue that tomorrow is going to be better than today through the wonders of technology and the exercise of reason and will. Peasants need to save their land and feed their families because there is an immediate present problem. Winter is always coming, the children are always sick, loved ones are always dying before their time. The world presents to 80 per cent of its people calamity of a personal sort from which it is hard to escape, with or without a political program. But the calamities we face are of vastly different types. Conservatives (really reactionaries) are fond of mistaking the *angst* of humanity, that which it feels because it is only human, for *furcht*, that fear and vulnerability which is socially caused. And in doing so conservatives play visionaries as dangerous fools who suffer and cause others to suffer as well, as if the social structure is a given, a natural phenomenon which cannot be changed or tampered with. In his novel *Arrival and Departure*, one of Koestler's characters, a woman psychoanalyst, says to the political activist hero who is committed to revolutionary change,

> I am sick of all their talk about the future. . . . It is a drug; people who become addicted to it don't live. The point is to make the present autarkic, with protective tariffs all around. "Look, Petya," she said, biting into the banana and munching it slowly, with an air dreamily lascivious, "There is more reality in this mouthful of fruit than in the whole future."[4]

Yet for all its literary cleverness the material reality is that bananas are eaten quickly, someone must pick them and a social structure of someone else's reality is involved in that banana which is palpably harsh and real. We (humanity) must act on the bananas or they will rot. The question remains, what is the social structure which states how we pick, distribute and share in our food? In other words, how we act towards each other as we (humanity) find ways of surviving. If we seek freedom we are condemned to choice and action. And by the nature of the present, past, and future we are always acting in and for the future. Human beings do nothing but think thoughts that of necessity are either about the past or the future. Thus we are condemned by the nature of physical reality and human existence to prepare future activity, or become part of the practico-inert, trapped, controlled, and thrown.

It is of course true that Marx, for other reasons, had doubts about visionaries and programs for a future. He stated in his *Critique of the Gotha Programme* that no society emerges ahistorically. It "emerges from capitalist society; which is thus in every respect, economically, morally and intellectually still stamped with the birthmarks of the old society from whose womb it emerges".[5] One must be careful, and those committed to reconstruction should be careful that such language is not a *moral* evasion

319

justifying new offences in terms of the old society and its habits.

Nevertheless, there is still reason to be hesitant about a programme. Political programmes, unless lived, are merely a set of rhetorical statements. They are metaphors. They are not lived experiences. So people should take them with a grain of salt or analyze them critically in terms of surprise and the unintended. Those of us who have lived through the revolutions, struggles and wars of this century as witnesses or indeed have been part of causing human tragedy are chary about all visions because the thrust towards freedom and progress gives no guarantees. So an important question remains. If we are uncertain of outcomes why bother to initiate any political actions? One reason is that the danger of not acting far outweighs the risks attendant to active confrontation and the re-routing of rational thought to humane results. Others are acting to build and buttress social institutions that are pathological and risk civilization's end. One may be certain about the outcome to this civilization if people do not act against powerful institutions which have allowed violence or oppression to gain the upper hand. We cannot cut deals any more with mindless authority hoping that by remaining passive and accepting the status of victim-hostage we will be able to maintain our tattered shred of dignity and trust of authority. (Nor can we swallow whole the assumptions of Faustian progress.) Our situation reminds me of a story in the tradition of gallows humor and Yiddish despair and trust.

Two Jews were in front of a Nazi firing squad. The lieutenant was about to give the order to shoot when one of the condemned Jews yelled out, "Wait, I'd like a blindfold please." at that moment the other condemned man poked him in the ribs with his elbow and said, "Shh, don't make trouble." By telling this story I do not mean to make light of the problems which are faced when we do not cooperate with the forces of reaction or authority's lackeys. Nor do I mean to suggest that those of us who believe in reconstruction argue that the progress of the kind we have had is unalloyed. In any case, what choice is there in a democracy but to give humane dimension to progress? After all, democracy is a system of political action which seeks to discover the depths of humankind and add political protections to us as human beings, as individuals and in our social context. In this sense reconstruction is based on transcending revolutionary errors and reactionary parochialisms. It is attentive to the fragility of human progress.

Reconstructive paths recognize that the task of the politics and inquiry of the common good is to add new rights to people as we learn more about those attributes of individual and group life which define us as human and humane. This is one aspect of the meaning of human progress. Yet we cannot dismiss out of hand other views. The molecular biologist, Gunther Stent, must be taken seriously when he said that there may be nothing more to be done around "progress" if we mean by that term the accumulation of happiness and the rights to protect that happiness. He asks the conventional but important question whether, as he puts it, "were the medieval serfs more or were they less happy than the denizens of present-day megalopolitan suburbia? – the definition renders belief in progress as an act of faith, one not subject to verification or disproof."[6]

The medieval serf would not have had a consuming interest in conquering nature or believing that this was useful or possible. In our time both Faustian socialism and Faustian capitalism champion the importance of having power over events in the "now"; and knowing how to yield positive results in the future. In our time, and this is the essence of modernity, we believe that to control and guide is "man's fate" once he decides to be part of the world – if he decides to act. (When people act politically for reconstruction, they risk and seek liberated status so that all may guide rationally.) But there is a terrible paradox about our present situation. This meaning to progress is now empty. Progress now requires a totally different character to it. Where, historically, it has been predicated on the fetishization of things and the accumulation of more, whatever the more was, now progress must be conceived of as a wholly humanistic project which of necessity includes the emancipation of women and the Third World. The purpose is to create human activity which allows for both error and the exercise of judgment. *Curiously the progressive undertaking of modern civilization is the task of transforming ourselves from being Faustian*. It is on this that a program of democratic reconstruction is premised. It will help us reject the conventional meaning of progress which teaches us to will into reality what too often should be rejected summarily. As I have said, our task is also related to the moral action of renunciation, of what under any circumstances should not be done. In a modern democracy, we learn about renunication through dialogue in the public space. These concerns are not abstract matters without consequences. There are the Dionysians who will fight tooth and nail to keep "the Empire" and keep their definition of control over "the free world." This means that they will fight to keep people out of history and out of their chance for subject-actor status. And there will be those who will fight like tigers, and military scientists to do their experiments and technological "improvements," insisting that it is only through an unreflective and uncritical technology that the common good can be achieved. This is Faustianism gone mad. One should not forget its seductive quality.

Faustianism is the very fiber of modern time for it has reflected one powerful aspect of the thrust for liberation. Marx swore by Faustianism and in effect wanted everyone to have the consciousness of Faust. He wanted and believed mightily that knowledge would be unpoisonous once the class struggle came to an end. For him as for other children of the Enlightenment man was worth saving only because he had consciousness of himself and others. For Marx, God gave Adam and Eve an important gift – the problematic of their humanity as they were kicked out of the Garden of Eden. This was their first moment of freedom for they were now in charge of their destiny, having acquired the obligation of choice. They generated a society by their own internal principles rather than those laid out by God. But to defend themselves they needed, like God, power. They had to change nature, for it was no longer passive and nice, they had to change each other, and they had to fabricate a will to power against things, animals, and people so they would survive. God's children had become beasts of prey in Western civilization.

Marx was turned on his head and it became national socialism so well prefigured in Oswald Spengler's *Decline of the West*. Here deformation was championed in which the few should control the many; that the real culture and progress resides in the whites and a few northern races of Europe; that whites will not and should not stop at anything, whether war, deception, tricks of organization to get their way. Whether our teachers were Spengler or Marx, Kennedy or Lenin, Hitler or Churchill, Reagan or Mitterrand, Western man was taught to

> laugh at all bounds of time and space, which indeed regards the
> boundless and endless as its specific target, subject whole continents to
> itself, eventually embrace[ing] the world in the network of its forms of
> communication and intercourse, and transforming it by the force of its
> practical energy and the gigantic power of its technical processes.[7]

This idea of Faustian power saw its fruition in the atomic explosions of 1945. It sees its continuation in star wars. At the testing of the first nuclear bomb Oppenheimer spoke through the lines of the Bhagavad Gita for the new peril which egocentric Faustian man had achieved with his deformed meaning to progress. "I have become the destroyer of worlds." The need to conquer and control, the need to be as God when even God could not control or conquer is the assumption of modern knowledge and modern state power. According to the American statesman it is necessary to have nuclear weapons, or so it is thought to maintain American hegemony or defeat Russians, Germans, and Japanese just as it was thought by the German statesmen that they had to have concentration camps and "scientific" medical experiments to eliminate the unwanted, to answer their paranoid fears. How did things go so wrong?

Before Lord Bacon (described by the imperial saint, Albert Schweitzer, as a somewhat wormy character), there was little thought of human progress in the way those committed to the common good might think of it. Human time was the enemy of the person, for the person could not recognize any cumulative change either in material or spiritual terms. The human condition seemed eternally damned. Indeed, if the person were an Indian he was kept in his place by those myths which insisted that certain limits should not be crossed because the next world was a time of paybacks.

In this world women, like slaves, saw no chance for themselves. (Indeed, the revolutionaries Marx and Engels lost sight of half the human race, as Delores Hayden pointed out, by concentrating on organizing workers, and restricting the meaning of work to production outside the home.)[8] At best women were keepers of cycles. On the other hand, emphasis on repetitive cycles, for example the productive system of agriculture which women carried out, was necessary if humankind intended to survive. Memory of suffering concentrated attention as a way of escaping physical need, of making things and growing crops. Nature itself had to be uniform and it had to repeat itself if humankind were to live in the world.

The Jewish and Christian definition of time was mixed together with progress. But it was a progress which moved to a common destiny. The destiny of humankind, therefore, was to transcend material time and become "timeless." If many could escape time through his thoughts, then he could approach God. Thus, to many people (including Socrates in the Phaedo) one's own death is the culmination of progress for it means that one would return to God, and the possibility of having escaped human time and the misery of the flesh.

But the definition of time changed for humankind when people sought self-definition. This meant that people would act in different ways at different times and in different circumstances, with the result that there was change which could be judged in the person. This change could then be seen as either progress or regression. In the Renaissance, progress was achieved through the immediate activity, action or project which found its authority in the end to be achieved or the pursuit of excellence which the actor sought to manifest in how he carried out his project or enterprise. Erich Kahler has said that the detachment of "man from the authority of the past" was accomplished through new scientific and technological discoveries which no longer made it obligatory to know about the past, be intimidated by the seasons, or believe in tradition.[9] It was no longer necessary to live a life of holiness either in thought or spirit. Where once there was a self-interest, everyday purpose to the holy life, man was now able to serve God by finding solutions to immediate disasters which God and the Devil presented to humankind. People acquired a new dignity through their own thought and actions. They were a welcome tonic to religious teachings of the Christian variety which started by seeing people as lying, posturing sinners (even modern theologians such as Reinhold Niebuhr were never far from this view). It is hardly surprising that people sought escape from a system of thought which continuously asserted their sinfulness. And it is no wonder that people came to embrace those who said that they could transform what was once called sinfulness through a kind of social alchemy now known as science and technology.

With the emergence of modern science and democracy sins were changed into problems to be solved and people crossed the chalk marks of fear. Those marks had warned man that his life and his world could never be more than a vale of tears. For now it became possible, through science and technology, to understand and control one's surroundings. Progress could be judged through one's own eyes and senses, measured by how much it was possible to control events and natural forces. People no longer had to dream of heaven or "perfect forms of government." They did not have to be tortured in the name of God. As Macauley said, these dreams made way for

> dreams of wings with which men were to fly from the Tower to the Abbey, and of double keeled ships which were never to founder in the storm. All classes were hurried along by the prevailing sentiment. Cavalier and Roundhead, Churchman and Puritan were for once allied. Divines, jurists, statesmen, nobles, princes, swelled the triumph of the Baconian philosophy.[10]

And of course, the arts now took second place in people's minds and actions as to what was described as "hard," "real," "measurable," and "predictable." Since art could only imitate nature, but technology and science could change it, and in the process appear to provide material well-being to human beings, it soon came to pass that there was no contest as to which sort of intelligence and sensibility would capture the modern age. Progress was inextricably linked to science and technology.

Scientists and technologists in their work detached themselves from those moral purposes which were obvious and necessary. They embraced a closed system with its own standards and proofs. In a way their autonomous standards embraced the epistemology of Machiavelli, a man whose influence went well beyond politics. For him politics, another synonym for power, was to be governed by amoral rules which its practitioners readily understood, but which outsiders could not quite fathom. It is hard to believe for the outsider but Hitler, Stalin, Kennedy, Nixon and Lyndon Johnson were playing by the same set of rules, amoral and in the final analysis quite brutal ones. As James Watson pointed out in *The Double Helix*, scientific endeavor now plays by an amoral set of rules.

In our time democratic politics and science cannot allow for an autonomous politics or science which excludes the citizens, and those acted upon. The victims will be heard, even before they are victimized. In other words, in a time of mass destruction no rational activity and no politics can serve the common good without a principle of inclusion and without a clear understanding of what caring and empathy mean in practice, or how generosity and social bonding are to be expressed. This must become true in all endeavors. It is in these conceptions, made operational in the way we consider "problems and sin" which will cast the light necessary to generate a world civilization. This is the most sensible way to have progress without constraining ourselves with pathological choices that will lead to civilization's end; a guarantee if we continue with Faustianism as our underlying ideology.

This bit of expansive language does not tell us how to recognize rational progress which starts from empathy and sustains this common attribute throughout the process of change. There are some who believe that progress is to be measured by certain social democratic principles as reflected in the well-organized, but supposedly joyless, society of Sweden. Others say that the progress of world civilization cannot and should not be measured by the North European belief in calculated rationality or the American fetish of individualism or the socialist totem of collectivism. In our time progress towards the common good would better be measured in terms of individual and collective responsibility. Facing up to responsibility helps a people change their status from victims and executioners to free people who set limits for themselves. This form of responsibility and freedom allows a people to come to themselves. It enables them, as I have said, to understand what they will never do for if they do cross these limits they become something else.

When we consider moral consequences we are searching for limits and ways to determine them. These limits do not have to come from the deterrent fear of what will happen to us in the next world, or in this one. They must come to us in the context of situations where we have been entrapped or enslaved and where we can be the active agents for life-affirming alternatives. The nuclear scientist in the laboratory, the soldier who accepts orders for destruction of others, either out of fear or false responsibility, the woman who accepts male-defined social roles and institutions, and the black worker who passively accepts unemployment are now called upon to fashion a new moral sensibility.

Since democracy is the people's social instrument to bring all of us into history, it, above all other forms of governing, needs a moral ethic which will guide and frame public action. The democratic forum enables us to retrace our steps and then consciously choose as a society and then as a world civilization what oppressors must no longer do and the oppressed no longer accept. The common good is now dependent on a conscious willingness to choose short-term "losses" as they might be so judged in the nationalist frame of reference, rather than become beastly in the process of seeking victory. Before we can progress we must interrupt institutions that encourage our inertial and masking processes for they help us to evade what we are doing and what is being done to us. Such taking stock will cause its own disruptions because it means that activities which people are dependent on, as deformed as they might be, do frame their lives and give them some measure of stability and economic security. As an example without proper planning a termination of the arms race for the United States would throw an additional 8-10 million people out of work. This is why a program of reconstruction is so crucial.

It is not enough to stop the arms race, for it has become a way of life which is comforting and comfortable adding meaning and purpose to its proponents and participants. Saying "no" is not enough to convince economically insecure workers seeking another direction. Politics and plans must be drawn and be ready. It is in the context of new plans that the more basic humanistic point can be made, namely, that our writ as human beings is to lower the quantum of human suffering in the world, not add to it through war preparations, or end civilization through war.

This "message" cannot be heard unless we have an empathic awareness of the Other, whether nature, animal or the person. Such awareness is of the kind that emphasizes interlinked, webbed, layered and necessary relationships, knowing full well that they can be natural or quite deformed. The brilliant comedian, Richard Pryor, has given us a comic sketch in which various parts of the body refuse to respond to the needs of other parts of the body. And the audience laughs uproariously at a situation in which the legs say "To hell with you, ribs, you are on your own."[11] The audience laughs because of the truth and madness of this situation, for no life can function without a harmonious relationship between the parts, and this harmonious relationship cannot develop unless the individual part can approach its natural fullness. The problem is that much more infinitely complex when we seek to bring together harmonious relationships between people, restore mind/body balance within the person and find a means of building a world civilization that is non-exploitive and just. After all, a harmonious relationship is not ethically sound if it embraces dominance as its purpose as in a situation where the cell of the person or the group's appetite like a cancer metastasizes and destroys the host.

I have said that the affirmation and reverence for life is the means by which people find their ethical duty and their intersubjective harmony with others. This ethical duty which people feel innately does not come from a Kantian measuring rod external to the person's feelings. Rather, ethical duty emerges from a consciousness in which direct affective relationships of hope, loving, empathy and caring are linked together and may be expressed directly in public and private activities. It is what women have done and must teach men to do. Without these sentiments paramount there can hardly be peace or harmony; nor can there be a progress which serves empathic justice linked to social bonding. This is true for a simple reason.

Empathic justice means recognition of the human Other. If there is no such recognition, if the Other is either used as an instrument, objectified or turned into a commodity or colonized, there can be no justice. For justice as the Melians long ago learned can only be present among equals. Perhaps we are required to have an animistic belief that all of nature lives to understand the importance that justice plays towards all things and beings. Just as hope

326

is God's gift to us so empathic justice is the gift of sharing one's humanity with another. As property gifts are not often missed for we do not know that they are supposed to be there. Nevertheless, once we know of their existence they take on special meaning for they are our unacknowledged but necessary link to each other. The gift of justice is a capacity within us and can be catalyzed into action once people have a consciousness of choice, of what they can shape. But justice alone is an empty vessel unless it is filled with empathy, what Herder chose to call *einfuhling*, a characteristic which grows out of life itself, one's body as well as one's mind.

When we seek to mystify justice and say that it grows out of abstract laws, or from the mind alone, as Kant said, or from the social role which persons happen to occupy, as Max Weber hoped, or the calculative rationality of democratic utilitarians, people's propensity to justice turns into shackles for it falsely assures humankind that passion rather than "reason" are more corruptible. It is reason as the rationalizer of our passions which needs to be redirected. And for the sake of the common good the most important purpose for which reason can be directed is to find ways of stimulating the empathic and caring sense. According to the empirical studies of Carol Gilligan women hold the key to the caring sense as it includes rights and responsibilities:

> For women, the integration of rights and responsibilities takes place
> through an understanding of the psychological logic of relationships.
> This understanding tempers the self-destructive potential of a self-critical
> morality by asserting the need of all persons for care.[12]

If these sensibilities are not raised up to dominant characteristics in our civilization, surely our civilization will end like the Iks who were reduced to operating on the most primal and deformed level. That on an individual basis the fittest may survive does not necessarily mean the species will survive as a species. Or to put it another way, what is good for the individual may not be good for the species.

Raising selfishness to a principle of ethics may be forced upon people because of terrible social and geographical conditions. However, the result of extreme individualism is to further destroy the people as a group, and therefore, the individual. The classic example of selfishness and individualism is that of the uprooted Ik tribe:

> The Ik, aware that there is simply too much demand and too little
> supply, have developed a non-social system that keeps the two elements
> in balance. As long as any person, young or old, can fill his stomach, that
> person is good. When he or she can no longer do this, the goodness is
> ended and there is no ground for further consideration of or for that
> person. The children, by taking food out of the mouths of their

grandparents are merely helping them to be what all old people should be, dead. Parents letting their children die if they cannot fend for themselves once they have left home at the age of three, are merely encouraging the survival of the fittest.[13]

Unless we find a means of making active the empathic sensibility without understanding of justice the survival of the *basest* will govern social and political relationships. This is the real terror which grips modern civilization. Human beings in their institutional functions and social roles will act like beasts without knowing that that is what they are doing. Modern social organizations reflect this tragic situation. They reinforce and "insist" that people act according to principles of organization that are utterly species destructive.

Can politics get civilization out of its species destructive course? Politics as ordinarily defined hardly seems up to the task. Politics is a relationship among people which continuously seeks to redefine human association. Its method is *ad hominem* and therefore politics is often unfair. It is based on judgments that are predicated on friendship, authority, or, as the saying goes, who you know rather than what you know. Political practitioners (the politicians) are of course far more interested in the question of who says it than what is said. The correct assumption of politics is that no one person can know everything. But each person believes that he or she can judge the worth of a friend or who should be respected. Political organizers and politicians exploit this usually harmless tendency and they will say and use almost anything to get their way if they are cynical enough. Acting as brokers, they believe only in the detail which can be used for present advantage. Therefore the quality of any action or argument is less important than the immediate end to be obtained. But even cynical action may have had a good motive and purpose behind it. Political actors know that alliances shift once there is political freedom or relative equality of power among the contestants, for politics is not like the immovable struggles of trench warfare or the set piece battles of we and they.

In politics lines are not clearly drawn and consequently politicians, .when they undertake "progressive acts," play in the force field of moral ambiguity. There is an instructive story about Earl Long who was once Governor of Louisiana and who practiced the politics of moral ambiguity. He was approached by black leaders to get jobs for black nurses in seregated hospitals. Long used a time-honored method of seeking a reform by appearing reactionary and playing on vicious prejudice. He told the black leaders that he would get black nurses in the hospitals, but this could only be accomplished in a way they would find distasteful. Shortly thereafter, he took a tour of the hospital system. Not to anyone's surprise, he found white nurses taking care of black patients. Long called in the press and railed that it was shocking to him that white nurses were taking care of black male patients. He said this practice was demeaning white women and had to stop. It was stopped within a matter of days. And black nurses were hired. No wonder literary purists who spoke about politics, Sartre for example, invariably felt betrayed by politicians and political movements. As one of his communist resistance leader characters said to his idealistic – and rigid – assistant, "We all have dirty hands, up to our elbows."

Political relationships and alliances shift on the basis of particular and immediate needs and practitioners of politics ply their trade by operating according to a disjunction between moral and political judgments. It is because of the problem of situational, moral ambiguity that those committed to the survival of humankind must be forever committed to ethical precepts as integral to political action. Politics then becomes the means of examining and cross-examining actions according to ends that must also be examined. This method does not necessarily point to ends so much as they observe limits. It is through limits on our behavior (for the most) part governmental and corporate behavior), constantly reevaluated in terms of the pain and consequences that result in the short and long term (so far as one may deduce these matters), that we define the practical points of linkage between politics and ethics. Without an ethical method to transform the disjunction of politics and ethics a program for the common good will founder.

Political programs which emerge out of a pragmatic people are often changed by the fixers, who under the guise of realism assert no hard edges between positions. They sell out for immediate gain or hold off participation on any level because they have no guideposts of what to accept or reject. Because they do not comprehend the dialectical nature of change in which one recognizes that change is a cumulative process of incremental steps which result in radical change they miss the step between theory, ideals and practice. They are caught up in the rightness of their cause, cut their moorings to any guideposts and swim to a shore that does not exist. Discovering their error they join various sects that once dotted our landscape such as the Weathermen, or they become members of our professional middle class that seek a grounding in the "light and source" of another like Werner Erhard's EST or those like Jim Jones reminiscent of Cipollo in Thomas Mann's *Mario and the Magician*. Others falsify the past and flagellate themselves in public like the ex-communists thereby hoping to curry favor with the powerful and the fashionable. Each of the groups suffered from the same malady: that of uncritical belief.

Activists and citizens attracted to progress and social reconstruction must be prepared to explore ideology, not consume it, just as they are required to see social change as a process rather than discrete events that can be judged like a horserace or football game. We must state honestly that each action and policy in social reconstruction when lived in practice will bring a different problem, conflict and contradiction. But social problems can be framed to yield humane and progressive solutions, by publicly reevaluating what we know, what can be done and what should be held dear. I do not mean to say that we will escape sin and error through the political dialogue or by raising everyone from a victim to citizen. I am saying that in a modern democracy where the distribution of power is more equal the sins and errors made are our own. They are not the mistakes, sins and errors of the few who then lay them on the rest of society as if they had to be. I have already spoken to the fact of everyone's interdependence. But now that interdependence must be made explicit. This allows for a full discussion in the public space as well as revitalization of it. It allows for an interruption of choices and decisions made privately which have profound public implications. Thus, this system must eschew ideological loyalty or secret means to exclude participation. This method, like science itself, is an open and busybody one.

Where this method is followed it becomes possible to live with mistakes since the likelihood is that the choices made through public dialogue would be mad or pathological is not great. It is not likely, therefore, that a nation, if it took a referendum, would choose to make aggressive war or use nuclear weapons. It is more likely that such choices would be made in secret and then foisted on the rest of the society. This was surely the history of the use of nuclear weapons. The public's business must be conducted publicly for judgment and justice are social activities that require the participation of many.

Many people together can gauge the prudential question of forswearing immediate incremental gains for later greater success. They will be better able to judge whether a particular policy of present denial for a greater good or pleasure later on is equitably distributed, is necessary, or in fact is a mere exercise in sadism. A politics of the common good, therefore, must make obvious sense, not contradicting what people know about themselves, others, or the world. It must not overburden people and it must allow progress to become a natural activity. It is to be consistent with hard-learned, moral and political lessons of history, and it is to match living nature's own cyclical function. For human beings these include our need to love, our need to explore and foster complementary relationships of egalitarian interdependence between each other, irrespective of gender, our need to eat and employ ourselves, our need to grow or prepare food for ourselves and to make things of beauty and functional utility. In a parallel sense, the cultural discovery in the 1960s of William Morris and Prince Kropotkin cannot be dismissed as an aberration. The principles which emerged from the democratic use of technology and the search for democratic technology were meant to rediscover human limits which in turn would liberate people. There is now a ready recognition by most people not utterly entrapped in the military or mammoth corporate nexus that progress can only be attained by accepting, metaphorically speaking,

330

the cycles of the seasons and of humankind. To do otherwise is to deform civilization, make human societies – and nature itself – into that which it should not be. If we understand the principle of cyclical recurrence we can then fit progressive reconstruction to it. We should also be aware of the political implications of this method.

Once we judge an action as leading to greater equity or participation and security among the citizenry we may then understand that all changes, whether great or incremental, bring into question the entire system of inequity, hyper-individualism and deformed notions of security. Karl Popper, whose sworn enemy is Marxism, speaks for incremental change rather than what he thinks is revolutionary or totalitarian change. While he is absolutely correct in criticizing those absolutists of history who believe they speak for the future as if there can be only one future, rather than different possibilities, he is wrong in understanding the question of change in politics. Incrementalism or a more comprehensive approach to politics is not dictated by theory but the clash of people and groups in practice. Often an incremental approach might end up unravelling an entire government or system. This is of course the fear that reactionaries and conservatives have of *any* incremental reform. It is they who present reform and reconstruction with the politics of authoritarianism conditioned by the holistic, all controlling (totalitarian?) nature of the market which governments are to secure by war, if necessary. This is why British Marxists are correct when they say that each minimum reform brings into question the entire system itself if the political system is unable to respond to minimum demands. Ralph Miliband, the English writer and editor of *Socialist Register*, has said that his kind of reformism entails

> first a concern with the day to day defense of working-class interests and
> the advancement of reform of every kind and secondly, a thorough
> involvement in the politics of bourgeois democracy, with the intention
> of achieving the greatest possible degree of electoral support, and
> participation in parliamentary and other representative institutions –
> local councils, regional assemblies and the like.[14]

This is what André Gorz means by "non-reformist reforms" for they change cumulatively – and radically – the economic, social and political system.[15]

Such thoughts are compatible with the struggles that occurred in the United States by the various movement groups which emerged in the 1960s and which sought to generate, without saying so, a new humanism. That humanism began from the principle of inclusion. No one person, but no necessarily that person's institutional role, was to be left out of the society or considered as Enemy. In a way this struggle was one which John Ruskin wrote of when he talked of a society struggling to be born. In any case, those who act for others must be sure that it is the kind of society they want

331

to see born. And of course an inner voice says to me that there are no such assurances anymore than there are when children are born. You take your chances and hope through daily nurturing to have strong, creative and healthy children, just as we hope that systemic change will yield the common good, if we act out of caring and empathy with conscious intention in the public and private span. What people expect of political thought is direction and a frame of reference for themselves in society. But society, when thought of as a whole, is a construct. No set of ideas can encompass the richness or diversity of humanity. That is why I say that a political program must be eclectic with strong elements of democratic, socialist and libertarian thoughts to it, for it is in those ideas that humankind can have its space and develop shifting boundaries.

Any ideological appellation, however, only begins the discussion for abstract words do not tell us what we mean. As I have said, they cannot existentially tell us about a lived experience. Perhaps I am ending where I began. Jacob Burckhardt once said that the twentieth century would be the time of the Great Simplifier. When we see a television commentator confidently saying "That's the way it is" after a telecast as if what he reported is the *world reality*, we know that Burckhardt had a handle on how our reality would be described to us. But from simplification comes ambiguity and while the twentieth century began with simplifiers, the end shows how only ambiguity can result from those who believe in simplicity. Slogans have failed us as well as one word descriptions. When we use a word like socialism without unpacking its meaning we will buy much under that particular label which we did not intend, just as people have throughout history bought and paid dearly for ideas of justice, equality and God's will. They never knew their own feelings nor could they accept or get others to accept their problems of ambiguity. And so they drowned in the attempt to give meaning and emotional coherence to these words. Jim Jones who led his community into mass suicide and murder also believed in "God's socialism" and believed he was practicing it, and Hitler thought he was practicing national socialism. Erich Fromm thought he was a socialist as did Martin Buber.

Perhaps I expect too much: that we be the pragmatists and have universalist ideals not governed by the situation, while our ideals should not lose sight of the person. I do not want humankind to think that there are no limits to what can be done and yet I believe in progress. Who can deny that we should have a reverence for the physical universe which is out there, separate from us, with its own rules and laws known only to itself and not by mind? Yet we live in a century which rightly believes that the physical universe is quite pliable.

Where, then, can the reader say a program for the common good comes from? Political programs grow out of people's needs. Is it a sign of *hubris* to believe that this program or one similar to it is necessary because I do not see how humanity is to survive and *be* human without effecting this or a variant of it? I don't think so.

A program of the kind I have outlined is necessary because of what we sense, in the way animals sense danger, and what we sense as human beings attempting to find answers to gnostic questions of who we are in this world. It is not only what is "objectively" necessary but what we make necessary.

I can see the grim smile on the face of the more technocratically oriented reader who says, "It is not enough to want, but to show things rigorously." But in a time of rigor we try everything and understand almost nothing. What we try is done with just enough manipulative knowledge which gives the belief to ourselves and anyone we care to influence that we understand in technical terms what is going on. Yet what we know is limited by operational methods that assert a difference between measurement and substance. An organic understanding of the world, which crosses the boundaries of what is inside and what is outside (*res cogitans res extensa* and *in corpore*) will only occur where there is enough cumulative fear and felt need which forces this feeling on everyone. Certain music in the first half of this century expressed this fear. The masters Berg and Schoenberg highlighted humankind's suffering and tenuous hold on earth. Their music warned us by reaching inside of us. It still mocks us and reminds us of our personal terror. Is it too much to say that our Cartesian methods or our belief in Baconian objectivity defeated us? It is not mathematics and calculative "rigor" which explain either our dilemma, moral choice or the content of things to us. Instead it is music which captures our weakness. We are frightened and convulsed by *Wozzeck* because it mirrors our own uncontained panic. Part of the panic we experience is the distancing method in our "awake" state which is filled by our consuming marketplace and the type of public policy and technology which seeks to make a virtue out of breaking our lives into little pieces that are then offered for sale. The convulsions which attack us now are brought on by our realization that there is something profoundly wrong with our methods of rational discourse. Our feeling-emotive sense registers "danger" for humanity just as the music of Berg and Schoenberg sought to warn us.

Our technologies are entrapped in the methods which cut human feeling from what supposedly we see in the experiment, or how we describe the universe. And we are justly skeptical of our senses, deformed as they are through roles and functions which are meant to limit what we see and understand. No wonder we perpetuate the same catastrophic grooves. No wonder we seek to mold within ourselves a biological need which requires us to find an organic and hopeful explanation of the world; that it is a positive spirit. No wonder we seek to construct metaphors, myths and organic forms which we favor over others, believing that these myths are as important to defining reality as seeing what is already "out there."

We are past the stage of believing that scientists understand the

333

fundamental propositions of the universe more than theologians just because they invent certain operations from which they can predict similar results from those operations. Scientific work does not tell us cause, why it works. As the platitude goes, "You get out what you put in" and this view is certainly true of scientific experiment. We can only know what we seek to know and we are bound by our language of description which is socially determined, and only partially by the phenomena we see. After we know everything and the rules for it, to paraphrase Wittgenstein, life still remains a puzzle.

What I have implied in the political program is that we would do better to fix our interest on raising and resolving political ethical questions much the way Socrates and the Athenian sophists sought to do for the ruling class of Athens. But in a modern democracy everyone must do it for each other. Why must this be so? The current problem caused by technology and class, race and sex gender and institutional fascism have decentered and thrown all of humankind just as the impulse to liberation rejects the reaction of authoritarianism. These are reasons enough for us to formulate a lived political practice and ethic that begins from circumscribing the limits of what is to be known and which publicly debates research direction and its practical development with "Everyone."

One wonders whether it is almost too late for such discussion since scientific results have begun to present us with a peculiar sort of dream world which has the most dire real consequences. Take the dream of nuclear reactors as a clean and cheap energy source. We know that this is false through experience. And while there is a small chance that something of enormous proportions might go wrong with any particular reactor, the statistical possibility is real and frightening, especially if we keep adding more of them. The result is that all sorts of safety, security and insurance procedures must be in place and operating in case something goes wrong. This prudential way of operating is understandable. The liberal and prudent response to possible disaster is increasing safety and precautionary staff. Their task is actively waiting and preparing for disaster. They are like characters in a Beckett play living their lives as "waiters." The new procedures adopted are costly. They become part of our everyday life, robbing us of our most precious possessions, time and space. They put people even more than they already are into an "as if" and artificial world where millions of lives are spent waiting and preparing for disaster. Society becomes like an army in peacetime which operates and prepares, living an as if reality in the meantime. But what happens when an increasing amount of all of our time, energy and life is governed by this *as if* reality? Once people waited for the Messiah. Now they prepare and wait for the Eschaton.

Our political and philsophic task is to break this artificial fantasy world by making judgments and helping others make judgments on what we do not want because of the intrinsically horrifying nature of what others have created and we are complicit with if we do not join in confronting it. Our confrontation can be most successful and humane where we recognize the yin-yang and complementarity of life and nature and where we will devise a scientific method linked to ethics. Those who seek to limit the phenomena under analysis or our relations to it, or who do not seek to refashion humankind's relationship to the earth and other living beings (*adam* and *adama*) prevent our understanding of what should and can be done. Under the guise of logic they miss what should be considered and what is really happening. Sometimes, as I have said, the changes for civilization are simple ones but they are very powerful in terms of their effects on humankind, as when man and woman began facing each other in the act of love, or when man started urinating on a fire to put it out. A similar point can be made about deciding how to categorize certain actions. Categorization becomes an important instrument for ethical progress. Take the following example.

The program for the common good states that nuclear war plans should be filed under genocide and criminal law rather than diplomacy and game theory in our libraries. Then we would be able to give a resounding "no" to the millions involved in this criminal activity. I wonder whether librarians could rise up and make this moral judgment about categorizing.

How we categorize can help us organize energies for the common good, thereby within a time certain we can be alerted to dangers as we reduce human suffering. This is also the minimum we can expect out of a progressive program. We must also expect the practice of liberation and at least a social downpayment on everyone's individual happiness.

As I have said, too many of those who believe in progress detach themselves from the past by denying its importance and by attaching themselves to a future aim. But these aims, which are often spelled out as plausible through quantitative description (so many houses this year, so many cars the next year), may not pan out as we hope, even if the production goals are achieved and with hindsight judged to be valuable. One reason is that each step of the way there will be a great struggle to bring the purpose of equity into lived reality and no matter if we think otherwise – or wish otherwise – the fears and interests of many hold to the comforts of class. People are not prepared to surrender their present comforts or those knowledges which helped them achieve such comforts either for the protection of humanity, the building of a world civilization – let alone egalitarian interdependence.

As Andrew Levine has pointed out,

Nowadays, hardly anyone, including even the ideological descendants of Burke and de Tocqueville, would deny the enormous historical advance, registered by the French revolution, despite its excesses and the extravagantly naive claims of many of its militants and ardent defenders. The French revolutionaries did not usher in an era of human perfectability; but they did advance human history.[16]

The fact that a movement for the common good may fail is no reason not to try. If we are successful, it means that reconstructive change and democracy can come into being without bloody civil war, and changes in what we think about and how we act can be made in new social spaces we create by our actions and through institutions rather than against them. We will all stand as guides to assure the future of humankind. In any case, the execution and implementation of this program will not be without struggle and pain. It will be like the pain which accompanies birth. For American society it will be "pain" which is necessary and blessed.

Notes

Introduction

1 Wilhelm Reich, *The Mass Psychology of Fascism*, New York, Farrar, Straus & Giroux, 1970.
2 Daphne Greenwood, "An Estimation of U.S. Family Wealth and Its Distribution from Microdata, 1973," *Review of Income and Wealth*, Colorado Springs, University of Colorado, 1983, pp. 23-43.
3 "Money, Income, and Poverty Status of Families and Persons in the U.S., 1983," *Current Populations Reports Series*, Bureau of the Census, US Dept of Commerce, No. 146, Tables 15 and 17, August 1984.
4 "Falling Behind: A report on how Blacks have fared under the Reagan Policies," Washington, D.C., Center on Budget and Policy Priorities, October 1984, p. 3.
5 Roger Alcaly and David Mermelstein (eds), *Fiscal Crisis in American Cities*, New York, Vintage Books, see esp. "Planning New York," Robert Fitch, pp. 246-85.
6 Mark Green and Norman Weitzman, *Business War On the Law: An Analysis of the Benefits of Federal Health Safety Enforcement*, Corporate Accountability Research Group, 1969, pp. 96-122.
7 See chapter by Edward S. Herman, "The Institutionalization of Bias in Economics," in *Shifting the Gaze* by Marcus G. Raskin and Herbert Bernstein, New Jersey, Rowman & Littlefield, 1987. Cf. Sam Peltzman, "An Evaluation of Consumer Protection Legislation: The 1962 Drug Amendment," *Journal of Political Economy*, September/October 1973, and "The Effects of Automobile Safety Regulations," *Journal of Political Economy*, August 1975.
8 Membership in trade unions has stayed roughly the same, fluctuating between 13.2 and 14.2 million since 1975. However, the work force has increased from 87,524,000 to 108,665,000 in the same period. Information from *Employment and Earnings*, monthly periodical of the Bureau of Labor Statistics. Also the American Federation of Labor-Congress of Industrial Organizations (1985).
9 James O'Connor, *The Fiscal Crisis of the State*, New York, St Martin's Press, 1973.
10 Lewis Mumford, *The City In History: Its Origins, Its Transformations and Its Prospects*, New York, Harcourt, Brace & World, 1961, p. 367.
11 Marcus G. Raskin, *Being and Doing*, New York, Random House, 1971. See especially "The Dream Colony" chapter.
12 5 February 1985, posture statement by Caspar Weinberger to the House Armed Services Committee. For arguments for and against ballistic missile defense systems, see *Issues in Science and Technology*, Fall 1984. Sidney D. Drell and Wolfgang Panofsky, "The Case Against Strategic Defense," James C. Fletcher, "The Technologies For Ballistic Missile Defense," George A. Keyworth II, "The Case for Strategic Defense," pp. 13-65.

13 Richard J. Barnet, *The Lean Years*, New York, Simon & Schuster, 1980.

14 Holly Sklar (ed.), *The Trilateral Commission and Elite Planning for World Management*, Boston, South End Press, 1980.

15 William Cannon, *The Budget: The Cockpit of the New Society*, Washington, D.C., Institute for Policy Studies, 1986. Vicente Navarro, "The 1980 and 1984 U.S. Elections and the New Deal: An Alternative Explanation," Baltimore, Johns Hopkins University, February 1985, unpublished.

16 James Livingston, "Politics, Ideology and the Origins of American Revolutions," *Socialist Revolution*, 36:7-36.

17 Robert N. Bellah, *Beyond Belief*, New York, Harper & Row, 1970 and *The Broken Covenant*, New York, Seabury Press, 1975.

18 Wygandt vs. Jackson, Board of Education. Doc. 841340-US Supreme Court. On appeal from sixth circuit 10/25/84.

19 Basil Davidson, "Angola: A Success That Changes History," *Race and Class*, Summer 1976, Vol. 18, no. 1, pp. 23-37, especially pp. 73-4.

20 Institute for Policy Studies Budget Study, 2 February 1983, Marcus G. Raskin (ed.).

21 Johan Huizinga, *Homo Ludens: A Study of the Play Element in Culture*, New York, J. & J. Harper Editions, 1970.

22 Antonio Gramsci, *Selections from Political Writing*, Vol. 1 1910-1920, Vol. 2, 1921-26, Quinton Hare (ed.), International Publishers, England, 1978. Central to Antonio Gramsci's ideas was the generation of workers' councils which would create management skills for all workers and instill a self-motivating discipline including services to the people at large. Note the editorials from Ordine Nuovo (1919-20) when Gramsci served as editor.

23 Carol Gilligan, *In a Different Voice*, Cambridge, Mass. Harvard University Press, 1982.

24 Ivan Illich, *Toward a History of Needs*, New York, Pantheon Books, 1978.

25 Cf. Garry S. Becker, *A Treatise On the Family*, Cambridge, Mass., Harvard University Press, 1981 and *The Economic Approach to Human Behavior*, Chicago, University of Chicago Press, 1978, Chapter 1.

26 For a thorough account of such projects now under way in the United States I would urge the reader to study *Economic Democracy*, by Martin Carnoy and Derek Shearer, edited by M.E. Sharpe, Armonk, N.Y., 1980.

27 Leo Huberman, *We The People*, New York, Harper, 1932. Howard Zinn, *A People's History of the United States*, New York, Harper & Row, 1980.

28 Leszek Kolakowski, *Main Currents of Marxism*, Oxford, Oxford University Press, 3 Vols, 1978.

29 Hannah Arendt, *Crises of the Republic*, New York, Harcourt Brace Jovanovich, 1972.

30 George F. Kennan, *Democracy and the Student Left*, Boston, Little, Brown, 1968.

31 Gary Hart, *A New Democracy*, New York, Quill, 1983.

32 *The Federalist*, from the original text of Alexander Hamilton, John Jay and James Madison, introduction by Edward Mead Earle, New York, Modern Library, 1941.

33 Navarro, *op. cit.*

34 Martin Buber, *Paths In Utopia*, Boston, Beacon Press, 1985.

35 Marcus G. Raskin, "Futurama", *Partisan Review*, Vol. 44, 1977, pp. 387-414.

36 Werner Jaeger, *Paideia: The Ideals of Greek Culture*, New York, Oxford University Press, Vol. 1, 1945, pp. 327-31. The dialectic between severe laws and belief in natural passions served as the basis for a societal transformation. The sophists had eliminated the old concept of *aidos*, secret shame, for the balance between "public severity and private toleration." In our time the concept of

personal secret shame, as against the "superego" or laws, can only be integrated in people's lives through the awareness of what is shared with others and how each is dependent on others. Shame is then transformed into responsibility for self and others. Thus, as Kant would have it, there is no conflict between morality and politics.

37 Wilhelm Reich, *Sex-pol.*, New York, Vintage Books, 1972 and *The Mass Psychology of Fascism*, op. cit.

1 The common good

1 Simone Weil, *The Simone Weil Reader*, New York, McKay, 1977. Paul Goodman, *Drawing the Line*, New York, Free Life Editions, 1977. Marvin E. Gettleman and David Mermelstein, *The Great Society Reader*, New York, Random House, 1967.
2 Martin Buber, *Between Man and Man*, New York, Macmillan, 1965. Goodman, *op. cit.*
3 *The Federalist*, from the original text of Alexander Hamilton, John Jay and James Madison, introduction by Edward Mead Earle, New York, Modern Library, 1941.
4 Thus, for example, imagine a nun in the Catholic church who brings an action against the church because she is discriminated against since she cannot become a bishop. Can she bring a successful action in civil court against such discrimination under civil law? Would the church in self-protection allow nuns to become bishops if enough nuns brought actions? Can civil politics change ecclesiastical behavior?
5 John D. Bernal, *Science In History*, Harmondsworth, Penguin, 4 Vols, 1969.
6 Often this will affect how we treat our parents. During the war in Vietnam the son of the Secretary of Defense Robert McNamara asked if he could come and work with me. Since I was an antagonist of his father on the war, the son's actions could have been taken as a personal rebuke of his father. I asked the young man to talk it over with him. And the young man never returned. One may respect the old, indeed, has to respect them. But it is not necessary for the young to *listen* to the old. It is enough to have access to the culture of the old. By having access to it and learning of its implications they are able to honestly reject it.
7 As I will suggest in Chapter 3 this principle operates in practical terms when we sustain and establish an old age pension system which also recognizes the non-material needs of old people. We might imagine a computerized registry fund which is run through a decentralized social security system that serves as a broker to bring old and young people together even with pets. Bringing them together in this way recognizes the relatively rootless nature of our society, where old people have sacrificed their geographical, social and employment roots.
8 Erich Kahler, *Man The Measure, A New Approach to History*, New York, Pantheon, 1943, p. 464 ff.
9 Richard P. McKeon, *Freedom and History: The Semantics of Philosophical Controversies and Ideological Conflicts*, New York, Noonday, 1952.
10 There are four different definitions of freedom, sometimes parallel, sometimes intersecting or contradictory: (a) The right to be wrong; (b) the right only to be right; (c) the right to think anything; (d) the right (and power) to act.
11 Such a guarantee does not require that the government guarantee an audience to the artist. However, the guarantee of artistic freedom does include the right to get an audience. In the modern society this means subsidized and guaranteed access to TV, film, newspapers and journals.

12 Walt W. Rostow, *The Stages of Economic Growth*, Cambridge, England, Cambridge University Press, 1971. Charles Bettelheim, *Class Struggles in the USSR*, New York, Monthly Review Press, 1976.

13 Norbert Wiener, *I am a Mathematician*, Garden City, N.Y., Doubleday, 1956, pp. 327-8.

14 Pope John Paul II, "On Human Work" (Encyclical Laborem Exercens), Third Encyclical Letter, Washington, D.C., United States Catholic Conference, 1981, p. 43.

15 Friedrich August von Hayek, *The Constitution of Liberty*, Chicago, Regnery, 1972.

16 Michael Albert, *What is to Be Undone?*, Boston, P. Sargent, 1974.

17 Hannah Arendt, *The Origins of Totalitarianism*, New York, Harcourt Brace Jovanovich, 1973. Franz L. Neumann, *Behemoth: The Structure and Practice of National Socialism*, New York, Oxford University Press, 1942.

18 Hannah Arendt, *Thinking*, New York, Harcourt Brace Jovanovich, 1978.

19 Bernard J.F. Lonergan, *Insight, A Study of Human Understanding*, Philosophical Library, 1971, pp. 173-209.

> For common sense not merely says what it means, it says it to someone; it begins by exploring the other fellow's intelligence; it advances by determining what further insights have to be communicated to him; it undertakes the communication not as an exercise in formal logic, but as a work of art; and it has at its disposal not merely all the resources of language but the support of modulate tone and changing volume, the eloquence of facial expressions, the emphasis of gestures, the effectiveness of pauses, the suggestiveness of questions, the significance of omissions. (p.177)

20 *Ibid.*

21 Plato, *The Laws of Plato*, New York, Arno Press, 1976. Karl R. Popper, *The Open Society and Its Enemies*, Princeton, N.J. Princeton University Press, 1963.

22 Booker T. Washington, *The Booker T. Washington Papers*, Louis R. Harlan (ed.), Urbana, University of Illinois Press, 1972.

23 William Ernest Hocking, *Types of Philosophy*, New York, Scribner, 1959.

24 Decency is there, all around us. But it must be heard from those who are not usually listened to. In talking with my children and their friends I would tell them stories that were famous legal cases and ask them to think of how they would decide the case. I would ask them to give their reasons as well. Once I told several friends of my children the story of the *Cow* case, a case which has bedeviled generations of law students trying to learn the relationship of contracts to markets. A farmer bought a cow from a neighboring farmer. Within a few months the cow happened to give birth to a calf. The farmer who sold the cow demanded the calf saying he did not sell the other farmer the calf. The farmer who bought the cow said that he bought the entire cow, including eventualities. And nothing was stipulated otherwise. Children, when they are told this story, usually give the various answers and arguments advanced by lawyers. But one Black child, apparently not yet defined by the market system, gave me the most extraordinary answer which I had heard. He said, "Well, the farmer who best takes care of the calf, who is nicest to the calf, should get it." The other children quickly agreed. Such a sensibility must be the one that the common good could begin to reflect where we concerned ourselves more precisely with the concrete elements of our situation, how and what we cared for and how to live with nature.

25 Richard H. Tawney, *History and Society*, London and Boston, Routledge & Kegan Paul, 1978.

26 John Rawls, *A Theory of Justice*, Cambridge, Mass. Belknap Press of Harvard University Press, 1971.
27 In this sense Rawls's position could be construed as a recipe for continuous revolution since unequal income, race discrimination, and unequal power are social arrangements which add to inequality. The brutal fact is that institutions creating these conditions do and will continue to exist for the foreseeable future. The question is whether exemplary politics can change these conditions, whether through different modes of organizing which recognize the importance of reaching to the core of a person's existence, a core which includes trust and empathy, institutions which are equitable and non-authoritarian can be established.
28 In state socialist nations such as the Soviet Union this characteristic is even worse. The Soviet thinker, Nalimov, has pointed out that the educational system is so specialized and the research institutes and libraries so restricted that books are not available to scholars outside of their immediate field of study.
29 Max Horkheimer, *Eclipse of Reason*, New York, Oxford University Press, 1947.
30 *Ibid.*, p. 143.
31 Konnilyn G. Feig, *Hitler's Death Camps: The Sanity of Madness*, New York, Holmes & Meier Publishers, 1981.
32 Stephen Jay Gould, *Ever Since Darwin: Reflections in Natural History*, 1st edn, New York, Norton, 1977.
33 Friedrich Engels, *The Origin of the Family, Private Property and the State, in the Light of the Researches of Lewis H. Morgan*, Moscow, Progress, 1968.
34 *Ibid.*
35 C.L.R. James, *A History of Pan-African Revolt*, Washington, D.C., 2nd revised edn, Drum & Spear Press, 1969, pp.13-14.

2 Becoming leaders and organizers

1 In a society where there is conflict, public concern and openness, more authentic forms of leadership manifest themselves. In the last generation we have witnessed the emergence of citizen leaders round a particular issue. They struggle around that issue and then return to their own work. Such people are less "political" leaders than they are good citizens who speak and act on what they know and feel. They act either out of a surplus of pain or a surplus of consciousness. This is the kind of spontaneous, and then sustained, action which gave impetus to women leaders such as Gloria Steinem or anti-war activists such as pediatrician Benjamin Spock. Their struggle changed and deepened the meaning of citizenship in America giving us a clue about the type of leadership we should encourage.
2 Hannah Arendt, *On Revolution*, New York, Viking Press, 1963. Garry Wills, *Inventing America*, New York, Vintage Books, 1979.
3 Holy Bible, Henry James Version, New York, New American Library, 1974. Genesis 30:24 ff., esp. pp. 39-50.
4 Cf. *The Age of Charisma, Arthur Schweitzer*, Chicago, Nelson Hall Publishers, 1984.
5 Noam Chomsky, *Problems of Knowledge and Freedom*, New York, Pantheon Books, 1971.
6 René Dumont, *Socialism and Development*, New York, Praeger, 1973.
7 Even in the program of social reconstruction we must be aware that the line between the public and private space in the productive and consumptionist sense

must be drawn. The individual exists prior to the social group, but his or her existence still is premised on the group's existence. Using the toilet at home is a private activity but we use the community's water, public sewage system, and toilet paper made by others.

8 Charles Bettelheim, *Class Struggles in the USSR*, New York, Monthly Review Press, 1976.

9 Ivan Illich, *Toward a History of Needs*, New York, Pantheon Books, 1978, p. 55.

10 "Italian and French Communist Parties, Declarations," *Socialist Revolution*, 27:69-74. "Italian Communism and the American Left," *Socialist Revolution*, 31:7-23. Santiago Carrillo with Regis Debray and Max Gallo, "Spain, Today and Tomorrow," *Socialist Revolution*, 34:37-63.

11 William Z. Foster and Earl Browder, *Technocracy and Marxism*, together with *The Technical Intelligentsia and Socialist Construction*, by V.M. Molotov, New York, Workers Library Publishers, 1933.

12 Arendt, *On Revolution, op. cit.* Carmen Claudin-Urondo, *Lenin and the Cultural Revolution*, Hassocks, England, Harvester Press, Atlantic Highlands, N.J., Humanities Press, 1977.

13 There are some people who despair at non-violence. Their point of view is dangerous and foolish on moral and strategic grounds. Changes which come through violence threaten and frighten most people. Armed struggle changes the very character of the movement into a hotbed of police agents, sadists and irrational activists – the latter reaching for easy, short-term solutions and using the shield of politics to settle old scores or conflicting ambitions. Vengeance is not politics. For some violence is an exciting means that soon becomes its own end. It invariably prepares the way for dragnet operations and the state's violence against the people. In other words, violence becomes its own sanction (in both meanings of that word).

14 Rudolf Bahro, "A New Approach for the Peace Movement In Germany," *Exterminism and Cold War*, London, NLB, New Left Review (ed.), 1982, pp. 87-8.

15 Melvyn A. Hill (ed.), *Hannah Arendt, The Recovery of the Public World*, New York, St Martin's Press, 1979, p. 227. Especially see the essay "Thinking Without a Ground: Hannah Arendt and the Contemporary Situation of Understanding" by J.G. Gray.

16 Robert Bellah, *The Broken Covenant*, New York, Seabury Press, 1975.

17 Robert L. Patterson, *Philosophy of William Ellery Channing*, New York, Bookman Associates, 1952. William Ellery Channing, *Works of William Ellery Channing* and *The Life of William Ellery Channing*.

18 Paul Tillich, *The Socialist Decision*, Washington, D.C., University Press of America, 1977.

19 Hannah Arendt, *Eichmann in Jerusalem*, New York, Penguin Books, 1976

20 Milton Mayeroff, *On caring*, New York, Harper & Row, 1971, p.1.

21 Aristotle, *The Politics of Aristotle*, books i-v, New York, Arno Press, 1976.

22 While it is usually taken for granted in the laws of property that a person or corporation may destroy his or her own property *almost* with impunity, or use it according to his or her own purposes, there are clear exceptions. The state may regulate through zoning or otherwise the use of the property. Squatters may even gain adverse possession of it. An argument may be extended further which surely has Lockean roots rather than the capitalist's *bête noire*, Marx. Since corporations are granted licenses and charters on the ground that they are serving the common "weal" or "good" can others take over property which is not being run·productively, or is allowed to decay or is constructively abandoned if legal procedures may inhibit or consecrate such action?

23 Fritjof Capra, *The Turning Point*, Simon & Schuster, 1982. Percy W. Bridgman, *The Way Things Are*, New York, Viking Press, 1959, p. 135. Stillman Drake, *Galileo*, Oxford, Oxford University Press, 1980. René Descartes, *Discourse on Method*, New York, Modern Library, 1958. Leo Steinberg, *Other Criteria*, London, New York, Oxford University Press, 1975.

24 John Berger, *Art and Revolution: Neizvestny and the Role of the Artist in the U.S.S.R.*, Harmondsworth, Penguin, 1969.

25 Marcus G. Raskin, *New York Times*, 28 December 1975, op. ed. Copyright © 1975 by the New York Times Company. Reprinted by permission.

26 For moral philosophers science and technological invention are beside the point in the face of questions like, "Does he cheat?" Once I asked Herbert Marcuse if he let students cheat on tests and Marcuse said, "No. If they would cheat on tests they would cheat on the central committee after a revolution." I was surprised by his answer since I believed that central committees and punishment for natural activities are linked whereas cheating is the essence of a positive social activity which asserts how each person can help another.

27 Franz L. Neumann, *Behemoth: The Structure and Practice of National Socialism*, New York, Oxford University Press, 1942.

28 It is likely that the Dutch, French and British would have held on to their Asian empires had it not been for the Second World War. The US would not have rebuilt Japan because it would have been an economic competitor and pressures from the other imperial powers would have kept Japan as one of several contenders.

29 Connecticut General Life Insurance Co. vs. Johnson, Supreme Court, No. 316 (1937), pp. 3-4, but note Justice Black's dissent.

30 Pope John Paul II, "On Human Work" (Encyclical Laborem Exercens), Third Encyclical Letter, Washington, D.C., United States Catholic Conference, 1981.

31 Reinhold Niebuhr, *Young Reinhold Niebuhr, His Early Writings*, New York, Pilgrim Press, 1982.

32 Martin Buber, *Moses: The Revelation and the Covenant*, New York, Harper, 1958.

33 Harold D. Lasswell, *Propaganda and Promotional Activities*, Chicago, University of Chicago Press, 1969 and "Propaganda" in *International Encyclopedia of the Social Sciences*, New York, Free Press Publishers, 1933.

34 Jacques Derrida, "The Principle of Reason", Vol. 10, No. 1, *Graduate Faculty Philosophy Journal*, New School for Social Research, 1984, pp. 5-27. Marcus G. Raskin and Herbert Bernstein, "Towards a New Political Science" in *Shifting the Gaze*, New Jersey, Rowman & Littlefield, 1987.

35 Henry Tundor, *Political Myth*, London, Pall Mall Press, 1972. Ernest Cassirer, *The Myth of the State*, New Haven, Yale University Press, 1963. Roland Barthes, *Mythologies*, Hill and Wang, New York, 1984, see especially "Myth Today," pp. 109-59. In his impressive essay Barthes says that only the revolutionary can dispense with myth. "The bourgeoisie hides the fact that it is the bourgeoisie and thereby produces myth" (p. 146). The left needs myth because it is reconstructive. Myths can be artistic and practical statements of the world to be made and to be!

36 Joseph Weizenbaum, *Computer Power and Human Reason*, Harmondsworth, Middlesex, England, New York, N.Y., Penguin, 1984, p. 15.

37 Rudolph Sibert, *Encyclopedia Moderna*, Institute for the Philosophy of Sciences and Peace of the Yugoslav Academy of Sciences and Arts and Yugoslav Pugwash Congerence, Zagreb, Yugoslavia, 1976. p. 104.

38 Ruth L. Sivard, *Women . . . A World Survey*, Washington, D.C., World Priorities, 1985, pp. 15-16.

39 Marvin E. Gettleman and David Mermelstein, *The Great Society Reader*, New York, Random House, 1967. Edward C. Banfield, *The University City Revisited*, Boston, Little, Brown, 1974. Amitai Etzioni, *The Neo-Conservatives*, Partisan Review, 1977, Vol. XLIV, pp. 431-7.

40 Leo Strauss, *What is Political Philosophy?*, Westport, Conn., Greenwood Press, 1973 and *Liberalism, Ancient and Modern*, New York, Basic Books, 1968. For a seering review of "Studies in Platonic Political Philosophy" by Leo Strauss read M.F. Burnyeat, "Sphinx Without a Secret," *The New York Review of Books*, 30 May 1985.

41 Saul Landau and Frank Diamond, *Quest For Power*, Film made for VARA Television, The Netherlands, 1982. Available through New Times Films, New York.

42 Stephen Jay Gould, *Ever Since Darwin: Reflections in Natural History*, 1st edn, New York, Norton, 1977.

43 L.B. Taylor, *The New Right*, New York, Watts, 1981.

44 Ivan Illich, *Medical Nemesis*, New York, Pantheon Books, 1976. Cf. "The Industrialization of Fetishism or the Fetishism of Industrialization: A Critique of Ivan Illich," by Vicente Navarro, *International Journal of Health Services*, Vol. 5, No. 3, 1975, pp. 351-71.

3 Social caring

1 All left parties saw an increased role for the state, either the old state as in the case of Bernstein or a post-revolutionary state with new machinery as in the case of Lenin (at least until the state withered away). Eduard Bernstein, *Evolutionary Socialism*, New York, Shochen Books, 1961. Vladimir I. Lenin, *State and Revolution*, Westport, Conn., Greenwood Press, 1978. Morton G. White, *Social Thought in America*, London, New York, Oxford University Press, 1976. Sigmund Neumann (ed.), *Modern Political Parties*, Chicago, University of Chicago Press, 1956.

2 *Nathan G. Glazer and Irving Kristol, The American Commonwealth, 1976*, New York, Basic Books, 1976.

3 William E. Channing, *Works of William Ellery Channing*, Vol. 1, p. 698. Noted in Robert L. Patterson, *Philosophy of William Ellery Channing*, New York Bookman Associates, 1952, p. 118.

4 "Infrastructure: A National Challenge," Hearing before the Subcommittee on Economic Goals and Intergovernmental Policy of the Joint Economic Committee, 29 February 1984, Washington,.D.C., US G.P.O. 1984, p. 1. *Hard Choices: A Report on the Increasing Gap between America's Infrastructure Needs and our Ability to Pay for Them*, A study prepared for the use of the Subcommittee on Economic Goals and Intergovernmental Policy of the Joint Economic Committee, Congress of the United States, Washington, D.C., G.P.O., 1984.

5 With Susan Walter, Durham, N.C., Duke Press Paperbacks, 1983, c.1981.

6 *New York Times*, 11 September 1981, p.17.

7 Martin Heidegger, *Being and Time*, Oxford, Blackwell, 1967.

8 Channing, *op. cit.*, p. 767. Channing understands this question as a matter of class consciousness.

9 John Myles, "The Trillion Dollar Misunderstanding," *Working Papers*, July/August 1981, p. 30.

10 Statistical Abstract, 1983, p. 382, Table No. 627.

11 The social democratic principle of equity and decency engaged the attention of

civil servants, trade unionists and liberals. It fitted well with a Weberian notion of bureaucracy which was to be staffed with disinterested experts whose purpose was to supply services to passive consumers.

As passive consumers they were to be treated as members of interest groups whose only concern was to broaden and increase the size of benefits. In the United States, at least since the beginning of the twentieth century, Edward Alsworth Ross's book *Social Control*, (Cleveland, Ohio Press of Case Western Reserve University, 1969) made clear that it was "better" for all concerned to accept the quasi-Platonic model in which bureaucrats and elite would mediate the differences and achieve incremental social welfare gains as defined in terms of services granted and expenditures made. The character of economic hardship among many groups left sincere government officials and social democrats to argue that supplying economic benefits and "services" was more important than enabling people to "enter history" and be active participants in shaping their society. The political effect of this point of view is to reproduce a class of people who believe that their knowledge and technical expertise, often profoundly conservative when applied, can keep the wheels of progress inching forward. It is true, of course, that revamping the social welfare conception of society will not in and of itself guard against the emergence of an arrogant technocratic elite. But as the reader will see, assuring direct participation of the people in the deliberation, investment and oversight of social welfare programs could have a marked and positive effect on a technocratic elite setting itself off from the citizenry.

12 Channing, *op. cit.*, Vol. 1, p. 182.
13 Gilbert Steiner, "The State of Welfare," Washington, D.C., Brookings Institution, 1971, p. 6.
14 Working Paper of the National Commission on Social Security, February 1981, Milton Gwirtzman, Chairman.
15 Working paper prepared for the Progressive Alliance by William Cannon, 1979.
16 In a society where income and wealth disparity is present and where social security payment is not a necessity to high income persons, such beneficiaries would not lose their benefits. Instead, their minimum social security incomes would be converted into a credit. This credit would be activated where the person joined with several others to begin projects of a public nature which benefited others and fell within the exemption provisions of the tax laws. This program would encourage high and middle income families to use their minimum income credits as part of a financing system for economic and social projects in local communities.
17 Friedrich August von Hayek, *The Constitution of Liberty*, Chicago, Regnery, 1972, p. 299.
18 L.K.Y. Ng and J.J. Banica, "Pain, Discomfort, and Humanitarian Care: Proceedings of NIH Conference," Holland, New York, Elsevier, 1980.
19 Erich Fromm, *The Anatomy of Human Destructiveness*, New York, Holt, Rinehart & Winston, 1973, 134n. The character of daily work existence has changed "man."
20 Note especially John Hamowy, "Early Development of Medical Licensing", *Journal of Libertarian Studies*, Vol. 3, no. 1.
21 In pointing out the effects of patient dependency it should be stressed that it is not the responsibility of the physician to interrupt this epidemic of self-absorption. For when the doctor does so without being part of an ethos of caring we will find that medical professionals will be pressured to surrender life protection as their primary concern and substitute another standard, that of manufactured and inauthentic forms of scarcity and zealotry. Where a society has already committed itself to a form of "patientism" it is not the medical person

who should be given the responsibility of interrupting this process and deciding who lives or dies. Such decisions remain cultural and political ones which may as easily be decided by juries of one's peers or by the person and the family.

22 This view directly contradicts the Reagan administration dogma that health care is a commodity which should be governed by the market and that there are "too many" health workers.

23 Louise Lander, "National Health Insurance" in *The Federal Budget and Social Reconstruction*, Institute for Policy Studies, Marcus g. Raskin (ed.), New Brunswick, N.J., Transaction Books, 1978, pp. 287-314.

24 National Health Service Act, HR 2049, introduced in the 99th Congress by Rep. Ron Dellums, D-CA.

25 Victor W. Sidel and Ruth Sidel, *A Healthy State*, New York, Pantheon Books, 1977, p. 267.

26 Alain Enthoven and Roger Noll, *Issues*, Fall 1984, Vol. 1, No. 1. "Prospective Payment Revolution: Will It Solve Medicare's Financial Problems?"

27 Marcus G. Raskin, *Being and Doing*, New York, Random House, 1971.

28 Such an education would not be enough. Schools in various parts of the nation could grow and prepare their own food from publicly controlled farms or in co-ownership with farmers. Such food would be used for school lunches for themselves and others. There are schools in North Dakota where such educational projects have been initiated. But these projects should be accompanied by an esthetic purpose.

29 Roger Garaudy, *The Alternative Future*, New York, Simon & Schuster, 1974, pp. 98-9, discussion of esthetics.

30 Michael W. Apple, *Education and Power*, Boston, Routledge & Kegan Paul, 1982.

31 Raskin, *Being and Doing, op. cit.*

32 Information from the National Center for Education Statistics Bulletin, US Department of Education, Office of the Assistant Secretary of Educational Research and Improvement, May 1985.

33 I also suggested the establishment of a tool and book allowance for each child. These allowances would be used to build up a school age child's individual book library or tool "shops". Not only would such a program serve as a way of broadening the skills based on cultural level of the society, it would change the relationship which government had with the people.

34 The naming of various things, phenomena in nature according to Latin names, should be switched to common names so that the jargon of a particular discipline will no longer remain inaccessible. Even the Catholic Church has decided that its services should be conducted in Vulgate.

35 Milton Friedman, *Capitalism and Freedom*, Chicago, University of Chicago Press, 1962.

36 A word should be said about the assumptions of the Educational Testing Service. A system of standardized aptitude tests is used to help determine entry into various schools and universities. Often such tests are determinative. They encourage a young person to internalize his or her score as being what that person's actual worth in a particular subject is, or that person's aptitude for a particular course of study and finally, that person's intellectual worth.

But this entire system is predicated on a number of outrageous notions. The usual pattern in our schools is something like the following: the student takes an examination. He receives the examination which he usually keeps either when he takes the examination or when he receives the grade. Once having taken the examination with his answers the teacher, or machine grades the student's paper. The student has access to three parts: the grade, the examination and his own answers which he is able to check against the grade and exam. In the ETS system the examinee takes the test, but he loses control over his answers. He is awarded a number which he is to take on faith. He is to believe that this number is the proper score and representative of how he did on the test. But there is no possibility of checking. This is a most extraordinary mystification. It would seem that the person taking the test would have access to (a) methods of scoring; (b) the exam; and (c) the questions as a matter of consumer and property right. As a result of Ralph Nader's efforts some inroads are being made in ending ETS terrorization.

37 Quoted in Max Planck, *Where is Science Going*, New York, Norton, 1932, pp. 204-5.

38 Frederick Winslow Taylor, *Scientific Management*, Westport, Conn., Greenwood Press, 1972.

39 Wilder Penfield, *The Mystery of the Mind*, Princeton, N.J., Princeton University Press, 1975, pp. 12-13.

40 The post-revolutionary situation in Russia was one of intense political struggle in which the communist party proclaimed that its leaders were not secular theologians but in fact were the creators of the new science of Marxism. Even Bukharin, the great theoretician of the communist party, who believed in spontaneous activity of peasants and who lost his life in the dialectical battle with Stalin as to how to industrialize Russia and transform its agricultural system, concluded that scientific purpose could be administered and directed. The Bolsheviks imported Frederick Taylor's notions of scientific management which were merely a more subtle form of exploitation. It is no wonder that some have said that Henry Ford's assembly line methods had more to do with developments of the Soviet Union than Karl Marx.

41 John Dewey, *Reconstruction in Philosophy*, Boston, Beacon Press, 1948, p. 173.

42 Charles A. Beard, and Mary R. Beard, *The Rise of American Civilization*, New York, Macmillan, 1930.

43 There is a further difficulty which is that the number of housing units available for renting is dropping. Contrary to the views of Housing and Urban Development (HUD) the condominium boom and its slum clearing policies are greatly affecting the possibilities of decent housing for people in the middle, working and poor classes.

44 Chester Hartman and Michael Stone, "Housing: A Socialist Alternative" in *The Federal Budget and Social Reconstruction*, Institute for Policy Studies, Marcus G. Raskin (ed.), New Brunswick, N.J., Transaction Books, 1978, p. 224.

45 Chester Hartman and Michael Stone, "Housing: A Radical Alternative" in *The Federal Budget and Social Reconstruction, op. cit.*., pp. 205-48.

46 Paul Goodman and Percival Goodman, *Communitas; Means of Livelihood and Ways of Life*, New York, Vintage Books, 1960. Lewis Mumford, *The City in History: Its Origins, its Transformations, and its Prospects*, New York, Harcourt, Brace & World, 1961.

47 Elliot Sclar, "Land Use and Transportation" in *The Federal Budget and Social Reconstruction, op. cit.*

48 David Morris, "The City as a Source of Raw Materials," unpublished manuscript, 1977, Washington, D.C.

4 Economy for the common good

1 But this is an extremely dubious assumption. Surely we cannot mean that Michelangelo would not create unless great wealth were given to him or won

through plunder, that Einstein would not think or discover the laws of the universe unless he would know that he could become a multimillionaire, that Tom Paine would not have been a revolutionary without promise of massive fortunes, that Marx wrote and acted to acquire real estate in downtown London, or that even organizational geniuses like Carnegie would not act in the world without being granted ownership to it. Once people have knowledge or develop a process for knowing, they are prepared to use their skills in both productive and unproductive ways. They want to work because it is the essence of life itself.

2 Discussion with Richard Emery, Congressional Budget Office, 1985. There are 149 public enterprises which represent 8.7 per cent of outlays. There are sixty intra-governmental units which use revolving funds; they represent 8.6 per cent of government obligations and 0.9 per cent of outlays. (1985 CBO Report.)

3 A word should be said about our definition of deformed bureaucracy. The deformed bureaucracy keeps people from acting in history as subjects, keeping them – instead – as claimants. By deformed bureaucracy we should be understood to mean a set of artificial rules which interrupts rather than extends natural behavior, the reasonableness and decency of people. The standard which should be used to judge bureaucracy is whether it furthers shared participation and an equitable sharing of resources. This is a simple but direct standard for thinking about administration and bureaucracy.

4 Bertrand Russell, *Political Idealism*, London, Unwin Books, 1917, 1963, pp. 58-76, esp. pp.73, 74.

5 The question to be asked around social activities is whether they fall within the public or private realm. Should education be public, defense be "public"? Admittedly, the distinction between the public and private is blurred. For example, a particular activity may be privately financed, but be public in its intention, purpose and generalized benefit. In the past certain hospitals fell into this cateory. On the other hand, the activity may be publicly financed and be private in terms of who gains. For example, military weapons factories are public enterprises for personal gain. Workers in military and defense industries are public even though they may be nominally employed by a private corporation.

6 Eli Ginzberg, "The Mechanization of Work," *Scientific American*, September 1982, pp. 66-75.

7 The costly agricultural policies followed in the early 1960s by the Kennedy and Johnson administrations which exacerbated the problems of the American cities could have been avoided through a national deliberative process.

8 Seymour Melman, *Profits Without Production*, New York, Knopf, distributed by Random House, 1983.

9 Oskar Lange and Fred M. Taylor, *On the Economic Theory of Socialism*, New York, Benjamin Uppincott (ed.), A.M. Helley, 1970.

10 Cf. James Boggs and Grace Lee, *Revolution and Evolution in the Twentieth Century*, New York, Monthly Review Press, 1974, pp. 9-25. The Boggs' see the relevance of such a party for obtaining power.

11 Derek Shearer, "Dreams and Schemes: A Catalogue of Proposals," *Working Papers*, Fall 1975, p. 45.

12 The increase in Congressional capability for long-term study through the Congressional Budget Office, the scientific assessment groups and the General Accounting Office suggests the possibility of a new type of Congressional responsibility when connected to the Congressional jury process.

13 Federal and municipal governments have given charters to corporations that operate in the public sector – utilities, for example, or hydroelectric dams – for up to fifty years. The intention of the original drafters of this legislation was to

give Congress and the public the legal power to debate and analyze change and shape the methods of economic enterprise necessary to create a minimum life of decency and public participation. Consequently, each economic change should be reviewed through the electoral and dialogic referendum process at specific twenty-five-year intervals. But to make this choice meaningful the federal government must be prepared to lend funds to communities to operate facilities after licenses are terminated, successfully challenged, or lapse.

14 Among large firms, changes in style, packaging or advertising are made to grab off pieces of the market. This system does not necessarily result in positive changes for the product. Aggressive advertising and selling – usually a function of competition – has deleterious effects on the social system as a whole since it plays on all desires and wants, attempting to turn those appetites into basic needs. We have the advertising industry to thank for this situation. It operates at $100 billion a year.

15 Data from Work Force Analysis and Statistics Division of the Bureau of Labor (from an as yet unpublished Work Year and Personnel Costs Report).

16 The complaints of small businessmen about regulation and undue paperwork should be taken seriously because such regulation causes needless discontent and malaise.

17 Nina Easton and Ronald Brownstein, "Small Business in the 1980s," Report prepared for the Institute for Policy Studies, 1982.

18 The government would establish spare parts depots. Many problems of small firms stem from an inability to obtain replacement parts because they are controlled by large industrial firms. Federal programs should be initiated to secure a stronger spare parts and machine tool industry. The machine tool industry has fallen on hard times in the US because of the magnetic draw of national security and defense work. This is a central reason why there is decay in our consumer goods sector.

19 Hazel Henderson, *An Alternative to Economics*, New York, Putnam, 1980.

20 Dorothy Nelkin, "Science as a Source of Political Conflict," *Ethics for Science Policy*, 1979, p. 22. It is usually taken for granted that the community should provide security of the physical person. Although the present conservative trend seeks to disinter its nineteenth-century roots security for the modern person is quite different from its meaning as told to us by Ricardo, Adam Smith and Dicey. The nation was to secure a person's rights (especially if he was from the upper classes) from being waylaid on the highway between the city and country.

21 As Russell pointed out in his critique of state socialism, using railways as an example:

> The only truly democratic system would be one which left the internal management of railways in the hands of the men who work on them. These men should elect the general manager and a parliament of directors if necessary. All questions of wages, conditions of labor, running of trains and acquisition of material, should be in the hands of a body responsible only to those who actually are engaged in the work of the railway. (Political Ideals, New York, Barnes & Noble, 1917, p. 54).

Russell's thoughts presage the worker control model in Yugoslavia. There is an important, if not fatal, shortcoming to this model. The worker control model which is an important form of participation and planning of production does not take account of consumer interests through consumer participation. This flaw can be corrected through their inclusion at different stages of the productive and distributive process either directly or with a strong consumer protection agency

349

as its surrogate.

22 Milton Friedman, *Capitalism and Freedom*, Chicago, University of Chicago Press, 1962, pp. 31-55. Friedrich August von Hayek, *The Constitution of Liberty*, Chicago, Regenery, 1972.

23 Frances Fox Piven and Richard A. Cloward, *New Class War: Reagan's Attack on the Welfare State and its Consequences,* New York, Pantheon, 1982.

24 Interest paid in billions of dollars in 1983:

487 – corporate business	65 – individuals
50 – non-farm, individual business	152 – governments
17 – farming	50 – foreigners
137 – real estate	

Source: Survey of Current Business, US Government, Dept of Commerce, Table 8.7, July 1984, p. 95.

25 Full Employment and Balanced Growth Act, PL95-523, 1978. The act was almost immediately interred by President Carter after signature.

26 Marcus G. Raskin, *Notes On the Old System: To Transform American Politics*, New York, David McKay Co. Inc., 1974.

27 On the other hand, that a new rationale may be required does not mean that education should lose its place as a collectively paid for public good once we accept the principle that each of us is responsible, and the society as a whole is responsible for giving people the tools of their human dignity.

28 On an economic level even though there is a cumbersome indexing procedure for taking account of inflation in present social security legislation, self-insuring private pension fund schemes do not account for inflation. Where private pension funds have been won through union bargaining, or other means, workers are surprised at the hidden clauses, poor investment, and administrative entanglements when they attempt to get those funds. This is not to mention the low yield but socially useless nature of the investment.

29 Metropolitan Planning and Housing Coalition.

30 J.M. Keynes, *How to Pay For the War*, printed in USA, Harcourt, Brace & Co. Note especially Chapter IX, pp. 57-78.

31 Marcus G. Raskin, *Being and Doing*, New York, Random House, 1971.

32 Eliot Sclar, "Land Use and Transportation" in *The Federal Budget and Social Reconstruction. op. cit.*, p. 355.

33 Delores Hayden, *The Grand Domestic Revolution*, Cambridge, Mass., MIT Press, p.1.

34 Jonathan P. Sher, *Education in Rural America*, Boulder, Colo., Westview Press, 1977, p. 302.

35 *Ibid.*, p. 336, National Emergency Council, "Report on Economic Conditions in the South."

36 Senator James Abourezk bill, 93rd Congress, S-1349, introduced 3/22/73, "A bill to require the Secretary of Agriculture to carry out all rural housing programs of the Farmer's Home Administration."

37 Alice Lynd and Staughton Lynd, *Rank and File: Personal Histories By Working-class Organizers*, Princeton, N.J., Princeton University Press, 1981, p. 4.

38 Erik Wright, Cynthia Costello, David Hachen and Joey Sprague, "The American Class Structure," *The American Sociological Review*, Vol. 47, December 1982, p. 722.

39 One can better see the use of individuality through elitist examples. The art critic, Bernard Berenson, more than any other person, made individuality and authentication into a market, thereby moving the concern of buyers and art lovers from the art work to the name of the painter. After he established the art

market around the names of the artists, he wanted to stop the practice, saying that it was corrupt. He would ban the names of all artists from art works so that people could concentrate on the intrinsic truth and meaning of the art work. The practical effect of this was to freeze those pieces of art which he and his friends owned as the true art pieces while the rest would not have a market because they had no authentication.

5 Securing the nation: an alternative foreign and defense policy

1 Readers familiar with military affairs will understand that I am arguing that the 1970s concept by former Secretary of Defense, James Schlesinger, of a missile force triad on land, sea and air is irrelevant as a means of assuring American security. Whether it has perceptual utility other than creating insecurity is of course debatable.

2 For an alternative view on the development of a cooperative international law and the limits of the UN see Wolfgang G. Friedmann, *The Changing Structure of International Law*, New York, Columbia University, 1964, pp. 366-81.

3 It is not likely that the fundamentalist views of Ayatollah Khomeini represent the future. His political success was not based on what he would do but who he got rid of.

4 Hans Morgenthau pointed out in a 1946 *American Political Science Review*, pp. 988-9, that "realism maintains that universal moral principles cannot be applied to the actions of states in their abstract formulation but that they must be filtered through the concrete circumstances of time and place." Note, Marcus G. Raskin, "Morgenthau, The Idealism of a Realist" in *Truth and Tragedy*, New Republic Books, Washington, D.C., 1977.

5 Note transnational efforts such as sit-ins at the South African embassy in Washington, D.C. (1984-5) which generated national sit-ins and a change in US Congressional attitude and policy.

6 Charles Austin Beard's definition of national interest is pertinent. He suggests in his book *The Idea of National Interest*, with the collaboration of G.H.E. Smith, Westport, Conn., Greenwood Press, 1977, c. 1934 that a definition of this term emerges from conflict between a class which historically has power, and a contending nascent group, perhaps a class which is contending for power. In Reagan's government there is confirmation of this view where establishment "moderates" seek to fend off the right-wing ideologues who have not known executive power directly.

7 It can be argued with justification that there is a rather flimsy character to UN resolutions and that they are less than useful as a basis for world law as, for example, in the case of the anti-Zionist resolutions. Some would say that they carry almost no operational significance and are merely a rhetorical flourish behind which *realpolitik* functions. It is painfully true that the sort of UN "internationalism" which dominated many of the UN's activities since the Second World War was little more than a mask for partying and spying. But this reality can be shifted.

8 One should not forget, however, that even the proponents of world law of the 1950s were suspect in their purposes. Those who favored the development of world law, so long as it could be on solely American terms, became less partisan in this cause after 1957 when many Third World, non-aligned nations entered the UN. Neither attitude which dominated the Cold War period has helped the US in the solution of its own domestic problems, in increasing its national security and

in integrating the US into a world civilization which it could help to shape, but not control.

9 Hedley Bull, "The Grotian Concept of International Society," from *The War System*, Richard A. Falk and Samuel Kim (eds), Boulder, Colo., Westview Press, 1980, pp. 613-35.

10 Another challenge is to find ways that it can get other nations, namely the Soviet Union, to play a similar, minimal role. This can be accomplished by conducting negotiations with the Soviet Union inside the framework of the UN and by making clear that all bilateral discussions have to fit a framework of laws and purposes that are generally shared.

11 Nevertheless, there is a strong pacifist strain in the United States. See Robert A. Divine, *Roosevelt and World War II*, Baltimore, Johns Hopkins Press, 1969, pp. 8-10, which explains even Roosevelt's difficulties in overcoming isolationism and pacifism.

12 Eugene Rostow, *Policy Review*, Fall 1978, p. 59.

13 William M. Arkin and Richard W. Fieldhouse, *Nuclear Battlefields: Global Links in the Arms Race*, Cambridge, Mass., Ballinger Pub. Co., 1985. Michael T. Klare, *The American Arms Supermarket*, Austin, Tex., University of Texas Press, 1984. Richard J. Barnet, *The Giants: Russia and America*, New York, Simon & Schuster, 1977. Paul Mattick, *Anti-Bolshevik Communism*, White Plains, N.Y., M.E. Sharpe Inc., 1978.

14 Quincy Wright, *A Study of War*, Ill., University of Chicago Press, 1942, Vol. 2, p. 1328.

15 Morris Janowitz, *The Professional Soldier, A Social and Political Portrait*, Glencoe, Ill., Free Press, 1960, pp. 241-54.

16 Note the history of ambivalent feelings which business has had towards the military. Arthur A. Ekirch Jr., *The Civilian and the Military*, New York, Oxford University Press, 1956.

17 In 1979 I testified before the National Security Task Force of the House Budget Committee and the chairman asked the witnesses whether there would be a military coup if the defense budget were cut by $20 billion. I did not know what to answer. Where the United States military and secret intelligence organizations have had a hand in making coups in other countries it is usually accomplished by dividing the military officer class and urging their adherents to break with constitutional authority and those in the armed forces who favor democratic constitutional control. This was the situation under Allende, although other examples abound such as Guatemala, Brazil and the Dominican Republic. For example, in Chile the right encouraged military officers to isolate and then kill those Chilean military leaders (Prats, Schneider and Araya) who supported the Chilean constitution. This was done with the direct aid and encouragement of the United States. It is hard to know what the military (with their nuclear weapons and missiles) would do if a program of democratic reconstruction had wide support and was implemented through the government (c.f. Philippines, 1986).

18 Quincy Wright noted in 1942, "The United States, which has perhaps somewhat unjustifiably prided itself on its peacefulness, has had only twenty years during its entire history when its army or navy has not been in active operation someday somewhere." *Study of War*, Vol. I, p. 236. At least three out of every four years the US has been involved in war since its existence. Note P. Sweezy and H. Magdoff, "Imperialism," *Monthly Review*, February 1970.

19 The Japanese attempted to surrender several months before the dropping of the atomic bomb with the condition that they be allowed to keep the emperor as their symbol. This condition was accepted by the US after the bomb was

dropped. For incisive discussion see Gar Alperovitz, *Atomic Diplomacy*, Viking, New York, 1985.

20 Gabriel Kolko, *Main Currents in Modern American History*, New York, Pantheon Books, 1976, pp. 236-8.

21 I.F. Stone, *The Hidden History of the Korean War*, New York, Monthly Review Press, 1969. Richard E. Neustadt, *Presidential Power*, New York, Wiley, 1980, pp. 120-40. Bruce Cumings (ed.), *Child of Conflict: The Korean-American Relationship, 1943-1953*, Seattle, University of Washington Press, 1983. Note especially pp. 3-66, essays by Cumings and Lloyd Gardner. The North Koreans had been involved in an on again off again guerilla war with the South for a several year period before 25 June 1950 although a lull occurred before the North Korean onslaught across the 38th parallel:

> Stalin had a policy similar to Acheson's in regard to Socialist allies along the containment periphery. Support them, if Russian interests are not hurt, abandon them (e.g., the Greek guerillas) if they are, but in any case leave a realm of ambiguity that does not commit Soviet might. Above all, make a mess here, make a mess there (Korea, Indochina) in hope that the Americans would be drained in a hemorrhage of blood and treasure. (p. 48)

Richard Barnet and Marcus Raskin, *After Twenty Years*, New York, Random House, 1965.

22 *Ibid.*

23 Herbert F. York and Jerome Wiesner, *Race to Oblivion: A Participant's View of the Arms Race*, New York, Simon & Schuster, 1970.

24 Saville Davis, "Recent Policy Making in the United States Government," *Daedelus*, (Journal of the American Academy of Arts and Sciences), Fall 1960, vol. 89, Note 4.

25 Marcus G. Raskin, *Being and Doing*, New York, Random House, 1971.

26 Marcus G. Raskin and Bernard Fall, *The Viet-Nam Reader*, New York, Random House, 1965. James William Gibson, *The Perfect War*, to be published by Atlantic in 1986. Richard M. Pfeffer, *No More Vietnams?*, New York, published for the Adlai Stevenson Institute of International Affairs by Harper & Row, 1968. Richard J. Barnet, Marcus G. Raskin and Ralph Stavins, *Washington Plans An Aggressive War*, New York, Random House, 1971.

27 B. Louis Sohn, *Phasing of Arms Controls: The Territorial Method*, Summer Study on Arms Control, 1960, American Academy of Arts and Sciences, pp. 265-71.

28 Richard Falk and Robert J. Lifton, *Indefensible Weapons: The Political and Psychological Case Against Nuclearism*, New York, Basic Books, 1982. Daniel J. Arbess, "The International Law of Armed Conflict in Light of Contemporary Deterence Strategies: Empty Promise or Meaningful Restraint?," *McGill Law Journal*, 1984.

29 Earl Ravenal, "The Dialectic of Military Spending" from *The Federal Budget Study and Social Reconstruction*, Institute for Policy Studies, Marcus G. Raskin (ed.), New Brunswick, N.J., Transaction Books, 1978, pp. 139-75.

30 Article 1, section 9 of the US Constitution prohibits any state from entering "into any agreement or compact with another state, *or with a foreign power* . . . without the consent of Congress."

31 Note Article 237 and Article 238 of the Yugoslav Constitution which prohibits surrender if invaded.

32 The Great Power arms race has had profound exemplary effect on the Third World where there is an 18-30 per cent yearly increase in armaments capability.
The implications of such arming is an increase in the ferocity of border wars

(because of arms sales), the militarization of smaller countries and the interlocking of the military elites in small countries to the military and technological elites of large countries. They operate according to obedience and hierarchy as, for example, in the communist countries where party organizations, or in the Catholic nations of Latin America where the church has, until Vatican I, laid out principles that secure obedience and anti-reform. The modern geopolitical result is one in which armed forces and states are involved in strategies for minerals, goods, etc., which supposedly define each nation's place in the international pecking order. This mode of international politics sees the struggle for power as continuous whether fought through means of war or threat. Military actions are not considered *value* questions that have profound ethical consequences. They are calculated according to military capability and convenience.

33 10 USC Sec. 976 1977. P.L. 95-610 renumbered P.L. 96-107 sec. 821, P.L. 98-414.

34 The present unstable situation can easily be made worse because of weakened national authorities which do not command the loyalties of their populations, or significant – even insignificant – minorities. In these cases, and they exist from Ireland to Iran, small nuclear weapons could be introduced with considerable direct effect and immediate destabilizing results.

35 Disarmament Forum, W. von Bredow, Economic and Social Aspects of Disarmament, p. 79.

36 Noam Chomsky and Edward S. Herman, *After the Cataclysm, Postwar Indochina and the Construction of Imperial Ideology*, Boston, South End Press, 1979. John Stockwell, *In Search of Enemies: A CIA Story*, New York, Norton, 1978. Marcus G. Raskin, *Politics of National Security*, New Brunswick, N.J., Transactional, 1978. Robert Borosage, Morton Halperin and Christine Marwick, *The Lawless State*, Penguin, 1976.

37 Klare, *op. cit.*

38 Amnon Neubacn and Yoram Peri, *Military-Industrial Complex in Israel*, International Center for Peace In the Middle East, 1984. In addition *US Assistance to the State of Israel*, The Uncensored Draft Report, prepared by Staff U.S. G.A.O., 1984. Distributed by the Arab Anti-Discrimination Committee.

39 Some psychiatrists have argued that the present framework of "security" is a collective system of psychoneurosis. National bureaucracies are like neurotics who when they seek to escape their personal difficulties often take decisions which entrap them even further in the very dynamics that are at the heart of their difficulties. So it is with the arms race. As the distinguished psychoanalyst Karl Menninger has said, mankind is committing collective mass suicide.

40 Richard P. Stebbins (ed.), *Documents On American Foreign Relations*, New York, Harper & Row, 1962, pp. 473-85 for President Kennedy's address.

41 For an analysis of the feedback effects between politics and economics on the character of Third World states see Eqbal Ahmad, "The Neo-Fascist State: Notes on the Pathology of Power in the Third World," *First Harvest: The Institute for Policy Studies, 1963-1983*, edited by John S. Friedman, New York, Grove Press, 1983, pp. 68-78.

42 Raskin, *Politics of National Security, op. cit.*

43 Private dealings in gold by American banks have adversely affected the dollar as the international measure. And there is little doubt that it will be replaced in the next decade as the major unit of exchange. This reflects a profound change in how the US will have to conduct itself internationally. The change may be seen as a positive one.

44 André Gunder-Frank, *Crisis in the World Economy*, New York, Holmes & Mercer,

1980, p. 48.
45 Library of Congress Bulletin Working Paper on International Monetary System, 1978.
46 Wassily W. Leontief, *et al.*, *The Future of the World Economy: A United Nations Study*, New York, Oxford University Press, 1977, p. 20.
47 Paul Tillich, *The Socialist Decision*, New York, Harper & Row, 1977, pp. 150-1.
48 This ideal system is not likely because there is no constitutional means for such a national referendum. On the other hand, through the allocative tax system described in Chapter 6, direct participation could occur.
49 Hans Wolfgang Singer, *Technologies for Basic Needs*, Geneva, International Labour Office, 1977. Illich, *op. cit.* Seymour Melman, *Profits Without Production*, New York, Knopf, distributed by Random House, 1983. Vijai Pillai, "Approaches to Development," *Alternatives*, VIII, 1982, pp. 351-68. René Dumont with Macel Mazoyer, *Socialism and Development*, London, Andre Deutsch, 1973.
50 Commission on the Organization of the Government for the Conduct of Foreign Policy, 1975. Comments by Robert Bowie, consultants to the Commission, G.P.O., June 1975. Robert D. Murphy Commission.
51 Interdependence without internationalism and transnational institutions has fostered a number of ideological ironies. In the mid 1970s the French champion of the Concorde, the plan of the international ruling elite, was the French Communist party ostensibly because it created a number of production and servicing jobs for the French worker. The losers in this battle were working-class neighborhoods near airports where inhabitants complained bitterly about the noise, safety and pollution emission of that plane. One can imagine that in a period of new internationalism the groups most directly concerned from both nations, the workers and neighborhoods would initiate talks through a UN mediation team. The continued generation of subject actor status requires an added set of actors from the local level on to the international political scene.

6 The next stage of democracy

1 As noted in Chapter 5, note 16, the US has been involved in war on an almost continuous basis since its inception. Since 1941 the character of its involvement changed *causing* significant internal changes in the economic governing and military structure.
2 Ronald Radosh, "Robert A. Taft and the Cold War" in *Prophets on the Right*, New York, Simon & Schuster, 1975, pp. 147-95. Robert A. Taft, *A Foreign Policy for America*, New York, Doubleday, 1951.
3 The Republican party's last national leader against intervention and military expansion abroad was Robert Taft. Since his death the conservative constituency was absorbed by Senator Goldwater, a reserve general. Its concerns were transformed as its leaders genuflected before the altar of the marketplace, joining the "liberal" wings of the two parties in encouraging US corporate expansion abroad, continuous military engagements and huge subsidies to defense industries. For an interesting vision of post Second World War world economic and political organization, see *Prefaces to Peace*, especially "The Problems of Lasting Peace" by Herbert Hoover and Hugh Gibson, New York, Simon & Schuster, 1943.
4 William O. Douglas, *Go East, Young Man: The Early Years*, New York, Random House, 1974; *The Court Years, 1939-1975: The Autobiography of William O. Douglas*, New York, Vintage Books, 1981 and *Towards A Global Federalism*, New

York, New York University Press, 1968.
5 Herbert Gintis, "Communication and Politics," *Socialist Review*, Vol. 10, No. 2/3, p. 188 ff.
6 Indeed, some liberals such as Arthur Schlesinger supported the war on grounds of the "whole traditions of Stimsonianism and of liberal evangelism" but then adopted a cost-effective attitude about the "enterprise." Richard M. Pfeffer, *No More Vietnams?*, New York, Harper & Row, 1968.
7 Paul M. Sweezy and Harry Magdoff, *The Dynamics of US Capitalism*, Part 1, "Corporations, Expansion, and Stagnation," New York, Modern Reader, 1972, pp. 1-113.
8 Ronnie Dugger, *On Reagan: The Man and His Presidency*, New York, McGraw-Hill, 1983. The social and intellectual roots of the Reagan presidency run deep. While its star is a film actor, his lines were taken from conservative and reactionary intellectuals who needed a star with mass appeal to confront them with self-hating and selfish real choices. Milton Friedman, Friedrich Hayek, and more recently, George Gilder, Jude Waninski, and William Buckley are the right's most popular script writers. They are joined by such former socialists as Irving Kristol.
  For further explication of the Reagan administration's domestic program see *The Reagan Record* edited by John L. Palmer and Isabell V. Sawhill, Cambridge, Mass., Ballinger, 1984.
9 Marcus G. Raskin, "Democracy Versus the National Security State," *Law and Contemporary Problems*, Summer 1976, Vol. 10, No. 3, p. 189.
10 Marcus G. Raskin, *Politics of National Security*, New Brunswick, N.J., Transactional, 1978. Richard J. Barnet, *Roots of War*, New York, Atheneum, 1972. Executive Orders in Times of National Emergency, Special Committee on National Emergencies and Delegated Emergency Powers (June 1974).
11 Raymond Williams, *Keywords*, New York, Oxford University Press, 1976, p. 84.
12 Luther v. Border 7 How 1, (1849).
13 *Public Interest*, a magazine of the neo-conservatives put forward a bicentennial issue which cautioned against excessive democracy (Fall 1975, No. 41).
14 Cf. Barrington Moore, *Social Origins of Dictatorship and Democracy: Lord and Peasant in the Making of the Modern World*, Boston, Beacon Press, 1966, pp. 413-32. Moore sees the democratic form as primarily concerned with questions of modernization.
15 Gintis, *op. cit.*
16 This section was enriched by discussions with Jamin Raskin.
17 J.V. Stalin, *History of the Communist Party of the Soviet Union*, International Publishers.
18 There is one time when leaders do not want to have access to the citizenry. It is when they are making war. Clark Abt, a social scientist, stated that it is of utmost importance that the public be unable to reach the leaders when they are making nuclear war. In such circumstances, the President must be barricaded from the emotional citizenry in order to be able to continue the way.
19 Raskin, *Notes on the Old System: To Transform American Politics*, New York, David McKay Co. Inc., 1974, for discussion of the jury system as instrument for public deliberation. For further contrary discussion on the tenth amendment see Bernard Schwartz, *The Powers of Government*, New York, MacMillan, Vol. 1, p. 40, 1962.
  Note as well Jane Mansbridge who argues in her important work *Beyond Adversary Democracy*, New York, Basic Books, 1980, for a form of non-adversarial democracy which transcends quantitative equality. "It has to do with

subjective relations among human beings, with the tone, the nature, the kind of bond between them. . . . Equal respect need not depend on equal ability. It can arise from moments of emotional indentification. . . . To feel that all women were sisters meant that all other differences faded into insignificance. . . . Women found too much in each other to respect." In egalitarian interdependence one must begin with the Other's humanity and respect for it. Ironically, modern life defies adversarial relations in a fundamental way forcing us to reach to a deeper humanity.

20 Marbury v. Madison stood for the accepted proposition that government officials cannot "sport away the vested rights of others." 1 Cranch at 166. Further, the Alien and Sedition Acts were considered obnoxious just because they restricted citizen participation in the public space to *assenters*.

21 People deliberate at the work place how best to get the job done, often irrespective of hierarchic planning and demands. In the "private" sphere a person often deliberates about ends as well as means; an important, perhaps critical activity. Should I marry x? Why?

22 Each of these questions contains moral, technological and economic factors which can be publicly discussed in a new epistemological framework of policy. Marcus Raskin and Herbert Bernstein, *Shifting the Gaze*, New Jersey, Rowman & Littlefield, 1987; specifically, "Toward a New Political Science."

23 Oswald Spengler, *Man and Technics: A Contribution to a Philosophy of Life*, Westport, Conn., Greenwood Press, 1976, pp. 86-7.

24 Raskin, *Notes On the Old System, op. cit.*, Chapter 9.

25 Not surprisingly environmental impact statements became the most popular participatory form just because they included deliberation and implementation.

26 Modern market definitions of rationality are limited to means not ends. Therefore economic modes of cost/benefit are insufficient tools just because they mask value considerations or come to grotesque or comical conclusions. The "objective" stance of conservative judges such as Richard A. Posner, one of the right's intellectual legal battleships who leads in attempting to insert "objective" economics into law, makes the same errors Fredric Bastiat made, namely that "all economic categories are only so many names for what is always the same relations." As Marx points out, the content and the extent of purchase, and the capitalist's capacity to exchange money, interest, and things for many different products and possibilities is the critical question about supposedly economically value neutral "commodities" such as money. Note Karl Marx, *Grundrisse*, New York, Vintage Books, 1973, pp. 247-51.

27 Immanuel Kant, *Perpetual Peace*, New York, Garland Pub., 1972, p. 114.

28 The UN Declaration on Human Rights comprised the thoughts of John Dewey and Jacques Maritain. The combination of pragmatism and natural rights is not without its internal policy logic. However, in its declaration the United States, among other nations, considered declarations on human rights as aspirations and a "positive" direction, not necessarily concrete goals to be implemented.

29 Victor E. Frankl, *From Death Camp to Existentialism*, Boston, Beacon Press, 1959, p. 67.

30 Where there is a potential human being as in the case of the unborn fetus it is the mother who decides for the group (society) when access to her body may be had by others to reach the fetus. She is the principal with absolute authority to control access to her body, and therefore the potential life of a next generation. She is its human link.

31 The constitution begins "We the people," rather than "We the states" as Patrick Henry would have had it. Schwartz, *op. cit.*, Vol. 1, p. 14.

32 Before 1790, there were not thirty corporations, by 1800 there were over 300, but these were mostly turnpike, bridge, canal or fire companies. Bank and insurance companies numbered sixty-seven by 1800, and there were only six incorporated manufacturing companies before the nineteenth century. Henry A. Wallace, *Whose Constitution?*, New York, Reynal and Hitchcock, 1936, p. 155 ff.

33 Edward H. Levi, "The Sovereignty of the Courts," University of Chicago, Law School, 15 July 1981.

34 *Ibid.*

35 The responsibility of the federal courts is not invented out of whole cloth. It is founded and created by understanding that there is an architectonic of rights which the society as a whole is to make part of people's individual consciousness. Marbury v. Madison 1 Cranch 137 (1803).

36 Hannah Arendt, *The Recovery of the Public World*, Melvyn A. Hill (ed.), New York, St Martin's Press, 1979. Note especially Michael Denneny, "The Privilege of Ourselves: Hannah Arendt on Judgement," pp. 245-74. Elizabeth Young-Bruehl, *Hannah Arendt – For Love of the World*, New Haven, Yale University Press, 1982.

37 Intervention is not a casual matter. It must first be debated within the governmental departments to ascertain how many of the government's respective activities do positive harm (lessening the value and humanity of people) by the way its programs are structured, its hiring and housing policies, the defense adopted, or the classes favored.

38 It should be noted in passing that the federal government is remarkably small for the work that it does. At the federal level government workers in the non-defense sector remain approximately at the same level which it had achieved in 1956 although the number of programs has increased in dollar terms from 70 billions to 832 billions. During this same period the population grew by 60 million people. The problem of government programs is that they are *privately* administered. They then require enormous red tape because of accountability demands that Congress makes. Furthermore, private corporations take on aspects of the government which in other nations would be public responsibilities that could never be contracted out to management consultants, private hospitals or entrepreneurial groups. Curiously, groups like the National Association of Manufacturers whose members depend on governmental largesse and which have impinged on the governing function complain bitterly about government regulation.

It is true that at the state and local level government employment has greatly increased over the last two decades as their tasks have increased under a theory of "decentralization" in which the federal government devolves responsibility to the states and local cities. Thus, in 1956, the total number of government employees on the state and local level was 5,068,500 while in 1985 the total number increased to 13,235,000. Is it better that local and state employment increase as against federal employment? There are several theories behind the answer to this queston. It is said that local and state systems are more responsive to the needs of the people. But this claim varies with the historical time. It should be remembered that federal power gained in stature because the local oligarchies were able to wield great power in state and local government to the detriment of the poor and working class. On the other hand, when the progressives and populists operated at the local and state level, there was greater concern with people's needs. Thus, local and state government controlled by the La Follettes or "sewer socialists," as they were called in Wisconsin, appeared to be closer to the people. From 1870-1920, while Congress's legislation often read otherwise, the executive and especially the federal judiciary served as the primary means to organize property relationships in the society for the expanding corporations. Even the vaunted anti-trust laws were a means to get corporations to play according to the capitalist rules of competition. While capitalists talked about social Darwinism and survival of the fittest, they intended to orchestrate the market in such a way as to allow those with the greatest power with government to survive.

Until the eve of the New Deal city governments did not know where to turn for help. The major strength of the Democratic party came from its ability to get Congress and the federal government to recognize the cities as central, necessary and needing entities in American life. Much of the federal government's strength (and that of the Democratic party) comes from the people's belief that the government will intercede for the middle, working and poorest classes, organizing the "economy" and the services system in the society for them.

Supposedly the government is the protector against special interests – at least taming their appetites to the extent that what they need in terms of profit and privilege can be dressed up as rational and good for the society as a whole. Unfortunately, the federal government appears to be organized as a holding company for the large corporations. For example, energy corporations such as Exxon have nothing to fear from the government since it has not defined a public interest, nor can it in the present restricted framework. Reconstruction is a method by which the citizenry is involved in all aspects of governing through the jury system and the promulgation of a separate program which is presented to Congress.

Part of the reason for the government's impotence stems from the common belief that the government of the United States should be separate from the people. The fear is that if government is throughout society the society will end as a totalitarian one. But the totalitarianism comes from the reverse situation. Totalitarianism is most apt to occur when government is reduced to interest group brokering or an interest group itself thereby losing sight of the purpose of government for society. There is no reason that a government infused with citizen participation should be less democratic than one which sits in isolation. Democratic citizenship can be a fundamental activity of American life for it has as its purpose achieving the common good by constantly reshaping the governmental enterprise according to clearly defined but perpetually and critically examined values.

39 Franz Neumann, *The Democratic and the Authoritarian State*, Glencoe, Ill., Free Press, 1957, pp. 216-33.
40 In all communities there is invariably great concern about the "outsider." The outsider is usually one who is of another geographic place. But he or she may be of a different race, color, or sex as well. If a person is discriminated against on those grounds, that person's citizenship rights are directly jeopardized and it is then that the federal apparatus has a positive obligation to intervene.
41 Max Horkheimer, *Eclipse of Reason*, Oxford, Oxford University Press, 1947, p. 178.
42 Robert J. Pranger, *The Eclipse of Citizenship*, New York, Holt, Rinehart, & Winston, 1968.
43 From private correspondence with Michael Apple.
44 Virginia Held, Kai Nielsen, and Charles Parsons (eds), *Philosophy and Public Action*, New York, Oxford University Press, 1972. Note essays on the choice between reform and revolution by Kai Nielsen, pp. 17-52; reform and revolution by Peter Caws, pp. 72-105.
45 Barrington Moore Jr "Moral Outrage," *New York Review of Books*, 1 June 1978,

vol. 25, p. 35.

46 Hannah Arendt, *Crisis of the Republic*, New York, Harcourt Brace & Jovanovich, 1972.

47 Frank Browning and John Gerassi, *The American Way of Crime*, New York, Putnam, 1980, chapters 1-3.

48 Brown v. Mississippi, 297 US 278, 56 S.Ct. 461, 80 L.Ed. 682 (1936).

49 In the past twenty-five years citizens have been used unwittingly as guinea pigs in LSD and cancer experiments, undeclared wars, hostile acts, and seduced into paying for genocidal policies which turned them into hostages. The managers of the state have seen no need to apply criminal law to themselves for such acts.

50 Criminal Code Reform Act of 1977. Senate Judiciary Committee p. 867.

51 In a case involving three executives of film recovery systems the prosecutors proved successfully that Stefan Golub died of hydrogen cyanimide fumes which came from hazardous chemicals. The employers willfully allowed unsafe conditions to obtain in the work place. At the very least the defendants allowed a "willingness to risk killing", in the words of Norval Morris, quoted approvingly by Alan Dershowitz. *Washington Times*, 20 June 1985.

52 For a period immediately after Watergate and the Indo-China war Congress favored the principle of openness as reflected in the Freedom of Information Act. This law created a new awareness among the citizenry about the activities of the government on them. By 1980, however, the state apparatus returned to its old habits and closed the curtain. To be political in the sense of seeking the common good can only be achieved in the public – without secrets where no difference exists between private and public action, and where scrutiny by the public is always present.

53 Rose Goldsen, "The Great American Consciousness Machine: Engineering the Thought Revolution" in *Journal of Social Reconstruction*, 1980, Vol. 1, No. 2, pp. 87-102.

54 P.L. 98-473, Title 2, Comprehensive Crime Control Act of 1984.

55 Whatever their ideological hue, nations find that it is exceedingly difficult to wean themselves from the death penalty. Some might say that there is a collective need to extirpate the Devil within us by allowing the state to murder for us. Americans are no exception to this apparent need, although we seem to assume that the poor, black and wretched are the devilish part of ourselves and body politic. Consequently, they are the likely clientele assigned to Death Row.

There are two reasons for the death penalty. One is politically motivated. In the history of nations, the death penalty is used to get rid of political enemies, troublemakers, or those bent on pursuing class conflict. The second reason for the death penalty is psychological, for the act of state murder contains within itself a combination of guilt, vengeance and blood sacrifice. In a modern society which has examined critically its psychological and anthropological motivation, the use of the death penalty would be acknowledged as a collective admission of failure. We assert that certain people are evil, never having done good, and never being capable of any act of generosity or decency. When the death penalty is administered through its collective apparatus, the government is expected *not* to recognize decent attributes in defendants, thus allowing the society to perform collective murder as its symbol of communal authority and rectitude. Some have said that punishment, especially capital punishment is the way solid citizens control their own tendencies toward sinfulness – namely, by scapegoating others. People bolster their own indignation and repress themselves, believing in crime and punishment procedures that are supposed to inoculate the society against the "virus of crime." I do not mean to be snide about evil and crime. In a society committed to the common good, social limits on individual behavior are necessary. However, the most important limits that people must set are those that relate collective power to restrain its most powerful institutions. This translates into a democratic society always being a society of risk for the individual, and personal responsibility of the kind which accepts an injustice or loss rather than executing such a deed on another. Citizen responsibility also means recognizing and querying institutionalized and legitimated criminality in various aspects of our lives, be it the manufacture of defective autos, maiming and killing drugs, foul air, etc. They are all elements of institutionalized manslaughter which are *there* but which we choose not to recognize because it would mean that we might have to initiate substantial changes in the social structure. In other words, our personal responsibility is to know collectively as a society what we would never do irrespective of the particular situation, and what we would seek to change and punish through legal action and dialogue.

56 The pertinent study on the relationship of crime and unemployment was conducted by Harvey Brenner of Johns Hopkins University:

> The following data I will be talking about represent the estimated impact of a 1 per cent increase in unemployment on a sample of crimes and criminal justice statistics. These data were based on equations prepared by myself in separate studies for the National Institute of Mental Health HEW, the United Nations Social Defense Research Institute, the National Institute on Drug Abuse, the Joint Economic Committee of Congress and relevant hearings. These samples of relationships between criminal justice system data and national economic indicators are presented here for the first time.
>
> Now crimes coming from arrest data as reported by the FBI for the period 1952 to 1975; the year 1970 the FBI reported 468,146 instances of arrests for narcotics. Based on relationships with unemployment, we observed that an increase of 1 per cent in unemployment is associated with 40,056 of those arrests, coming to a total of approximately an 8.7 per cent increase for narcotics arrests. There were 832,.624 larcenies in 1970, 23,151 for 2.8 per cent are attributed to only a 1 per cent increase in the unemployment rate.
>
> Looking at burglary for the same year, where we start with a base of 385,785 arrests, the association with unemployment on a 1 per cent increase results in approximately 8,646; there's a 2.2 per cent increase for each 1 per cent increase in unemployment.
>
> For robbery, it is a 5.7 per cent increase, or an increase of close to 7,000 arrests.
>
> Now, from studies over the last twenty or thirty years, the suicide rate is so finely tied to change in unemployment through time, that the rate is one of the better economic indicators for the United States. It is better than probably many that we find, including the Dow Jones Index, for example.
>
> The stress involved in unemployment we then observe to befall many of our countrymen but this is not by any means limited to the United States. This relationship of suicide to unemployment is found in virtually all countries in which the attempt has been made to investigate it. The power of loss of employment is such that it appears that a very sizable number of persons are willing to destroy themselves rather than bear the humiliation of dealing with the consequences of loss of job and income.
>
> These kinds of studies began with suicide and mental hospitalizations; that is, specifically in the mental health area. Since then, attempts were made to look into stress-related disorders of the sort that affect very large populations,

such as heart disease, which takes a toll of some 60 to 70 per cent of all deaths in this country.

And once again the very sharp and profound impact of changes in unemployment, with a log of within five years, is found for heart disease, cardiovascular disease generally, including stroke and renal diseases.

Following that, the question arose as to whether if we looked at a phenomenon which should be relatively rare in this country by now, namely, infant mortality, which once people believed was highly tied to the state of the economy, still was tied to it in a very affluent society. And what was observed there, again was that the rate of infant mortality was intimately tied to the rate of unemployment. "Unemployment and Crime" serial no. 47, House Judiciary Committee 95th Congress, also "Unemployment and Crime" 97th Congress serial 6D, Subcommittee on Crime and Subcommittee on Education (Joint Hearings) (1979).

57 Computer technology has been adopted in most developing nations. It is usually used for control over citizens and national security, defense purposes. From Chile to the Soviet Union computers for police work are thought of as necessary and efficient. They buy such computers from the United States.

58 A subsidiary issue which is raised by the doctrine of *property right in one's name* is that it may inhibit research, free speech, and press. But here again there are saving exceptions which do not destroy the fundamental rule. There is a strong right to privacy which is meant to control the invasion of anyone into the private affairs and lives of another. And where the person through his or her own actions becomes a public figure the character of the person's property right changes. Where research is done by name on the living and it is to be published, there is no reason why permission should not be requested from the person being studied. If it is the case that a person or business must pay a newspaper to run an ad, there does not seem to be good reason why the media should not have to ask permission of those whose names they use who are not "public figures."

59 A Report of the American Bar Association, *Special Committee to Study Federal Law Enforcement Agencies* (1976).

60 For example, presidential power includes the power of intimidation, and commitment to warmaking activity, as we have all learned in recent years. Indeed, under one Supreme Court case (Neagle in/re, 135 US I(1908)) "the rights, duties and obligations growing out of the Constitution itself, our international relations and all the protections implied by the nature of the government under the Constitution" has been so interpreted by American Presidents, and those surrounding them to include unlimited power. In this context public officials view themselves as serving presidents and presidencies, the laws and their own personal needs. The use of counterintelligence as a means of breaking up political activities of individuals and groups is a critical question in a time of social transformation. Thus, the police should always be limited to named crimes and ending criminal behavior of policing institutions.

7 Progress and the common good

1 The Frankfurt School, notably Max Horkheimer, had taken the view that philosophy should *not* be integral to action in the sense that it could provide a formula. Horkheimer *et al.* sought to transcend the problematic and pragmatic school of Dewey which assured that program and philosophy can be made "scientific." Experience would show that both schools are right and wrong; the

Frankfurt School theorists were right in attempting to save philosophy by articulating deeper understandings and seeking non-obvious connections. They were wrong in assuming that because of their marginal position it would not be necessary to have a program which at least could serve as a "myth" understanding of reality to sustain liberation. On the other hand, the pragmatist's notion of a program was an ensemble of ideas which justified the project of the dominant social forces in the society. This direction could only lead to disaster for neither facts nor values were understood in a larger framework which would show their true meanings.

2 Ivan Supek, "Humanistic Morality" in *Encyclopaedia Moderna*, Institute for the Philosophy of Sciences and Peace of the Yugoslav Academy of Sciences and Arts and Yugoslav Pugwash Conference, Zagreb, Yugoslavia, 1976, pp. 71-80.

3 Mircea Eliade, *Myths, Dreams and Mysteries*, New York, Harper, 1960, p. 30.

4 Arthur Koestler, *Arrival and Departure*, Berkley, Medallion, 1943, p. 32.

5 Karl Marx, *Critique of the Gotha Programme*, Moscow, Progress Publishers, 1971, p. 15.

6 Gunther S. Stent, *Paradoxes of Progress*, San Francisco, W.H. Freeman, 1978, p. 27.

7 Oswald Spengler, *Man and Technics: A Contribution to a Philosophy of Life*, Westport, Conn., Greenwood Press, 1976, p. 79.

8 Delores Hayden, *The Grand Domestic Revolution*, Cambridge, Mass., MIT Press, 1981, p. 7.

9 Erich Kahler, *Man the Measure, A New Approach to History*, New York, Pantheon, 1943, p. 464 ff.

10 *Ibid.* p. 475.

11 *Richard Pryor Live On the Sunset Strip*, Columbia Pictures, 1982.

12 Carol Gilligan, *In A Different Voice*, Cambridge, Mass., Harvard University Press, 1982, p. 100.

13 Colin M. Turnbull, "Human Nature and Primal Man," in *Social Research*, Vol. 40, No. 3, Fall 1973, pp. 511-30.

14 Ralph Miliband, *Marxism and Politics*, Oxford, Oxford University Press, 1977, p. 164.

15 Where a political system is too brittle then even minimum reforms are seen as a challenge to the social economic and political system as a whole. Thus reformists sought to contain slavery within specific boundaries before the American Civil War but it was clear that the system had become so inflexible and rigidified that it could not afford any change. This situation could easily develop within the United States around capitalism if there is deepening depression and inflation or a national security system which does not accept limits. For example, the modest reforms which were proposed for the CIA by President Carter and President Ford are now thought to be too stringent. Cuts in the defense budget are fought on the grounds that they will damage badly the defense-oriented American economy.

16 Andrew Levine, *Arguing For Socialism*, Boston, Routledge & Kegan Paul, 1984, p. 229.

Index

abolitionists, 210
Abourezk, James, 189
access, in democracy, 278-9, 282, 283
Acheson, Dean, 270
advertising techniques, 78
agriculture, 187-8
alliance, forming, 8-11
American Federation of Labor-Congress and
    Industrial Organizations (AFL-CIO), 147,
    153
anarchism, 24
Anderson, Eddie, 36
Angell, Norman, 197
apartheid, 220; domestic, 221
Apple, Michael W., 118, 297-8
architecture, 184-6
Arendt, Hannah, 35, 56, 293
Aristotle, 32, 57
arms race, 6; citizen action, 209; control,
    226-30; as deterrence, 217-18;
    disarmament, 13, 211-19, 230-55;
    economic interests, 13; effect of, 27-8; as
    mutual problem, 200-1; spending, 19, 212,
    215, 218; termination, 325-6; and world
    economy, 224-6
arts, and progress, 324
associate class, 269, 270
associative relationships, 23
atomic bomb, as blunder, 207
attributes as rights, 286

Bacon, Lord, 127, 322
Bahro, Rudolf, 53
Bakke decision, 125
banks: reorganization, 178-80; and shelter,
    133
Beard, Charles, 18, 132
Being and Doing (Raskin), 9
Bellarmine, Cardinal, 126
Bennett, William, 116
Benny, Jack, 36

Berg, Alban, 333
Bernal, J.D., 28
Bernstein, E.M., 257
Bettelheim, Charles, 259
bonding, 83-5, 86, 120-1; crime and re-
    bonding, 308-10; ersatz, 311-12; in foreign
    relations, 195-7; and security, 302
Bretton Woods agreement (1944), 257
Bricker, Senator, 198
Bryan, William Jennings, 203
Buber, Martin, 24, 55, 76, 332
Buchanan, President, 132
budgeting, 181-2
Bull, Hedley, 199
Burckhardt, Jacob, 332
bureaucracy: in democracy, 284; restraining,
    304
bureaucratic institutional reconstruction,
    149-51
bussing, 11

Cannon, William, 98
capital, monopoly, 13
capitalism: and cooperation, 14-15; shaky,
    180-2; small scale, 15; and the state, 143-4
caring, 53, 56-9, 326-7; definition, 89-91; by
    government, 88, 93; value of, 90
Carter administration, 98, 152, 198, 226, 256;
    260
Castro, Fidel, 300
categorization, 335
change, incremental, 331
Channing, William Ellery, 55
characterization, 290
China, socialism, 16
Choate, Pat, 90
CIA, 313, 314
cities: gentrification, 138; planning, 139-41;
    productive, 140
citizen class, 269
citizenship, 13, 275, 296-8; false, 299

civil disobedience, 17, 298-300
civil war, 6
Clark, Ramsey, 315
coercion, 23-4
COINTELPRO, 314-15
college education, 123-5
colonialism, 117
common good, 23, 25-6, 27; and care, 89; as natural propensity, 30-1; and social security, 100-1; strategies towards, 70-8
common sense and common good, 34-7
community: and the criminal, 307; and economy, 146-7; in international relations, 195; participation in planning, 139-41, 147, 154; questioning, 132
Comprehensive Crime Control Act (1984), 305-6
conflicts in society, 4-5, 9
Congress, 73-5
Constitution, American, 291-3; and democracy, 290-4; function, 290
cooperation, as need, 14; *see also* interdependence
corporations, 2, 13, 73; crime, 303-4; foreign competition, 180-1; multinational, 265-8
Costello, Cynthia, 190-1
courts, neighbourhood, 310-11; *see also* judiciary
covenant: American, 7-8; new, 11, 12, 13-14
covert activities: domestic, 221; foreign, 219
crime, in democracy, 302-5; punishment, 306, 307-8, 309; and re-bonding, 308-11
criminal code, in national security state, 305-7
Cuban missile crisis, 208
currency, separate, 257-8
cycles, 28, 29, 330-1

defense: budget, 212, 215, 218; common, 214-16
deliberation, in democracy, 282-4
Dellums, Ron, 202
democracy, 26, 37, 124, 273; attributes, 275-85; and common good, 275; Conservative attitude to, 274; and constitution, 290-4; defining, 273-4, 276; and economic distribution, 166-7; foreign policy in, 193, 209; function, 274-5, 277, 288; importance of, 12; modern, 275, 276, 277; moral ethic, 325; and personal recognition, 288-90; power in, 307; US as, 270-2, 273
dependency, international system, 197; *see also* interdependence
design, 184-6
deterrence *see* arms race
de Tocqueville, Alexis, 15, 264
development, international, 258-67

Dewey, John, 39-40, 52
dialogue, in democracy, 36, 283, 330
dignity, 8, 286-7
disarmament *see* arms race
Disney, Walt, 117
doctors: drugs, use of, 105; in national health service, 112; role, 106; standards, 106; training, 104-5
dollar standard, 255
Doty, Paul, 226
Douglas, William O., 270
Dulles, John Foster, 199, 208

ecology, caring for, 89, 303-4; disasters, 2, 13, 183, 303
economic distribution, 164-6
economic order, new international, 260, 261
economic security, 12-13, 27
economic system: and common good, 145-6; international, 5
economy, international: and arms race, 224-6; and international development, 258-67; money market, 255-8; social reconstruction, 255
economy, national: and full employment, 169-72; problems of, 167; protective tariffs, 186; public nature, 146-7; reconstructive reforms, 182-9; reorganization, 149-54; Zone One, 155-8; Zone Two, 158-60; Zone Three, 160-1; Zone Four, 161-4
education: centralization, 121-2; and common good, 115-25; community participation in, 120-1; federal participation, 121; function, 120-1; funding, 118-20; higher, 123-5; tests, 123; vouchers, 118-19
Einstein, Albert, 48, 126
Eisenhower administration, 256
Eliade, Mircea, 318
elitism, 36
empathic justice, 326-7
employment, full, 169-72; and inflation, 168-9
Engels, Friedrich, 44
Enthoven, Alain, 114
equality, as interdependence, 13, 83, 288, 289
esthetics, 117
ethical duty, 326

Falwell, Jerry, 6
family as role-carrier, 24
fantasy world, 334
Faustianism, 320, 321-2
favoritism, 199-200
FBI, 313
Feyerabend, Paul, 128
Flexner Report (1910), 105
foreign policy: bonding, need for, 195-7; covert activities, 219; forward strategy,

210-11; general principles, 219-24; irrationality in, 203-4; militaristic, 202-3; nonintervention, 195, 219-21; participation in, 194; positive peacekeeping, 221-2; themes, 193-4, 195, 201, 204; UN resolutions as, 198-9; violence in, 196; *see also* arms race; security, national
freedom and common good, 29-30, 317
free goods, 172-3; and need, 174
free trade, 265
Friedman, Milton, 103, 159
Fromm, Erich, 332
Fulbright, J. William, 271
fund, common, 261

Galileo, 126
Garaudy, Roger, 117
George, Henry, 133, 134
GI bill, 123
Gilligan, Carol, 12, 57, 327
Gintis, Herbert, 271, 275
Ginzberg, Eli, 159
God, 76-7, 323
Goldwater, Barry, 272
Goodman, Paul, 24, 141
Goodman, Percival, 141
Gorz, André, 331
Gould, Stephen, 128
government: attitudes to, 3; crimes of indirection, 303-4; direction of economy, 142-3; function, 290-1; participation in, 284, 293-4, 316; reorganization, 294-6; *see also* state
government workers, 75
Gramsci, Antonio, 11
Great Power, role, 200, 202, 272
Greenwood, Daphne, 1
Grotius, 195
Guevara, Che, 318

Hachen, David, 190-1
Haig, General, 206
Hamilton, Alexander, 17
happiness, 20-1, 26, 107
Harris, Fred, 187
Hatfield, Mark, 137
Havana Charter, 259-60
Hayden, Delores, 185, 323
Hayek, F.A. von, 101, 144
health: dangers to, 2-3; and market economy, 104, 111; and social reconstruction, 102-15
health system: funding, 107-8, 110-11, 112, 113-14; organization, 107-15
health workers, 104, 106, 107, 108-9, 113
Hegel, G.W.F., 20, 31
Heidegger, Martin, 90-1
Helms, Jesse, 6
helping, capacity for, 14

Herder, J.G., 327
heroism, 54
history, 28; and progress, 322-3
Hitler, Adolf, 295, 332
Hocking, William, 37
Homestead Act, 132
Hook, Sidney, 40
Hoover, Herbert, 218
Hoover, J. Edgar, 313
Horkheimer, Max, 40, 296
housing: community trust, 134-7; finance, 133, 135; private, 136; public, 133-6
humanism, new, 331
Hume, David, 31
Huntington, Samuel, 226
hydrogen bomb, as blunder, 208

identification, international, 197
ideology: change, and interests of state, 203; current, 2, 10-11, 88
Ik tribe, 327-8
Illich, Ivan, 51, 103
imagination, 11
imperialism, 220-1
implementation, in democracy, 284-5
income, minimum, 93, 94; redistribution, 96-7
incrementation, 331
inflation: causes, 168, 256; and full employment, 168-9; international, 255, 256
insecurity, personal, 300-1
institutions, social: and social disorder, 4; opening, 7
interdependence, 34, 194-5, 200, 326; equal, 13, 83, 288, 289; explicit, 330
International Labor Organization, 266-7
International Monetary Fund, 257
Iran, 197

James, C.L.R., 45
James, William, 41
Janowitz, Morris, 205
Japan, defense spending, 218
Jefferson, Thomas, 132
John Paul II, Pope, 32, 73
Jones, Jim, 332
judgement, 53, 55-6
judiciary, 309
jury system, 282
justice, 326-7

Kahler, Erich, 323
Kant, Immanuel, 31, 56, 285, 327
Kastenmeier, Robert, 74
Katz, Julius, 261
Keller, Evelyn Fox, 126
Kellogg, Francis, 203
Kennan, George, 17, 201

Kennedy Administration, 202, 227
Keynes, Lord, 257
King, Martin Luther Jr, 48, 54
Kissinger, Henry, 16, 49
knowledge, evaluating, 123-4; reconstructive, 125-31
Koestler, Arthur, 319
Korea, US intervention, 207
Kropotkin, Prince, 330

La Guardia, Fiorello, 74
laissez-faire economy, 142-3
land ownership, 132-3
Lands and Shelter Trust, 135-7, 138
Lange, Oscar, 152
Lasswell, Harold, 20, 78
law; criminal code, 305-7; democratic revision, 307-8, 310; redrafting, 306; and revolution, 295-6; and security, 301-2
leadership, 47-8; American, 49; aversion to, 47; and common good, 6, 49; innate, 48-9; methods, 49; moral purpose, 48; revolutionary, 49-51
Lenin, V.I., 50
Levi, Edward, 291
Levine, Andrew, 335
liberalism: critics of, 17; origins, 303
library system, 122, 335
life boat strategy, 5
linked principles, 83-5
Lippmann, Walter, 283
local government, 295
Lonergan, Bernard, 35-6
Long, Earl, 328-9
Long, Huey, 94
Lovestone, Jay, 153
Lukács, Georg, 295
Lynd, Alice, 190
Lynd, Robert, 40
Lynd, Staughton, 190

Macaulay, Lord, 324
McCloy, John, 272
McCloy-Zorin Agreement, 227, 230
McNamara, Robert, 56, 208
Machiavelli, Niccolo, 324
maiming, social, 304-5
Marcuse, Herbert, 317
market system, inhumanity, 14
Marxism: British, 331; and the common good, 38; Faustian, 321-2; and human unpredictability, 318-20; and myths, 79; and science, 192-31
Mather, Cotton, 302
medical schools, 104, 108
men, dominance, 23
middle class ideology, 9-10
Miliband, Ralph, 331

militarism *see* arms race, disarmament
military, attitudes of, 204-5
money, 171-2, 178-80
money market, international, 255-8
monopolies, natural, 155-8
Moore, Barrington, 299
Morgenthau, Hans, 203
Morris, David, 140
Morris, William, 330
Mumford, Lewis, 4
Murphy, James Gardner, 126
music, modern, 333
Muste, A.J., 76
Myles, John, 91, 96
myths and the common good, 78-93

National Education Insurance Fund (NEIF), 120
National Health Planning and Resources Act (1974), 110
National Health Service Corps, 110, 112
National Institutes of Health (NIH), 103, 114
nationalization, 152
National Security Act (1947), 272
national security state, 272-3; criminal code, 305-7
national socialism *see* Nazism
nature, caring for *see* ecology
Nazism, 43, 286, 322
need, 174; recognition of, 25
neighborhood courts, 310-11
Niebuhr, Reinhold, 76, 323
Nixon, Richard, 74, 206, 257
Noll, Roger, 114
nonintervention, 195, 219-21
non-profit activities, 161-4
nuclear freeze *see* arms race
Nuremberg Charter, 211, 212, 216

Occupational Safety and Health Administration (OSHA), 103, 141
oligopolies, 155-8
ordinariness, and social reconstruction, 11
organizers, 47; functions, 60-1; political, 52-3, 59-62; qualities, 61; rules for, 62-8; strategic tasks, 69-78
Other, awareness of, 326
ownership, shared, 148

paper identity, 311-12
participation, 324; and civil disobedience, 298-300; and democracy, 277, 279-81, 282, 283, 316; in education, 120-1; in government, 284, 293-4, 316; in law revision, 310; in planning, 139-41, 147, 154; workers, 15, 145, 148, 161-4
past, domination of, 322-3, 335
peacekeeping, positive, 221-2

Index

Penfield, Wilder, 129
pension funds, 147-8, 176
personal recognition, 288-90
personhood, 31, 287
Philippines, 197
phone tapping, 305
planning: importance of, 326; participation in, 139-41, 147, 154; urban, 139-41, 184-6
Plato, 31, 36, 79
police: arming, 313; obligations, 312-16
politics, 32-3, 328-9; and common good, 330; new, 19-22; as solution, 328
pollution, 303-4
Popper, Karl, 331
power, 19; in democracy, 307; Faustian, 322; of individual citizen, 312
pragmatism and common good, 39-42
prices, 148, 171, 173; international, 261-2
prison sentences, 309-10
private interests and common good, 37-9, 73
programmes and unpredictability, 318-20
Program Treaty for Security and General Disarmament, 230-55
progress, 317, 320-1; definition, 321, 325; and science, 323-4
property: and common good, 12-13, 21; fundamental right, 312; and voting, 276
protective tariffs, 186
prudentialists, 210, 334
Pryor, Richard, 326
public and private, 2, 10, 146
public interest sector, 13, 146, 155-8
public service sector, 158-60
punishment, 306, 307-8, 309

quality of life, 8

racism, 11, 24
rationality, 53, 59, 324, 325
Rawls, John, 38
reactionary views, 5-6
Reagan administration, 5, 86; and Congress, 74-5; and democracy, 271; economy, 143, 169; education, 118, 120; foreign policy, 197, 201, 209, 218-19; health, 111, 113; internal security, 300, 301; private space, 138; social policy, 11; Third World, 263; underclass, 36
reconstructive knowledge, 125-31
reform, minimum, 331
Regan, Donald, 168
regulation, economic, 183-4
rehabilitation, 308
relationships, interdependent, 326
religious movements, 76-7; and progress, 323
Renaissance, progress in, 323
repression and security, 300, 301
republic, US as, 269-70, 272

revolution, 317-18
rights: attributes as, 286; conflicting, 285-6; natural, 276
Roosa, Robert, 257
Roosevelt, President, 203, 313
Rouse, James, 137
rural life, 187-9
Ruskin, John, 331
Russell, Bertrand, 145, 165

salaries, 171
Sartre, Jean-Paul, 329
Schelling, Thomas, 226
Schlafly, Phyllis, 6
Schoenberg, Arnold, 333
schools, role, 116-17; see also education
Schweitzer, Albert, 322
science and technology, 323-4
Sclar, Elliott, 139
security: internal, 300-2; Program Treaty, 230-55; world arrangement, 209, 210, 222-4, 230-55
security, national: internal activities, 305; blunders, 207-8; general principles, 219-24
self-definition, 323
selfishness, 327-8
sentencing, 306, 309
sexism, 24; and architecture, 185
Shearer, Derek, 154
shelter, 131-41
Sher, Jonathan P., 188
Sibert, Robert, 80
Sidel, Ruth, 112
Sidel, Victor, 112
simplification, 332
sins, 323-4
skills, 13, 119, 120-1, 305
small business, 160-1
Smith, William French, 301
social class: conflict, 10; interests, 9; shared values, 124
socialism: and common good, 15; and compulsion, 15-16; perversion of, 300; state, 15-17, 30, 144-5
social reconstruction, 11-18; caring in, 88-9; education in, 115-16, 119; political organizers, 52-3, 61-2, 77-8; program for, 6-7, 8, 85; value of, 26-7
social security, 91, 92, 93, 94-101; financing, 97-9, 175-8; investment trusts, 175-8
Social Security Act (1935), 94
Social Security Trust, 137
Socrates, 287
Sohn, Louis, 211
South Africa, 220
Soviet Union, 15-16
space, use of, 140
Spengler, Oswald, 283-4, 322

Sprague, Joey, 190-1
Stabilization of Export Earnings (STABEX), 261
Stalin, Joseph, 279, 287
Stassen, Harold, 208
state, views of, 24-5
Steiner, Gilbert, 94
Stent, Gunther, 320-1
stockholders, 191
Stockman, David, 168
strategy, 69
surveillance, 313-15

Taft, Robert, 198, 199, 218, 270, 272
Tawney, R.H., 38
taxation, 180-2; cuts in, 182; voting by, 182-3
Taylor, F.W., 127-8
Taylor, General Maxwell, 202-3, 208
teachers, 119, 120-1, 122
Third World, aid, 258-65
Thomas Aquinas, St, 35, 38
Tillich, Paul, 55
time and progress, 322-3
timing, 69, 70
Tolstoy, Leo, 280
torture, 302-3
Townsend Plan, 94
trade unions, 3, 73
transportation, 139, 184, 192
triumphalism, 202
truckdrivers, regulations, 192
Truman, Harry, 270
trust, and common good, 42-5
trusteeship, and common good, 33-4

understanding in foreign policy, 194
unemployment, 169
United Nations: Charter, 219, 231; Conference on Trade and Development, 260, 262, 263; delegitimation, 198-9; Force, 242; Human Rights Declaration, 286; international security plan, 222-3; International Trade Organization, 259-60; misuse, 207; strong, 194, 196, 198
universality, timeless, 30-3
university education, 123-5
urban design, 184-6

utilitarianism, 38, 39

values: and health system, 109-10; humane, 14; international consensus, 200
victims of crime, 310
Vietnam, 16; War, 208, 271
Virchow, Rudolph, 103
voluntarism, 51-2
voting, and property, 276

wages, 171
war, American attitude to, 201; and morality, 216-17
Washington, Booker T., 37
Washington, George, 186, 194, 195
Watergate, 206
Watson, J.B., 78
Watson, James, 324
wealth, distribution of, 1-2
Weber, Max, 79, 327
Weil, Simone, 24
welfare, American system, 88, 91-3; *see also* caring; social security
Western Europe, American protection, 207-8
Weyrich, Paul, 83
Wiener, Norbert, 32
Wiesner, Jerome, 208
will, 53-5
Wilson, Justice, 273
Wilson, Woodrow, 202
Winthrop, John, 54, 77, 302
women: and design, 185; dominance, 23; employment, 81, 190-1; ethical duty, 326, 327; and progress, 323
worker-community control, 146-7
workers, anonymity, 191-2; and common good, 189-92; control and participation, 15, 145, 148, 161-4
working conditions, 102, 104, 115
Wright, Erik, 190-1

York, Herbert, 208

zonal disarmament, 211-14
zoning, 139
Zorin, Valerian, 208